Peter Warr was educated at Cambridge and Sheffield Universities and is currently employed at the Institute of Work Psychology at Sheffield University. As a visiting professor he has taught at the universities of Princeton, Colorado and California, USA, Canterbury in New Zealand, and Curtin in Australia. In 1969 he was awarded the Spearman Medal of the British Psychological Society for distinguished research, and in 1982 he received the Presidents' Award of the same society for his outstanding contributions to psychological knowledge.

Professor Warr has carried out research investigations in a range of areas of applied psychology. He has written widely and has served on many editorial boards for journals and books to promote the understanding of psychology. He has published nineteen books, including *Thought and Personality* (1970), *Work and Well-being* (1975), *Work, Unemployment and Mental Health* (1987) and *Training for Managers* (1993). He is the editor of *Personal Goals and Work Design* (1976), and a co-author of *The Experience of Work* (1981) and *People and Computers* (1988).

Psychology at Work

Fourth Edition

EDITED BY
PETER WARR

PENGUIN BOOKS

To the memory of Sir Frederic Bartlett and
Dr Donald Broadbent

PENGUIN BOOKS

Published by the Penguin Group
Penguin Books Ltd, 27 Wrights Lane, London W8 5TZ, England
Penguin Books USA Inc., 375 Hudson Street, New York, New York 10014, USA
Penguin Books Australia Ltd, Ringwood, Victoria, Australia
Penguin Books Canada Ltd, 10 Alcorn Avenue, Toronto, Ontario, Canada M4V 3B2
Penguin Books (NZ) Ltd, 182–190 Wairau Road, Auckland 10, New Zealand

Penguin Books Ltd, Registered Offices: Harmondsworth, Middlesex, England

First published in Penguin Books 1971
Second edition 1978
Third edition published in Pelican Books 1987
Reprinted in Penguin Books 1991
Fourth edition 1996
1 3 5 7 9 10 8 6 4 2

Typeset, from data supplied, by Datix International Limited, Bungay, Suffolk
Printed in England by Clays Ltd, St Ives plc
Set in 9.5/11.5pt Monophoto Times

Contents

Introduction

Peter Warr

Applied psychology in work settings has made considerable progress in the past twenty-five years. Around 1970, when this book was first envisaged, most people viewed the subject almost entirely in terms of practical problem-solving, without a concern for wider understanding or contributing to academic knowledge. The extremely pragmatic emphasis of work psychology at the time was disliked by the university community, and students of psychology were rarely taught about the methods and findings of applied research. At that earlier time very few students looked for careers in the area of this book, and there was almost no interchange between psychologists active in pure or basic research and those whose interests were more applied.

It was that absence of interaction which gave rise to the first edition of *Psychology at Work*, in 1971. In the late 1960s introductory psychology books were of two quite different kinds. On the one hand were students' texts, packed with detailed experimental findings and brimming with enthusiasm for a single scientific method defined in restricted, laboratory-oriented terms. Practical issues of everyday concern found no place there. On the other hand, many popular books described applications of psychology in more sensational terms, very much of the 'how to make friends and influence people' variety. Whatever their value to the lay reader, these pragmatic books made no scholarly contribution, and they were routinely excluded from student reading lists.

This situation was characterized in the Introduction to the 1971 edition as follows:

> It is extremely easy (and correspondingly common) for academic [psychology] teaching and research to become divorced from problems which are important outside the university

1

environment ... Able students within the cultural framework which rewards laboratory investigation tend to develop into able teachers in that same framework ...

Meanwhile, back in the world there are some 'applied' psychologists who are trying hard to tackle the pressing human problems of the day. These ... lack status and influence within the profession, so that they are rarely in a position to get at the root of this problem of imbalance – the teaching and the climate within university departments.

In brief, pure psychology is too pure and applied psychology is too applied; and much academic psychology is barricaded within its fortress of purity.

The first edition of *Psychology at Work* set out to help remedy that situation. The goal was to communicate the intellectual excitement of applied research, and to make it clear that applied psychologists can be as concerned to develop and test theories as their 'purer' counterparts.

Applied investigators are by definition primarily concerned with issues arising in a particular setting of everyday life – work organizations in the present case. However, there are, of course, differences between applied psychologists in the importance they attach to practical versus theoretical objectives. Some applied psychologists employed within a company are valuably engaged entirely in solving problems and devising practical improvements, for example in systems of personnel selection or training. Many others, especially within academic institutions, are primarily concerned to develop broad generalizations and systematic theories. Their inquiries are addressed to real-life situations (in that sense their work is 'applied'), but they set out to understand and influence these situations through the creation of models and by testing predictions against the facts. For instance, an academic applied psychologist may be interested in the consequences of explicit goal-setting at work, and he or she is likely to examine those through studies in organizations, setting out to contrast alternative predictions. Academic applied researchers' concern for sound research methods can be very similar to that of their counterparts in basic research; the key difference is in the site of their investigations.

The first edition of *Psychology at Work* argued that a healthy, pure psychology was unquestionably needed, but it deplored the fact that academic psychologists overvalued pure research to the detriment of applied work. It pointed out that applied psychology was not necessarily short-term and localized. Applied research is that which examines issues of practical concern, but the examination can be either pragmatic and localized or of wider theoretical interest. Chapters were therefore written to fill the gap which existed between the two types of book described above; practical issues were addressed by applied psychologists, but the authors set out to illustrate theoretical development as well as the empirical richness of their field.

And that remains the present aim. 'Applied' psychology is defined in terms of the source of the issues to be addressed, outside the academic's laboratory. It may have a purely pragmatic focus, but equally it may seek to develop models and test predictions as rigorously as do 'pure' psychologists.

There have been enormous advances in knowledge and method in the area covered by this book since 1971, and the present material is considerably different from that in the first edition. Associated with a welcome expansion of factual understanding, marked improvements have occurred in research procedures, in the creation of focused models and broad conceptual frameworks, in the application of statistical procedures, and in the sophisticated use of computing power.

The book's environment has also changed, with a widespread acceptance of the scholarly importance of applied research. This is seen in growing pressures from governments in many countries for universities to remedy their neglect of applied research. Many more students and their teachers now take it for granted that energy and creativity should be directed towards issues of the kind described in the chapters which follow. Most university Departments of Psychology now recognize that their discipline requires excellent applied researchers (which was certainly not the case when the first edition was written), and undergraduate and graduate teaching in the area of this book has expanded greatly.

Professional bodies and scientific networks are now firmly established, after a period of considerable growth. For example, the number of members of the British Psychological Society's Section of Occupational Psychology has increased by more than four times since the first edition of this book. The corresponding division of the American Psychological Association has approximately doubled in size. And the European Association of Work and Organizational Psychology, founded in 1991, is now flourishing. Employment opportunities have expanded, and new entrants to the field are of a generally high calibre. Psychology at work has come a long way since 1971.

SIR FREDERIC BARTLETT

Yet the field still owes a major debt of gratitude to a figure who was influential some fifty years ago. This is Frederic Bartlett (1886–1969), who was Professor of Experimental Psychology at Cambridge University between 1931 and 1952, and an active Professor Emeritus until his death. The fourth edition of this book, like its predecessors, is dedicated to his memory.

Bartlett's career has been well summarized in several published tributes (e.g. Broadbent, 1970; Conrad, 1970; Buzzard, 1971). He had tremendous influence in building what was then a young discipline and successfully bringing together theoretical insights and practical concerns. For more than fifty years he directed applied psychological work, nurtured the careers of younger psychologists, and worked to ensure that needs of government departments and others for psychological investigations and recommendations were met.

Bartlett's publications covered almost all the topics addressed in this book. He wrote articles and books about skills, noise, perception, human–machine interaction and other aspects of ergonomics, fatigue, learning and remembering, accidents, training, personnel selection, interviewing, leadership, financial incentives, morale, older workers, group working, and aspects of culture. 'His life covered precisely the birth, childhood, adolescence and early maturity of occupational psychology, and no man has done more to nurse and strengthen it' (Buzzard, 1971, p. 1).

Bartlett believed that the most fruitful development of psychology depended upon its involvement in day-to-day problems, arguing forcibly that the major theoretical advances were likely to come from those researchers whose prime concern was with genuinely practical problems. The juxtaposition of 'theoretical' and 'practical' here is most important. Bartlett's notion was that we certainly need a theoretical structure, but that this has to be built upon a foundation of practical importance rather than solely on the basis of what academics happen to find interesting.

As illustrated in the opening paragraphs of this Introduction, such a view was extremely unfashionable in the academic climate of the time. The position can be illustrated through a pair of quotations. The first comes from a symposium held in 1947, in which Bartlett asserted:

> No matter what 'kind' of psychologist a person is, he is a student of human behaviour. To my mind the history of psychology shows that if he shuts himself up narrowly in any particular small sphere of conduct inside or outside the laboratory (but specially inside), he will tend to get over-immersed in a terrific lot of detail about behaviour problems which he cleverly imagines for himself, and will approximate to a sort of puzzle solving which is often extremely interesting and, in a debating sense, intellectually attractive, but which leaves him revolving round and round his limited area. This works both ways, and if it is true that the general, or the laboratory, psychologist must be prepared to keep his problems alive by going outside the study or beyond his immediate experimental settings, it is equally true that the field psychologist must seek his executive solution* with loyalty to that rigour of scientific method and that honest sense of evidence which only the study and the laboratory appear to instil (Bartlett, 1949, pp. 215–216).

The second quotation comes from an appreciation written after Bartlett's death in 1969:

> He would sometimes say that no good psychologist should be interested only in psychology. This made him friends outside his

---

* In the context of the discussion from which this is taken, an 'executive solution' was a set of practical activities to solve a problem. This was contrasted with a 'fundamental solution', an explanation in terms of cause and effect.

own subject, and also guaranteed to his professional writings a realism and contact with life sometimes lacking in academic psychologists. His ideas concerning psychology stemmed not from the criticism and development of abstract ideas, but from pondering on the mechanism which could produce an efficient stroke at cricket or explain why an African tribesman could remember perfectly the details of a number of cows sold a year previously. From a purely scientific point of view this made his ideas more original and more productive than those of the abstract theoretical schools, and from a worldly point of view he doubtless made psychology more acceptable to the representatives of other fields (Broadbent, 1970, pp. 1–2).

The present volume is a contemporary assertion of Bartlett's philosophy. The authors have tried to show how investigations into jobs and organizations can be as intellectually stimulating and theoretically challenging as research from a starting point which is 'pure' in academic terms.

DR DONALD BROADBENT

Bartlett's approach was carried forward with outstanding success and wide-ranging impact by Donald Broadbent (1926–1993). Soon after graduating with qualifications in both engineering and psychology, Broadbent took up employment in Bartlett's Cambridge department. He has indicated that around this time 'the centre of the excitement was Bartlett' (Broadbent, 1980, p. 48), who was 'a tremendous inspirational figure' (Kitzinger, 1991, p. 409) and 'my old master' (Broadbent, 1980, p. 66).

Broadbent worked at Cambridge in a research and supervisory capacity for twenty-five years up to 1974, after which he moved with a research team to Oxford. In this period he carried out a large and influential programme of work. In laboratory studies he was particularly interested in processes of information-processing, decision and control, with a principal focus upon attention and memory. Outside the lab he conducted investigations into the impact of noisy environments, factors influencing communication between workers, the influence of job characteristics on worker well-being, personal vulnerability to stress, and self-reported as well as actual mental functioning (e.g., Baddeley and Weiskrantz, 1993; Long, 1995). Unusually among academic psychologists in his area (who typically investigate average scores rather than the behaviour of individual people), he had a strong interest in patterns of individual differences and their effects on mental processes (e.g., Broadbent, 1958, chapter 7; Revelle, 1993).

Bartlett's approach to research influenced Broadbent throughout his career. The latter's basic orientation was 'that the test of intellectual excellence of a psychological theory, as well as its moral justification, lies in its application to concrete practical situations' (Broadbent, 1973, p. 7). 'Most great scientific advances have originated in practical problems . . . By looking at difficulties that arise in real life, one is forced to think more rigorously and to consider variables which it is easy to forget while in the fastnesses of theory' (Broadbent, 1973, pp. 124–125). His colleagues have emphasized how this orientation determined the nature of his own work and also the investigations of those who collaborated with him (see chapters in the book edited by Baddeley and Weiskrantz, 1993). For example, in that book Shaffer illustrates his applications of 'the principle that Donald Broadbent taught me thirty years ago, that good research begins and ends in the real world' (p. 150). As pointed out in his citation from the American Psychological Association accompanying its Distinguished Scientific Award (1975), 'his consistent emphasis on the interrelation of theory and application has strengthened both'.

Around the time of the first edition of this book (1971) psychology in British universities was expanding considerably. As indicated earlier, very few academic psychologists at that time were interested in the practical problems of everyday living. For that reason Broadbent had reservations about this expansion of his discipline. 'About fifty well-equipped, and sometimes splendidly housed, university schools shifted the main centre of the subject firmly toward conceptual and theoretical problems, rather than practical and empirical ones' (Broadbent, 1980, p. 67). As he saw it, research in that period 'was certainly academic rather than applied, and *for that reason*, contained serious intellectual weaknesses. It could slip over into excessive rationalism, where theories were devised for behaviour that human beings do not in fact show, or into a mandarin-like concern with small experimental paradigms' (p. 68, italics in the original). The first edition of *Psychology at Work* explicitly sought to counterbalance that contemporary emphasis.

Broadbent was active on many national committees and decision-making bodies, working to develop and strengthen the infrastructure of applied psychology. Yet his importance to our discipline derives not only from his influence on national policy and his academic publications. 'His achievements should be seen not simply in terms of the many excellent books and papers that he published, but more by his personal example. Possibly his greatest contribution was his development and consistent championing over the years of an approach to psychology that blends sophisticated theorizing with careful experimentation and a commitment to solving real world problems' (Berry, 1995, p. S2).

Psychology in general, and psychology at work in particular, would have advanced much less slowly without the contributions of Donald Broadbent and his source of inspiration, Frederic Bartlett. This book is dedicated to their memory.

WORK AND EMPLOYMENT

The chapters which follow examine psychology in settings of paid work, but the notion of 'work' itself is wider than merely 'employment'. Examples of *unpaid* work include housework, voluntary work, and domestic repair and decorating work. Definitions of the term in its general sense vary somewhat across time and between cultures, but most often they contain the assertion that work is an activity directed to valued goals beyond enjoyment of the activity itself. (That does not mean that work cannot be enjoyed; merely that enjoyment is not part of the definition.) In addition, there are suggestions that it is required in some way, and that it implies effort and difficulty, a need to labour or exert oneself against the environment.

One important type of work is examined in this book. We are here primarily concerned with people in their jobs, when they are working for financial gain. This usually means being employed by someone else, with terms and conditions embodied in an explicit or implicit employment contract. 'Self-employed' people are in the minority in most developed countries, comprising between 10 and 20 per cent of the work-force.

Jobs may be considered as 'socially acceptable means of earning a living' (Garraty, 1978, p. 10), thus excluding activities which are defined as illegal. Those which are referred to as 'full-time' typically take up between thirty-five and forty-five hours in a week, but travelling to and from a place of employment adds, on average, a further 10 per cent. 'Part-time' jobs may of course vary in their weekly duration, but thirty hours per week is often taken as their upper limit for statistical and survey purposes.

Paid work has long been a cornerstone of society. It is a source of social cohesion and material welfare; and for the individual it is often crucial to both physical and mental health. It warrants study by psychologists for its enormous societal importance, but also for the contribution which increased understanding of job activities and relationships can make to the development of psychology itself.

TYPES OF PSYCHOLOGY

The subject-matter of psychology is wide-ranging, and some specialization into branches has naturally occurred. For example, individual psychologists may be principally interested in child development, in perceptual or cognitive process, in animal behaviour, or in statistical models. Others devote their attention mainly to physiological correlates of behaviour, or to personality differences, the structure of attitudes, mental illness, or features of social interaction.

That branch of psychology which deals with people at work has been variously labelled as 'industrial', 'occupational', 'work' and 'organizational' psychology. Each of these terms has merit, but each has its own limitation. 'Industrial' excludes the large number of non-industrial settings in which people are employed (hospitals, schools, government departments, etc.); in the United States of America this difficulty is avoided by use of the term 'industrial/organizational (I/O)' psychology. The second term, 'occupational' psychology, is mainly applied within the United Kingdom, and it is unfamiliar or unknown elsewhere. Despite that, the label is an appropriate one to cover all employment settings and processes. The third description, 'work' psychology, widely used in certain countries of continental Europe, is also a useful one; but, as we have seen, 'work' has wider reference than merely paid employment. Finally, 'organizational' is often applied primarily to issues at the level of groups, institutions or entire organizations, with an emphasis on social interaction, culture and group structure. Additional labels for people who investigate workers in job settings include ergonomists, human factors specialists, applied cognitive psychologists, applied social psychologists, behavioural scientists, and organizational behaviour (OB) specialists. This book covers the activities of all these groups.

CONTENTS OF THE BOOK

The chapters which follow have been specially prepared for this volume. They are directed primarily at students of psychology, business and management, but members of educational and professional study groups are also likely to find material which arouses their interest. So will the many managers and other employees who are not 'students' in a strict sense, but who share a curiosity and concern for the developing science of psychology and for what it can offer them in their day-to-day work.

Work organizations and behaviour at work are complex and can be viewed from many angles. The diversity of topics to be covered is thus quite considerable. As a result, each reader is likely to find certain parts of the book more interesting than others. The material is arranged in a sequence which, roughly speaking, moves from an emphasis on the individual, through the study of groups, to the examination of complex organizations as a whole. This sequence is a straightforward one, but it is not necessarily the most suitable path for all readers to follow. Course teachers may wish to emphasize certain features or recommend a particular sequence, and the general reader may prefer to dip into a selection of individual chapters.

The authors are all experienced and influential in their fields. They have provided substantial and up-to-date summaries, but have written in a style which makes clear their personal approach and their preferred interpretations. Topics have been chosen because of their importance for the field and in order to reflect developments occurring within psychology and within society more broadly. In general, the book seeks to identify growth points and to anticipate some future developments.

We hope that readers will come to share our enthusiasm. The topics addressed in this book impinge on the daily lives of millions of individuals. We are convinced that work psychology can improve those lives in many ways, and would like more people to study and make use of its achievements.

REFERENCES

Baddeley, A. and Weiskrantz, L. (eds.) (1993). *Attention: Selection, Awareness and Control. A Tribute to Donald Broadbent*. Oxford: Clarendon Press.

Bartlett, F. C. (1949). What is industrial psychology? *Occupational Psychology*, 23, 212–218.

Berry, D. (1995). Donald Broadbent and applied cognitive psychology. *Applied Cognitive Psychology*, 9, S1–S4.

Broadbent, D. E. (1958). *Perception and Communication*. Oxford: Pergamon Press.

Broadbent, D. E. (1970). Sir Frederic Bartlett: An appreciation. *Bulletin of the British Psychological Society*, 23, 1–3.

Broadbent, D. E. (1973). *In Defence of Empirical Psychology*. London: Methuen.

Broadbent, D. E. (1980). Donald E. Broadbent. In G. Lindzey (ed.), *A History of Psychology in Autobiography*, vol. 7, pp. 39–73. San Francisco: W. H. Freeman.

Buzzard, R. B. (1971). Sir Frederic Bartlett, 1886–1969. *Occupational Psychology*, 45, 1–11.

Conrad, R. (1970). Sir Frederic Bartlett, 1886–1969: A personal homage. *Ergonomics*, 13, 159–161.

Garraty, J. A. (1978). *Unemployment in History*. New York: Harper and Row.

Kitzinger, C. (1991). Donald Broadbent: Defending empirical psychology. *The Psychologist*, 4(9), 408–410.

Long, J. (1995). Commemorating Donald Broadbent's contribution to the field of applied cognitive psychology. *Applied Cognitive Psychology*, 9, S197–S215.

Revelle, W. (1993). Individual differences in personality and motivation. In A. Baddeley and L. Weiskrantz (eds.), *Attention: Selection, Awareness, and Control*, pp. 346–373. Oxford: Clarendon Press.

1

Skilled Performance and Mental Workload

Robert Hockey

We generally use the term 'skill' to refer to high levels of expertise in areas of behaviour that we value highly or regard as very difficult to attempt ourselves. Within the world of work we readily think of traditional craftsmen, surgeons or pilots, but less often of assembly line workers, shop assistants or bus drivers. This everyday attribution of skill is also heavily biased towards those who work with their hands or bodies (jugglers, acrobats, mechanics or plasterers), and not those whose work is primarily mental. Yet, within a psychological framework, almost all human behaviour may be considered skilful at some level, in the sense that even the simplest action requires the co-ordination of many components, both mental and bodily, and the selection of one out of many possible actions at the right time.

In accordance with accepted usage within cognitive psychology, the term 'skill' refers in the present chapter to this general character-istic of an organized action sequence. A primary defining feature of a skilled action is that it is influenced by learning (so does not include simple reflexes), though it may range from simple acts like pressing a key in response to a light on a panel, to driving a Formula 1 car or managing a nuclear power plant. While the demands on skilled per-formance made by working in complex human–machine systems (e.g., in air traffic control or nuclear power plants) provide a focus for much of the material considered in the chapter, many of the broad conclusions apply equally to skill in everyday activities.

The chapter first considers the nature of skill in terms of its relation to human error and expertise. Even highly developed skills may let us down under certain conditions, typically when we are under pres-sure, either from other work demands (workload) or from various external factors in the work environment or in our general lives (stressors). It next reviews the impact of workload and stressors on

13

the stability of practised skills. These are major limiting features of the design of workplaces, though the mechanisms of performance decrement are quite complex. Finally, it examines some of the ways in which work design may help in the maintenance of skilled performance by providing support to an operator within the task structure.

THE NATURE OF SKILLED ACTION

Work tasks may be considered to be made up of sequences of *actions* carried out to achieve certain *goals*. The extent to which a person's actions satisfy these goals is usually assumed to reflect his or her level of skill in the task. Well-learned skills enable us to operate efficiently, even in such demanding work environments as intensive-care nursing, nuclear-plant management and air traffic control. However, an individual's performance may sometimes be inadequate to meet work goals, even when skill level is demonstrably high, resulting in reduced quantity or quality of output, missed signals, and so on. In some conditions these failures will lead to accidents.

Much of our current understanding of skilled action comes from the study of behaviour in the laboratory, mainly in the post-war period and up to the 1970s (Holding, 1981). The kinds of activity investigated were based on real-life tasks such as those found in the operation of military and industrial equipment, and focused on manual control, the dominant mode of industrial work during the post-war period. While much of this research is still highly relevant to the design and use of complex control systems, the emphasis in modern work has increasingly moved towards cognitive activities and away from manual skill. In keeping with this shift in the broader environment, the emphasis in laboratory studies of skill has switched to cognitive activities such as planning, decision making and problem solving. It is now clear that the differences between manual and cognitive work are a matter of degree rather than of kind. Some overt actions are always necessary, even in highly cognitive work, and some internal information processing precedes actions in all manual activity.

A distinction may usefully be made between the attained level of skill acquisition (or *competence*) and observed level of skill proficiency (*performance*). Thus, a chemical plant process operator may be known to possess the knowledge and operational experience to act appropriately when a particular fault occurs, but may nevertheless fail to bring the system under control when the critical situation arises. Competence is usually established by appropriate training (see Chapter 3), and it is important to establish that any observed skill failures are not simply the result of inadequate learning. Performance levels are affected by factors such as motivation, which restrict the ability or willingness to sustain the use of this learned skill under prevailing work conditions, and by the opportunities and constraints built into the work system.

The quality of skilled performance is measured in terms of various attributes, depending on goal requirements, though some aspect of either speed or accuracy is usually involved. If speed of action is an important objective, performance may be measured in terms of *reaction time* (RT), the time taken to react to a critical event by (say) a key press or verbal response. Speed may also be measured indirectly, in terms of output, as the average number of actions carried out in a given time (e.g., lines of computer program checked in a minute). If accuracy is a major criterion, error rates may be a more appropriate performance index. The two measures are not independent, however, and may be influenced by the individual's understanding of the relative importance of acting quickly and of not making errors. A key feature of speeded reactions of all kinds is that they are likely to be subject to a *speed–accuracy trade-off*. In general, faster responses may be achieved only at the expense of a loss of accuracy, and an increased emphasis on accuracy often implies a willingness to tolerate a slower rate of response. In some cases the design of the task will itself determine the speed–accuracy relationship. In cockpit systems, for example, responses to auditory displays are known to be both faster and more error-prone than those to visual displays (Wickens, 1992).

Human Error and Expertise

While speed and error are, in general, complementary, in most practical contexts error avoidance is the main criterion of performance.

When a major accident occurs (for example, capsized car ferries, train collisions or plane crashes), human error is commonly assumed to be at the root of the problem. It has been estimated that human error is the major contributory factor in between 50 and 80 per cent of all accidents (Spettell and Liebert, 1986). The qualitative analysis of error, both in accidents and in everyday life, has attracted much interest (e.g., Norman, 1981; Reason, 1990), and been shown to reveal important aspects of the cognitive basis of skilled actions.

A fundamental distinction (Reason, 1990) is that errors may occur because of failures of either intention (*mistakes*) or execution (*slips* and *lapses*). Mistakes may occur in situation appraisal, planning or goal selection. A driver may incorrectly judge that he or she has enough space to overtake before a bend, or an officer on a ship's bridge may fail to give way (as required) when a vessel on the starboard bow is detected by the radar as being on a collision course. In Rasmussen's (1986) 'skill–rule–knowledge' framework, mistakes are further separated into *knowledge-based* (a failure to understand situations and their requirements) and *rule-based* errors (an inappropriate application of old solutions to new situations). Slips and lapses are referred to in Rasmussen's model as *skill-based* errors. With slips the intention is correct, but the action is executed badly. Most errors in laboratory experiments are of this kind (indeed, they are often immediately detected as errors, and corrected where possible). Pressing the wrong button on a telephone or computer keyboard is an everyday example of a slip, where the consequences are usually trivial; pressing the accelerator instead of the (intended) brake in a driving emergency may be a more costly slip. *Lapses* are failures of attention or memory rather than of action. An operator may miss a critical change in an indicator or lose track of where he or she is in a sequence of actions.

In general, we expect that all kinds of errors are eliminated by extended practice or experience ('practice makes perfect'). The literature of human error reveals, however, that expertise is more complex than this. By the end of a training programme errors have normally been reduced to an acceptable minimum, though continued practice over an extended period will continue to show further improvement in terms of timing, precision and economy of effort. While we take it

for granted that experts 'know more' than novices, research on expertise has shown that there are qualitative as well as quantitative differences between the two groups.

Much of what we know about expertise comes from the study
of skill in chess (e.g., Charness, 1991). For example, expert players
(masters) are known to access stored knowledge more effectively
(than club players), have a more abstract representation of problem
situations, make more efficient use of working memory and are
better at evaluating alternative search options. These advantages
allow them to make better decisions: they respond more efficiently
to new problems, and explore promising rather than unproductive
solutions. In addition, from work in other areas of expertise (e.g.,
computer programming, mathematical problem solving, medical diagnosis and decision making) experts also appear to be more efficient
than novices in monitoring the environment for task-relevant information, and make more use of active hypothesis-generation in
deciding upon appropriate actions (see Ericsson and Smith, 1991).

From this, it may seem that experts are very unlikely to make
errors, though that is, of course, not the case. Ironically, since increased responsibility tends to go with expertise, major accidents
tend to involve human error at the highest level: the captain of an oil
tanker; the pilot of a 747; the process engineer in a nuclear plant.
As Reason (1990) suggests, because of their extensive and flexible
domain-specific knowledge, many of these errors are likely to be
rule-based or skill-based (slips and lapses), rather than knowledge-
based. However, the complexity of accident scenarios is such that
experts may be working at the limits of even their highly developed
competence. Mistakes may therefore arise from incomplete
understanding or limited experience with the prevailing unfamiliar
conditions. Roth and Woods (1988) showed that more experienced
operators in nuclear power plants preferred an 'open loop' mode of
control (making use of feedback only to carry out later adjustments).
While allowing more effective moment to moment management of
the system, such a strategy is more prone to error because of its high
demands on working memory and planning. Such knowledge-based
problem solving is the hallmark of expert skill, but it is a vulnerable
activity at the limits. Chess is a finite (if complex) game, whereas
controlling a nuclear plant or skippering an oil tanker is subject to

perturbations from many external events. These more open skills may require emergency reactions to situations which not only have never occurred before, but which could not have been predicted.

MENTAL WORKLOAD

A major reason for the failure of skilled action, for experts and novices alike, is excessive *mental workload*: an individual may be 'overloaded' or have too much to do. In everyday language workload is often used to refer to how busy someone is, or the number of things that he or she has to do. In some jobs the term has taken a specific meaning (e.g., the 'caseload' in social work, medicine and law). How we define mental workload (often referred to here simply as workload) is important. Although various definitions exist, a number of general principles are agreed. These have significance not only for the academic analysis of work and skilled performance, but also for the design and implementation of work systems. For example, Wickens (1992) points out that decisions about staffing in civil aviation may soon be based on a standard workload analysis for individual aircraft. Techniques to measure workload are increasingly being used to compare different system and job designs, and to assess the impact of environmental load, training and other features of the work environment.

Mental Work, Capacity and Resources

By analogy with physical work, the term mental work implies that a supply of 'energy' is needed to maintain cognitive activity and skilled behaviour. The energy metaphor has a long history within the study of mental function and has remained closely identified with the development of 'energetical' aspects of human information processing, such as a person's resources, capacity, effort and alertness (e.g., Hockey, Gaillard and Coles, 1986; Kahneman, 1973). Workload has thus come to be considered primarily in terms of competition for a limited resource – mental energy, mental capacity or mental workspace, depending on a writer's theoretical emphasis. In terms of

18

cognitive theory, the most generally accepted model of resource competition is that of a limited computational workspace, based on Broadbent's (1958) concept of a limited-capacity 'bottleneck' located in the central information-processing system. The form of the limited-capacity model has undergone various transformations and modifications (e.g., Broadbent, 1971; Kahneman, 1973; Treisman, 1993), though it remains a central assumption of most approaches to skilled performance. In current theory the idea is most strongly associated with limitations of working memory, and the central executive process in particular (Baddeley, 1986).

A requirement for a person to carry out two tasks simultaneously, both of which use the same mental workspace, is likely to lead to competition for processing space, and result in a performance decrement (errors or delayed response in one or more of the activities). Looked at more closely, however, the evidence suggests that the problem of high workload is not simply that of competition for a general supply of processing space. Explanations of workload in these terms provide a reasonable account of the effects of increased demands of the same type, but not of interference between tasks of different types. Such effects are known to depend less on their overall level of demand, and more on their structural and temporal interrelationships. Some studies have demonstrated this lack of dependence of skilled performance on overall workload even for highly complex performance, which would appear to demand maximal processing space. For example, Allport, Antonis and Reynolds (1972) showed that expert pianists could simultaneously carry out sight-reading of music and auditory shadowing (repeating spoken text) without decrement to either task; Shaffer (1975) found the same effects for expert typists simultaneously typing and shadowing.

Results of this kind have led to the view that cognitive resources may not be undifferentiated, but located in a number of more specific components or *multiple resources* (Wickens, 1984); e.g., visual versus auditory input channels; verbal or spatial forms of representation; manual or voice output channels. In dual-task situations having low structural interference (e.g., visual and auditory inputs, requiring manual and vocal outputs, as in the above studies of skilled pianists and typists), there is an absence of competition for use of the same processing resources, and interference is minimal. Conversely, when both activities demand access to, say, visual input or manual output, performance is likely to be impaired. Such effects may occur even at quite low levels of overall demand (workload), as the result of 'cross-talk' or 'confusion' between input or output channels (Wickens, 1986): the response for one task becomes attached to the input for the other, or errors occur in the identification and selection of relevant input or output.

These structural features of dual-task interference have been largely side-stepped in recent research on workload, though they have an important role in applications of workload methodology. In general, demonstrated differences between tasks or systems in terms of workload also require us to show that there are no important differences in structure between the two configurations. Thus, the term 'workload' implies a concern with an overloading of capacity *within a particular resource* or set of resources, and explicitly not interference between tasks in terms of their structural properties. The distinction has important practical consequences. While both may be examples of poor work design, they have different remedies. In the first case the overall level of demand on the operator (required rate of work, level of concentration, etc.) has to be reduced. In the second, (say) one stream of information should be presented visually rather than both in the auditory mode, or a control modified to allow separate manual and voice outputs.

Levels of Control

A rather different theoretical development within workload considers the *level* of cognitive control required for effective performance. The idea that mental activity is organized in terms of levels of control goes back at least to Bartlett (1932), and has become a strong feature of later models of attention and skill, as exemplified by Schneider and Shiffrin's (1977) demonstration of 'automatic' and 'controlled' modes of visual search (detecting a target letter in an array of other letters). In unpractised tasks search is controlled by the constraints of limited attentional resources: search speed is slower when there are more targets to look for and when there are more 'distracter' letters. With extended practice with the same kind of materials, however, the skill becomes progressively 'automated' and apparently effortless: under these conditions (of 'constant mapping') search speed is independent of the number of targets and distracters in the display.

The general distinction between automatic and controlled processing is a major assumption of current cognitive theory, through the work of theorists such as Broadbent (1977), Norman and Shallice (1986) and Posner (1978). Put simply, such models assume that skilled action may be controlled either by (automatic) triggering of well-learned routines and procedures, or by the use of general-purpose mechanisms (executive or supervisory systems) which allow planned sequences of actions to be maintained under (effortful) voluntary control. High levels of control are required, for example, when skills are not well learned or when actions require real-time processing of (unpredictable) environmental events.

The most effective application of control level theory to workload analysis has come from approaches based on Rasmussen's (1986) analysis of complex diagnostic and control activity in process operators. As mentioned earlier, Rasmussen distinguishes three levels of control activity, *skill-based*, *rule-based* and *knowledge-based*, increasing in control requirements. Skill-based actions are routine responses to common signals (equivalent to automatic processing). Rule-based control will normally be effective in familiar variable work contexts, where appropriate condition–action procedures are available. Knowledge-based control (problem solving) is often required in unfamiliar or unexpected situations, or where rule-based procedures are not available.

Assessment of Mental Workload

In everyday conversations jobs are often referred to as if they themselves had a 'high workload' or were 'mentally demanding'. At a conceptual level this is misleading, however. Current theory emphasizes the interactive or *transactional* nature of mental workload (e.g., Gopher and Donchin, 1986): it is a product of the interplay between task and individual characteristics, as well as the environmental and motivational context in which the work is carried out. Checking a set of accounts or monitoring a radar display may be perceived as demanding or not, depending on such factors as the skill, effort capacity and motivational level of the operator, his or her level of training and familiarity with the work, the ambient environmental conditions (noise, heat, etc.), and so on.

In view of the multifaceted nature of mental workload, it is not surprising that a number of different ways of measuring it have evolved. These include methods based on primary and secondary task performance level (referred to later as 'performance-based techniques'), and on psychophysiological and subjective assessments (referred to as 'indirect indicators'). While the use of different methods does not always lead to the same conclusions, there are clearly advantages for both researcher and practitioner in having a range of techniques at his or her disposal. Different methods may be suitable for different work environments, as well as revealing potentially different features of the workload assessment problem.

The choice of which method to use is often dictated by criteria such as *sensitivity*, *diagnosticity* and *unintrusiveness* (O'Donnell and Eggemeier, 1986). Sensitivity refers to the extent to which a method will detect any change in mental workload, irrespective of its source. In contrast, diagnosticity refers to the extent to which a measure can pinpoint the source of the problem in terms of specific information-processing resources (e.g., having too much information to take in from displays, as opposed to having too many actions to carry out). On a practical level, any method may be unsuitable if it interferes with the work being measured. The intrusiveness of a technique refers to the extent to which it impinges directly on work, interfering with the task or job being assessed. Other desiderata, particularly for field studies, include *ease of use* and *acceptability*. Subjective scales are easy to use in that they can be administered reliably without extensive training or specialized equipment, in contrast to most secondary task and psychophysiological methods. The characteristics of which techniques are acceptable will vary, though operators generally have less tolerance for methods which take extra time to complete, or involve wires attached to the head or chest. Table 1.1 summarizes the various workload techniques in terms of their general performance on these five criteria.

Table 1.1 Comparison of workload assessment techniques in terms of criteria for selection. The entries for each cell are to be read as 'the more stars the better'

Workload assessment technique	Criteria				
	sensitivity	diagnosticity	unintrusiveness	ease of use	acceptability
Primary task	★	★★	★★★	★★	★★
Secondary task	★★	★★★	★	★	★
Subjective	★★★	★	★★★	★★★	★★★
Psycho-physiological	★★★	★★	★	★	★★

Performance-based techniques

Mental work may conveniently be separated into primary and secondary tasks, in terms of their priority in relation to overall task goals. This may be done informally or, for very complex jobs, following a task analysis (see Chapter 3). In driving, for example, speed regulation and steering/collision avoidance may be thought of as primary, and traffic information monitoring and efficient use of controls as secondary. The most obvious implication of the workload approach to the analysis of skill is that more demanding tasks are more difficult to carry out.

Assessment of *primary task* performance provides a direct measure of the effect of demands on the main work tasks of the individual, so should always be carried out in addition to any other measures. For example, we might expect to find increased manoeuvring errors or perceptual failures in driving under heavy traffic loads or with fatigue from prolonged driving (e.g., Hicks and Wierwille, 1979). However, primary task measures are rarely sufficient as measures of mental workload. Performance while driving a car and a heavy goods lorry may prove to be equally good in terms of error rates, though this cannot be taken as evidence that they impose equal demands on drivers. For example, differences in error rates may be obscured by spare mental capacity in both tasks, and driving performances may not be strictly comparable because of differences in vehicle handling characteristics.

Various *secondary task* methods provide an indirect measure of primary task load in terms of spare capacity or 'spill-over' from primary task demand. In many practical contexts a standardized task is added to the primary task, with instructions to respond to it only when the primary task permits. Demands of different primary tasks may then be compared by examining performance on the standard secondary task. A variant of this approach is the use of the secondary task *probe*, in which operators respond to discrete events, such as tones presented over headphones, or light signals in driving mirrors, by making rapid manual or vocal responses. Differences in spare capacity are then inferred from reaction times (RTs) to the probes or from measures of how well they are detected. A third version of the dual-task method is the *loading task* procedure. In this case, operators are required to give priority to the additional task itself, allowing differences in primary task load to be measured directly as resources are drawn away from it. Secondary tasks have been used extensively in laboratory settings as a powerful technique for the study of attention, time-sharing and multiple resources, though they have also been used to measure workload in many field contexts. They are sensitive to general capacity demands, and may also be diagnostic if they are designed to test spare capacity for quite specific processing components (Wickens, 1992).

Indirect indicators of workload
In many cases the use of a secondary task is impracticable. Asking air traffic controllers or fighter pilots to carry out a second (to them, unnecessary) task may actually result in an impairment of performance on the primary task, compromising safety and reliability. In such cases, in addition to primary task performance, subjective and psychophysiological methods are often preferred.

Measures of *subjective workload*, in the form of self-reports from operators, are probably the most widely used of the various workload assessment techniques. In field contexts they are favoured because of their ease of use and low intrusiveness, but they are also generally sensitive to even small changes in perceived demand. Although the use of simple scales measuring undifferentiated workload levels is still common, recent techniques have emphasized the multi-dimensionality of the construct, based on laboratory-based analyses of different kinds of task. The two best known procedures are

SWAT (*Subjective Workload Assessment Test*) and NASA-TLX (*Task Load Index*), both developed within the aviation/space context. SWAT (Reid and Nygren, 1988) defines the subjective workload of a task in terms of three separate kinds of load: (1) its demands on the use of time, (2) its requirement for mental effort, and (3) its impact on feelings of stress. Thus a task may seem demanding because it keeps you busy most of the time, because it demands high levels of concentration, or because it causes anxiety, confusion or frustration in trying to achieve task goals. The NASA-TLX (Hart and Staveland, 1988) includes six sub-scales, four of which have clear links with the three SWAT dimensions (temporal demand; mental demand; mental effort; frustration level), and two additional variables (physical demand, performance). Both methods have proved sensitive to a broad range of between-task manipulations of demand, particularly in aviation (see Wierwille and Eggemeier, 1993), though the potential diagnosticity of their use of multiple scales has been demonstrated only rarely in applications to date.

The use of *psychophysiological* measures to estimate workload (see Kramer, 1991) is often motivated by a desire to minimize intrusiveness, since the subject or operator is not required to carry out any additional task, though there may be problems of unacceptability associated with the use of electrodes or recording equipment. Measures of brain activity, particularly event-related potentials (ERPs), are usually assumed to measure information-processing demands in terms of the amplitude and timing of the brain response to a standard secondary task. Such methods are moderately diagnostic and may reflect specific sources of demand in terms of different processing stages. Measures of physiological processes cannot be interpreted as indices of workload in an unequivocal way, however, since bodily processes are determined by many other functions. It may be more realistic to regard them as reflecting the degree of resource activation or energy mobilization (mental effort) associated with the individual's response to work tasks. The use of autonomic indices, such as suppression of heart rate variability (HRV) or increased pupil dilation, is based on the well-established shift towards sympathetic dominance in autonomic nervous system activity under conditions of mental challenge and involvement (Kahneman, 1973; Kramer, 1991). HRV suppression has been shown to be a reliable index of increased levels of mental effort and controlled processing demands, such as that associated with knowledge-based problem-solving (Tattersall and Hockey, 1995). Measurements of the level of stress hormones (e.g., adrenaline and cortisol) are also used as markers of the costs of work tasks, though the need to collect blood samples or urine sometimes makes them intrusive and unacceptable. Such techniques may have diagnostic value, however, in differentiating between active and passive forms of engagement with task demands (Frankenhaeuser, 1986; Hockey, Payne and Rick, 1995).

In general, indices of the psychophysiological state of the person are important in revealing the impact of the work on the underlying physiological system, though they also provide an independent measure of the level of engagement of the individual with the task (the effort applied to maintaining task goals). Because they are only indirect measures of workload they are best used in conjunction with either performance-based techniques or subjective measures, allowing inferences to be made about the effort required to attain measured performance levels (or the brain processes affected by changes in task structure), and the relation between energy mobilization and perceptions of mental demand.

DECREMENTS IN SKILLED PERFORMANCE

Prevention of breakdown in skilled performance is a major goal of the design of work and human–machine systems, though threats to the maintenance of stable levels of performance are found in many aspects of the work environment. As discussed in the previous section, high levels of workload are an obvious problem, causing overload in one or more parts of the task. Disruption of primary activities will normally be more serious than failures in subsidiary features of the work, particularly where task features are relatively independent, or where only one of them may be carried out at any one time. In more complex tasks, however, overall safety and reliability often depend critically on a high level of integration between task elements.

A second major threat to performance stability is any change in the general background state of the individual. We generally believe that being tired, anxious or emotionally aroused will impair skilled performance, particularly when the task is a demanding one. Such effects have been surprisingly difficult to demonstrate under controlled laboratory conditions. Certainly, environmental stressors such as noise and time pressure have been shown to reduce the overall quality of performance across a range of skills, though the effects are often quite subtle ones (Hockey, 1993). As observed in relation to workload, manifest breakdown in primary task skill under externally imposed stress is unusual, and rarely greater than 10 per cent of normal functional levels. Does this mean that the breakdown of performance under high demand is a myth, and that job design should no longer be concerned with controlling the factors which help to generate stress?

Latent Degradation in Performance

As noted earlier, compensatory effort can serve to recruit additional resources for the protection of the primary task under stress or acute additional load. This effect was attributed by Kahneman (1971) to the effectiveness of attentional control in maintaining dominant action plans. Maintaining selectivity of attention under high demand or environmental distraction has obvious adaptive value, in preserving high priority goals, but it may result in a pattern of *latent* degradation. While primary performance may not be manifestly affected, the level of available resources is partially depleted in overcoming the imposed threat, and this may leave the individual vulnerable to disruption from further or more extreme demands. If appropriate measurements are taken, the impact of latent degradation can be revealed as changes in secondary features of performance or in the ways in which tasks are carried out: cutting corners in information processing, taking risks and so on. Such effects compromise safety and reliability by leaving no margin of error (e.g., for unexpected demands or emergencies). Consequently, the use of performance decrement as a measure of the impact of stressors or sub-optimal working environments may lead to misleading inferences about the threat to stable work performance.

Table 1.2 summarizes the various patterns of latent degradation in skilled performance observed under high levels of task or environmental demand. The first type of effect, *secondary decrement*, has already

Table 1.2 Patterns of latent degradation in skilled performance under demanding task and environmental conditions

Source of latent degradation	Typical changes observed
Secondary decrement	reduced performance on secondary aspects of work tasks or on imposed secondary tasks
Strategic adjustment	changes towards the use of high selectivity or low effort modes of information processing, reduced use of planning and working memory
Compensatory costs	increases in sympathetic activation, increased effort and increased expenditure of mental energy
After-effects	preference for use of low effort strategies on tests administered after completion of work

been discussed in connection with mental workload as a more sensitive (and usually more diagnostic) marker of changes in primary task load. Similar changes are also found, however, as a consequence of environmental demand factors such as noise and time pressure, or internal state changes such as sleep deprivation and fatigue. In general, decrements in primary task performance under such conditions are rare, and typically small (see Hockey, 1993), while secondary task decrements are more common. As mentioned above, this may or may not have serious consequences for task performance, depending on the closeness of the relationship between task elements.

A second, more subtle, effect on performance may be described as *strategic adjustment*. Even in simple laboratory tasks, conditions such as noise, time pressure and perceived danger are associated with a shift in the speed–accuracy trade-off function, towards a faster but less accurate pattern of responding (Hockey, 1986). In general terms, strategy shifts reflect the use of simpler or less effortful processing modes under high demand conditions, preserving the primary task goals at the expense of secondary priorities. One of the best-known forms of strategy shift is an increase in selectivity (funnelling or narrowing of attention) under high levels of perceived threat or anxiety. This takes the form of a maintenance (or even enhancement) of central or primary goals, with a relative neglect of low priority features. Such effects have been found under both laboratory and field conditions for the effects of noise, deep-sea diving, threat of shock, and many other environmental and work variables (Baddeley, 1972; Broadbent, 1971; Hockey, 1979). In more complex cognitive activities, withdrawal from effortful information processing operations appears to involve a reduced dependency on the vulnerable working memory resource. Sperandio (1978) found that air traffic controllers adapted their work pattern when the number of aircraft contacts increased beyond the individual's typical limit. Under the high load, controllers switched from individual routing of all planes to a fixed, routinized procedure for all contacts, hence reducing the load on planning and working memory while maintaining primary work goals such as safety. A series of studies by Schonpflüg and his colleagues (e.g., Schonpflüg, 1983) found similar changes in a simulated office task. When subjects had to work under time pressure or loud noise they made more reference to externally available information before making decisions, rather than storing it in memory. As with the Sperandio study, reducing the load on working memory helped maintain accuracy goals, though at the expense of increased time costs.

The third type of latent degradation in Table 1.2 is referred to as *compensatory costs*. These may be thought of as the unwanted side-effects of the compensatory behaviour which helps to maintain primary performance under stress and high workload. Although there has been little systematic research on this problem to date, two general kinds of cost can be distinguished: increased activation in energetic psychophysiological processes, and increases in subjective effort and strain. For example, in a study of sleep deprivation Wilkinson (1962) found that decrements in arithmetic computation were smaller for subjects who showed greater increases in muscle tension during testing under the stress condition. Similarly, as part of a series of studies of effects of noise on mental work (e.g., Lundberg and Frankenhaeuser, 1978), noise was found to impair performance in one study but had no effect in another. The two different sets of results were associated with different patterns of cost. When performance was maintained under noise in one experiment, levels of adrenaline and subjective effort were found to be increased; in the other, noise impaired performance and no such costs were observed. A field study (Rissler and Jacobson, 1987) measured the costs incurred during a busy period of continued overtime and intense time pressure associated with the implementation of a new computer system in an organization. Although there was no disruption of performance during this period, measured levels of adrenaline and cognitive effort were found to be increased. Such effects illustrate the role of compensatory regulation in the protection of performance, and may be seen as a trade-off between the protection of the primary performance goal and the level of mental effort that has to be invested in the task. These and other more recent studies (see Hockey, 1993) indicate that the regulation of effort is at least partially under the control of the individual, rather than being an automatic feature of task or environmental conditions.

Finally in Table 1.2, degradation from overload may appear only after tasks have been completed, in terms of decrements on tasks presented at the end of the work period. These *after-effects* have also been studied very little, and then normally within a workload/fatigue paradigm (see Hockey, 1986), though they are equally appropriate as a response to working under demanding environmental conditions (Hockey, 1993). Given its long-recognized importance, work fatigue has been studied extensively since the early days of psychology, though the search for a sensitive test of the carry-over effect of sustained mental work to the performance of new tasks has proved elusive (Broadbent, 1979). Holding (1983) showed that fatigue may be revealed as a disposition towards activities which make less demand on effort, particularly where subjects are provided with a choice of alternative ways of carrying out the task. It may be apparent from what has been said above about compensatory control that, where no options are available (as is usual in such studies), we would expect to see increased costs associated with maintained performance levels. It appears that these have not been measured.

DESIGNING FOR SKILL MAINTENANCE

Issues concerned with skilled performance and its breakdown under demanding operational environments present major challenges to the design of work, and of complex human–machine systems in particular. Work tasks need to be designed to minimize the load placed on operators, particularly on the more vulnerable parts of the information-processing apparatus, such as our limited working memory and computational power.

Rouse and Morris (1987), among others, have argued that systems should be designed to be 'error-tolerant'. Good design can assist in identifying and rectifying slips if the effects of the incorrect actions are made clearly visible (e.g., by providing feedback on the effects of actions), and by building in reversibility. In personal computer systems, for example, it is now routine for critical file management actions such as 'deleting' to require confirmation, and for all screen changes to be readily 'undone'. It has even been suggested that some errors are inevitable, and that they should not be prevented entirely or 'trained out'. This would have the effect of allowing operators to explore the limits of possible actions to enhance learning, try out strategies, test hypotheses, and so on. Permitting errors would not incur serious costs if the system were error-tolerant, though such behaviour has been known to lead to complications or accidents when it was not supported by on-line decision aids or action monitoring facilities (Hockey and Maule, 1995; Reason, 1990).

While systems may be designed to minimize general levels of workload, many complex work tasks have continually varying demands, with peak load sometimes changing from zero to some unmanageable amount within minutes. The vulnerability of working memory and attention in complex tasks has been recognized most clearly in the provision of decision support systems (see Chapter 4). Decision aids are usually designed to be optional, so that the operator may make use of them only if he or she requires assistance (for example when there are high demands for different kinds of action, or when there are competing demands on working memory and attention). Generally, these may be seen as providing an 'external memory' for the human operator, allowing him or her to use recognition rather than recall, and so minimize the load on (internal) working memory. For example, in modern Windows-driven programs for personal computers, the provision of menu displays for the most commonly used functions helps us to navigate our way around quite complex tasks without having to remember what we need to do next. In troubleshooting tasks operators may be provided with alternative hypotheses about the meaning of a set of fault symptoms, summarized information about the history of the process or updated information about effects of recent actions on process parameters.

The concept of error-tolerance introduced above is not confined to compensating for routine slips of action. As envisaged by Rouse and Morris (1987), it assumes some form of intelligent adaptive control between human and machine. The problem of allocation of function is central to problems of automation. In addition to reducing the contribution of the operator to the overall control of the task, supervisory systems are usually designed in such a way that the functions that are available to the human are fixed. Rouse and Morris describe a flexible system that makes inferences about the current capabilities and performance of the operator, providing relevant feedback and information, monitoring actions and so on. Only if the operator steps outside acceptable boundaries does the computer system intervene by reasserting control. Such a system could, in principle, also take account of information about the operator's subjective and psychophysiological state, allowing the computation of performance–cost trade-off functions. Thus, although the operator's output is within limits, he or she may be showing relatively high levels of effort or fatigue, or signs of cardiovascular strain. Under these conditions the computer may signal this information to the operator, or resume control and maintain it until the operator state has stabilized.

These features are particularly necessary in jobs which make use of highly automated systems. While humans and computers share the control of the process in all automated systems, most complex work (for example, in chemical and power plants, jet aeroplanes and modern manufacturing) makes use of the highly developed form of automation known as *supervisory* control (Moray, 1986; Sheridan, 1987). This kind of system restricts the information-processing role of the human operator to that of monitor and troubleshooter for the automatic controller, effectively 'designing the operator out of the control loop'. The inability to interact actively with the process reduces the opportunity to develop an effective understanding of the (changing) system, and makes it more difficult to intervene appropriately when something goes wrong (Wiener, 1984). This is not to deny the obvious value of advances in automation, and there are strong arguments to support their critical role in both productivity and safety. It is, however, increasingly being accepted that the role of the human operator in supervisory systems needs to be supported by better design of decision-making, and more flexible means of allocating control between human and automatic elements of the job (Hockey, Briner, Tattersall and Wiethoff, 1989; Sheridan, 1987; see also Chapter 12).

SUMMARY

Skilled performance has been presented as an interplay between goals, mental resources, motivation and the control of action. A critical distinction was made between competence (or potential skill level) and performance (actual achieved level). A major goal of the application of psychological knowledge and methods to work is to minimize this difference, and to achieve stability of skilled performance in operational environments. High levels of workload may compromise performance, either by making excessive demands on the limited mental resources available, or by causing specific interference between task elements which use the same sensory or motor channels. Workload can be assessed by several measurement techniques, making use of different levels of task performance, subjective reports or psychophysiological indices of the response to demand. The choice of appropriate method depends on a number of theoretical and practical criteria: sensitivity, diagnosticity, unintrusiveness, ease of use and acceptability.

In addition to their use in workload evaluation, these techniques were also shown to be important in detecting effects of threats to performance from outside the task, such as those associated with changes in operator state and environmental conditions. Compensatory effort typically ensures that primary goals are maintained under stress. Thus performance may be only minimally affected, though various forms of latent degradation in skill may be observed: secondary task decrements, strategy changes, compensatory costs and aftereffects. It seems likely that the impact of workload and stress may be reduced by appropriate system design. A number of possible design features were outlined, based on the concepts of error-tolerance and adaptive control, which address the problem of reducing threats to performance.

FURTHER READING

The most generally useful companion volume to the material in this chapter is provided by the excellent second edition of *Engineering Psychology and Human Performance* by C. D. Wickens (1992). A highly readable and theoretically developed account of *Human Error* is given by J. Reason (1990), and a valuable recent set of papers on expertise in the volume *Towards a General Theory of Expertise*, edited by K. A. Ericsson and J. Smith (1991). A summary of the innovative and influential work of Jens Rasmussen is provided by his monograph *Human Information Processing and Human Machine Interaction* (1986). A broad account of the extension of workload analysis methods to problems of performance decrement under operator state changes is given in chapters by G. R. J. Hockey in the volume *Attention, Selection, Awareness and Control: A Tribute to Donald Broadbent*, edited by A. D. Baddeley and L. Weiskrantz (1993), and in Volume 2 of the *Handbook of Perception and Performance*, edited by K. Boff, L. Kaufman and J. P. Thomas (1986).

REFERENCES

Allport, D. A., Antonis, B. and Reynolds, P. (1972). On the division of attention: A disproof of the single channel hypothesis. *Quarterly Journal of Experimental Psychology*, 24, 255–265.

Baddeley, A. D. (1972). Selective attention and performance in dangerous environments. *British Journal of Psychology*, 63, 537–546.

Baddeley, A. D. (1986). *Working Memory*. Oxford: Oxford University Press.

Bartlett, F. C. (1932). *Remembering*. Cambridge: Cambridge University Press.

Boff, K., Kaufman, L. and Thomas, J. P. (eds.) (1986). *Human Computer Interaction (Interact '87)*. Amsterdam: Elsevier-North Holland.

Broadbent, D. E. (1958). *Perception and Communication*. Oxford: Pergamon Press.

Broadbent, D. E. (1977). Levels, hierarchies and the locus of control. *Quarterly Journal of Experimental Psychology*, 29, 181–201.

Broadbent, D. E. (1979). Is a fatigue test now possible? *Ergonomics*, 22, 1277–1290.

Charness, N. (1991). Expertise in chess: The balance between knowledge and search. In K. A. Ericsson and J. Smith (eds.), *Towards a General Theory of Expertise: Prospects and Limits*, pp. 39–63. Cambridge: Cambridge University Press.

Ericsson, K. A. and Smith, J. (eds.) (1991). *Towards a General Theory of Expertise: Prospects and Limits*. Cambridge: Cambridge University Press.

Frankenhaeuser, M. (1986). A psychobiological framework for research on human stress and coping. In M. A. Appley and R. Trumbell (eds.), *Dynamics of Stress: Physiological, Psychological and Social Perspectives*, pp. 101–116. New York: Plenum.

Gopher, D. and Donchin, E. (1986). Workload: An explanation of the concept. In K. Boff, L. Kaufman and J. P. Thomas (eds.), *Handbook of Perception and Performance*, vol. 2, pp. 41/1–49. New York: Wiley.

Hart, S. G. and Staveland, L. E. (1988). Development of NASA-TLX (Task Load Index): Results of empirical and theoretical research. In P. A. Hancock and N. Meshtaki (eds.), *Human Mental Workload*, pp. 139–183. Amsterdam: North Holland.

Hicks, T. G. and Wierwille, W. W. (1979). Comparison of five mental workload assessment procedures in a moving-base driving simulator. *Human Factors*, 21, 129–143.

Hockey, G. R. J. (1979). Stress and the cognitive components of skilled performance. In V. Hamilton and D. M. Warburton (eds.), *Human Stress and Cognition: An Information Processing Approach*, pp. 141–177. Chichester: Wiley.

Hockey, G. R. J. (1986). Changes in operator efficiency as a function of environmental stress, fatigue and circadian rhythms. In K. Boff, L. Kaufman and J. P. Thomas (eds.), *Human Computer Interaction (Interact '87)*, pp. 44/1–49. Amsterdam: Elsevier-North Holland.

Hockey, G. R. J. (1993). Cognitive-energetical control mechanisms in the management of work demands and psychological health. In A. D. Baddeley and L. Weiskrantz (eds.), *Attention, Selection, Awareness and Control: A Tribute to Donald Broadbent*, pp. 328–345. Oxford: Clarendon Press.

Hockey, G. R. J., Briner, R. B., Tattersall, A. J. and Wiethoff, M. (1989). Assessing the impact of computer workload on operator stress: the role of system controllability. *Ergonomics*, 32, 1401–1418.

Hockey, G. R. J., Gaillard, A. W. K. and Coles, M. G. H. (eds.) (1986). *Energetics and Human Information Processing*. Dordrecht: Kluwer.

Hockey, G. R. J. and Maule, A. J. (1995). Unscheduled manual interventions in automated process control. *Ergonomics* (accepted for publication).

Hockey, G. R. J., Payne, R. L. and Rick, J. T. (1995). Intra-individual patterns of hormonal and affective adaptation to work demands: An n = 2 study of junior doctors. *Biological Psychology* (accepted for publication).

Holding, D. H. (ed.) (1981). *Human Skills*. Chichester: Wiley.

Holding, D. H. (1983). Fatigue. In G. R. J. Hockey (ed.), *Stress and Fatigue in Human Performance*, pp. 146–167. Chichester: Wiley.

Kahneman, D. (1971). Remarks on attentional control. In A. F. Sanders (ed.), *Attention and Performance III*, pp. 118–131. Amsterdam: North Holland.

Kahneman, D. (1973). *Attention and Effort*. Englewood Cliffs, NJ: Prentice-Hall.

Kramer, A. F. (1991). Physiological metrics of mental workload: A review of recent progress. In D. L. Damos (ed.), *Multiple-Task Performance*, pp. 279–328. London: Taylor & Francis.

Lundberg, U. and Frankenhaeuser, M. (1978). Psychophysiological reactions to noise as modified by personal control over noise intensity. *Biological Psychology*, 6, 55–59.

Moray, N. (1986). Monitoring behavior and supervisory control. In K. Boff, L. Kaufman and J. P. Thomas (eds.), *Handbook of Perception and Human Performance*, vol. 2, pp. 40/1–51. New York: Wiley.

Norman, D. A. (1981). Categorisation of action slips. *Psychological Review*, 88, 1–15.

Norman, D. A. and Shallice, T. (1986). Attention to action: Willed and automatic control of behavior. In R. J. Davidson, G. E. Schwartz, and D. Shapiro (eds.), *Consciousness and Self-regulation: Advances in Research and Theory*, vol. 4, pp. 1–18. New York: Plenum Press.

O'Donnell, R. D. and Eggemeier, F. T. (1986). Workload assessment methodology. In K. Boff, L. Kaufman and J. P. Thomas (eds.), *Handbook of Perception and Performance*, vol. 2, pp. 42/1–49. New York: Wiley.

Posner, M. I. (1978). *Chronometric Explorations of Mind*. Hillsdale, NJ: Erlbaum.

Rasmussen, J. (1986). *Human Information Processing and Human Machine Interaction*. Amsterdam: North Holland.

Reason, J. T. (1990). *Human Error*. Cambridge: Cambridge University Press.

Reid, G. B. and Nygren, T. E. (1988). The subjective workload assessment technique: A scaling procedure for measuring mental workload. In P. A. Hancock and N. Meshkati (eds.), *Human Mental Workload*, pp. 185–218. Amsterdam: North Holland.

Rissler, A. and Jacobson, L. (1987). Cognitive efficiency during high work-load in final system testing of a large computer system. In M. J. Bullinger and B. Shackel (eds.), *Human Computer Interaction (Interact '87)*. Amsterdam: Elsevier-North Holland.

Roth, E. M. and Woods, D. D. (1988). Aiding human performance, I: Cognitive analysis. *Le Travail Humain*, 51, 39–64.

Rouse, W. B. and Morris, N. M. (1987). Conceptual design of a human error-tolerant interface for complex engineering systems. *Automatica,* 23, 231–235.

Schönpflüg, W. (1983). Coping efficiency and situational demands. In G. R. J. Hockey (ed.), *Stress and Fatigue in Human Performance*, pp. 299–330. Chichester: Wiley.

Schneider, W. and Shiffrin, R. M. (1977). Controlled and automatic human information processing I: Detection, search and attention. *Psychological Review*, 84, 1–66.

Shaffer, L. H. (1975). Multiple attention in continuous verbal tasks. In P. M. A. Rabbitt and S. Dornic (eds.), *Attention and Performance V*. New York: Academic Press.

Sheridan, T. B. (1987). Supervisory control. In G. Salvendy (ed.), *Handbook of Human Factors*, pp. 1243–1268. New York: Wiley.

Sperandio, A. (1978). The regulation of working methods as a function of workload among air traffic controllers. *Ergonomics*, 21, 367–390.

Spettell, C. M. and Liebert, R. M. (1986). Training for safety in automated person-machine systems. *American Psychologist*, 41, 545–550.

Tattersall, A. J. and Hockey, G. R. J. (1995). Level of operator control and changes in heart-rate variability during simulated flight maintenance. *Human Factors* (accepted for publication).

Treisman, A. (1993). The perception of features and objects. In A. D. Baddeley and L. Weiskrantz (eds.), *Attention, Selection, Awareness and Control: A Tribute to Donald Broadbent*, pp. 5–35. Oxford: Clarendon Press.

Wickens, C. D. (1984). Processing resources in attention. In R. Parasuraman and D. R. Davies (eds.), *Varieties of Attention*, pp. 63–102. New York: Academic Press.

Wickens, C. D. (1986). Gain and energetics in information processing. In G. R. J. Hockey, A. W. K. Gaillard, and M. G. H. Coles (eds.), *Energetics and Human Information Processing*, pp. 373–390. Dordrecht: Kluwer.

Wickens, C. D. (1992). *Engineering Psychology and Human Performance*, 2nd edn. New York: HarperCollins.

Wiener, L. (1984). Beyond the sterile cockpit. *Human Factors*, 27, 75–90.

Wierwille, W. W. and Eggemeier, F. T. (1993). Recommendations for mental workload measurement in a test and evaluation environment. *Human Factors*, 35, 263–281.

Wilkinson, R. T. (1962). Muscle tension during mental work under sleep deprivation. *Journal of Experimental Psychology*, 64, 565–71.

2

Body Rhythms and Shiftwork

Simon Folkard

Humankind has evolved as a diurnal species – one that is habitually active during daylight hours and sleeps at night. Since the Industrial Revolution, however, an increasing proportion of our workforce has attempted to overcome this natural bias, and to work at night. This colonization of the night can result in a number of problems both for the individuals concerned and for the organizations employing them. This chapter summarizes these problems and the manner in which researchers from many disciplines, including psychologists, have attempted to solve them. Following an account of variations in psychological variables over the normal day, the concept of an underlying 'biological clock' is introduced. The characteristics of this clock are then considered in some detail to provide a framework within which the major problems associated with shiftwork are subsequently considered.

TIME-OF-DAY EFFECTS IN PERFORMANCE AND AFFECTIVE STATE

Psychologists have long recognized that people's efficiency at performing mental tasks is not constant, but varies over the course of the day. Early theorists ascribed these variations to either a build-up of 'mental fatigue' with increased time awake (e.g., Thorndike, 1900) or to an underlying 'sleepiness rhythm', which was independent of whether people had actually slept (e.g., Michelson, 1897). As we shall see below, recent evidence suggests that both the duration of time awake and an underlying rhythm contribute to variations in 'alertness' or 'fatigue' over the day.

Task Demands and the Arousal Theory

Many of the early studies on time of day and performance were concerned with the optimization of work schedules in industrial and educational contexts. These, and subsequent studies, have indicated that at least for some types of task there are fairly consistent trends in efficiency over the day, but that the nature of the trend varies according to task demands. This is illustrated for three different types of task in Figure 2.1, in which the normal curves in body temperature (top curve) and in subjectively rated alertness (bottom curve) are also shown. In the case of performance, the efficiency at each time of day has been expressed as a percentage of the overall mean for the day.

Inspection of Figure 2.1 suggests that the performance trend over the day for a given task may depend on the short-term memory load involved in carrying out that task. Simple serial search speed, such as that involved in 'proofreading' (the second curve), involves little, if any, memory component and reaches a maximum in the evening. On more complex, 'working memory' tasks, such as logical reasoning, performance tends to improve to about midday and then declines (the middle curve). These tasks require the use of a working memory system which involves a number of different cognitive sub-systems (e.g., short-term storage, information processing, throughput, etc.) and it is likely that the pattern observed for this type of task is the outcome of a combination of different trends associated with the different cognitive mechanisms involved. When the task is one of 'immediate retention' which emphasizes memory mechanisms and requires people to memorize digit strings or passages of text, then immediate recall tends to be best early in the day and to steadily decline over the rest of the day (see the fourth curve in Figure 2.1, and Folkard and Monk, 1980).

The apparent parallelism between performance on simple tasks and the temperature rhythm led to an early view that diurnal variations in temperature were responsible for those in performance (Kleitman, 1939). However, this hypothesized link between performance and temperature was discredited when it was realized that when time of day was controlled for, residual variations in temperature were unrelated to those in performance (Rutenfranz, Aschoff and Mann,

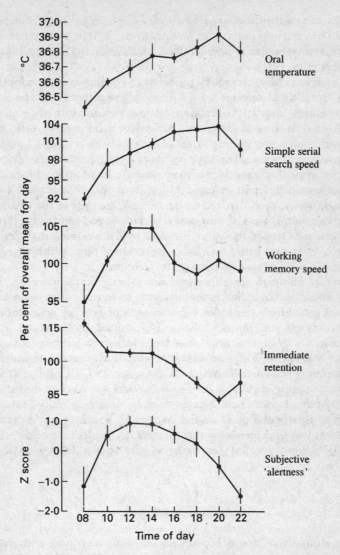

Fig. 2.1 Time-of-day trends averaged from a number of independent studies for temperature, three different measures of performance, and subjective ratings of alertness. (See Folkard, 1983, for details of the individual studies.)

1972). It was then thought that time-of-day effects in performance could be explained in terms of an underlying rhythm in sleepiness or 'arousal' that tended to parallel the diurnal variations in temperature (Colquhoun, 1971).

One reason why this arousal model was so enthusiastically adopted was that it could account for the many different trends observed. It assumed an inverted U-function relating performance to arousal such that, as arousal increased, performance on a given task improved until some optimal level of arousal was reached. Further increases in arousal beyond the optimum were thought to result in a decline in performance due to 'over-arousal'. In addition, the model hypothesized different inverted U-functions for different levels of task difficulty, such that the easier the task, the higher the optimal level of arousal. Thus, the arousal model could account for the three performance trends shown in Figure 2.1, if it assumed that 'serial search' tasks were easier than 'working memory' ones, which were, in turn, easier than those of 'immediate retention'.

In fact, although immediate retention is better in the morning, the available evidence indicates that delayed (seven days or more) retention is generally better following afternoon or evening presentation (see Folkard and Monk, 1985a). The arousal model could also account for this interaction, since there was some independent evidence that although high arousal at presentation impaired immediate retention, it benefited delayed recall (Eysenck, 1982). Unfortunately, this explanatory power of the arousal model was also its downfall. Many sets of data could be explained by assuming individuals to start at a particular point on the inverted U, but there was no independent way of determining this. Further, as we shall see below, this model cannot account for many of the results from shiftwork studies.

Individual Differences

The arousal model also encounters problems in coping with individual differences in people's trends in performance over the day. It has long been known that the trends for individuals may differ considerably from one another, and attempts have been made to link these differences to scores on personality measures. There is some evidence that the performance of introverts on simple tasks may reach a maximum somewhat earlier in the day than that of extroverts, and that this is paralleled by similar differences in body temperature (Blake, 1971). However, rather greater differences in the performance trends for simple tasks are associated with the personality dimension of 'morningness–eveningness', and these are not paralleled by a similar difference in the temperature rhythm as the arousal theory would suggest (see the review by Kerkhof, 1985).

'Morning' and 'evening' types are usually identified by means of a self-assessment questionnaire (e.g., Horne and Ostberg, 1976; Smith, Rilley and Midkiff, 1989). This type of questionnaire attempts to distinguish between those who wake early and quickly, but who also feel tired relatively early at night ('morning types') and those who take some time to get going properly in the morning but happily stay up late at night ('evening types'). The performance of extreme morning types on a simple detection task has been found to deteriorate over most of the day, while that of evening types tended to improve (Horne, Brass and Pettit, 1980). In contrast, the time of the maximum body temperature in these two groups differed only by about one hour, which is insufficient, if it reflects arousal level, to account for the difference in the performance trend.

It seems probable, but as yet unproven, that 'morningness–eveningness' is a stable trait rather than a reflection of recent habit, and there is a slight tendency for both women and older people to score more highly on morningness scales. While it has yet to be established whether there are consistent gender differences in the trend in any kind of performance over the day, there is some evidence that females may perform a working memory task rather better than males in the morning (Baker, Holding and Loeb, 1984). Further, if these various individual differences reflect different trends in arousal level (despite the failure of the temperature rhythm to do so), then the nature of the differences in diurnal performance trends should depend on the demands of the task. Thus, if morning types are better than evening types on a simple detection task in the morning due to a higher level of arousal, they should be worse at that time on a more memory-loaded task that is thought to be impaired by high arousal. This possibility has received little attention, but the few studies that have been conducted suggest that the differences associated with both introversion and morningness are not dependent on task demands (Eysenck and Folkard, 1980; Petros, Beckwith and Anderson, 1990).

Some Complications in Deriving Practical Recommendations

These differences in the performance trend over the day associated with task demands and individual differences complicate any recommendations for the scheduling of work over the normal day. Indeed, to some extent this complexity was recognized by early educational researchers in this area, who, on the basis of the different trends found in immediate memory and simple performance measures, suggested that more 'mentally taxing' school subjects should be taught in the morning (e.g., Gates, 1916). This recommendation is clearly questionable in the light of the superior delayed retention following afternoon presentation (Folkard, Monk, Bradbury and Rosenthall, 1977) and the finding of superior examination results by students who attend classes in the afternoon or evening rather than in the morning (Skinner, 1985).

The situation is further complicated by two other factors. First, some, but not all, authors have found a temporary decrease in simple (non-memory-loaded) performance in the early afternoon, which has been interpreted as reflecting a similar decrease in arousal (Colquhoun, 1971). This temporary decrease appears to be only partially dependent on the ingestion of food (see Folkard and Monk, 1985a) and may thus affect early afternoon performance whether or not individuals eat at lunch time. Secondly, there are a large number of jobs, such as those involving simple manual dexterity or complex decision-making, for which no consistent performance trend over the day has been established. Thus, although we know that task demands affect performance trends, we cannot as yet make specific recommendations as to the best time of day to perform most given tasks.

Finally, even for those tasks for which consistent diurnal trends have been established (e.g., as in Figure 2.1), it is important to consider the contribution to these trends of the mental fatigue associated with the time elapsed since waking rather than by the underlying sleepiness rhythm. Thus, for example, the trend for immediate retention shown in Figure 2.1 might imply that people should get up earlier than normal in order to perform such tasks at 08.00. However, if they did so, and the trend were largely dependent on mental fatigue associated with time since waking, then their ability may have deteriorated by 08.00. Such considerations become far more important when people change their sleep/wake cycle by up to twelve hours in order to work on a night shift. Before considering performance under these conditions, we thus need some understanding of the factors underlying trends in performance over the day.

CIRCADIAN RHYTHMS

Life on Earth has evolved in an environment subject to regular and pronounced changes produced by planetary movements. The rotation of the Earth on its own axis results in the twenty-four-hour light/dark cycle, while its rotation around the sun gives rise to seasonal changes in light and temperature. The combined influence of the moon and sun leads to variations in gravitational pull on the Earth's surface that are reflected in complex but predictable tidal movements of the sea approximately ($\sim$) every 12.4 and 24.8 hours. These resultant tides themselves vary in magnitude every $\sim$14.7 and $\sim$29.5 days according to the phase of the moon.

During the process of evolution these periodic changes have become internalized so that they allow organisms to anticipate changes in their environments. Such an anticipatory ability clearly has an adaptive value for most species, and has presumably been strengthened through natural selection (Cloudsley-Thompson, 1980). It is now widely accepted that living organisms possess 'body clocks', such that the environmental changes mentioned above are not merely responded to by organisms, but are actually anticipated by them.

This 'anticipation' of environmental events is mediated by regular cyclic changes in body processes. In humans, the most pronounced of these are the approximately twenty-four-hour 'circadian' ('around a day') rhythms that occur in almost all physiological measures (Minors and Waterhouse, 1981a). The most important characteristics of such rhythms are (a) their period, which is the time taken for one

45

complete cycle of the rhythm (normally twenty-four hours), (b) their phase, which is a measure of their timing with respect to some external criterion such as clock time, and (c) their amplitude, which is usually measured as the difference between the maximum value and the average value over a complete cycle.

The Body Clock(s)

The best evidence that human circadian rhythms are at least partially controlled by an internal, or *endogenous*, body clock comes from studies in which people have been isolated from their normal environmental time cues, or '*zeitgebers*' (from the German for 'time-givers'). In their pioneering studies Aschoff and Wever (1962) isolated individual subjects from all environmental time cues in a 'temporal isolation unit' for up to nineteen days, while Siffre (1964) lived in an underground cave for two months. In both studies people continued to wake up and go to sleep on a regular basis, but instead of doing so every twenty-four hours, they did so approximately every twenty-five hours. The circadian rhythms in other physiological measures, including body temperature and urinary electrolytes, typically showed an identical period to that of their sleep/wake cycle.

However, about a third of the people that have subsequently been studied in this way have spontaneously shown a rather different pattern of results that has important theoretical and practical implications. In these cases the sleep/wake cycle and body temperature rhythms have become 'internally desynchronized', such that they run with distinctly different periods from one another. The temperature rhythm continues to run with an average period of approximately twenty-five hours, while the sleep/wake cycle shows either a much shorter or a much longer period than either approximately twenty-five hours or twenty-four hours (Wever, 1979). Interestingly, this phenomenon of 'spontaneous internal desynchronization' has been shown to occur more frequently in older people, and in those with higher neuroticism scores (Lund, 1974). Further, while women are more likely to desynchronize by shortening their sleep/wake cycle, men are more likely to do so by lengthening it (Wever, 1984). These individual differences may relate to the dimension of 'morningness' (see above) and may have important implications for the adjustment to shiftwork (see below).

At a more theoretical level, the fact that the temperature rhythm and sleep/wake cycle can run with distinctly different periods from one another has been taken to suggest that the human 'circadian system' comprises two, or perhaps more, underlying processes. The first of these is a relatively strong 'endogenous' (internal) body clock that is dominant in controlling the circadian rhythm in body temperature (and in other measures such as urinary potassium and plasma cortisol) and is relatively unaffected by external factors. The second is a weaker process that is more 'exogenous' in nature (i.e., more prone to external influences) and is dominant in controlling the sleep/wake cycle (and other circadian rhythms such as those in plasma growth hormone and urinary calcium). There is some debate as to whether this second process is clock-like in nature, but there seems to be general agreement that some circadian rhythms are dominantly controlled by the endogenous body clock, while others are more influenced by external factors.

These two processes are thought to be asymmetrically coupled such that the endogenous clock exerts a considerably greater influence on the weaker exogenous process than vice versa. Thus, for example, internally desynchronized subjects show such a strong tendency to wake up at a particular point of the temperature rhythm, irrespective of when they went to sleep, that their sleeps can vary in duration from four to sixteen hours (Czeisler, Weitzman, Moore-Ede, Zimmerman and Kronauer, 1980; Zulley, Wever and Aschoff, 1981). Further readings in this complex but fascinating area are suggested at the end of the chapter. The important points to bear in mind are (1) that circadian rhythms in different measures are not all controlled by a single system, so that different rhythms may adjust at very different rates from one another when people work at unusual times of day, and (2) that sleep is likely to be disrupted unless the temperature rhythm has adjusted to such a change.

Entrainment by Zeitgebers

Under normal circumstances both the endogenous body clock and the weaker exogenous process will be entrained to a twenty-four-

47

hour period by strong natural zeitgebers, including the light/dark cycle, and, in the case of humans, knowledge of clock time and the behaviour of other members of society. As a result, all our circadian rhythms normally show a fixed phase relationship to one another. For example, our urinary adrenaline level reaches a maximum around midday, while our body temperature peaks at about 20.00. Similarly, all other circadian rhythms will reach their maxima at their appointed time, allowing us to fall asleep at night and waking us up in the morning. The occasional late night may affect those rhythms controlled by the weaker process, but are less likely to upset the strong oscillator and hence our body temperature rhythm and the time at which we spontaneously wake up.

However, this inherent stability in the human circadian system can pose problems if a mismatch arises between our internal timing system and our external time cues. The simplest example of this occurs when people fly across time zones, since all the zeitgebers change. A flight from Europe to North America involves crossing several time zones, so that on arrival our timing system is five to nine hours too early for the local zeitgebers. Although people seldom experience problems falling asleep after their arrival, their body temperature rhythms usually take about a week to delay their timing by the appropriate amount (Wegmann and Klein, 1985). For the first few nights, this often results in people waking up in the early hours of the morning and being unable to get back to sleep. The rhythms in other processes adjust at different rates, presumably depending on the degree to which they are controlled by the endogenous clock or the weaker exogenous process. As a result, the normal phase relationship between rhythms breaks down and is only slowly re-established as the various rhythms adjust to the new time zone. This internal dissociation between rhythms is thought to be responsible for the 'jet-lag', feelings of disorientation or general malaise, experienced by many people after flying across time zones.

These feelings of jet-lag are normally worse following an eastward flight, which requires an advancing of the body's timing system, than following a westward one requiring a delay. This directional asymmetry effect is thought to be related to the fact that the endogenous period of our circadian system is slightly greater than twenty-four hours. Thus, in the absence of any zeitgebers our rhythms will tend to delay rather than to advance. This bias towards a delay will assist adjustment to westward flights but inhibit it to eastward ones. As we shall see below, this difference has implications for the design of shift systems.

When shiftworkers go on to the night shift, most environmental zeitgebers remain constant and discourage adjustment of the circadian system. The natural light/dark cycle, the clock time, and most social cues do not change, while the timing of shiftworkers' work can be delayed by up to sixteen hours, and that of their sleep by up to twelve hours. From what we have learnt so far, it is clear that the adjustment of a shiftworker's body clock to these changes is likely to be very slow, if indeed it occurs at all. We shall return to this and associated problems later in the chapter.

Experimental Manipulations of Zeitgebers

In view of their important theoretical and practical implications, a large number of studies have examined the role of different zeitgebers in entraining the circadian timing system. For most lower animals, the light/dark cycle appears to be the most powerful zeitgeber. Light impinging on the retina results in messages being sent to the suprachiasmatic nucleus (SCN) of the hypothalamus, which in turn sends messages to suppress the secretion of melatonin by the pineal gland. The SCN and the secretion of melatonin are thus seen as playing crucial roles in controlling circadian rhythms. Until recently, however, this process in humans seemed rather more complex.

In his pioneering studies Wever (1979) found that some individuals' circadian rhythms could not be entrained by an artificial twenty-four-hour light/dark cycle unless they were specifically requested to go to bed when the lights faded, and to get up at 'dawn'. This was interpreted as indicating that for humans the most effective zeitgebers were of an essentially informative or social nature (e.g., Hughes and Folkard, 1976). However, it has now been shown that if a considerably higher level of illumination is used than is necessary for other mammals, but still less than normal daylight, melatonin secretion can be suppressed in humans (Lewy, Wehr, Goodwin, Newsome and Markey, 1980), and their circadian rhythms can be entrained (Wever,

49

Polasek and Wildgruber, 1983). Indeed, further research has shown that both exposure to bright light (Czeisler, Kronauer, Allan, Duffy, Jewett, Brown and Ronda, 1989) and artificially 'feeding' melatonin (Lewy, Ahmed, Jackson and Sack, 1992) can 'reset' humans' circadian rhythms, with the extent and direction of the resetting depending on the precise timing of their administration. Bright light administered in the morning (05.00 to 11.00) will advance the body clock to an earlier phase, while the same light administered at night (21.00 to 03.00) will set it to a later phase. These findings have generated considerable interest in the potential uses of bright light and melatonin in alleviating shiftwork and jet-lag problems, and this will be returned to later.

Despite these recent developments on the influence of bright light, artificial zeitgebers, including dim light, can be used in experimental settings both to simulate the abrupt changes associated with shiftwork and jet-lag, and to enforce internal desynchronization. Thus, for example, people can be exposed to artificial zeitgebers that are progressively shortened or lengthened by a small amount each 'day'. It has been found that the sleep/wake cycle follows these changes in the zeitgeber period very closely over a wide range of periods. However, circadian rhythms in body temperature, and in various other physiological functions such as urinary potassium, have a far more restricted range of entrainment and, under normal levels of artificial illumination, can only be entrained down to a period of approximately twenty-three hours or up to approximately twenty-seven hours. Outside this range, rhythms that are dominantly controlled by the endogenous body clock 'break out' from the sleep/wake cycle and free-run with their endogenous period. Thus, by using artificial 'day' lengths of less than twenty-three hours or greater than twenty-seven hours, internal desynchronization can be induced in everyone.

This type of study is important because it allows the behaviour of the rhythms in different measures to be compared. Thus rhythms that are dominantly controlled by the endogenous body clock described above should behave in a similar manner to one another and to that in body temperature, while those that are more dependent on the weaker exogenous process should follow the sleep/wake cycle for longer. Similarities in the behaviour of different rhythms may thus tell us something about their causal relationship (Wever, 1983) and may allow us to extrapolate from one to the other in shiftwork situations. For example, the rhythm in simple serial search speed has not only been found to behave in a very similar manner to that in body temperature in abnormal day length studies (Folkard, Wever and Wildgruber, 1983) but has also been found to adjust to shiftwork at a similar rate (Monk, Knauth, Folkard and Rutenfranz, 1978). The importance of this is that body temperature measures, which are relatively easy to obtain, could be used as an indirect measure, or 'marker', of simple serial search speed, which is rather more difficult to assess in most shiftworking situations. Conversely, the rhythms in performance on more memory-loaded cognitive tasks, and in subjective ratings of alertness, behave rather differently from that in body temperature, indicating that the latter may be a rather poor 'marker' for these processes (Folkard *et al.*, 1983; Folkard, Hume, Minors, Waterhouse and Watson, 1985).

Dissecting Rhythms

Measurements of any physiological or psychological variable reflect not only the activity of our endogenous circadian timing system, but also a number of exogenous factors. These factors may themselves show an approximately twenty-four-hour pattern and thus enhance or diminish the magnitude of the overt circadian rhythm, depending on their phase relationship to the endogenous component. Thus, for example, body temperature is known to fall when we go to sleep, and to rise as a result of physical (and perhaps mental) activity, quite independently of any endogenous circadian rhythm. This can result in spuriously fast estimates of the adjustment of the body temperature rhythm to shiftwork.

Some rhythms, such as those in urinary noradrenalin and pulse rate, appear to be almost entirely due to variations in activity level, i.e., they are exogenous in origin, while others, such as those in body temperature, urinary adrenaline and potassium, and subjectively rated alertness are at least partially controlled by the endogenous body clock. In these latter cases the size and shape of the endogenous and exogenous components can be estimated from various types of

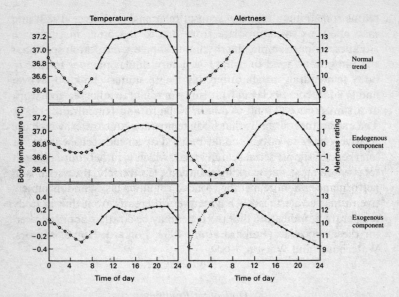

Fig. 2.2 The normal trends in temperature and alertness over the twenty-four-hour day (top panels) broken down into their endogenous (middle panels) and exogenous (lower panels) components. The dotted lines (open points) indicate readings taken or estimated during sleep. The discontinuity in the normal trend in alertness, and in its exogenous component, on awakening reflects a 'sleep inertia' effect. (Derived from Folkard, 1988, and Folkard and Akerstedt, 1992.)

temporal isolation studies. This is illustrated in Figure 2.2 for the circadian rhythms in temperature (after Folkard, 1988) and alertness (after Folkard and Akerstedt, 1992).

Two important points emerge from inspection of Figure 2.2. First, the normal or 'overt' rhythms in both these variables reflect both endogenous and exogenous components that are of similar magnitude to one another. Secondly, however, for temperature these two components are approximately 'in phase' with one another such that the exogenous component (bottom panel) enhances the amplitude of the endogenous component (middle panel) in 'producing' the normal rhythm (top panel). In contrast, the two components of the normal rhythm in alertness show somewhat different phases such that the normal rhythm in alertness is of approximately the same amplitude as its endogenous component.

This difference in the phase relationship between the endogenous and exogenous components of these overt rhythms will result in them responding rather differently to the abrupt changes in the timing of sleep associated with shiftwork. The temperature rhythm of shiftworkers will tend to flatten when they move on to the night shift, since the normally phased endogenous and the shifted exogenous components will tend to cancel each other out. However, the alertness rhythm, which normally can be measured only when people are awake, is less prone to this cancelling-out effect because the two underlying components differ in their normal phase. It would appear that this is why these two rhythms have been shown to behave rather differently in abnormal day length studies (Folkard *et al.*, 1985) and why temperature cannot be used as a 'marker' for alertness (see above).

Even without this complication of the phase relationship between the endogenous and exogenous components of an overt rhythm, it is clear that some rhythms will be virtually entirely dependent on the timing of sleep and wakefulness, and the concomitant timing of activity and meals. Others will be relatively uninfluenced by these factors and will depend more on the strong endogenous oscillator, which, as we have seen, is likely to adjust rather slowly, if at all, to the shifts of the sleep/wake cycle associated with night work.

SHIFTWORK

There is no doubt that shiftwork can result in a variety of problems for the individual worker. These range from difficulties with sleep that depend, at least in part, on a disturbed circadian timing system, through impaired subjective (and perhaps objective) measures of health, to an impoverished social life. These problems are often reflected in general feelings of malaise and may result in various consequences for both the individual and the employer (Waterhouse, Folkard and Minors, 1992).

It is generally assumed that disturbed circadian rhythms are central to the problems experienced by an individual shiftworker, and, indeed, Reinberg, Andlauer, De Prins, Malbec, Vieux and Bourdeleau (1984) provided dramatic evidence to support this view. They found that workers who had medical and social problems as a result of shiftwork tended to show internal desynchronization between their body temperature rhythm and sleep/wake cycle, while those who were better able to tolerate shiftwork did not.

The problems of shiftwork do not, however, arise equally in all individuals. Indeed, it has been estimated that about 10 per cent of shiftworkers may positively enjoy their pattern of working, while about 60 per cent are able to tolerate it reasonably well. It is only a minority (20–30 per cent) of shiftworkers who positively dislike shiftwork and hence are most likely to be 'at risk' (Harrington, 1978). Nor do all shift systems result in equal problems for (some of) the individuals employed on them. As we shall see below, there is a great diversity of shift systems, and it appears to be primarily those that necessitate a change in the timing of sleep that cause trouble (Kogi, 1985).

The Nature and Prevalence of Shiftwork

The prevalence of shiftwork has increased considerably over the past fifty years in most industrialized countries, and is currently rapidly increasing in the developing countries (Kogi, 1985). There appear to be three main reasons for this, which can be broadly classified as social, technological and economic. There is an increased demand for the provision of twenty-four-hour services such as medical care and transportation, while technological advances have resulted in the use of continuous processes in, for example, the steel and chemical industries. However, the major reason for this increased prevalence appears to be economic, in that shiftwork can improve the return on capital investment.

In view of this, it is not surprising that the prevalence of shiftwork varies dramatically with both the size and nature of the organization concerned. Recent European statistics indicate that the incidence of night work is twice as high in larger organizations, i.e. those employing more than fifty individuals, and that the involvement in night work varies from about 5 per cent in building and civil engineering to about 40 per cent in transport and communication (Wedderburn, 1993). Interestingly, over 10 per cent of those employed in banking and finance worked at night at least 25 per cent of the time, and this figure is expected to increase in the future.

Comparisons between countries are complicated by inconsistencies in their criteria, but some 5 per cent of employees in the European Community work at night 'all', or 'almost all', of the time, while 17.6 per cent do so 'at least 25 per cent of the time'. These figures will, of course, underestimate the overall incidence of shiftwork since they exclude shiftworkers who seldom or never work at night. Statistics for developing countries are not normally available, but the incidence of shiftwork in these countries appears to be increasing for primarily economic reasons (Ong and Kogi, 1990). Economic factors also appear to be resulting in the spread of shiftwork out of traditional shiftworking industries into white-collar jobs, such as computer operating, although there are few statistics on the prevalence of shiftwork in these jobs.

This sizeable minority of the workforce is engaged on a wide variety of shift systems. These can be classified according to their key features (see Kogi, 1985), the most important of which is whether the system involves a displacement of normal sleep time. Other features include whether an individual always works on the same shift (e.g., evening or night) or rotates from one shift to another, and, if so, the speed and direction of rotation. However, even most so-called 'permanent' night workers typically rotate from a nocturnal routine on their work days to a diurnal (i.e., day-oriented) one on their days off. Thus, in terms of their endogenous circadian timing systems, the label of a 'permanent' shift system is somewhat misleading. Finally, it is also worth noting that the speed and direction of rotation of a shift system determine how fast or slow an individual's circadian system would have to run in order to stay adjusted to it.

Disturbed Rhythms and Sleep

Studies of the effects of shiftwork on circadian rhythms in physiological functions have been largely confined to the body temperature rhythm. This is mainly due to the ease with which temperature

55

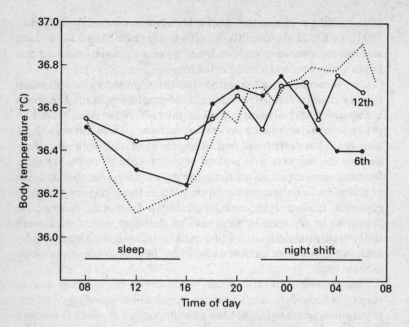

Fig. 2.3 The disturbance of the body temperature rhythm on the sixth and twelfth successive night shifts. The dotted line shows what a totally adjusted temperature rhythm would look like. (Derived from Colquhoun, Blake and Edwards, 1968.)

rhythms can be measured, and is perhaps unfortunate in view of the fact that the endogenous and exogenous components enhance one another in producing the overt rhythm (see Figure 2.2). Nevertheless, there is considerable agreement that whereas the body temperature rhythm is often disturbed by working at night, it rarely adjusts completely over a normal span of night duty and rapidly reverts to its normal state when the individual has a rest day or changes to a different shift. Indeed, any adjustment to night work that is observed could simply reflect a shifted exogenous component and an unaltered endogenous one. Thus, the temperature rhythm typically shows a 'flattening' or reduction in amplitude but little evidence of a real phase shift. An example of this is shown in Figure 2.3 from a simulated shiftwork study of Colquhoun, Blake and Edwards (1968).

On the sixth successive night shift (heavy line), temperature continued to fall rather than rise over the work period. By the twelfth night shift (light line) the rhythm had flattened to such an extent that any estimate of phase would be fairly meaningless. Subsequent modelling of these data has suggested that the changes in the measured rhythm simply reflected a changed timing of the exogenous component rather than any phase shift of the endogenous one (Folkard, 1988). Further, large-scale surveys carried out in Germany and Japan have indicated that it is extremely rare for people to work more than six or seven successive night shifts (Kogi, 1985) and this will clearly limit the amount of adjustment that might occur. Studies of other physiological rhythms for which there is evidence of an endogenous component (e.g., urinary potassium and plasma cortisol) typically show a similar pattern of results to body temperature. In contrast, some rhythms, such as pulse rate and urinary noradrenalin, may show relatively good adjustment to night work, but this presumably simply reflects their largely exogenous origin (Akerstedt, 1985).

One of the major complaints of shiftworkers is that their day sleeps between successive night shifts are disturbed. They often attribute this to increased environmental noise (Rutenfranz, Knauth and Angersbach, 1981) and that may well be a contributing factor. However, it seems probable that the major cause of disturbed day sleeps is that they take place at an inappropriate phase of the endogenous timing system (see above). Thus, unless this system has adjusted to night work, day sleeps will be of reduced duration compared to night sleeps. This has been confirmed using both objective sleep measures (Akerstedt, 1985) and large-scale survey measures (Kogi, 1985).

In Figure 2.4 the solid line shows the reported sleep duration of shiftworkers as a function of the time of day at which they fell asleep (Kogi, 1985). It is clear from this figure that normal length sleeps (i.e., of eight hours) were obtained only when the shiftworkers went to sleep between about 21.00 and 01.00. Later sleep onsets resulted in a progressive shortening of sleep duration to a minimum of about two hours for sleeps started between 13.00 and 17.00. Clearly these data might potentially reflect not only the influence of the body clock, but also a wide variety of other factors, including environmental noise levels and social and family pressures. However, a very

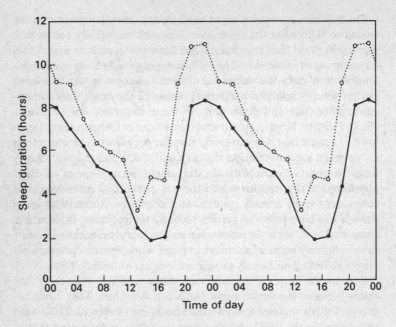

Fig. 2.4 The dependence of the sleep duration of shiftworkers on the time of day at which they went to sleep (solid line) and the influence of the endogenous body clock on the sleep duration of internally desynchronized people (dotted line). Both curves are 'double-plotted' to emphasize their rhythmic nature. (Adapted from Folkard, 1988.)

similar pattern of sleep has been observed in internally desynchronized people who were removed from all external influences (dotted line) and must, therefore, reflect only the influence of their endogenous body clocks. The similarity between the shapes of these two curves clearly suggests that the sleep duration of shiftworkers is largely determined by their endogenous body clocks (Folkard, 1988), while the generally longer sleeps of the internally desynchronized people simply reflects the fact that they only went to sleep once every thirty-three hours.

On average, the day sleeps of shiftworkers taken between night shifts are between one and four hours shorter than normal night sleeps, and this is largely due to a reduction in Stage 2 and rapid eye movement (REM) sleep, rather than in the deeper slow wave sleep (SWS). Loss of SWS, but not that of REM or Stage 2 sleep, is typically 'made up' on recovery night sleeps taken on 'off days'. Thus, largely due to the influence of their body clocks, night workers will show a cumulative sleep deficit over successive night shifts, which is only partially restored on their rest days (Akerstedt, 1985).

Associated Medical and Social Problems

These disturbances of circadian rhythms and sleep undoubtedly contribute to the other major complaints of shiftworkers, namely impaired health and impoverished social life. The general feelings of malaise experienced by shiftworkers are similar to those associated with jet-lag and are reflected in an increased incidence of various psychosomatic conditions (Rutenfranz, Haider and Koller, 1985; Bohle and Tilley, 1989). There is also fairly clear evidence for an increased incidence of gastro-intestinal disorders, including ulcers, in shiftworkers and increasing evidence for a greater cardiovascular risk (Waterhouse *et al.*, 1992). However, as yet there is no clear evidence that this is a direct consequence of the disturbance of circadian rhythms associated with shiftwork.

It is important to recognize that the adverse effects of shiftwork may take many years before manifesting themselves in impaired health (Rutenfranz *et al.*, 1985). Further, the impact of shiftwork is likely to depend on a large number of intervening variables, such as housing conditions, work conditions, and the quality of social life, which may in turn be influenced by the type of shift system. Rotating shiftworkers are less likely to be members or office-holders in various organizations, including political parties and parent–teacher associations. They tend to have fewer friends than day workers, and those they do have are largely restricted to fellow shiftworkers (Colligan and Rosa, 1990). Even contact with members of their own family tends to occur at unusual and often inconvenient times of day. The main advantage of night work, often cited by those 10 per cent who positively enjoy it (see above), is an enhanced ability to pursue solitary hobbies (e.g., gardening or fishing) during daylight hours.

Impaired Productivity and Safety

In view of the disturbed rhythms, partial sleep deprivation, general feelings of malaise and impoverished social life of nightworkers, it is perhaps not surprising that most of the available evidence suggests that the night shift is associated with impaired productivity and safety. However, the body of evidence to support this is not large, since it has proved extremely difficult to obtain the necessary, uncontaminated, measures needed to assess the extent of this problem. Thus, for example, in many shiftworking situations impaired nighttime productivity or safety could reflect the use of less efficient or more dangerous machines since their maintenance is often confined to the day shift (see Meers, 1975). Nevertheless, a number of studies have managed to obtain relatively continuous measures of performance speed or accuracy over the twenty-four-hour period, and these are summarized in Figure 2.5. It is clear from this figure that job performance is low over most of the night shift, reaching its minimum at about 03.00.

With regard to safety, a number of authors have pointed out that many major catastrophes, such as those at Three Mile Island and Chernobyl, have occurred at night (Mitler, Carskadon, Czeisler, Dement, Dinges and Graeber, 1988), but there appears to be only a single study that has managed to examine accident (injury) frequencies across shifts in a situation where the a priori risk appeared to be constant. Rotating shiftworkers showed a 23 per cent increase in overall risk on the night shift relative to the morning shift, and this figure increased to 82 per cent when only the more serious injuries incurred by self-paced workers were considered (Smith, Folkard and Poole, 1994). These figures clearly support the view that safety may be impaired on the night shift, a topic of particular concern in situations such as nuclear power and transport where there may be a risk to the general public, but they give little indication as to the underlying cause(s) for this increased risk.

The results from laboratory studies, and from field studies in which shiftworkers have voluntarily performed various tasks for the researchers, suggest that the reduced safety and performance efficiency at night may in part be due to disturbed circadian rhythms, and in part to the cumulative sleep deficit that accrues over successive night

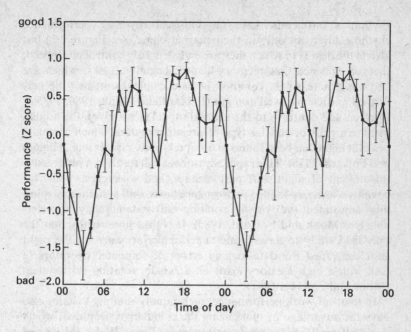

Fig. 2.5. The mean trend (and standard deviations) in job performance measures based on a Z transformation of the results from six published field studies of shiftworkers' performance. The curve is 'double-plotted' to emphasize its rhythmic nature. (See Folkard and Monk, 1979, for details of the studies concerned.)

shifts. Some researchers in this field emphasize the parallelism found between the circadian rhythm in body temperature and that in performance efficiency on some tasks (see above). They argue that permanent shift systems will maximize the adjustment of temperature, and hence performance, rhythms as well as resulting in longer sleeps between night shifts (e.g., Wilkinson, 1992). However, this perspective fails to take account of either the rapid readjustment that occurs on days off or of the cumulative sleep debt that builds up over the longer spans of successive night shifts involved on permanent shift systems (Folkard, 1992).

In addition, as we have seen, the concept of a single performance rhythm is erroneous. Like physiological rhythms, performance rhythms differ not only in their normal phase (see Figure 2.1) but also in the degree to which they are endogenously controlled. Indeed, there is evidence that memory-loaded, cognitive tasks, which are becoming increasingly common in paid employment, may be performed particularly well at night (Folkard and Monk, 1980, 1985a). Further, and contrary to the arousal model (see above), the adjustment to night work of this type of circadian rhythm, which normally peaks at night, has been found to occur relatively rapidly (e.g., Hughes and Folkard, 1976). This rapid adjustment will result in a progressive impairment of night-shift performance, and so suggests that, for cognitive, memory-loaded performance tasks, shift systems that minimize adjustment (i.e., rapidly rotating shift systems) may be preferable (see Monk and Folkard, 1985). It is thus noteworthy that the only field study to have found superior performance on the night shift concerned the data-logging errors of computer operators (a task with a high memory load) on a rapidly rotating shift system (Monk and Embrey, 1981).

In terms of work performance, such rapidly rotating systems also have the advantage of minimizing the cumulative sleep debt which can itself result in impaired performance (Tepas, Walsh, Moss and Armstrong, 1981; Tilley, Wilkinson, Warren, Watson and Drud, 1982; Wilkinson, 1965). Indeed, Vidacek, Kaliterna, Radosevic-Vidacek and Folkard (1986) have shown that even for a simple job requiring manual dexterity, the beneficial effects of circadian adjustment may be outweighed by the detrimental effects of cumulative sleep debt after only three successive night shifts. There is also evidence that this sleep debt may affect productivity and safety, not only directly, but also indirectly through a short-lived, temporary, 'night-shift paralysis' (probably a waking form of 'sleep paralysis'). Although rare, the incidence of this paralysis peaks at about 05.00 and increases in an approximately exponential manner over successive night shifts. When it does occur it may totally prevent workers from performing their job for up to five minutes (Folkard, Condon and Herbert, 1984; Folkard and Condon, 1987). In general, it would thus appear that, unless the shiftworker is engaged in a particularly crucial task and is willing to remain on a nocturnal routine on his or her rest days, the advantages of permanent shift systems may be outweighed by their disadvantages. The alternative of using rapidly rotating shifts will minimize the cumulative sleep debt and may be particularly advantageous for the night-time performance of the increasingly common memory-loaded, cognitive tasks (Folkard, 1990).

Possible Interventions

There are a number of possible interventions that may help to alleviate the problems associated with shiftwork. First, and foremost, the shift system can be tailored to suit the needs not only of the particular requirements of the job, as we have just seen, but also of the individuals and organizations concerned. The earlier bias towards permanent systems, assuming that complete adjustment of circadian rhythms would occur, has now been virtually reversed in Europe; the bias is now in favour of rapidly rotating systems that should minimize the disruption of such rhythms. Theorists tend to agree that slowly rotating shift systems are probably undesirable, and that shift systems that delay (i.e., in the order: morning–evening–night) result in fewer problems for the individuals concerned than those that advance (night–evening–morning) (e.g., Czeisler, Moore-Ede and Coleman, 1982; Barton and Folkard, 1993).

The choice between rapidly rotating and permanent systems needs to be considered, not only in relation to performance efficiency (see above), but also in relation to medical and social criteria. Unfortunately, there are insufficient medical data available for any valid comparison to be made, although it is arguable that the reduced sleep deprivation and undisrupted circadian rhythms associated with rapidly rotating systems may make them the lesser of two evils. Further, when social criteria are considered, a widespread resistance to change results in most shiftworkers favouring their current system. Nevertheless, when rapidly rotating shift systems have been introduced, they have usually proved highly acceptable, since they allow at least some normal social activity every week (Walker, 1985). Other important features of shift systems include the timing and duration of shifts, the duration of the rest period between shifts, and the accumulated hours worked before a rest day (Folkard, 1992; Knauth,

1993). While many researchers in this area agree that there is probably no single 'best' shift system for all situations, most would support the move towards placing specific limitations on various features of shift systems (Council of the European Union, 1993).

In the future a second form of intervention may well be to try to maximize the adjustment of an individual's circadian rhythms to his or her work schedule by the use of appropriately timed administrations of bright light or melatonin. Recent advances (see above) suggest that this is certainly a possibility and there have been a few experimental trials on real shiftworkers (e.g., Eastman, 1990; Folkard, Arendt and Clark, 1993) that have shown that these manipulations may improve circadian adjustment and reduce sleep problems. However, the long-term consequences of adjusting individuals' circadian rhythms to their shifts and then readjusting them back to normal for their rest days are unknown. A plausible explanation for many of the health problems associated with shiftwork is that they stem from exactly this continual adjustment and readjustment of individuals' rhythms; manipulations that maximize that process may well exacerbate the problems. Clearly, there is a strong need for research on the potential long-term effects of the use of these manipulations before they are recommended for widespread use. Indeed, it seems probable that they will prove most applicable on permanent and very slowly rotating shift systems, and this might result in an eventual reversal of the current trend towards more rapidly rotating ones.

Two final forms of intervention are more concerned with the individual, and are based on individual differences in tolerance to shiftwork, and on the development of appropriate coping strategies. It is obvious that individuals differ substantially from one another in their ability to tolerate shiftwork, and individual difference measures have met with some success in predicting these differences in a longitudinal research programme (e.g., Vidacek, Radosevic-Vidacek, Kaliterna and Prizmic, 1993; Kaliterna, Vidacek, Radosevic-Vidacek and Prizmic, 1993). These results tend to agree with evidence from cross-sectional studies that individuals with flexible sleeping habits, and those who can easily overcome drowsiness, are better able to tolerate shiftwork (e.g., Barton, Costa, Smith, Spelten, Totterdell and Folkard, 1995). While there is a clear need for further longitudinal studies in this area, even if the predictive validity of these individual-difference measures can be established they could not readily be used for personnel selection purposes since candidates might well fake desirable scores on them. However, these measures might be useful in counselling individuals as to whether they would be likely to tolerate shiftwork and, if so, how best to develop adequate coping strategies.

A number of authors have argued that the adoption of appropriate coping strategies should reduce the problems that an individual encounters as a result of shiftwork (e.g., Wedderburn, 1991; Monk and Folkard, 1992). These coping strategies are primarily concerned with the scheduling of various activities, such as sleep and meals, that are under voluntary control. However, there is only limited evidence for the efficacy of coping strategies (e.g., Adams, Folkard and Young, 1986) and even this may have been confounded by differences between individuals in whether they had chosen to work on their particular schedule (Barton, 1994).

Nevertheless, it is clear that sleeps taken at a regular time are likely to stabilize circadian rhythms, while an irregular sleeping pattern may disrupt them. Indeed, it has been shown that four hours' sleep taken during the night, in combination with an additional four hours taken at an irregular time of day, is sufficient to prevent the disruption of most rhythms (Minors and Waterhouse, 1981b). In practice, many night workers do take a night-time nap (often unofficially), although this is seldom of four hours' duration (Kogi, 1985), while most go to bed as soon as they can after their night shift, i.e., at about the time when their endogenous body clocks will be 'telling them' to wake up. This may well account for the difficulty they experience in falling asleep. Unfortunately, if they delay their sleep until the early afternoon, when it would probably be easier for them to fall asleep, their sleep duration is likely to be considerably shortened (see Figure 2.4). Finally, in addition to sleep, the timing of meals, the scheduling of social contacts and leisure activities, and improving physical fitness have all been suggested as ways in which individuals may improve their tolerance to shiftwork (Wedderburn, 1991). While these suggestions would seem sensible, there is a strong need for further research in this area to identify the most effective way(s) for people to cope with their shift system.

SUMMARY

A substantial proportion of our workforce is employed on some form of shift system. This can result in a variety of problems for both the individuals concerned and the organizations employing them. Central to these problems is the fact that we have evolved as a diurnal species with an internal body clock that sends us to sleep at night. This internal body clock is disrupted when people work at abnormal times, and this disruption is thought to mediate many of the shiftworkers' problems. Consideration of the nature of our body clocks allows a better understanding of these problems as well as suggesting ways in which they may best be alleviated.

FURTHER READING

Most of the topics covered in this chapter are considered in greater detail in S. Folkard and T. H. Monk (1985b) *Hours of Work: Temporal Factors in Work Scheduling* and in A. J. Scott (1990) *Shiftwork*, both of which also have extensive bibliographies for those wishing to pursue this area in greater detail. More 'popular' accounts of the shiftwork area include T. H. Monk and S. Folkard (1992) *Making Shiftwork Tolerable* and M. Moore-Ede (1993) *The 24 Hour Society*. General introductions to human circadian rhythms and their practical implications include D. S. Minors and J. M. Waterhouse (1981a) *Circadian Rhythms and the Human*, M. C. Moore-Ede, F. M. Sulzman and C. A. Fuller (1982) *The Clocks that Time Us*, and L. Lamberg (1994) *Bodyrhythms: Chronobiology and Peak Performance*.

REFERENCES

Adams, J., Folkard, S. and Young, M. (1986). Coping strategies used by nurses on night duty. *Ergonomics*, 29, 185–196.

Akerstedt, T. (1985). Adjustment of physiological circadian rhythms and the sleep-wake cycle to shiftwork. In S. Folkard and T. H. Monk (eds.), *Hours of Work: Temporal Factors in Work Scheduling*, pp. 185–197. Chichester: Wiley.

Aschoff, J. and Wever, R. A. (1962). Spontanperiodik des Menschen bei Ausschluss aller Zeitgeber. *Naturwissenschaften*, 49, 337–342.

Baker, M. A., Holding, D. H. and Loeb, M. (1984). Noise, sex and time of day effects in a mathematics task. *Ergonomics*, 27, 67–80.

Barton, J. (1994). Choosing to work at night: a moderating influence on individual tolerance to shiftwork. *Journal of Applied Psychology*, 79, 449–454.

Barton, J., Costa, G., Smith, L., Spelten, E., Totterdell, P. and Folkard, S. (1995). The standard shiftwork index: a battery of questionnaires for assessing shiftwork related problems. *Work and Stress*, 9, 4–30.

Barton, J. and Folkard, S. (1993). Advancing versus delaying shift systems. *Ergonomics*, 36, 59–64.

Blake, M. J. F. (1971). Temperament and time of day. In W. P. Colquhoun (ed.), *Biological Rhythms and Human Performance*, pp. 109–148. London: Academic Press.

Bohle, P. and Tilley, A. J. (1989). The impact of night work on psychological well-being. *Ergonomics*, 32, 1089–1099.

Colligan, M. J. and Rosa, R. R. (1990). Shiftwork effects on social and family life. *Occupational Medicine: State of the Art Reviews*, 5, 315–322.

Cloudsley-Thompson, J. L. (1980). *Biological Clocks: Their Function in Nature*. London: Weidenfeld and Nicolson.

Colquhoun, W. P. (1971). Circadian variation in mental efficiency. In W. P. Colquhoun (ed.), *Biological Rhythms and Human Performance*, pp. 39–107. London: Academic Press.

Colquhoun, W. P., Blake, M. J. F. and Edwards, R. S. (1968). Experimental studies of shiftwork II: stabilized 8-hour shift system. *Ergonomics*, 11, 527–546.

Council of the European Union (1993). Council directive 93/104/EC of 23 November 1993 concerning certain aspects of the organization of working time. *Official Journal of the European Communities*, L 307, 18–24.

Czeisler, C. A., Kronauer, P. E., Allan, J. S., Duffy, J. F., Jewett, M. E., Brown, E. N. and Ronda, J. M. (1989). Bright light induction of strong (type 0) resetting of the human circadian pacemaker. *Science*, 244, 1328–1333.

Czeisler, C. A., Moore-Ede, M. C. and Coleman, R. M. (1982). Rotating shiftwork schedules that disrupt sleep are improved by applying circadian principles. *Science*, 217, 460–463.

Czeisler, C. A., Weitzman, E. D., Moore-Ede, M. C., Zimmerman, J. C. and Kronauer, R. S. (1980). Human sleep: its duration and organization depend on its circadian phase. *Science*, 210, 1264–1267.

Eastman, C. I. (1990). Circadian rhythms and bright light: Recommendations for shift work. *Work & Stress*, 4, 245–260.

Eysenck, M. W. (1982). *Attention and Arousal: Cognition and Performance*. Berlin: Springer.

Eysenck, M. W. and Folkard, S. (1980). Personality, time of day, and caffeine: some theoretical and conceptual problems. In Revelle *et al.*, *Journal of Experimental Psychology: General*, 109, 32–41.

Folkard, S. (1983). Diurnal variation. In G. R. J. Hockey (ed.), *Stress and Fatigue in Human Performance*, pp. 247–272. Chichester: Wiley.

Folkard, S. (1988). Circadian rhythms and shiftwork: adjustment or masking? In W. Th. J. M. Hekkens, G. A. Kerkhof and W. J. Rietveld (eds.), *Trends in Chronobiology*, pp. 173–182. Oxford: Pergamon Press.

Folkard, S. (1990). Circadian performance rhythms: some practical and theoretical implications. *Philosophical Transactions of the Royal Society* (London) B, 327, 543–553.

Folkard, S. (1992). Is there a 'best compromise' shift system? *Ergonomics*, 35, 1453–1463.

Folkard, S. and Akerstedt, T. (1992). A 3-process model of the regulation of alertness-sleepiness. In R. J. Broughton and B. D. Ogilvie (eds.), *Sleep, Arousal and Performance*, pp. 11–26. Boston: Birkhauser.

Folkard, S., Arendt, J. and Clark, M. (1993). Can melatonin improve shiftworkers' tolerance of the night shift? Some preliminary findings. *Chronobiology International*, 10, 315–320.

Folkard, S. and Condon, R. (1987). Night shift paralysis in air traffic control officers. *Ergonomics*, 20, 1353–1363.

Folkard, S., Condon, R. and Herbert, M. (1984). Night shift paralysis. *Experientia*, 40, 510–512.

Folkard, S., Hume, S. I., Minors, D. S., Waterhouse, J. M. and Watson, F. L. (1985). Independence of the circadian rhythm in alertness from the sleep/wake cycle. *Nature*, 313, 678–679.

Folkard, S. and Monk, T. H. (1979). Shiftwork and performance. *Human Factors*, 21, 483–492.

Folkard, S. and Monk, T. H. (1980). Circadian rhythms in human memory. *British Journal of Psychology*, 71, 295–307.

Folkard, S. and Monk, T. H. (1985a). Circadian performance rhythms. In S. Folkard and T. H. Monk (eds.), *Hours of Work: Temporal Factors in Work Scheduling*, pp. 37–52. Chichester: Wiley.

Folkard, S. and Monk, T. H. (eds.) (1985b). *Hours of Work: Temporal Factors in Work Scheduling*. Chichester: Wiley.

Folkard, S., Monk, T. H., Bradbury, R. and Rosenthall, J. (1977). Time of day effects in school children's immediate and delayed recall of meaningful material. *British Journal of Psychology*, 68, 45–60.

Folkard, S., Wever, R. A. and Wildgruber, Ch. M. (1983). Multioscillatory control of circadian rhythms in human performance. *Nature*, 305, 223–226.

Gates, A. I. (1916). Variations in efficiency during the day, together with practise effects, sex differences, and correlations. *University of California Publications in Psychology*, 2, 1–156.

Harrington, J. M. (1978). *Shiftwork and Health: A Critical Review of the Literature*. London: HMSO.

Horne, J. A., Brass, C. G. and Pettit, A. N. (1980). Circadian performance differences between morning and evening 'types'. *Ergonomics*, 23, 129–136.

Horne, J. A. and Ostberg, O. (1976). A self-assessment questionnaire to determine morningness–eveningness in human circadian rhythms. *International Journal of Chronobiology*, 4, 97–110.

Hughes, D. G. and Folkard, S. (1976). Adaptation to an 8-hour shift in living routine by members of a socially isolated community. *Nature*, 264, 232–234.

Kaliterna, Lj., Vidacek, S., Radosevic-Vidacek, B. and Prizmic, Z. (1993). The reliability and stability of various individual differences and tolerance to shiftwork measures. *Ergonomics*, 36, 183–190.

Kerkhof, G. A. (1985). Inter-individual differences in the human circadian system: A review. *Biological Psychology*, 20, 83–112.

Kleitman, N. (1939, revised 1963). *Sleep and Wakefulness*. Chicago: University of Chicago Press.

Knauth, P. (1993). The design of shift systems. *Ergonomics*, 36, 15–28.

Kogi, K. (1985). Introduction to the problems of shift-work. In S. Folkard and T. H. Monk (eds.), *Hours of Work: Temporal Factors in Work Scheduling*, pp. 165–184. Chichester: Wiley.

Lamberg, Lynne (1994). *Bodyrhythms: Chronobiology and Peak Performance*. New York: William Morrow.

Lewy, A. J., Ahmed, S., Jackson, J. M. L. and Sack, R. L. (1992). Melatonin shifts human circadian rhythms according to a phase-response curve. *Chronobiology International*, 9, 380–392.

Lewy, A. J., Wehr, T. A., Goodwin, F. K., Newsome, D. A. and Markey, S. P. (1980). Light suppresses melatonin secretion in humans. *Science*, 210, 1267–1269.

Lund, R. (1974). Personality factors and desynchronization of circadian rhythms. *Psychosomatic Medicine*, 36, 224–228.

Meers, A. (1975). Performance on different turns of duty within a three-shift system and its relation to body temperature: two field studies. In P.

Colquhoun, S. Folkard, P. Knauth and J. Rutenfranz (eds.), *Experimental Studies of Shift Work*, pp. 188–205. Opladen, Germany: Westdeutscher Verlag.

Michelson, M. (1897). Uber die Tiefe des Schlafes. *Psychologische Arbeiten*, 2, 84–117.

Minors, D. S. and Waterhouse, J. M. (1981a). *Circadian Rhythms and the Human*. Bristol: Wright PSG.

Minors, D. S. and Waterhouse, J. M. (1981b). Anchor sleep as a synchroniser of rhythms on abnormal routines. In L. C. Johnson, D. I. Tepas, W. P. Colquhoun and M. J. Colligan (eds.), *Biological Rhythms, Sleep and Shift Work*, pp. 399–414. New York: Spectrum Publications.

Mitler, M. M., Carskadon, M. A., Czeisler, C. A., Dement, W. C., Dinges, D. F. and Graeber, R. C. (1988). Catastrophes, sleep, and public policy: consensus report. *Sleep*, 11, 100–109.

Monk, T. H. and Embrey, D. E. (1981). A field study of circadian rhythms in actual and interpolated task performance. In A. Reinberg, N. Vieux and P. Andlauer (eds.), *Night and Shift Work: Biological and Social Aspects*, pp. 473–489. Oxford: Pergamon Press.

Monk, T. H. and Folkard, S. (1985). Shiftwork and performance. In S. Folkard and T. H. Monk (eds.), *Hours of Work: Temporal Factors in Work Scheduling*, pp. 239–252. Chichester: Wiley.

Monk, T. H. and Folkard, S. (1992). *Making Shiftwork Tolerable*. London: Taylor & Francis.

Monk, T. H., Knauth, P., Folkard, S. and Rutenfranz, J. (1978). Memory based performance measures in studies of shiftwork. *Ergonomics*, 21, 819–826.

Moore-Ede, M. (1993). *The 24 Hour Society*. London: Piatkus.

Moore-Ede, M. C., Sulzman, F. M. and Fuller, C. A. (1982). *The Clocks that Time Us*. London: Harvard University Press.

Ong, C. N. and Kogi, K. (1990). Shiftwork in developing countries: current issues and trends. *Occupational Medicine: State of the Art Reviews*, 5, 417–428.

Petros, T. V., Beckwith, B. E. and Anderson, M. (1990). Individual differences in the effects of time of day and passage difficulty on prose memory in adults. *British Journal of Psychology*, 81, 63–72.

Reinberg, A., Andlauer, P., De Prins, J., Malbec, W., Vieux, N. and Bourdeleau, P. (1984). Desynchronisation of the oral temperature circadian rhythm and intolerance to shiftwork. *Nature*, 308, 272–274.

Rutenfranz, J., Aschoff, J. and Mann, H. (1972). The effects of a cumulative sleep deficit, duration of preceding sleep period and body temperature on multiple choice reaction time. In W. P. Colquhoun (ed.), *Aspects of Human*

Efficiency: Diurnal Rhythm and Loss of Sleep, pp. 217–229. London: English Universities Press.

Rutenfranz, J., Haider, M. and Koller, M. (1985). Occupational health measures for nightworkers and shiftworkers. In S. Folkard and T. H. Monk (eds.), *Hours of Work: Temporal Factors in Work Scheduling*, pp. 199–210. Chichester: Wiley.

Rutenfranz, J., Knauth, P. and Angersbach, D. (1981). Shift work research issues. In L. C. Johnson, D. I. Tepas, W. P. Colquhoun and M. J. Colligan (eds.), *Biological Rhythms, Sleep and Shift Work*, pp. 165–196. New York: Spectrum Publications.

Scott, A. J. (ed.) (1990). *Shiftwork: Occupational Medicine: State of the Art Reviews*, 5. Philadelphia: Hanley & Belfus.

Siffre, M. (1964). *Beyond Time*. (ed. and trs. H. Briffault) New York: McGraw Hill.

Skinner, N. F. (1985). University grades and time of day of instruction. *Bulletin of the Psychonomic Society*, 23, 67.

Smith, C. S., Rilley, C. and Midkiff, K. (1989). Evaluation of three circadian rhythm questionnaires with suggestions for an improved measure of morningness. *Journal of Applied Psychology*, 74, 728–738.

Smith, L., Folkard, S. and Poole, C. J. M. (1994). Increased injuries on night shift. *Lancet*, 344, 1137–1139.

Tepas, D. I., Walsh, J. K., Moss, P. D. and Armstrong, D. (1981). Polysomnographic correlates of shiftwork performance in the laboratory. In A. Reinberg, N. Vieux, and P. Andlauer (eds.), *Night and Shift Work: Biological and Social Aspects*, pp. 179–186. Oxford: Pergamon Press.

Thorndike, E. (1900). Mental fatigue. *Psychological Review*, 7, 466–482.

Tilley, A. J., Wilkinson, R. T., Warren, P. S. G., Watson, B. and Drud, M. (1982). The sleep and performance of shift workers. *Human Factors*, 24, 629–641.

Vidacek, S., Kaliterna, Lj., Radosevic-Vidacek, B. and Folkard, S. (1986). Productivity on a weekly rotating shift system: circadian adjustment and sleep deprivation effects. *Ergonomics*, 29, 1583–1590.

Vidacek, S., Radosevic-Vidacek, B., Kaliterna, Lj. and Prizmic, Z. (1993). Individual differences in circadian rhythm parameters and short-term tolerance to shiftwork: a follow-up study. *Ergonomics*, 36, 117–124.

Walker, J. (1985). Social problems of shiftworkers. In S. Folkard and T. H. Monk (eds.), *Hours of Work: Temporal Factors in Work Scheduling*, pp. 211–226. Chichester: Wiley.

Waterhouse, J. M., Folkard, S. and Minors, D. S. (1992). *Shiftwork, Health and Safety: An Overview of the Scientific Literature 1978–1990*. London: HMSO.

Wedderburn, A. A. I. (1991). *Guidelines for Shiftworkers. Bulletin of European Studies on Time No. 3.* Shankhill: European Foundation for the Improvement of Living and Working Conditions.

Wedderburn, A. A. I. (ed.) (1993). *Statistics and News. Bulletin of European Studies on Time No. 6.* Shankhill: European Foundation for the Improvement of Living and Working Conditions.

Wegmann, H-M. and Klein, K. E. (1985). Jet-lag and aircrew scheduling. In S. Folkard and T. H. Monk (eds.), *Hours of Work: Temporal Factors in Work Scheduling*, pp. 263–276. Chichester: Wiley.

Wever, R. A. (1979). *The Circadian System of Man: Results of Experiments under Temporal Isolation.* New York: Springer.

Wever, R. A. (1983). Fractional desynchronization of human circadian rhythms: a method for evaluating entrainment limits and functional interdependencies. *Pflugers Archiv*, 396, 128–137.

Wever, R. A. (1984). Sex differences in human circadian rhythms: intrinsic periods and sleep fractions. *Experientia*, 40, 1226–1234.

Wever, R. A., Polasek, J. and Wildgruber, Ch. M. (1983). Bright light affects human circadian rhythms. *Pflugers Archiv.*, 396, 85–87.

Wilkinson, R. T. (1965). Sleep deprivation. In O. G. Edholm and A. L. Bacharach (eds.), *The Physiology of Human Survival*, pp. 399–430. New York: Academic Press.

Wilkinson, R. T. (1992). How fast should the night shift rotate? *Ergonomics*, 35, 1425–1446.

Zulley, J., Wever, R. A. and Aschoff, J. (1981). The dependence of onset and duration of sleep on the circadian rhythm of rectal temperature. *Pflugers Archiv.*, 391, 314–318.

3

Training and the Acquisition of
Knowledge and Skill

Rob Stammers

When individuals begin a new job, whether it be a first or a subsequent one, they will bring to that situation a range of previous learning experiences. New learning experiences will also take place in the new role. The sum of these experiences will determine the effectiveness with which a person tackles the job's demands. This prior learning will in part result from the education, training, and work and life experiences they have already had. These may be relevant to the new job, indeed they may be the basis on which individuals were selected for it. Alternatively, their previous experience may be very limited or have little relevance to the new tasks, so that substantial new learning is required.

Learning in a new job will mainly be through formal training, but it will also involve other learning activities, generally under the heading of 'on-the-job experience'. That experience may be formally recognized by the organization, for example by supervision and logbooks etc., or it may be informal experience, coming from one or more encountered situations. The focus in this chapter will be on formal training activities.

ACQUIRING KNOWLEDGE AND SKILL

The most influential body of theory in the training field in recent decades has come from cognitive psychology, whereas earlier influences had been from the behaviourist school. An exception to this

73

has been the continued influence of skill theory, which at one time stood apart from the mainstream cognitive field but is now seen as very much part of it (see Chapter 1).

In everyday language we talk of our 'knowledge' and our 'skills'. These can be seen as knowledge about *things in the world* ('knowledge') and knowledge about *how to do things in the world* ('skills'). In more psychological terms these have been called 'declarative knowledge' and 'procedural knowledge' (e.g., Anderson, 1982). Psychologists' research into memory has concentrated on declarative knowledge, and has generally focused on how information is gained, stored and retrieved. For many years the tradition was to study unrealistic material (to control for contamination of results from previous experience), and to examine memory over short periods of time (typically seconds). More recently, memory for everyday events and over longer periods of time (e.g., hours, weeks and even years) has come into vogue (e.g., Neisser, 1982). The established view of memory is that we have a 'working memory' with a small, limited, 'capacity'. This capacity is used for storing information for brief periods of time and for carrying out mental operations on the information held. Beyond this, a vast and complex storage system retains acquired knowledge in long-term memory. It is generally assumed that this information is stored in complex networks, based on the meaning of the items and on their links to other items to which they are related (e.g., Anderson, 1990). Long-term memory is also the repository of our skills.

The study of skills has recently been extended to the world of *cognitive* skills (see also Chapter 1). These skills have received increasing attention because of the rise of automation and information technology, and a recognition of the need to study managerial and other non-manual skills. As a result, some of the traditional barriers between what is thought of as knowledge and what is thought of as skill are breaking down. This has given rise to a new vocabulary for describing activities and new ways of seeing the relationships between them. Anderson (1982) draws upon the earlier skill learning theory of Fitts (e.g., Fitts and Posner, 1967), and proposes a progression theory of skill acquisition. Any theory of how skills develop must account for such phenomena as the continued improvement of performance with practice, a concomitant reduction in the ability to describe activities, and the apparent increase in working memory capacity, manifest as a capacity to time-share between two or more tasks (e.g., to drive a car, converse with a passenger and listen to the radio).

In Fitts' theory the three phases of skill acquisition are cognition, association and automation. Anderson's interpretations are similar, and involve descriptions of the 'compilation' of knowledge. Fitts' first phase, the cognitive one, is where there is an initial communication of information to the trainee. This typically takes the form of verbal and/or visual instruction from a trainer or from some printed, written or recorded material. The learner must then attempt to put together a novel pattern of activities to meet the goal set. This could be a set of physical actions to carry out a task, a set of speech activities in learning a new language, a set of problem-solving strategies in some mental skill, or a set of perceptual skills for recognizing a pattern of sensory stimuli (e.g., sights, sound, tastes, fragrances). There is a need for some form of guidance from an instructor or from the training environment to prevent errors being made and some source of evaluation to provide feedback to the learner on progress. This evaluation, or extrinsic feedback, is the most powerful source of information for learning. Its main role is to lead the learner to utilize appropriate intrinsic feedback, that is feedback that will always be present in interactions with the task environment. Thus extrinsic feedback from a language teacher will comment upon how we are pronouncing a word, and intrinsic feedback will be how it feels to carry out the speech action and how the word sounds to us.

Anderson's (1982) interpretation is that in the initial phase the trainee acquires *declarative* knowledge, the instructional information described above. This information typically contains sets of concepts and rules to guide performance. In both theories the key to skill development is continued practice of the activities comprising the skill. There can then be a subtle shift to Fitts' associative phase, where correct patterns of activity are established through practice, and a learner comes to rely less on extrinsic feedback. Anderson's interpretation of Fitts' associative phase is that a process of 'knowledge compilation' is occurring. An analogy is drawn between the internal translation of a computer program from a user-oriented language into machine code in order for the instructions to be implemented. The compilation process for skill involves the conversion of declarative knowledge about how to do a task into a new form of storage, known as *procedural* knowledge or 'productions'. This term is borrowed from the world of computers, and is used to describe specific rules for carrying out tasks. These rules consist of 'condition–action' pairs of the kind 'If X occurs, then do Y.' In the artificial intelligence approach they are taken as models of how human knowledge may be stored. This is a form of knowledge that can direct activity without placing high demands on working memory capacity. In everyday terms, tasks can be executed out without 'thinking'.

According to Fitts, this development of skill is marked by a gradual move to the automation phase. At this last stage of skill acquisition, speed of performance continues to increase, few errors are made, and there is a greater capacity to carry out other tasks at the same time. In Anderson's terms, productions become responsible for controlling activities, and different productions can be put together to build larger, integrated wholes. There is also increasing resistance to interference from stress and other concurrent tasks. The difference between these types of learning can be illustrated by comparing our everyday use of speech 'without thinking' to our struggles to put together a simple phrase in a foreign tongue; repeated use of that phrase will eventually lead to it having the same automatic characteristics as our native language.

Another implication of this automatization or proceduralization of knowledge concerns its availability for teaching other people. It is a common experience that being skilled at a task does not necessarily make a person qualified to teach it to someone else. Although we can do a task well, the declarative knowledge that we initially used may not be available to us once proceduralization has taken place. It may be necessary for us to de-compile the knowledge back into a declarative form, by slowing down what we do, thinking it through or perhaps talking aloud as we carry out the task.

DETERMINING TRAINING CONTENT

It is increasingly common to view the training process as a 'system'. This places a particular emphasis on determining what the *objectives* of the system are. In the past the objectives of training have often been agreed merely on the basis of opinion or have not been stated in any detail. The increasing recognition that training must be based upon task analysis to determine its objectives has been a major achievement of psychologists in this area. The term 'task analysis' has a number of meanings. In general, it is taken to cover three main stages: information collection, information representation and information interpretation. The middle stage of representation is the key one and one to which the term is most commonly applied.

The first stage, information collection, is where techniques have to be selected and applied appropriately to the task in question. The aim is to gather information about the task from a range of sources. Very often direct observation will be used, sometimes supplemented with recording techniques, especially videotaping. The important thing to bear in mind is that these techniques can be very time-consuming, and care should be taken in planning such activities. Questioning and interviewing job incumbents is also commonly used, with audio-recording sometimes playing a useful role. People can also give running commentaries on what they are doing, termed 'verbal protocols'. Questionnaires can be used to collect information about task activities, and existing documentation (e.g., manuals) can yield additional information.

In the second stage there are many different approaches to representing task information (Kirwan and Ainsworth, 1992). Some use tables to organize different types of material, some use flow charts, others generate simple lists. One technique that is widely used in the United Kingdom is Hierarchical Task Analysis (HTA). This was developed by Annett and Duncan (Annett, Duncan, Stammers and Gray, 1971), but has undergone a number of revisions over the years (e.g., Shepherd, 1989). The approach uses the 'operation' as a unit of analysis, and represents tasks as hierarchies of operations. An operation is taken to be any component of activity that is defined by an objective. Thus a task will be initially described in fairly broad terms, such as 'Operate overhead projector' (see the example in Figure 3.1). The task is then progressively broken down into more detail to produce a typical hierarchy. As can be seen in the figure, some activities may be analysed into more detail than others.

The hierarchical diagram will show the analyst what tasks have to

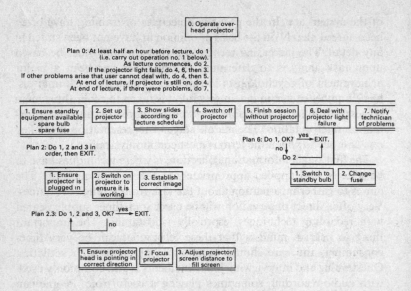

Fig. 3.1 Hierarchical task analysis: operations involved in operating an overhead projector during the course of a lecture (from Shepherd, 1989).

be carried out. In addition to task information on its own, it is also necessary to collect information about how the sub-groups of operations are organized. In Hierarchical Task Analysis terms, these are the 'plans' of a task. As the hierarchy is being developed, the analyst should specify what plans are needed. A plan is usually a set of rules that define under what circumstances the operations are carried out and in which sequence. The plans appear on the diagram in italics to the left of descending lines. Plans may be represented by statements of the rules for the task, as in Plan 0, or flow diagrams, as in Plan 2.3 (see Figure 3.1). They may need to be encoded in more complex forms, such as decision trees. Many are simple rules such as 'Do A, then B in a fixed order.' Others will be of the form 'If X occurs, do A; if Y occurs, do B.' As tasks become more complex, particularly if they are of a problem-solving nature, then the rules may need to be represented in separate diagrams showing more complex flow-charts.

As the tasks are broken down, it is suggested that the collection of unnecessary detail is prevented by there being rules for 'redescription'. Such rules ask predetermined questions about operations as they are isolated. Thus the overall description 'Operate overhead projector' is sufficient detail for an experienced lecturer. However, for the novice the extra detail provided by the full analysis is needed. Questions can be asked on whether the generation of more detail by redescription is needed to ensure efficient learning, safe operation or an effective reduction in costs. Decisions have to be made at each stage of redescription, and the analysis for different operations can cease at different levels. The aim is to reduce the amount of information collected which will be discarded as unnecessary later on. When description ceases for an operation, a line is written under the box (see Figure 3.1).

While the hierarchical diagram is a useful way of representing tasks, not much detail can be included in the limited space available to describe each operation in the diagram. It is usually necessary to supplement this with some form of table that can give fuller descriptions, and to which can be added notes and comments. It is particularly important to highlight specific operations where learning difficulties may occur for the trainee. These difficulties may be found in the perceptual side of the task, for example in the input cues that are used to determine that a particular action should take place or in the feedback cues that result from actions. Learning the actions themselves may also present difficulties for the trainee if new skills have to be acquired or old patterns changed. Another source of difficulty might be in learning the plans that have to be followed in the task. An example of this would be in a problem-solving task, where the rules for finding faults in equipment are sometimes very complex, whereas the actions needed to rectify the faults may be simple.

In the third stage, analysis of the information in the task analysis document can begin. The document forms the basis of the subsequent activity to design a training programme. It provides a summary of the required training content, and permits the trainer to specify standards of performance and to abstract the information needed to produce training material. In addition, the way the task is broken down in the analysis may suggest 'natural' components of the task that can then be used as the practice units in part-task training. It should also contain comments on areas of difficulty, as mentioned above, and may include suggestions made at the time of analysis for the choice of training media.

BUILDING LEARNING ENVIRONMENTS

There is a range of activities involved in producing a training programme of any complexity. Some of these are concerned with organizing the training content into an optimal sequence of activities for the trainees. Other activities determine the selection of appropriate media for the delivery of the content. These topics are dealt with in the next two sections.

Instructional Activities

The theoretical analysis outlined above of the difference between declarative and procedural knowledge suggests a basic dichotomy of training activities. One type of training is concerned with the communication of declarative knowledge in 'instruction' activities, the other is concerned with the development of procedural knowledge in a 'practice' environment. In the first case there is a concern with factual material, to be retained and used for its own sake, and to be used as a foundation for further declarative communications or as the basis for the subsequent developments of skills. On the other hand, the practice environment must allow for the establishment of procedural knowledge by providing a context in which the skill can be practised, initially in a supported way but ultimately merely in a self-monitored way.

The task analysis will provide the basis for defining the content of training. In skill-based areas, it is possible to be specific about what an individual needs to be able to do. Similarly, in specific knowledge areas definite statements can be made about training content. The definition of content is more difficult where there is a requirement to identify knowledge and competencies that can be generalized to new situations after the training activities. Under these circumstances there is a need to provide information that will give a conceptual underpinning for what will be coming later. For example, for the controllers of complex industrial processes the underlying physics and chemistry could be taught, while those learning first aid procedures may be taught basic anatomy and physiology. However, it has been demonstrated in a number of real-world contexts that, in training for fault diagnosis, coverage of the underlying theory does not in fact enhance performance (Schaafstal, 1993). In addition, studies by Berry and Broadbent (1984) have shown that under some conditions there is no clear relationship between effective task performance and the extent to which individuals can access explicit knowledge of the task. For example, practice at some tasks can lead to improvements in performance without improvements in ability to ask questions about what is involved in the task. This could be explained on the basis of the declarative knowledge of the task no longer being available after it has been compiled into procedural knowledge.

However, it is unlikely that only task-specific information will be provided in training situations. Some form of scene-setting, or general theoretical background, is likely to form part of an initial instruction phase. It is important that this material has some demonstrated link to the more focused training material, and that it serves an explicit purpose rather than being there without a clear rationale. One way of determining the appropriate knowledge-content of training is to examine what is required at the task performance level, and to work back from that to the knowledge a person must acquire to support that performance.

It can be useful to think of three 'levels' of knowledge that can be described when defining training content. At the performance level it is possible to describe 'task' knowledge. This is concerned with the basic concepts and rules of the task, how it is carried out and with what items. It involves the direct interface of the trainee with the equipment of the task; or, in interpersonal skill situations, it prescribes what behaviour is required of him or her in that situation, including, for example, how to deal with customers and clients.

At the next level 'functional' knowledge can be described. This makes clear to the trainee *why* the tasks have to be carried out. It consists of information putting the task activity into a broader context and shows the interrelationships between different components of a system. It typically takes the form of statements of the kind:

'The next task that is carried out is Y, since this follows on from X, and is done to meet this part of the overall objective of the task.'

The final level is 'general' knowledge. Here the functions that are carried out by individuals are put into a broader context of the overall system in which the individuals are working. It also attempts to draw parallels with the prior knowledge that individuals will bring to the learning situation. As an example, if someone is learning to use a computer to carry out a record-keeping task, then the task knowledge would consist of instruction on how to use the computer. The functional knowledge would cover the nature of the records being maintained and the importance of such features as accuracy and confidentiality. At the general level, the role of records for the efficient running of the system could be covered as well as such topics as the nature of relevant computer systems.

It may sometimes be difficult to justify the need for underlying general knowledge with any certainty. However, such knowledge may be important in helping to establish supporting 'cognitive structures' for new knowledge. Cognitive structures can be taken to mean the form in which we hold information in memory. It has been found that such structures, termed 'schemas', once in place and activated, make the acquisition of new knowledge more effective (Mayer, 1979). While provision of such supporting structures can be defended as an appropriate training strategy, the evidence cited above about the limited role of basic theory should not be forgotten. Another justification that could be advanced for including background information is that it might provide the basis for a generalization of knowledge to a new or emergent situation. The need arises when individuals have to be able to cope with novel situations, for which training has not been received, by bringing to bear on it knowledge of a general nature. It is also likely that knowledge gained from general experience will have a role here. However, if this need for generalization of training is a feature of the system in question, it is better to isolate the nature of this need in a task analysis and address it directly through training. This would be more effective than relying on non-specific training acting as a form of insurance. However, there are particular problems associated with training for infrequently occurring tasks, and these are addressed in the final section of this chapter.

Determining training content is likely to be most effective when it proceeds in a bottom-up manner. Task knowledge can be examined initially, then functional knowledge can be specified, and in turn used to determine the general knowledge required. It is then more likely that instruction in this knowledge will be conducted in a top-down manner, proceeding from the general to the specific. This would be in line with a number of theories of instruction which advocate approaches of that kind (Reigeluth, 1983; West, Farmer and Wolff, 1991).

A basic theme running through cognitive theories of instruction is that some introductory material benefits the learner by providing a schema or outline structure into which new knowledge can be fitted. This material may serve to activate existing schemas or, with more unfamiliar material, may provide a new schema for the learner to use. In some cases the outline material may cause some reorganization of an existing structure. Such an outline could draw upon existing knowledge and, perhaps by using it as an analogy, provide a structure to which new material can be added. The value of this approach has been demonstrated empirically on a number of occasions (e.g., Patrick and Fitzgibbon, 1988). The material used in describing such a structure may not always be in words, since the value of diagrammatic material can be high.

As new information is presented, it is assumed that the cognitive structure to which the new knowledge is added becomes increasingly complex. Analogies have been drawn with the building of a more and more complex web, which as it grows in complexity also grows stronger. Questions arise over what is the best sequence in which the material should be presented. A fixed order of presentation allows for control of the learning experience by the trainer, whereas a user-determined sequence permits the learners themselves to gauge the best order for them (e.g., Stanton and Stammers, 1990). This makes the point that learners come to training with their own styles of learning which may need to be accommodated. There is also the possibility of training in effective learning strategies that precede the instruction proper and make it more efficient (e.g., O'Neil, 1978; Schmeck, 1988).

The above mostly refers to the instruction phase, and while a clear-cut distinction between this and the practice phase cannot always be drawn, there are often very different activities and learning variables at work. The key requirement for skill development is to allow for practice of the task activities. A practice environment is required, in actual settings or in simulated environments; the latter are discussed in the section below. However, practice on its own is not sufficient in the absence of extrinsic feedback (see above). There are also questions about the optimum size of practice units, associated with the classic problem of 'part versus whole' training. In other words, is it better to be faced with the completeness of the practice task, or is it preferable to practise with sub-components of it? It appears that where there is a cross-flow of information between parts, then 'whole' methods will be more appropriate. Part-learning has been shown to be more beneficial where the parts have limited cross-flow of information and where poor performance on an earlier part in the sequence will disrupt practice conditions for a later part. These and other topics on skill learning are well reviewed by Patrick (1992).

Training Media

A wide range of media can be used for training, extending from the 'talk and chalk' of the traditional classroom situation through to advanced simulators and the world of 'virtual reality'. In between are the various print and graphical media, video and audio recordings, and the increasing use of computers, sometimes with integration of other audio and visual displays, the so-called 'multimedia' approach. Which particular medium is used in a training project will depend on a number of factors. These factors include: the experience of the trainer, the availability of material suitable for use, time, the preferences of trainees, corporate policy, and the suitability of the medium for the task.

In considering this issue, it is important to view training as a communication activity. If this is done, it becomes possible to see the problem of choosing an appropriate training medium as paralleled by ergonomic principles for choosing aspects of any human–technology interface (some illustrations are set out in Chapter 4). To extend the analogy, a learner can be seen to be faced with a range of tasks to complete. These are not the typical fixed tasks of an unchanging system, but are what can be termed 'learning tasks'. They concern the acquisition of knowledge and skill, and involve transitions from one stage of learning to another. The training system has to be able to adapt to these changes, and perhaps offer different forms of interaction with training material at different times. Ergonomics-inspired questions can then be asked of each medium. For example, is the displayed material ambiguous or intelligible, does it appear at too fast or too slow a pace, is it compatible with the learner's understanding so far? On the input side, one might ask whether actions have to be initiated or whether the learner remains passive. A trainee may know the answer to a question, but if it is difficult to type this into a computer or if the simulator does not allow for a particular type of activity to be practised, then the usability of these media should be questioned.

With this approach, various forms of training media can be assessed for their value as communication devices. Perhaps the most widely used medium is the traditional classroom situation, where a group is faced by a trainer who will describe a body of knowledge or a process. The lecture, or lesson, is a well-established method, with its advantages and disadvantages. On the plus side it is an approach with which the trainees are usually familiar and to which they often bring a set of learning strategies for collecting information. They will have note-taking skills of varying efficiency and will use the lecture to gain detailed information or background knowledge, to gain the flavour of a field or be entertained. From the lecturer's point of view advantages may again lie with familiarity and with the possibility to rapidly update material and give current examples. Disadvantages can arise from it being a passive situation for the learner. It can also be adversely influenced by the style and limited competence of the teacher.

Another widely used learning medium is printed material, both words and pictures. The principal value lies in its permanence and the opportunity that this gives for repeated examination as learning proceeds. Books, notes and handouts are typically used for the instruction phase, but handbooks, diagrams and manuals may also be used to guide initial performance of a task during a practice phase. Design of printed material in the training field will benefit from the application of sound principles of design and layout established for other written material (Wright, 1988).

The use of video and sound recording media is widespread. However, this field is undergoing a major revolution in terms of quality, power and versatility of reproduction. One development concerns videotape recording and playback facilities. This technology is important for rapidly capturing information. It allows for the easy collection of information from live action situations, and a library of items can be created for presentation to trainees. Another key role is to record trainees' performances as they make attempts in learning tasks or in the final evaluations of their performance. Activities can be quickly recorded and played back. On the basis of this feedback further attempts can be made and tapes can be reused. Given that feedback on actions is a key factor in the acquisition of skills, this medium can be seen to be a very powerful one.

A second major development field concerns digital recording techniques. Video disks and CD-ROMs can offer high-fidelity recordings of an immense range of material. Interactivity is increasingly feasible with developing computer technology, in that following a response by the learner, further information that is individually tailored to his or her current state of knowledge can be presented. In addition, there are the capabilities of computer graphics themselves and the possibility of rapid communication between devices in different locations by cable and by satellite.

It is all too easy to get carried away with these possibilities and be swept up by the enthusiasm of those researching the technology and of those marketing it. The role of the psychologist is to reflect upon these activities, and to ask questions about the trainees' needs and their learning processes. After the initial entertaining role, what do the more expensive media offer over existing, cheaper solutions; more importantly, what do they offer beyond other methods that will justify them in cost-effective terms?

One key issue, mentioned above, is interactivity between a medium and a learner. Those psychologists involved in the early developments in computer-assisted learning in the 1950s and 1960s were quick to see the advantages of computers here: quick and flexible display of information, the possibility of automatic evaluation of responses, the provision of tailored feedback, and the possibility of each individual carving a unique path through the training material. There is continuing increase in using computers in this way, and, as mentioned above, in linking them to the advanced storage systems becoming available. Computer-assisted learning is an interesting medium, as it allows for both instruction and practice from the terminal. There are a number of examples of where the computer terminal has been used as a low fidelity training device. Direct interaction with a dynamic version of the task is possible with detailed performance measurement and feedback. For example, Crawford and Crawford (1978) showed that practice on a computer terminal could be as effective as working with a realistic simulator for learning a data manipulation task. There were very large cost-savings projected from these findings.

We can now turn to simulation in general. This is the principal approach to building practice environments. It is important to maintain a broad view of what a simulator can be; to focus on the process of simulation and the learning it supports, rather than on the simulator as a hardware device and how closely it resembles reality. The area is dominated by high-technology equipment such as aircraft simulators, but two examples of low-technology situations should make the general point about building effective learning environments. Role-playing exercises for learning of social interaction skills are widely used, in which trainees practise their skills playing out a role, whether it be as a sales person, an interviewer or a counsellor. A 'client' plays a role too and the whole proceedings may be video-recorded. Role-playing is one form of simulation: all the elements for an effective practice environment are in place in what is very cheap implementation.

A second example is seen when, in order to learn the mouth-to-mouth breathing skills and chest compression procedures of cardio-pulmonary resuscitation (CPR), first-aid trainees make use of life-size human manikins. Indeed, it is hard to envisage how such skills could be practised without these devices. It is not appropriate to carry out the procedures on other people, and the likelihood of trainees being able to practise on a collapsed person while under supervision is very low. This example serves to illustrate why simulations are often necessary. A real task environment often does not allow for effective practice, instruction alone will not permit effective learning, the tasks are critical and they require advanced skill to be successfully executed (Stammers, 1983).

Very often simulation training is required for tasks using advanced technology in industry and transport, such as electricity power generation and aviation. These situations present challenges to psychologists to specify what needs to be simulated and at what level of realism. While lower fidelity may be needed to establish basic learning, more realistic simulations may be demanded to allow for proficiency to be assessed and for trainees to build up confidence in their abilities. For example, aircraft evacuation procedures can be initially practised by cabin crews with co-operating passengers and without time pressure, etc. Ultimately, it will be necessary for the trainees to assess their competencies with passengers acting out panic reactions, in a smoke filled environment and with realistic time limits.

MAKING TRAINING DECISIONS

Earlier in this chapter, in considering task analysis, the importance of looking at the training function as an integrated system was emphasized. In turn, it is important to see the training system as part of a larger system. Research in training psychology has tended to focus on the improvement of learning efficiency and effectiveness. While this is undoubtedly an important area, to be effective applied psychologists must also understand the broader system context of their work. When this is done, many key decisions made within the system can have more impact if based upon psychological knowledge; in other cases, a need for psychological research may be revealed in order to answer key questions.

One approach is to use the methodologies of the subject to examine itself. Thus a task analysis of the training function (Shepherd, Stammers and Kelly, 1992) reveals the following top-level operations for the overall task of 'Manage and deliver training for the organization':

1. Promote and optimize training function
2. Design and develop training
3. Install new training

4. Provide training delivery.

Operation 4 refers to the need to ensure that established training activities are carried out. Operations 2 and 3 come into existence when a training need has been determined. Operation 1 is the key one, however, and one where the innovative training manager can make an impact, particularly through the use of the results of training research. If this operation is broken down further, it yields:

1. Promote and optimize training function
   1.1 Respond to organizational directives
   1.2 Monitor opportunities for training
   1.3 Communicate opportunities for training
   1.4 Anticipate costs and benefits of a potential training project.

Operations 1.1, 1.3 and 1.4 concern ways in which the manager can promote training in the organization. All the operations require concern for the overall strategy of that organization and the development of effective procedures to achieve strategic goals. Operation 1.2, however, is different in scope. It requires the manager, or indeed a team in a large organization, to monitor events in the outside world and within the organization for opportunities to exploit resources and innovations in technology and training practice. In more detail these operations are:

1.2 Monitor opportunities for training
   1.2.1 Monitor potential demand, e.g., new systems under development
   1.2.2 Monitor problems associated with incidents and observed drifts in operational achievements
   1.2.3 Monitor opportunities to extend training involvement in on-going projects
   1.2.4 Monitor the emergence of new training technologies
   1.2.5 Monitor general human resource environment
   1.2.6 Monitor unused training resources.

It is in operations 1.2.5 and 1.2.6 that training research ideas will most often enter the knowledge base of the training function. However, it is possible to find many other examples of how psychological

89

knowledge influences activity in this area. Two examples will be explored here. The first is the evaluation of training, the second is the long-term retention of information gained through training.

The question of evaluation of training is an ever-present one in many organizations. In order to assess the effectiveness of a training activity, its performance needs to be measured. The systems approach that has been referred to throughout has measurement of output as a basic principle. However, this is not as simple as it sounds. Firstly, there is often resistance on the part of those involved to develop and apply such measures. Secondly, there are sometimes real difficulties over what to measure and how to measure it.

A four-level approach to the evaluation of training in organizations has generally been advocated (e.g., Alliger and Janak, 1989). All too often training courses are evaluated only at a first level, merely in terms of the reactions they produce in the trainees: how enjoyable or how valid did they find their training? While trainees may sometimes be good judges of the usefulness of what they have received, this may not always be the case. Also, initial reactions may be different from those found after some job experience. It certainly is true that this should not be the only way in which a training outcome is determined.

A second level at which measurement can be made concerns whether or not learning has occurred during the training period. For some situations it will be fairly straightforward to measure what has been learned, many courses having some form of assessment at their end. In other cases it may be more difficult to determine what has been acquired, particularly when a training programme has multiple objectives.

The third level of evaluation should assess whether the learning that has occurred produces the desired changes in job proficiency. On return to the work situation after training, does the training received make a difference? The task analysis will have specified what is required. This can be investigated, and, if the desired behaviour is not achieved, the content and delivery of training needs to be examined. Evaluation at this level requires that it is possible to take the necessary measurements in a job context. Direct measurement may not be possible and some form of task simulation may have to be used. It may be possible to use supervisor ratings of individuals, taken in the job context. A range of measures can be used, but they must be tailored to the situation in question (Phillips, 1991).

The fourth level to which evaluation can be extended is concerned with whether the changes in job behaviour lead to changes in the overall effectiveness of the organization. Again such changes are difficult to measure directly. Recourse could be made to indirect measures of effectiveness such as labour turnover or absenteeism. Alternatively, it might be necessary to make estimates of resources needed to exploit some new situation, for example, in terms of human resource needs reflecting the state of training readiness. Within many organizations there is a need to make changes frequently and often quite rapidly. Indeed, the idea of the 'learning organization' is a current theme in management studies. The view is that all individuals should constantly be learning to improve both their own and the organization's progress towards goals. Such organizations should be better able to cope with planned or enforced change as a result (Pedler, Burgoyne and Boydell, 1992; see also Chapter 15). For any particular training project it is unlikely that measurements will be made at all four levels. However, it is important that assessments are made at more than the first level.

The second example of where psychology can help in training decisions is in the field of skill retention. In some cases what has been learned during training will be put into practice immediately afterwards in the job situation; this immediate application will encourage further learning and retention of the material. There are, however, a number of situations where this does not occur and where some time, possibly even a number of years, may pass before specific skills are called upon. This can arise for a number of reasons. One example is in fault-finding activities in complex systems such as industrial plant or aircraft. Luckily, such faults are rare, but when they do occur it may be critical that they are quickly put right by operators who have retained relevant knowledge. Other situations arise when training is given to people for a role that might have to be adopted at short notice as a change from their normal job. For example, there are often designated fire wardens or first-aiders in workplaces, and on a larger scale there are volunteer reserve military personnel who can be called up for duty at short notice.

There are also situations where training is given to people in periods of unemployment, with the intention that this investment will make them more employable when opportunities arise. In the light of this, it is not surprising that reviews of the literature on long-term skill retention have been commissioned by a number of agencies (e.g., Annett, 1979; Hagman and Rose, 1983). These reviews are consistent in their conclusions that skill loss over time is likely to occur across a range of tasks. However, it is also the case that relearning can be very rapid, that rehearsal activities can ameliorate skill loss, and that an initial investment in overlearning (practice beyond the normal criterion point) can be effective in producing skills that are more resistant to deterioration in the absence of practice.

SUMMARY

The objective of this chapter has been to show the relevance and contributions of psychology to the training that is carried out in organizations. A theoretical background on the acquisition of know-ledge and skills focuses on the way in which declarative and pro-cedural knowledge are used to support performance. The role of task analysis in the determination of training programme content is then reviewed, followed by an account of how training programmes can be designed to produce effective learning. This is in terms of both the types of training that are undertaken and the media that are used to deliver them. Finally, training as a management decision process is outlined, with examples of how methodology and results from psy-chology can aid decision-making.

FURTHER READING

An excellent coverage of the topic is provided by Patrick (1992), *Training: Research and Practice*. Key areas are also assessed in Morri-son (1991), *Training for Performance*. Research on perceptual-motor skills has been reviewed in *Human Skills*, edited by Holding (1989), and cognitive skills are covered in Colley and Beech (1989) *Acquisi-tion and Performance of Cognitive Skills*. Current cognitive psychology developments can be found in *Cognitive Psychology and its Implications* by Anderson (1990) and in Eysenck (1990), *Cognitive Psychology; A Student's Handbook*. A useful guide to the impact of cognitive psychology on training is given by West, Farmer and Wolff (1991) in *Instructional Design: Implications from Cognitive Science*, and a good introduction to the field of evaluation is provided by Bramley (1991), *Evaluating Training Effectiveness*.

REFERENCES

Alliger, G. M. and Janak, E. A. (1989). Kirkpatrick's levels of training criteria: Thirty years later. *Personnel Psychology*, 42, 331–342.

Anderson, J. R. (1982). Acquisition of cognitive skill. *Psychological Review*, 4, 369–406.

Anderson, J. R. (1990). *Cognitive Psychology and its Implications*, 3rd edn. New York: Freeman.

Annett, J. (1979). Memory for skill. In M. M. Gruneberg and P. E. Morris (eds.), *Applied Problems in Memory*, pp. 215–247. London: Academic Press.

Annett, J., Duncan, K. D., Stammers, R. B. and Gray, M. J. (1971). *Task Analysis*. Training Information Paper No. 6. London: HMSO.

Berry, D. C., and Broadbent, D. E. (1984). On the relationship between task performance and associated verbal knowledge. *Quarterly Journal of Experimental Psychology*, 36A, 209–231.

Bramley, P. (1991). *Evaluating Training Effectiveness*. London: McGraw-Hill.

Colley, A. M. and Beech, J. R. (eds.) (1989). *Acquisition and Performance of Cognitive Skills*. Chichester: Wiley.

Crawford, A. M. and Crawford, K. S. (1978). Simulation of operational equipment with a computer-based instructional system: A low cost training technology. *Human Factors*, 20, 215–224.

Eysenck, M. W. (1990). *Cognitive Psychology: A Student's Handbook*. London: Erlbaum.

Fitts, P. M. and Posner, M. I. (1967). *Human Performance*. Belmont, Calif.: Brooks Cole.

Hagman, J. D. and Rose, A. M. (1983). Retention of military tasks: A review. *Human Factors*, 25, 199–213.

Holding, D. H. (ed.) (1989). *Human Skills*, 2nd edn. Chichester: Wiley.

Kirwan, B. and Ainsworth, L. K. (eds.) (1992). *A Guide to Task Analysis*. London: Taylor & Francis.

Mayer, R. E. (1979). Twenty years of research on advance organizers: Assimilation theory is still the best predictor of results. *Instructional Science*, 8, 133–167.

Morrison, J. E. (ed.) (1991). *Training for Performance*. Chichester: Wiley.

Neisser, U. (1982). *Memory Observed: Remembering in Natural Contexts*. San Francisco: Freeman.

O'Neil, H. F. (ed.) (1978). *Learning Strategies*. New York: Academic Press.

Patrick, J. (1992). *Training: Research and Practice*. London: Academic Press.

Patrick, J. and Fitzgibbon, L. (1988). Structural displays as learning aids. *International Journal of Man–Machine Studies*, 28, 625–635.

Pedler, M., Burgoyne, J. and Boydell, T. (1992). *The Learning Company*. London: McGraw-Hill.

Phillips, J. J. (1991). *Handbook of Training Evaluation and Measurement Methods*, 2nd edn. London: Kogan Page.

Reigeluth, C. M. (ed.) (1983). *Instructional Design: Theories and Models*. Hillsdale, NJ: Erlbaum.

Schaafstal, A. (1993). Knowledge and strategies in diagnostic skill. *Ergonomics*, 11, 1305–1316.

Schmeck, R. R. (ed.) (1988). *Learning Strategies and Learning Styles*. New York: Plenum.

Shepherd, A. (1989). Analysis and training in information technology tasks. In D. Diaper (ed.), *Task Analysis for Human–Computer Interaction*, pp. 15–55. Chichester: Ellis Horwood.

Shepherd, A., Stammers, R. B. and Kelly, M. (1992). Taskmaster – A model of training functions to support the organization of effective training provision. In *Proceedings of the International Training Equipment Conference and Exhibition*, pp. 328–332. Luxembourg: International Training Equipment Conference and Exhibition.

Stammers, R. B. (1983). Simulators for training. In T. O. Kvålseth (ed.), *Ergonomics of Workstation Design*. London: Butterworths.

Stanton, N. A. and Stammers, R. B. (1990). A comparison of structured and unstructured navigation through a CBT package. *Computers and Education*, 15, 159–163.

West, C. K., Farmer, J. A. and Wolff, P. M. (1991). *Instructional Design: Implications from Cognitive Science*. Englewood Cliffs, NJ: Prentice-Hall.

Wright, P. (1988). Functional literacy: Reading and writing at work. *Ergonomics*, 31, 265–290.

4

Human–Computer Interaction

Andrew Monk

Computers are an important part of the working life of many people, not only in the office, but also in manufacturing processes, stock control and so on. Poorly designed computer systems can have a large negative impact on the efficiency of an organization and the well-being of the people who work in it. Recognizing this, the last ten years have seen a concerted research effort to understand human–computer interaction. The ultimate goal of this research is to help build computer systems that fit human and organizational requirements more closely.

Human–computer interaction (HCI) is now a research discipline in its own right. Its origins were in computer science and psychology, but many other disciplines have contributed. This chapter introduces the psychological perspective on HCI, which views the problem as one of understanding how individuals process information when working with computers. For a more organizational approach, see Chapter 12.

One can distinguish two kinds of knowledge that experimental psychology can contribute to an applied topic such as HCI. One is derived from theories of perception, cognition and social psychology; theory is applied to make predictions about what will be good or bad under what circumstances. The other is derived from methodologies for making experimental comparisons.

Both ways of applying psychological knowledge can be seen in the next two sections, which briefly review studies of some of the components of human–computer interaction under the headings 'The user interface' and 'Computer supported co-operative work'. They can also be seen in the attempts made to formalize procedures for evaluating and improving prototype designs. The section 'Evaluation and design' describes how experimental techniques have been adapted to this purpose. The section 'Models of human–computer interaction' describes some attempts to generate theoretical models of people using computers that can similarly be used to evaluate prototypes.

THE USER INTERFACE

The parts of a computer system that the user comes in contact with are known as the user interface. From the point of view of the engineer these are either displays and other output devices by which the computer communicates information to the user or input devices (e.g., the keyboard) by which the user communicates information to the computer. However, this is an over-simplified view of HCI.

Consider a modern graphical user interface (GUI – pronounced 'gooey'). Here the user can issue commands to the computer by manipulating the display. A mouse is used to change the position of a cursor on the display, and the position of this cursor, relative to the other contents of the display, governs what command is issued. Here the distinction between input and output becomes blurred. Instead, one can take a linguistic analogy and talk about human–computer dialogue: the pattern of actions by the user and responses from the computer that go to make up the human–computer interaction needed to complete a task.

Input devices, output devices and human–computer dialogue have all been studied by psychologists. These studies are the subject of this section.

Input Devices

Many of the early experimental studies in HCI were to compare alternative input devices. A classic example is the study by Card, English and Burr (1978) that compared the use of a mouse, an isometric joystick and a keyboard. This experiment, on the boundary between ergonomics and psychology, will be described in some detail to illustrate how one goes about making this kind of experimental comparison.

Users were required to move a cursor to randomly placed targets on a visual display unit screen, and the time it took to do this was measured electronically. The experimental task was designed to approximate to the kind of selection tasks a user might make while using a word-processor. The target was a small region of text, and the user pressed the space bar on the keyboard before positioning a hand on the input device and making the movement. This made it possible to estimate homing time, that is, the time it would take a user to shift from typing to selection using the input device in question. The distances moved could be 1, 2, 4, 8 or 16 cm on the screen, and each user made each movement many times until an asymptote in performance was reached. This turned out to require between 1,200 and 1,800 trials on each device. Card and colleagues were able to demonstrate an advantage for the mouse over the other two input devices, particularly for larger movements. They also showed that their data could be modelled using Fitts' Law, which predicts a logarithmic relationship between movement time and the distance moved.

As new input devices come along they are subject to the same sort of experimental examination. For example, some recent work has been concerned with evaluation of pen-based systems. These allow the user to write on a hand-held computer screen with a stylus. The movements of the stylus are recorded as a trace on the screen, which can be stored and transformed in various ways. Handwriting might be recognized as characters and transformed into printed text. In these systems commands are given with the stylus, and so the system must recognize gestures such as 'cross out' and 'select'. These devices have become available only very recently and this work is still at a very early stage, as the alternatives to be compared are not yet clear.

Output Devices

The majority of computer systems use cathode ray tube (CRT) displays to output information. Here knowledge from psychophysics, a part of the psychology of human perception, can be applied directly. The human visual system has limited temporal and spatial resolution. That is to say there is a limit beyond which a very fast temporal change in luminance cannot be seen. Similarly, there is a limit beyond

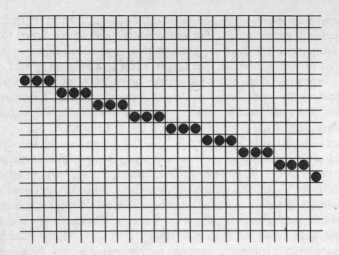

Fig. 4.1 'Jaggies' in a raster display; see text for explanation.

which a very small spatial change in luminance cannot be seen. It is possible to calculate the smallest spatial change in luminance and the fastest temporal change in luminance that can be detected, given various other physical data.

CRT displays depend on this limited spatial and temporal resolution. They work by briefly brightening a series of dots on the screen in a systematic scan from left to right and top to bottom; this is known as a 'raster' display. A typical computer screen consists of approximately 600 rows of 800 such dots, and it can take up to two-hundredths of a second to scan through them all, briefly brightening each. Some are brightened more than others and this gives the illusion of graphics on a steady background. This illusion breaks down when the visual system is able to detect the temporal changes and we see 'flicker'.

Similar problems arise when we can see spatial changes too well. Figure 4.1 demonstrates the problem of drawing a straight line with a raster display. The dots are arranged in a rectangular array. This means that, unless the line exactly fits a diagonal through this array, some dots will not be in the right place and the line will actually be jagged. Under the right conditions the human visual system will not be able to resolve these small spatial inaccuracies and the line will appear smooth. Under the wrong conditions the 'jaggies' will be visible. Information from psychophysics allows us to make strong predictions about how to maintain these two illusions that can be used directly in the design of CRT displays (Thompson, 1984). In the same way recommendations can be made about the use of colour and how best to allow for colour-deficient users (see for example Travis, 1991).

Computer hardware designers have been rather unimaginative in providing both input and output devices for computers. Buxton (1986) has pointed out that a physical anthropologist in the distant future trying to guess about the physiology of the humans of our era by looking at our computer systems would conclude that humans had one eye, a very limited auditory apparatus, one arm longer than the other and no feet! This lack of imagination is a particular problem for blind or visually impaired computer users (Griffith, 1990). Computer technology has been a blessing for many disabled people; however, the current popularity of GUIs that depend on hand–eye coordination present problems for many groups of disabled people.

Human–Computer Dialogue

Early interactive systems required users to type commands in response to a 'command prompt'. In these systems, for example the UNIX and DOS operating systems, the human–computer dialogue takes the following form. The computer indicates it is ready to receive a command by displaying a prompt, e.g., 'C:\ >'. The user types a one-line command. The computer executes the command, if it can be recognized, and then issues a new prompt. Other 'dialogue styles' are menus, form-filling and direct manipulation as in a drawing package.

With a menu, the responses the computer will recognize are spelt out explicitly as items in a list and users are able to select from these alternatives. Compared with recalling or constructing a command line, menus can reduce the requirement on the user to remember and reason about the form a command should take. There were many experimental studies of menu usage in the mid-1980s (for a review

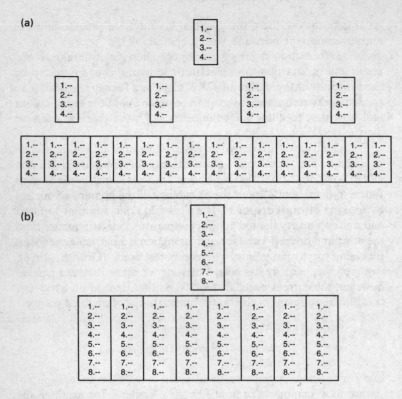

Fig. 4.2 Two ways of accessing sixty-four items via menus: (a) three layers of four-item menus, where the users choose from a four-item menu that takes them to another four-item menu, which takes them to another; (b) two layers of eight-item menus, where the users choose from one eight-item menu and then another.

see MacGregor and Lee, 1987), mostly concerned with how one should structure a hierarchical menu system (see Figure 4.2). Should one have several short menus or just a few much longer menus? The optimal number of items there should be in each menu is governed by (i) how fast the computer can put up a new menu and (ii) how fast the user can scan through the menu items and select a response. The latter depends on how easy it is to structure the material so that it makes sense to the user.

An insight into how people use the menus in graphical user interfaces, such as that for the Macintosh computer, is provided by an experiment by Mayes, Draper, McGregor and Oatley (1988). Users of MacWrite were asked to recall details from the screens they viewed each time they used this word-processor. A typical question was:

> *The menu bar is now as follows:* **'Apple' File Edit Search Format Font Style**. *Now please list the choices you have from each menu when it is pulled down.*

The average performance on this task was very poor. Even frequent users were able to recall only rather less than half of the menu items. This contrasts with their performance in a follow-up study, where users who had forgotten items or put them in the wrong menu generally found those items without hesitation. Asked to do a task with the user interface, they had no problem, but when asked to reconstruct the form of the user interface from memory they had considerable difficulty. This would seem to show that the behaviour of the users of this kind of menu system is driven by the appearance of the display rather than some learned representation of how it works. We will return to this finding in the section on models of human–computer interaction.

COMPUTER-SUPPORTED CO-OPERATIVE WORK (CSCW)

In the previous section we considered the problem of an individual working with a computer. However, work is a social activity and computer work will nearly always involve communication with colleagues. This communication may be an explicit function of the computer system or it may come about through the way the computer tool is used. Electronic mail and bulletin boards are the most obvious examples of computer systems explicitly designed for communication. A program for producing presentation slides or documents is a program for communication even if the eventual communication medium is not electronic. Even tools designed for apparently solitary activities, such as spreadsheets for financial calculations, have been found to have important communicative functions within an organization or business (Nardi and Miller, 1991). People pass around spreadsheets to support one another in their efforts to construct spreadsheets and also use them to structure discussions.

Video images contain enormous quantities of information, and radical improvements in the processing power of computer hardware and the potential capacity of telephone networks make it possible for computers to transmit video images to one another. This might take the form of a video image of someone you are talking to, so that the computer screen becomes a kind of video telephone, as in the Bellcore Cruiser system (Fish, Kraut, Root and Rice, 1993). It might be an image of some machinery that you are advising someone how to repair (Kuzouka, 1992). Displaying images of the work one is conversing about has become known as 'video as data' to distinguish it from displaying images of the person one is talking to. New inventions incorporating video in computer displays and digital communications are coming along so fast that there has yet been little systematic study of their use, either in experiments or field studies. However, video telephony has been studied by social psychologists in some detail.

Two of the most extensive and well-known series of studies were conducted in the early 1970s. Chapanis in the USA and Short, Williams and Christie in the UK performed a large number of experiments where pairs of people had to co-operate to complete some task. For example, in some of his experiments, Chapanis had pairs construct a 'trash-can transporter' from a do-it-yourself kit. One member of the pair had the instructions and the other had the kit. Within the experiment, different pairs communicated in different ways to complete this task. Some typed messages to each other, others wrote messages. Some could speak to each other because they were in the same room, because they had telephones, or because they were linked by television. Both Chapanis (1975) and Short, Williams and Christie (1976) found that, for information-transfer tasks of the kind described above, the main differences were between communication by writing or typing and communication by speech. There was little difference between pairs using, say, the telephone and pairs in the same room or communicating over a video link. This finding suggests that, of the two potential applications of video discussed above, images of shared work (video as data) are likely to be more useful than images of the face of the person one is talking to (video telephony).

Video communication via computers may become widespread in the future, but there are extensive and well-established text-based electronic communication systems already in place. Thanks to government initiatives in the USA and elsewhere, scientists have been using electronic mail or 'e-mail' for many years. There are also large communities of people who communicate via personal computers with modems attached to bulletin board systems or 'BBSs'. Rheingold (1994) provides a very readable account of how the use of e-mail and BBSs has developed. He also describes some of the other popular forms of text-based computer-mediated communication (CMC), such as multi-user dungeons (MUDs) and internet relay chat (IRC). The former originated as a kind of fantasy game that can be played simultaneously by hundreds of users but has been adapted for general multi-party interaction; the latter is a kind of text-based multi-person conversation.

E-mail allows someone with an account on a networked computer to send short messages to someone else with an account on that or another machine. Messages are stored in the recipient's 'in box', where they can be inspected at some later date. While typing is more effortful than speaking on the phone, there is more time to compose one's thoughts and the recipient does not have to be available when you send the message. One can still get a relatively fast answer to a query and it may be useful to copy textual information for use in other electronic documents. Increasingly, people are using e-mail to exchange documents. With the advent of networked personal computers, intra-company e-mail is also now becoming more common.

E-mail communication was studied in an experiment by Lea and Spears (1991). They described the effect of this medium as one of 'de-individuation'. Even though the source of each message is known, participants felt more anonymous, leading to more risky behaviour. This is congruent with the observation that people are often emboldened to send e-mail messages they might hesitate to communicate face-to-face, especially to someone senior to them in an organizational hierarchy (Sproull and Kiesler, 1991). Readers interested in computer-mediated communication should also look at the literature on computer-supported meeting rooms. Here the computer takes the role of a white board in a conventional meeting, with additional features to exploit the power of the computer for storing and sharing data. Tatar, Foster and Bobrow (1991), for example, discuss some of the problems users had with an early attempt to provide facilities of this kind at the Xerox PARC (Palo Alto Research Center).

EVALUATION AND DESIGN

The previous two sections have reviewed a selection of experimental studies of computer-based tools that may be used at work. The reason for doing this research is to inform design, and it is hoped that the new understanding gained is sufficiently practical to be applied by the designers of new computer-based tools so that they can build systems that are easier to use and easier to learn. These tools in turn enable their users to do things they could not do before. This section considers a more direct attack on the problem of building more usable systems. It describes how the techniques developed by experimental psychologists for eliciting and analysing behavioural data have been adapted for use as a part of the design process itself.

The design of software for modern computer systems is a large undertaking. Even though software is inherently flexible, it is very difficult to change a product once the design has been 'implemented' as a working system. For this reason software engineers, like other engineers, construct a 'specification' between ascertaining the requirements for the product and implementing it. A specification is a blueprint. It is built to be analysed, evaluated and changed until the designer is as certain as possible that the worst problems have been ironed out.

The specification for a user interface can take many forms. It is common to draw 'storyboards', as used in the film industry, that describe the major screens and how the user moves between them. It is also possible to build a working user interface with no underlying application below it. This can mimic some aspects of the eventual user interface and so specify how it should behave. Having built a prototype user interface, it is possible to test and improve it by having people typical of the eventual users work with it in simulated tasks. This has come to be known as 'user testing'. Of course, it is the prototype or specification that is being tested, not the user.

Quantitative Experiments

A great deal of user testing went into the development of the Xerox 8010 STAR Office Workstation, which was the predecessor to the Apple Macintosh. For example, Bewley, Roberts, Schroit, and Verplank (1983) describe how they compared seven different schemes for selecting text with a mouse. Seven different groups of four users each performed a standard set of tasks using one of the schemes. These could involve one, two or three mouse buttons used in different ways. One scheme, involving two buttons, resulted in significantly faster performance and was adopted in the final design.

Quantitative experiments of this kind are extremely expensive to perform. Software has to be built that will work in a sufficiently realistic way, and several users, twenty-eight in this case, have to be tested. To make this process practical one can test only selected components of an interface. It would take too long to train users to a reasonable level of competence on all aspects of the system. One may wonder what the effect of the missing context is. There is probably not too much of a problem with low-level questions about selecting text, as asked by Bewley and colleagues, or in the experiment by Card *et al.* (1978) described earlier in this chapter. However, imagine using the same method to test the effectiveness of alternative ways of wording the three most important menus in a system. Let us say there are three alternatives for labelling each menu. One could do three experiments. The first tests the alternatives for menu A, the second those for menu B, and the third those for menu C. This would require nine groups of users. However, there is the strong possibility that the way menu A is worded could change the effect of how menu B or C is worded. This means one has to use a factorial design where each alternative is combined with every other, i.e. $3 \times 3 \times 3 = 27$ groups. Such a comprehensive approach is clearly impractical.

Carroll (1990) describes this as the 'problem of infinite detail'. One simply cannot tell whether a small change somewhere else in the system will affect the results of an experiment of this kind. This is well recognized by cognitive psychologists, where each experimental finding is replicated with numerous subtle changes by different research groups. That process of replication may be acceptable for long-term research in a scientific community; though one may question its profitability given the small amount of agreed theory that has accumulated over the many years experimental psychologists have been doing this. It is not acceptable in the testing of a prototype design in the usability laboratory.

Quantitative experiments may have a place in a large research and development projects, such as the STAR Office Workstation discussed above, but most software development projects have much more modest objectives and resources. Rather than comparing alternatives to find out which is best, these designers have a single design and the question they ask of user testing is 'How can I improve it?' Quantitative experiments are of limited use in this case. Firstly, there are no alternatives to compare and, secondly, they provide very little in the way of information about what should be changed. Being told merely that a particular component scored low on some test is of little use. Watching users experiencing and explaining the problems they have is much more likely to provide ideas about what should be done.

Qualitative Techniques

Wright and Monk (1989) make a strong case for the use of qualitative data obtained from 'think aloud' protocols in user testing. Their analysis of the usability problems detected in an evaluation of a single user interface shows that many of the problems can be detected only if the users describe their thoughts as they undertake the task. Errors and unexpected behaviour can be detected only if the evaluator knows what the user is trying to achieve at a given moment; this cannot always be inferred from the user's prior actions on the system alone. Similarly, points where the user is behaving as the designer intended, but finding the experience very tedious or effortful, cannot be detected in any other way.

The use of verbal protocols has a long history in psychology (Ericsson and Simon, 1980), and the problems it poses are well understood. While thinking aloud undoubtedly changes a user's performance, this does not invalidate its use to determine the user's intentions at a given moment or when the user interface intrudes on experience. Monk, Wright, Haber and Davenport (1993) have used this argument to devise a user-testing methodology that encapsulates a think-aloud testing procedure in such a way that it can be easily learned and used by a software developer with no training in psychological methods. The method is inexpensive, in the sense that it requires little in the way of training and can be performed rapidly. Nevertheless, Wright and Monk (1991) were able to show that it is capable of detecting a reasonable proportion of the usability problems identified by more thorough and very much more costly procedures. In the practical context of software development a strong argument can be made for such 'discount' or 'bargain basement' approaches (see for example Nielsen, 1993).

The other advantage of these qualitative methods is that they can be used with more approximate prototypes. Two classic papers in this respect are by Gould, Boies, Levy, Richards and Schoonard (1987) and Good, Whiteside, Wixon and Jones (1984). Gould and colleagues were part of a team of engineers and human factors specialists charged with providing a voice messaging system for the 1984 Olympic Games in Los Angeles. A large range of prototypes was built. The team started by writing short user manuals. These leaflets were circulated amongst athletes and their families. The families could use the system from abroad to leave a message for an athlete; their instruction could thus be tested just using a normal telephone, before any code had been written or any hardware installed. A great deal was learned through this user testing and the system simplified accordingly. Another form of prototype was a mocked-up booth that looked as close as possible to the booths to be distributed around the Olympic village. This was placed in the entrance to the IBM T. J. Watson Research Centre. Though it was not connected to a proper working system, people passing by could read the instructions and try simple operations with it. Their comments were used to redesign the system yet again.

Each of the many forms of prototype built was tried out in this cyclical fashion. They were first tested with a few users. The behaviour and comments of these users gave the designers some new ideas that were incorporated into the prototype, which was then tested again. This procedure of repeatedly testing and changing the design has become known as iterative design. Iterative design recognizes the problem of infinite detail and minimizes it by retesting each design.

Good, Whiteside, Wixon and Jones (1984) also used iterative design. They set out to devise an e-mail system that could be used with little or no training. They were working at Digital in the early days of electronic mail, when few people had used such systems. First they specified a set of problems for their users to solve. This started off with a list of eight simple tasks, such as 'Get rid of any memo which is about morale' and 'Look at the contents of each of the memos from Dingee.' Later problems in the list were more complex, such as 'It turns out that the Dingee memo you got rid of is needed after all, so go back and get it.' They then built a command-driven system capable of providing these functions and user-tested it. The users were given no instructions apart from the problems and an exhortation to try to guess what commands the system was looking for. At first, as one would expect, the system was able to recognize only a few of the commands given it, and so, to provide an illusion of smooth human–computer dialogue, Good and colleagues used a hidden human operator. When the system was unable to recognize a command, the user's typing was displayed on a computer screen in another room. If the hidden operator judged that the command was reasonable, he would 'translate' it into a command that the system would respond to. Good and colleagues used the guesses of their users to expand the commands available. They would test two or three users, modify the system, test a few more, modify it again, and so on. Initially the system recognized only a small proportion of the commands issued to it. After several cycles of iterative testing, a total of sixty-seven users, it was able to recognize 76 per cent. Most of the changes made were small, such as allowing synonyms and variations in syntax.

The procedure of using a hidden human operator to simulate software that is not yet available has become known as the 'wizard of Oz' technique, after the character in the book of the same name. Another good example of what can be achieved in this way is provided by Gould and Hovanyecz (1983). Working at IBM, they performed some experiments on the feasibility of using automatic speech recognition to make a listening typewriter. At the time speech recognition algorithms were capable of recognizing only very small vocabularies of tens of words. Gould and Hovanyecz used a wizard-of-Oz technique to compare a system recognizing 1,000 words with one recognizing 5,000. The hidden operator typed in all the words spoken by the user, the computer had only to decide whether the word was in the recognition vocabulary. This system allowed the realistic simulation of problems such as how to allow a user to spell out unrecognized words and how to deal with homonyms (e.g., 'to', 'too' and 'two'). As well as looking at the effect of vocabulary size the investigators compared natural continuous speech with speaking each word separately. This makes speech much easier to recognize mechanically. They found that this was much less disruptive of performance than having a smaller recognition vocabulary. These very detailed experiments were carried out long before the technology became available that would make automatic speech recognition with such large vocabularies possible.

MODELS OF HUMAN–COMPUTER INTERACTION

The techniques described above for evaluating and improving a design all require that users are obtained and given an opportunity to work with a prototype. This is not always practical. Another problem is that it is seldom possible to train users to high levels of skill because the time they are available is limited. This means that iterative user testing is really good only at finding problems of comprehension, points where the system is confusing or hard to learn. Various authors have attempted to provide an alternative to user testing by creating models of a user working with a user interface. The analogy is with a civil engineer, say, making a mathematical model of some physical structure and calculating its strength and the loads it has to bear.

An influential book by Card, Moran and Newell (1983) contains two examples of this approach. The first is an attempt to summarize relevant theory from cognitive psychology and perception in a form where it could be used by designers. The Model Human Processor assumes a basic 'recognize-act' cycle. Perceptual processes activate working memory, which in turn activates motor processes, resulting in action. Cognitive processes may also change the contents of working memory. Formulae in the model allow a designer to compute average, best and worst times for certain parts of the cycle. Card and colleagues show how this model can be used to make reasonable predictions that could guide design. For example, were a designer to consider changing the position of a commonly used key on a handheld calculator, he or she could calculate the time advantage gained. To do this, the designer would enter the size of the keys and the average distance the finger has to move into a formula provided for this purpose.

The second influential contribution from the Card, Moran and Newell book is GOMS: Goals, Operators, Methods and Selection rules. The GOMS notation can be used to provide a kind of cognitive task analysis of what a user is presumed to be doing when he or she is working a computer-based tool, such as a word-processor. This is in some ways similar to hierarchical task analysis, which has a long history in human factors and ergonomics and has been used for designing training procedures amongst other things (see Annett, Duncan, Stammers and Gray, 1971). The two techniques, together with the similarities and differences between them, will be illustrated by an example.

Figure 4.3 is a hierarchical task analysis for part of a secretary's job. The top level task is to change the electronic form of a document on a personal computer in accordance with some editing marks made on a paper copy of the same document. This is achieved by repeating sub-task 1.1 until all the changes have been made (see the 'plan' in last line of Figure 4.3). Sub-task 1.1 is broken down into two sub-sub-tasks: finding the next change on the paper copy and making that change on the electronic copy. Each of these is decomposed in a similar way. Finally we get down to tasks that correspond to operations with the word processor, e.g., 1.1.2.1.1. (QS command and LF command are shorthand for two different ways of moving through the electronic document with this particular word processor.)

Figure 4.4 follows the most commonly used convention for writing

1. Edit electronic document on personal computer
  1.1 Do next change
    1.1.1. Find change marked on paper document
      1.1.1.1 Turn to next page
      1.1.1.2 Read change
      Plan: 1.1.1.2 preceded by 1.1.1.1 if at end of page
    1.1.2. Make change
      1.1.2.1 Locate line in electronic document
        1.1.2.1.1 Search with QS command
        1.1.2.1.2 Step through with LF command
        Plan: Use 1.1.2.1.1 if >10 lines, else 1.1.2.1.2
      1.1.2.2. Edit document
        1.1.2.2.1 Use Substitute command
        1.1.2.2.2 Use Modify command
        1.1.2.2.3 Verify edit
        Plan: 1.1.2.2.1 or 1.1.2.2.2; then 1.1.2.2.3
      Plan: 1.1.2.1, then 1.1.2.2
    Plan: 1.1.1, then 1.1.2
  Plan: Repeat 1.1 until there are no more changes to be made

Fig. 4.3 Hierarchical task analysis for the task of editing an electronic document with changes marked on a paper version.

Goal: edit-manuscript
  Goal: edit-unit-task *repeat until no more tasks*
    Goal: acquire unit task
      get-next-page *If at end of manuscript*
      get-next-task
    Goal: execute-unit-task
      Goal: locate-line
        [select: use-qs-method
                  use-lf-method]
      Goal: modify-text
        [select: use-s-command
              use-m-command]
      verify-edit.

Fig. 4.4 GOMS analysis of editing task (adapted from Card *et al.*, 1983, p. 142).

task analyses. Tasks are numbered to indicate the nesting relationship and a 'plan' is written for each level to indicate the rules for doing the tasks. A hierarchical task analysis is simply a record of the analyst's understanding of some work recorded for some specific practical purpose. As such it may be developed arbitrarily deeply. For one purpose, it may be convenient to stop at the level of broad tasks, e.g., at '1.1.1 Find change marked on paper document', and '1. Edit electronic document on personal computer' might be just one sub-task of some higher level task in the secretary's work. For another purpose it may be useful to go right down to the detailed analysis of keystrokes, e.g., '1.1.2.1.1 Search with QS command' would be further analysed to specify the actions required of the user.

The GOMS approach similarly decomposes tasks, but here the analysis is presented as a model of what is going on in the user's head rather than as an essentially arbitrary record of the analyst's understanding of the work. Figure 4.4 has been adapted from Card *et al.* (1983) and presents their analysis of the same task. Figure 4.3 was constructed from Figure 4.4 and Card and colleagues' description of what is happening. The GOMS analysis is based on models of problem solving from artificial intelligence (see, for example, Newell and Simon, 1972).

The notion of a user's goal is crucial to this approach. Having the high-level goal 'edit manuscript' leads the user to generate a sub-goal 'edit unit task'. This in turn leads to the generation of another goal 'acquire unit task', and so on until eventually some action is taken. If the action is successful, the immediately preceding goal may be 'satisfied' and can be removed from the list of goals to be achieved. When all the sub-goals of a goal are satisfied, that goal is itself satisfied and can also be removed. Action, then, is controlled by a constantly changing list of goals and the main determinants of detailed behaviour are the rules for adding and removing goals to and from this list.

GOMS has been used to carry out detailed cognitive analyses of various tasks. Gray, John, Stuart, Lawrence and Atwood (1990), for example, claim to have saved a phone company $3 million a year by their painstaking GOMS analysis of the work of toll assistance operators. This was achieved by shaving an average of one second off the time it took to complete each transaction. However, it is questionable whether GOMS analysis can be practical except for very short repetitive tasks of this kind. Also the significant insight that led to the saving came from a critical path analysis of parallel activities, which is not conventionally a part of the GOMS approach. To be fair, GOMS was put forward as an engineering approximation in the spirit of other components of the Model Human Processor and its creators make no claim that it should be applicable under all circumstances. More recent work has sought alternative theories and alternative approximations to those theories (see Polson, Lewis, Rieman, and Wharton, 1992).

Perhaps the most telling criticism of the GOMS approach is that it assumes that human behaviour is essentially 'planful', supposing that when one learns a new task what one learns is a way of generating plans to do it. Another possibility is that behaviour is driven by the environment. Take Suchman's (1987) influential analysis of people learning to use a photocopier. Suchman is an ethnographer coming from a sociological ('anthropological' in the USA) background. She presents a provocative anti-planning stance, claiming instead that all action is 'situated', i.e., embedded in a context of previous action and current circumstances. Her analysis is of how actions lead to perceptible changes and a context for further action, and ignores what is going on in the user's head. This is an extreme position and it is quite possible to build cognitive ('in the head') models that learn by modifying the way they react to changes in the environment.

A less extreme position than Suchman's is to assume that at some level behaviour is driven by goals and at other levels by the environment. Studies of highly practised work carried out by human factors engineers in the 1950s and 1960s showed that such skilled behaviour depends crucially on feedback from the environment (Fitts, 1964). However, it would seem reasonable to assume that these skills are put into practice in order to achieve some higher-order goal or plan. So at the very highest level behaviour is driven almost exclusively by a plan and at the very lowest levels by feedback from the environment. The question then is, what happens at levels in between these two extremes? For example, to what extent are apparently cognitive skills like using a word-processor driven by the environment rather than the user's plans and intentions?

The experiment by Mayes, Draper, McGregor and Oatley (1988), described above, suggests that more behaviour is driven by the environment than a GOMS analysis would lead us to believe. The reader will remember that in this study people had great difficulty recalling from memory the menus they used on a daily basis. Further, users who had recalled items in the wrong menu or confused them in other ways were able to find and use the item in the right menu, without hesitation, when given a practical task to do with the word-processor. The interpretation put on this result by Howes and Payne (1990) is that menu selections are made by semantic matching. Their account is as follows. Let us say one wants to save one's work onto disk. One scans the menu tabs at the top of the screen. An approximate match is obtained between the meaning of this goal and the meaning of the item named 'File'. Selecting this reveals another set of items containing the word 'Save'. This is similarly matched with the goal and selected. This is the sort of process that one might expect of someone exploring a new word-processor. Howes and Payne propose that the learning that occurs with continued experience with these menus is simply to automate this matching process. One does not learn a plan: 'To save one's work, select File, then Save.' One simply learns to do the semantic matching with what appears on the screen more effectively.

Howes (1994) has gone on to build a cognitive model, ayn, that learns how to format text into double columns in Microsoft Word using the same principles. A cognitive model is a computer program built to exemplify a theory of cognition. Running the program demonstrates that the theory is in some sense complete. It is also possible to compare the behaviour of the program with the behaviour of real users as a further test of the theory. The important thing to note about ayn is that, like Mayes and colleagues' users, it can do the task only by reacting to an accurate model of the displays generated by Microsoft Word. The model of the computer system generated by Howes to depict the behaviour of Microsoft Word is as important in determining the behaviour of the system as his model of what goes on in the user's head. One can thus argue that ayn displays 'situated' behaviour of the kind described by Suchman. The difference between this conception of how behaviour is generated and the more conventional viewpoint represented by GOMS is depicted in Figure 4.5.

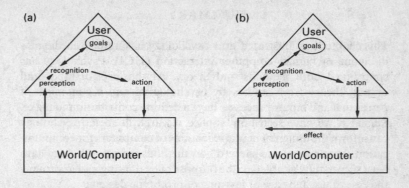

Fig. 4.5 Two ways of modelling human–computer interaction: (a) a conventional model as represented by GOMS; (b) a model including an account of how the computer reacts to the user's actions. The second approach is necessary to explain the cyclical display-based nature of much human–computer interaction.

One can think of (b) in that figure as a rapprochement between the cognitive and situated approaches.

As was noted above, the idea of situated action comes from ethnography, a branch of sociology, not psychology. Sociological explanations are couched at the level of the group or organization rather than at the psychological level of the individual. Again, this generates ideas and observations that psychologists might otherwise have missed. For example, Seifert and Hutchins (1992) have described the process by which a group with some common goal, navigating a ship in this instance, co-ordinate their behaviour. This is done through shared artefacts (displays, documents, etc.) and public communications.

Like the cyclical model of behaviour in Figure 4.5 the notion of 'distributed cognition' can be thought of as an attempt to translate ideas from social science into a more cognitive framework.

SUMMARY

This chapter has illustrated how psychology has influenced the new discipline of human–computer interaction (HCI). Psychology has contributed both methods and theory. At the level of input and output, theory from studies by psychologists and ergonomists of perceptual and motor processes have a definite contribution to make. Similarly, we have seen how applied research in social psychology can inform the design of new applications of computers for communication. The chapter also showed how methods from psychology have been successfully adapted to the purpose of evaluating and improving the ease of use and ease of learning of prototype designs.

However, the contribution of theory from cognitive psychology has been disappointing (see for example Landauer's (1987) discussion of the difficulties of applying work on learning and memory to the design of command names). Card *et al.*'s (1983) Model Human Processor was explicitly built to capture cognitive theory in a way that would make it useful for design. However, the influence of the Model Human Processor has been more on cognitive psychology itself than on the design of new systems. From the designer's point of view, most of the useful predictions that can be made are either obvious or not very relevant. On the other hand, the exercise of linking up research in cognitive psychology to produce an integrated model with quantitative predictive power in an applied setting made very apparent the weakness of much cognitive theory. Few of the experimental findings of thirty years of intensive research can be applied outside of the very specific and artificial experimental paradigms used. This has stimulated Newell (see Laird, Newell and Rosenbloom, 1987) and others (e.g., Anderson, 1993) to produce integrated 'cognitive architectures' in an attempt to provide, in Newell's words, a unified theory of cognition.

As was pointed out at the beginning of the chapter, psychology is only one of the disciplines that have contributed to the new discipline of HCI. As a psychologist myself I can say that I have found the influence of computer scientists, linguists, sociologists and anthropologists very stimulating. The practical problem of designing better computer systems forces scientists from these diverse backgrounds to communicate with each other when in the past they would probably have dismissed each other's work out of hand. The influence of ethnographers such as Suchman was discussed in the last section. Their point about action being 'situated' can be incorporated into a cognitive model, but only if the model includes a description of how the world reacts to the user's actions as well as how the user reacts to the world.

In the beginning HCI depended on psychology for concepts and methods, but HCI has now come of age. HCI has to be seen as a major source of new ideas and phenomena that challenge traditional psychological viewpoints. It is now up to psychology to respond to this challenge.

FURTHER READING

The short text by Lansdale and Ormerod (1994) presents an excellent discussion of the relationship between psychology and HCI. Preece, Rogers, Sharp, Benyon, Holland and Carey (1994) have written a full (773 pages) and well-structured HCI textbook with numerous illustrations and exercises. Many of the classic papers in HCI, including several of those referenced in this chapter, are to be found in the readings edited by Baecker and Buxton (1995).

Readers interested in the contribution of other disciplines to HCI should consult Monk and Gilbert (1995). Finally, readers looking for a guide on how to make better use of IT in business are referred to Clegg, Warr, Green, Monk, Kemp, Allison and Lansdale (1988).

REFERENCES

Annett, J., Duncan, K. D., Stammers, R. B. and Gray, M. J. (1971). *Task Analysis*. Training Information Paper No. 6. London: HMSO.
Anderson, J. R. (1993). *Rules of the Mind*. Hillsdale, NJ: Erlbaum.
Baecker, R. M. and Buxton, W. A. S. (1995). *Readings in Human–computer Interaction: A Multidisciplinary Approach,* 2nd edn. Los Altos, Calif.: Morgan Kaufman.
Bewley, W. L., Roberts, T. L., Schroit, D. and Verplank, W. L. (1983). Human factors testing in the design of Xerox's 8010 'Star' office

workstation. In *CHI '83 Proceedings*, pp. 72–77. New York: Association for Computing Machinery.

Buxton, W. (1986). There's more to interaction than meets the eye: Some issues in manual input. In D. A. Norman and S. Draper (eds.), *User Centered System Design: New Perspectives On Human-Computer Interaction*, pp. 319–337. Hillsdale, NJ: Erlbaum.

Card, S., English, W. and Burr, B. (1978). Evaluation of Mouse, rate controlled isometric joystick, step keys and text keys for text selection on a CRT. *Ergonomics*, 21, 601–613.

Card, S. K., Moran, T. P. and Newell, A. (1983). *The Psychology of Human–computer Interaction*. Hillsdale, NJ: Erlbaum.

Carroll, J. M. (1990). Infinite detail and emulation in an ontologically minimised HCI. In J. C. Chew and J. Whiteside (eds.), *CHI '90 Conference Proceedings: Empowering People*, pp. 321–327. New York: Association for Computing Machinery.

Chapanis, A. (1975). Interactive human communication. *Scientific American*, 232(3), 36–42.

Clegg, C., Warr, P., Green, T., Monk, A., Kemp, N., Allison, G. and Lansdale, M. (1988). *People And Computers: How To Evaluate Your Company's New Technology*. Chichester: Ellis Horwood.

Ericsson, K. A. and Simon, H. A. (1980). Verbal reports as data. *Psychological Review*, 87, 215–251.

Fish, R. S., Kraut, R. E., Root, R. W. and Rice, R. E. (1993). Video as a technology for informal communication. *Communications of the Association for Computing Machinery*, 36, 48–61.

Fitts, P. M. (1964). Perceptual motor skill learning. In A. W. Melton (ed.), *Categories of Human Learning*, pp. 244–285. New York: Academic Press.

Good, M. D., Whiteside, J. A., Wixon, D. R. and Jones, S. J. (1984). Building a user-derived interface. *Communications of the Association for Computing Machinery*, 27, 1032–1043.

Gould, J. D., Boies, S. J., Levy, S., Richards, J. T. and Schoonard, J. (1987). The 1984 Olympic message system: A test of behavioral principles of system design. *Communications of the Association for Computing Machinery*, 30, 758–769.

Gould, J. D. and Hovanyecz, T. (1983). Composing letters with a simulated listening typewriter. *Communications of the Association for Computing Machinery*, 26, 295–308.

Gray, W. D., John, B. E., Stuart, R., Lawrence, D. and Atwood, M. E. (1990). GOMS meets the phone company: analytic modelling applied to real-world problems. In D. Diaper, G. Gilmore, G. Cockton and B.

Shackel (eds.), *Human–computer Interaction – INTERACT '90*, pp. 29–34. Amsterdam: Elsevier.

Griffith, D. (1990). Access to computers by blind people: Human factors issues. *Human Factors*, 32, 467–475.

Howes, A. (1994). A model of the acquisition of menu knowledge by exploration. In B. Adelson, S. Dumais and J. Olson (eds.), *CHI '94 Conference Proceedings: Human Factors in Computing Systems – Celebrating Interdependence*, pp. 445–451. New York: Association for Computing Machinery.

Howes, A. and Payne, S. J. (1990). Display-based competence: towards user models for menu-driven interfaces. *International Journal of Man–machine Studies*, 33, 637–655.

Kuzouka, H. (1992). Spatial workplace collaboration: A shared view video support system for remote collaboration capability. In P. Bauersfeld, J. Bennett and G. Lynch (eds.), *CHI '92 Conference Proceedings*, pp. 533–540. New York: Association for Computing Machinery.

Laird, J., Newell, A. and Rosenbloom, P. (1987). SOAR: An architecture for general intelligence. *Artificial Intelligence*, 33, 1–64.

Landauer, T. K. (1987). Relations between cognitive psychology and computer system design. In J. M. Carroll (ed.), *Interfacing Thought: Cognitive Aspects Of Human–Computer Interaction*, pp. 1–25. Cambridge, Mass.: MIT Press,.

Lansdale, M. W. and Ormerod, T. C. (1994). *Understanding Interfaces: A Handbook of Human–Computer Dialogue*. London: Academic Press.

Lea, M. and Spears, R. (1991). Computer-mediated communication, deindividuation and group decision making. *International Journal of Man–Machine Studies*, 34, 283–301.

MacGregor, J. N. and Lee, E. S. (1987). Performance and preference in videotext menu retrieval: A review of the empirical literature. *Behaviour and Information Technology*, 6, 43–68.

Mayes, T. J., Draper, S. W., McGregor, M. A. and Oatley, K. (1988). Information flow in a user interface: The effect of experience and context on the recall of MacWrite screens. In D. M. Jones and R. Winder (eds.), *People and Computers 4*, pp. 275–289. Cambridge: Cambridge University Press.

Monk, A. F. and Gilbert, N. (1995). *Perspectives on Human–Computer Interaction: Diverse Approaches*. London: Academic Press.

Monk, A. F., Wright, P., Haber, J. and Davenport, L. (1993). *Improving Your Human–Computer Interface: A Practical Technique*. Hemel Hempstead: Prentice Hall, BCS Practitioner Series.

Nardi, B. A. and Miller, J. A. (1991). Twinkling lights and nested loops:

119

Distributed problem solving and spreadsheet development. *International Journal of Man–machine Studies*, 34, 161–184.

Newell, A. and Simon, H. A. (1972). *Human Problem Solving*. Englewood Cliffs, NJ: Prentice Hall.

Nielsen, J. (1993). *Usability Engineering*. New York: Academic Press.

Polson, P. G., Lewis, C., Rieman, J. and Wharton, C. (1992). Cognitive walkthroughs: A method for theory-based evaluation of user interfaces. *International Journal of Man–Machine Studies*, 36, 741–773.

Preece, J., Rogers, Y., Sharp, H., Benyon, D., Holland, S. and Carey, T. (1994). *Human–computer Interaction*. Wokingham, Surrey: Addison-Wesley.

Rheingold, H. (1994). *The Virtual Community*. London: Secker and Warburg.

Seifert, C. M. and Hutchins, E. L. (1992). Error as opportunity: Learning in a cooperative task. *Human–Computer Interaction*, 7, 409–435.

Short, J. A., Williams, E. and Christie, B. (1976). *The Social Psychology Of Communications*. London: Wiley.

Sproull, L. and Kiesler, S. (1991). Two-level perspective on electronic mail in organizations. *Journal of Organizational Computing*, 1, 125–134.

Suchman, L. A. (1987). *Plans And Situated Actions: The Problem Of Human–Machine Communication*. Cambridge: Cambridge University Press.

Tatar, D. G., Foster, G. and Bobrow, D. G. (1991). Design for conversation: Lessons from cognoter. *International Journal of Man–Machine Studies*, 34, 185–209.

Thompson, P. (1984). Visual perception: An intelligent system with limited bandwidth. In A. F. Monk (ed.), *Fundamentals of Human–Computer Interaction*, pp. 5–33. London: Academic Press.

Travis, D. (1991). *Effective Color Displays*. London: Academic Press.

Wright, P. C. and Monk, A. F. (1989). Evaluation for design. In A. Sutcliffe and L. Macaulay (eds.), *People and Computers 5*, pp. 345–358. Cambridge: Cambridge University Press.

Wright, P. C. and Monk, A. F. (1991). A cost-effective evaluation method for use by designers. *International Journal of Man–Machine Studies*, 35, 891–912.

5

Personnel Selection and Assessment

Ivan Robertson

Personnel selection and assessment activities are integral parts of organizational life, and almost everyone has experience of being a candidate for a job at some time. Although some form of assessment procedure is always used at the recruitment stage, it is also quite common for organizations also to use procedures, such as interviews or psychological tests, to evaluate individual members of staff for promotion. Many large organizations also use assessment procedures in a more developmental fashion, to provide feedback and guidance to assist individuals in their career development. This chapter is concerned particularly with the use of assessment methods for selection or placement purposes, rather than for personal development, although some attention is also paid to developmental issues.

The cornerstone of personnel selection and assessment is the demonstrated existence of measurable psychological differences between people that are of importance in determining job success. It is clear from research into the psychology of individual differences that people differ from each other in stable and noticeable ways. Some differences and their links with job performance criteria are easy to identify, at least at a fairly general level. For example, basic numerical skills are needed for shop assistants and manual dexterity is important for a plastic surgeon. Other features are less straightforward: is it important for a salesperson to be outgoing? What role does emotional stability play in the creative arts? For most jobs and people it is clearly quite difficult to be certain about the precise mix of psychological characteristics that are important for success.

The goal of much personnel selection research has been to establish specific links between individual difference variables and job success. For instance, work has explored relationships between intelligence and success in a wide range of occupational areas. Research has also investigated the links between personality variables and job success and between the biographical history of candidates and job-related criteria. Although the stimulus for much of this work has been a wish to improve personnel selection, the implications of some of the results extend beyond the narrow boundaries of the selection of people for jobs. Many findings provide information relevant to the understanding of the underlying determinants of behaviour in organizational settings.

The capacity to conduct the tasks of a job to a high standard is not the only ingredient in overall job success. A consistent person who performs to a modest standard and is rarely absent from work may sometimes be more useful to an organization than a person who is capable of outstanding performance but is given to frequent bouts of unexplained and unpredictably poor performance. Sporting personalities and entertainers sometimes provide graphic examples of such contrasting types of behaviour. Furthermore, different circumstances will often lead to emphasis being placed on different aspects of an employee's overall performance. At an early stage in the selection process systematic consideration needs to be given to the major job requirements (referred to from now on as 'criteria') that are important. Figure 5.1 indicates some of the major types of criteria that might need to be considered.

As the figure illustrates, there are several different criteria that might be important in any particular setting. It is not always clear which one should receive primary attention. The position is further complicated by the fact that the need for one criterion may not be compatible with the need for another. A small company with modest growth potential may find it difficult to recruit high-performing graduate trainees and hold on to them for much longer than two to three years, indicating a tension between the two different criteria of proficiency and tenure.

As far as personnel selection is concerned, the existence of different and interrelated criteria of job performance implies that, at an early stage, due consideration must be given to the purpose of a selection procedure (i.e., selection for what?). The basic elements of a procedure may be quite different depending on what kind of criteria the organization has in mind. The criteria used also help to determine

Performance/proficiency: effectiveness in conducting work tasks.
This might be examined by obtaining performance ratings from
supervisors, by observing work outputs, or by a variety of other means.

Attendance: reliable attendance at normal work times.
This may be particularly important in settings where absence is a
problem for the organization.

Tenure: length of stay in the job.
Long tenure is not always a target when personnel selection schemes
are developed. There are many positions where some staff turnover is
expected, or even desirable.

Progression: progress through relevant grades in the organization's
hierarchy.
Some personnel selection or assessment schemes are specifically
designed to identify 'high flyers'.

Training performance: effectiveness in assimilating and benefiting from
training provided by the organization.
New recruits in many jobs require training. Progress in training gives an
early indication of suitability.

Fig. 5.1 Criteria of job success.

the qualities that are to be looked for in candidates. Reliability
and agreeableness may be important if long-term tenure is the dominant criterion, whereas creativity and high analytical ability may be
important if outstanding job performance is the dominant criterion.

The extent to which criterion variables can be measured accurately
is of primary importance to the area reviewed in this chapter. This is
because personnel selection is essentially an attempt to predict job
success. Any checking on how successful this attempt has been (a
process of 'validation') requires that job success is measured accurately. A criterion variable that is not measured accurately is impossible to predict accurately; for example, it would be impossible to
work out how to predict language skills from factors such as number
of years residence in a country if no accurate measure of language
proficiency was available.

The balance of evidence from a substantial amount of psychological research makes it clear that behaviour is not determined solely
by either the person (i.e., individual differences) or the situation
(e.g., the work setting) (see Pervin, 1989). If situational factors such

as co-workers, supervision, organizational culture and job design help to determine work behaviour, then we should not expect to be able to predict precisely how well someone will do in a job (his or her performance, absenteeism, etc.) merely by evaluating aspects of the person at the selection stage. At least some aspects of work behaviour will be impossible to predict without adequate knowledge of the situation in which he or she will work.

This helps to make two points clear. First, it is important to have a good understanding of the job and organization in which a candidate will be working. Second, personnel selection decisions are very unlikely to be 100 per cent accurate. The inevitable uncertainty about behaviour does not mean that systematic personnel selection is pointless, simply that there are limits to the benefit that might be expected. Even the best procedure will necessarily produce some errors, but it will be more effective than random selection or less sophisticated alternatives. As a later section of this chapter will show, it is possible to obtain extremely useful gains from selection procedures that are far from completely accurate.

INDIVIDUAL DIFFERENCES AND PERSONNEL SELECTION PROCEDURES

It is obvious from the above that good personnel selection decisions cannot be made without consideration being given to the situation in which a person will work. Effective design of a personnel selection procedure begins with a detailed examination of the job in question (see below) and its organizational setting. Despite this important point, it is clear that the principal focus of attention at the personnel selection stage is on the person and his or her attributes. Everyday experience suggests that all people are not equally suited to all jobs. The differences between people, in terms of their abilities and personal qualities, mean that some people would be very ill-suited to some positions. For example, extremely withdrawn and introverted salespeople are not commonplace, and statisticians with poor numerical skills are not likely to be very successful.

In broad terms the major differences between people can be grouped into three major categories: cognitive ability (Kline, 1991),

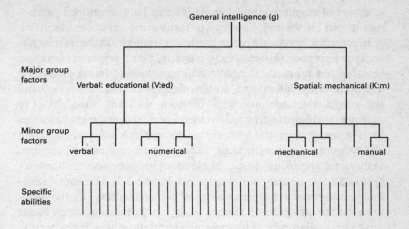

Fig. 5.2 P. E. Vernon's (1961) model of the structure of intelligence.

personality features (i.e., disposition and temperament; Mischel, 1993), and attitudes (Oskamp, 1991). As far as personnel selection is concerned, cognitive ability and personality are the most important categories.

The structure and measurement of cognitive ability have been central issues for psychological research and theory since early this century, and attention given to the area has produced a reasonable consensus amongst psychologists. This consensus was reached some time ago after an intense period of research and theorizing (see Kline, 1991). The structural view that underpins tests of cognitive ability used in contemporary personnel selection is consistent with Vernon's (1961) hierarchical theory (see Figure 5.2).

General mental ability (often referred to as 'g' or 'general intelligence') is seen as a fundamental attribute associated with a person's capacity to process, store and retrieve information. It is also closely linked to a person's capacity to learn from experience in formal training and elsewhere. As well as a general factor (g), Vernon's model proposes that there are major sub-factors of cognitive ability, such as spatial and verbal ability. Even more specific factors of ability lie at lower levels in the hierarchy. In parallel with exploring the structure of cognitive ability, psychologists have developed psychometric tests for the major and minor factors that have been identified.

In respect of personality, one particular framework, the trait factor-analytic approach (Kline, 1993), has dominated personnel selection research and practice. The statistical technique of factor analysis is a procedure for identifying underlying factors that help to explain the intercorrelations observed between different variables. For example, in studies conducted over a number of years, factor analyses have revealed that the pattern of correlations between different ability tests is consistent with underlying factors of both general ability and specific abilities. These analyses gave rise to Vernon's (1961) theory, already summarized in Figure 5.2. The trait factor-analytic approach to personality is complementary to the work done on the structure of mental ability. In both approaches factor analysis is used to explore underlying interrelationships. In the personality domain, factor analysis is applied to correlations that are found between people's responses to questions about their typical behaviour, usually derived from questionnaires that ask them to agree or disagree with statements relevant to the construct under examination.

Research on the factor-analytic structure of human personality has identified a number of underlying factors. In a long programme of research Eysenck isolated three major underlying factors: extroversion, neuroticism and psychoticism (Eysenck and Eysenck, 1985). Using similar research methods Cattell (1965) produced a model incorporating sixteen factors. In fact, differences between these models were more to do with preferences for different levels of analysis than with fundamentally different results. More recent factor-analytic studies have rationalized the position and produced a model involving five major factors (Digman, 1990: the so-called 'big five' factors, see Figure 5.3).

There is a reasonable degree of consensus amongst personality researchers about the big five as an underlying structure for personality. Personality inventories exist for measuring the big five and other, usually more detailed, personality traits (e.g., Costa and McCrae, 1985).

Although cognitive ability and personality are the major building blocks underlying differences between people, personnel selection

Extroversion: the extent to which a person is sociable and outgoing. Extroverts also tend to enjoy excitement and may be aggressive and impulsive.

Neuroticism: the extent to which a person is emotionally stable. Neurotics are generally tense and anxious with a tendency to worry.

Openness (to experience): the extent to which a person is imaginative and flexible, with a positive, open-minded response to new experiences.

Conscientiousness: the extent to which a person is well-organized, planful and concerned about achieving goals and deadlines.

Agreeableness: the extent to which a person is good-natured, warm and compassionate with others.

Fig. 5.3 The 'big five' factors of personality.

decisions are often taken with reference to less fundamental constructs such as skills or competencies. In recent years the term 'competency' has become important in personnel selection research, theory and practice.

Competencies are seen as psychological attributes that determine people's behaviour in a variety of settings (Boam and Sparrow, 1992). As an illustration, the competencies required by a first-line supervisor might emphasize persuasiveness and technical knowledge, whereas those for a senior manager might focus more on strategic thinking and analytical skills. Some competencies are quite similar to the kinds of cognitive ability referred to earlier in this chapter. Numeracy, for example, is often mentioned as a competency that is necessary for a variety of jobs. Other kinds of competencies resemble a mix between personality characteristics and cognitive abilities. For example, interpersonal skills, persuasiveness, analytical ability and good judgement are partly personality dispositions and partly connected to cognitive ability. Although competencies are widely used and now form a routine part of the design process for personnel selection procedures, there is considerable conceptual confusion concerning the term and there are practical difficulties when it comes to the measurement of some competencies.

At the root of the conceptual confusion is a lack of clarity about the meaning of a 'competency'. Definitions often include reference to the fact that competencies are forms of behaviour (e.g., Woodruffe, 1992). However, an examination of typical lists of competencies reveals quite clearly that many are in practice not behavioural (Boyatzis, 1982). As far as the measurement of competencies is concerned, a significant amount of work has shown that even trained judges working with apparently well-defined lists find it difficult to make clear and discriminating judgements about candidates' competencies. For example, problems arise in the overlaps between them. This difficulty is exemplified in research looking at the assessment of candidates with the aid of assessment centres, which is discussed in more detail later in the chapter. In brief, the studies make it clear that judges find it difficult to evaluate candidates on more than a small number of dimensions. When relatively large numbers of dimensions (more than about five) are used, substantial correlations appear between the supposedly different competencies, suggesting that for practical purposes, and as far as the judges are concerned, the competencies are not truly discrete. Psychological theory underpinning competencies is not particularly extensive, and, as indicated above, the conceptual confusion and measurement difficulties mean that there is some way to go before competencies can be successfully incorporated into a general psychological theory of human performance.

PERSONNEL SELECTION METHODS

Personnel selection methods are used to assess candidates in order to estimate the extent to which they possess attributes that are thought to be desirable for the job. The major methods in current use are defined in brief below; research relating to each is considered later in the chapter.

Selection Interviews

Personnel selection interviews take a variety of forms. Essentially, an interview is a conversation with a specific purpose. As a minimum there is one interviewer and one interviewee (job candidate), but some interviews use more than one interviewer. There are wide variations in the extent to which interviews are structured and in the kind of topics that are discussed during employment interviews.

Psychological Tests

Psychological tests are available for assessing the cognitive abilities and personality characteristics of candidates. These generally involve pencil and paper administration, although increasingly tests are available in computer-administered form. Candidates are required to answer a carefully derived set of questions, which may focus on specific aspects of ability (e.g., verbal ability, spatial ability) or general mental ability, or facets of personality. Information about norms is desirable, so that an individual candidate's score may be compared with those in some suitable reference group.

References

References are obtained by collecting information about candidates from previous employers. Sometimes the information is gathered with the aid of a structured form, but most reference requests are much more open-ended, permitting the referee to choose which attributes to cover or avoid.

Work-sample Tests

Work-sample tests involve identifying a sample of the job behaviour in question and requiring candidates to complete a realistic item of work within that sample. One widely used and well-known work-sample is the typing test. At the management level, a commonly used work-sample is the in-tray or in-basket exercise, where candidates are required to work through the contents of a typical in-tray or in-basket.

Assessment Centres

The assessment centre approach makes use of a variety of different methods such as interviews, work-sample tests, group discussions and psychological tests. Trained assessors (usually line managers from the organization in question) observe and evaluate the behaviour of candidates. Candidates are frequently studied in assessment centres in groups of four to six people.

Biodata

Biodata are systematically collected biographical information about candidates. Items may range from objective features such as date of birth, examination successes, positions of distinction at school, college or in previous jobs, through to items that resemble those that might be asked in a personality test, such as preferences for subjects at school and preferred characteristics of jobs. Biodata questionnaires frequently include in excess of 100 different items of information about candidates.

Other Selection Procedures

Other methods sometimes used in personnel selection procedures include the analysis of handwriting ('graphology'), self-assessments (requesting candidates to give evaluative information about themselves), and trainability testing. The latter is a specific form of work-sample test which involves candidates in a period of training, during which they are given an opportunity to learn how to conduct the tasks in question. Their performance on the relevant tasks is subsequently evaluated by trained assessors.

In recent years a substantial amount of information has been collected about the usage of different personnel selection methods. The first systematic evidence to become available in the United Kingdom was drawn from a questionnaire survey conducted in the early 1980s (Robertson and Makin, 1986). This original questionnaire has been used for more recent surveys, so it is possible to get an indication of how the use of selection methods has developed; note, however, that different samples were used in the various surveys so that inferences concerning changes across time must be tentative. A special issue of the *International Journal of Selection and Assessment* (vol. 12, no. 2, 1994) is devoted to the usage of selection methods in various countries. Table 5.1 provides an overview for some of the principal methods.

As this table shows, interviews are by far the most popular personnel selection method in all countries except Germany. References are also popular in some countries. Other methods of selection such as psychological tests or assessment centres are less widely used. Comparisons of results from the original survey (Robertson and Makin, 1986) and later ones using the same questionnaire (e.g., Shackleton and Newell, 1991) suggest that the usage of assessment centres has increased. There are some rather interesting differences in the application of personnel selection methods across different countries. For example, graphology is widespread in France and in subsidiaries of French companies in the rest of Europe. By contrast, references are more widely used in Germany and Great Britain than in many of the other European countries.

DESIGN AND EVALUATION OF PERSONNEL SELECTION PROCEDURES

Well-established procedures exist for the effective design and evaluation of personnel selection procedures (see Figure 5.4). The conventional design process begins with a detailed examination of the job for which selection decisions are to be taken. It is worth noting that, at least implicitly, this step presumes that a stable set of job demands exists, though in many practical settings a job may not yet exist, or may be expected to change over time. At the job analysis stage it is possible to make allowances for the dynamic nature of some jobs. This can be done by including current and anticipated future tasks in the initial description of the job. The need for fixed points of reference is nevertheless a potential limitation to the conventional personnel selection design and evaluation process.

Smith and Robertson (1993) identify nine different methods of job analysis, including structured questionnaires and checklists,

Table 5.1 Methods of selection used in several European countries

	Interviews	Application forms	References	Personality tests	Cognitive tests	Handwriting analysis	Bio-data	Assessment centres
Never								
Belgium (Flemish)	0.0	4.3	14.9	17.4	23.3	78.7	65.9	57.8
Belgium (French)	0.0	4.2	33.3	37.5	27.3	56.0	91.7	76.0
France	0.0	1.9	22.6	37.7	51.1	22.6	96.2	81.2
Germany	0.0	0.0	0.0	81.0	79.0	90.8	89.1	40.0
Great Britain	0.0	6.8	4.1	35.6	30.1	97.4	80.9	41.1
Italy	0.0	31.8	12.0	80.0	80.0	88.0	100.0	92.0
About half of the time								
Belgium (Flemish)	2.1	8.5	17.0	6.5	7.0	2.1	7.3	6.7
Belgium (French)	0.0	0.0	8.3	4.2	9.1	4.0	0.0	4.0
France	5.7	0.0	13.3	9.4	7.5	11.3	1.9	7.5
Germany	6.0	0.0	4.5	6.3	6.5	0.0	1.6	4.6
Great Britain	1.3	4.1	4.1	15.1	16.5	1.3	1.3	12.3
Italy	0.0	13.6	16.0	4.0	8.0	0.0	0.0	4.0
Always								
Belgium (Flemish)	91.5	74.5	14.9	34.8	30.2	2.1	12.2	2.2
Belgium (French)	100.0	91.7	12.5	25.0	31.8	12.0	4.2	0.0
France	94.3	88.6	11.3	17.0	7.5	17.1	0.0	0.0
Germany	59.7	83.3	75.8	1.6	1.6	0.0	1.6	3.1
Great Britain	90.5	70.0	73.9	9.6	12.3	0.0	4.2	4.2
Italy	96.3	45.5	32.0	8.0	8.0	0.0	0.0	0.0

Source: Abridged from Shackleton and Newell, 1991.

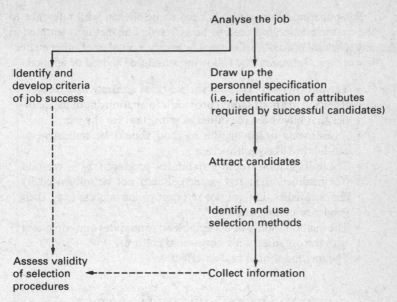

Fig. 5.4 The design and evaluation of personnel selection procedures.

interviews, diaries, observation, participation and critical incidents (Flanagan, 1954). The common feature of all methods is that they seek to provide a clear view of the principal job components. This picture of the job is then used to identify the characteristics that successful job incumbents will need to display (see also Chapter 3). The step from job analysis to person specification is an integral part of the traditional approach to personnel selection, but there is no foolproof way of translating knowledge of the job into knowledge of the attributes that lead to success in the job. Some job analysis methods produce an indication of the personal attributes that are suggested by the job analysis, but the decision rules linking job features with personal requirements in a job-holder are derived from a mixture of scientifically established knowledge, theory and judgement. Once decisions have been made about which candidate characteristics are thought to be desirable, attention may be given to the methods that might be used to assess candidates.

133

Personnel selection methods need to be chosen with reference to the characteristics that need to be assessed. The methods adopted in any selection procedure also need to satisfy a number of other evaluative criteria. In general the following standards should be applied.

- The information provided should be as accurate as possible.
- Selection methods should provide information about the qualities that have been identified as important for the job.
- Assessments based on the method should be indicative of candidates' likely job success.
- The information about candidates produced by a method (for instance, their test scores) should not be influenced by characteristics that are not relevant to job success (e.g., their gender or ethnic origin).
- The method should be acceptable to candidates and consistent with the organization's norms and culture.
- The method should be cost-effective.

VALIDITY AND RELIABILITY

The first three items in the list above concern the reliability and validity of the method. These features of personnel selection methods are the evaluative criteria that most personnel psychologists consider to be of prime importance.

'Reliability' refers to the extent to which a measurement procedure is free from unsystematic error. Various methods are available for assessing the reliability of a measure, including estimates of stability across time (e.g., test–retest reliability) and estimates of internal consistency (e.g., Cronbach's coefficient Alpha). For more information see Moser and Schuler (1989). The reliability of a measure is quantified by a reliability coefficient, which gives a direct indication of the proportion of variance in the measure that is free from unsystematic error. For example, a reliability coefficient of 0.85 indicates that 15 per cent of the measure's variance is random error. Essentially, the reliability of a measure refers to the consistency of the scores given by the measure. An unreliable measure is like a ruler that changes length in a random fashion: the same object would be measured as of

Face validity: the extent to which a measuring procedure seems 'at face value' to assess the qualities in question. Not really a form of statistical validity at all.

Content validity: the extent to which the items or procedures in a measuring instrument sample the domain of interest.

Construct validity: the extent to which the measure gives accurate information about the psychological construct that it is designed to measure.

Criterion-related validity: the extent to which the measure produces scores related to scores on a measure of some relevant criterion. In the case of personnel selection, the relevant criteria are usually indicators of job success, such as supervisors' ratings of job performance.

Fig. 5.5 Types of validity.

different lengths on different occasions. It is obviously crucial for psychological measurements to be as reliable as possible. In general, reliability coefficients of less than 0.8 are cause for some concern, and those less than 0.7 need improving if at all possible.

Although a measurement procedure cannot give accurate results if it is unreliable, it is perfectly possible for a measurement procedure to be reliable (i.e., free from random error) but still inadequate as an assessment instrument. The length of a person's hair could be measured with great accuracy, but it would be worthless as an indication of intelligence! On a more realistic level, a test involving answers to questions about behaviour at parties could also be reliable but may not give a good indication of someone's level of extroversion. The extent to which a measurement procedure gives appropriate information about the quality under investigation is referred to as the 'validity' of the measure. Validity may be looked at in a number of ways (see Smith and Robertson, 1993), as illustrated in Figure 5.5.

Both construct validity and criterion-related validity are of major importance for personnel selection. Information about construct validity can assist in understanding the psychological construct(s) assessed by the instrument. Criterion-related validity is measured in terms of the relationship between performance on a selection procedure and performance on some key criterion variable, such as overall job proficiency.

For many personnel psychologists criterion-related validity is the major yardstick by which any selection method should be judged. Like reliability, criterion-related validity is usually quantified by a coefficient: the validity coefficient. Criterion-related validity coefficients may be derived by two principal methods: predictive and concurrent data-gathering. In both cases the validity coefficient is calculated by computing the correlation between scores on the selection method and scores on a relevant criterion, such as work performance, absenteeism, salary increase or tenure. The concurrent method involves collecting selection scores for a sample of people who are already in the organization, that is, existing job incumbents. For the same sample of people, criterion scores, such as ratings by supervisors of work performance, are also collected. The validity coefficient may then be derived by correlating the two sets of scores.

Although the concurrent approach provides a speedier way of obtaining a validity coefficient than the predictive approach, there are some drawbacks. The first and most obvious problem is that there is a restriction in the range of people who are likely to be examined. Anyone who is already in the organization is likely to have achieved at least a minimum level of job competence. Otherwise, he or she would probably have been moved to other employment or have left the organization. A second concern is about the motivation and behaviour of individuals when the selection method scores are gathered. In a concurrent validation study members of the sample already have jobs in the organization. Their motivational state and need to do well on the selection method are likely to be somewhat different from those of real job candidates.

In the predictive approach to validation, selection method scores are collected on a sample of actual job candidates. Their scores are then stored for a suitable period of time. After the time period has elapsed, scores on a relevant criterion are collected for those selected applicants who are still employed in the company. The time period involved will depend on the complexity of the job and the length of time it might take for any successful candidate to be able to develop proficiency in the job.

There are several requirements that make conducting a predictive validity study much more difficult than a concurrent study. For example, it is desirable that the selection method scores are not used to make actual selection decisions. This is to ensure that a full range of scores on the selection method is available when the validity coefficient is calculated. Another requirement is that the scores obtained for candidates are not made available to anyone in the organization who is expected to provide follow-up information on job performance or any other criterion measure. This requirement is designed to ensure that later criterion scores are not contaminated by the expectations individuals may have, based on selection method scores.

Until the late 1970s results published from studies into the criterion-related validity of various personnel selection methods were not particularly encouraging. When the studies were reviewed (e.g., Ghiselli, 1973) the validity evidence for each personnel selection method appeared to be erratic, in as much as different studies tended to show different levels of validity for the same method. Another problem was that, in general, the validity coefficients obtained were quite modest. This led personnel selection researchers to a number of key conclusions.

The most important of these were that the validity of most methods, in general, was not particularly good and that for any particular application of a method, a specific local validation study was needed to check that the method was producing sufficiently good validity. This requirement seemed sensible in view of the considerable variation in the validity of methods from one study to another. However, with the benefit of hindsight it is now clear that these conclusions were not appropriate. Researchers at the time failed to pay sufficient attention to some features of the validation studies that had been published. The most important feature that was underemphasized was the fact that the validation studies were almost always conducted with the use of rather small samples (often less than 100 people).

Since the early 1980s a significant shift has occurred in the research base concerning the criterion-related validity of most personnel selection methods. Two American psychologists, Jack Hunter and Frank Schmidt, paid careful attention to the influence that sampling error and other artefactual features might have on the resulting validity coefficient. Most importantly, they developed statistical procedures that enabled researchers to combine the results from various individual, small-sample studies which had looked at the validity of any particular selection method (Hunter, Schmidt, and Jackson, 1982; Hunter and Schmidt, 1990). This technique, known as meta-analysis, enabled researchers to use the results from the many validation studies done on specific selection methods to derive overall estimates for the validity of each method.

Meta-analysis also allows investigators to control statistically for the effects of two further flaws that often arise in validation studies. One of these is range restriction. Range restriction occurs when the spread of scores on one of the measures (the selection method or the criterion) does not span the full spread that occurs in the population. As noted earlier, this is frequently the case for criterion scores when concurrent validation methods are used. There may be many other reasons why range restriction occurs in a validation study, such as the fact that selection decisions were, in fact, based upon data from the selection method. If candidates with selection scores above a specific cut-off were chosen, this means that criterion scores for candidates with low selection scores will not be available. The net effect of range restriction is to reduce the maximum possible magnitude of any correlation coefficient that is calculated. In other words, when a restricted range of scores is available, the magnitude of the maximum correlation coefficient (i.e., the validity coefficient) that might be obtained is reduced artificially.

Another factor that influences the possible magnitude of a correlation coefficient is the reliability of measurement. As reliability decreases, the amount of randomness in the scores for any particular variable will increase. The existence of this random error will necessarily reduce the probability that high correlations with other variables can be observed.

It is important to recognize that sampling error, range restriction and unreliability of measurement are all aspects of study design that can create misleading impressions of the underlying relationship between two variables (e.g., scores from a selection method and a criterion of work performance). If a study uses a small sample with a restricted range of scores derived from unreliable measuring instruments, the observed correlation between the selection method and the criterion is likely to be smaller than the true correlation between those two variables. What this means is that many validation studies are likely to give misleadingly low impressions of the validity of personnel selection methods.

Meta-analytic procedures have been used to cumulate and correct validity data for most of the major selection methods. When this was done, the results led to different conclusions from those that were drawn in the late 1970s. The results of this work are discussed in a later section of this chapter.

In addition to being valid and reliable, acceptable selection methods must be fair to all sub-groups of the population for which they are likely to be used. The purpose of selection is, of course, to discriminate between candidates, but this discrimination must not be based on attributes of candidates that are irrelevant to the job, such as age, gender or ethnic origin. It is important to recognize that a selection method is not necessarily unfair if members of a specific sub-group do less well on the test. Men are less likely than women to sing soprano well, and women are less good at singing bass notes than men. This does not mean that a test for one role or another that produces different numbers of successful males or females is unfair. A selection method is unfair only if it rejects or accepts members of a sub-group disproportionately, compared with their ability to do the job. This definition of unfairness was developed in the late 1960s (Cleary, 1968). It is the classical definition of fairness and is accepted as a reasonable view of fairness by both psychologists and employment lawyers. The definition may be expressed more technically: 'A test is biased for members of a sub-group of the population if, in the prediction of a criterion for which it was designed, consistent non-zero errors of prediction are made for members of the subgroup' (Cleary, 1968, p. 115). What this means is that a *biased* test is not as accurate for members of the sub-group as it is for the remainder of the population; that is, the validity of the test is different for different groups. When this arises it is referred to as 'differential' validity. Any selection method showing differential validity results in unfair disadvantage to one sub-group of the population. This approach to fairness may seem unnecessarily complex but it is important to recognize that adverse impact (i.e., the disproportionately low selection of members of a particular sub-group) is unfair only if it is based on *errors* of prediction.

The Financial Utility of Personnel Selection

The ability to use meta-analytic procedures to derive better estimates of the criterion-related validity of personnel selection methods was one of two significant methodological developments for personnel selection research since the mid-1970s. The second important methodological development concerned the use of 'utility formulae' to estimate the financial gain to be derived from personnel selection procedures (see Boudreau, 1989; Schmidt, Mack and Hunter, 1984). The main goal of any personnel selection system is to ensure that better selection decisions are made. If a personnel selection system ensures that an organization appoints only people who are very effective in their jobs, this will confer benefits on both the organization and the individual. The benefits to the individual may include greater job satisfaction, enhanced earnings and better career prospects. The most tangible benefit for the organization will be the financial gain derived from the improved effectiveness of job holders. However, in some settings improved selection procedures may be of little benefit. For example, when there are as many jobs as there are candidates and if the jobs need to be filled, selection is pointless, although placement (i.e., matching applicants to the available jobs) could be extremely important. At the other extreme, when there is a large field of candidates, the benefits from improved selection may be considerable. The selection ratio (i.e., the ratio of jobs to candidates) is thus an important determinant of the gain that can be realized from better selection.

To grasp the financial benefits to organizations of improved selection it is useful to identify the factors that influence these benefits. The key elements are:

- the selection ratio
- the accuracy of selection (i.e., the validity of the method(s) used)
- the financial gain obtained from improved job performance.

Consideration of a typical selection problem will help to make the role of each component clear.

When the selection ratio is small, there is a small number of jobs and a large number of candidates (e.g., with 10 jobs and 200 candidates the selection ratio would be 0.05). Under these circumstances the selection decision-maker is able to choose whichever candidates he or she thinks are the best ten (i.e., the best 5 per cent). When the selection ratio is more favourable to the candidates, a higher proportion of applicants will have to be chosen if the vacancies are to be filled. For example a selection ratio of 0.5 would mean that half of the candidates would have to be offered jobs. Even if the selection methods in use are good at identifying the best job performers, they will not be perfect, and even some of the top performers on the selection measures will be less than ideally suited to the job. In general, of course, the better the selection scores of candidates, the more likely it is that they will do well in the job. Choosing as many as half of the candidates will mean that some relatively poor performers will be given jobs. The performance of the selected group will be much better if job offers can be restricted to the top 5 per cent of applicants.

With perfect selection the best candidates would always be chosen. The benefits to the organization of selecting 'the best candidates' will depend on how much of an improvement these people bring about in terms of the organization's performance. With perfect selection and a large field of candidates, people who perform well on the selection measure (e.g., one standard deviation (SD) above average), will perform equally well (e.g., one SD above average) when it comes to work activities. Imagine a situation in which the organization has 20 jobs and 200 candidates. With this selection ratio (0.1) the organization can select the top 10 per cent of candidates. How well they actually perform at work will depend on the extent to which the selection procedure gives an accurate indication of candidates' job performance. When the criterion-related validity of the selection procedure is very poor, even selecting the top 5 per cent of performers on the selection procedure will not be certain to produce people who are good at the job. On the other hand, if criterion-related validity is good, performance on the selection procedures will be linked more closely to job performance. In other words the criterion-related validity of the selection procedure together with the selection ratio will determine the actual job performance of the selected group of applicants. The most favourable situation for the organization is good criterion-related validity and a small selection ratio, the worst is poor criterion-related validity and a large selection ratio.

The actual monetary gain derived from better selection will depend on the financial value of improvements in work performance. Obviously the financial gain from an improvement (e.g., one SD) in performance will vary from job to job. An improvement of one SD in the goal-scoring performance of a Premier League footballer would mean several more goals per season and could make the difference between winning major honours or not, resulting in a difference of several million pounds for the football club. For other jobs the differences may be less substantial. Several studies have attempted to derive estimates of the financial values associated with improved performance, and a conservative estimate, for typical jobs, of the financial value of one SD improvement in performance is 40 per cent of salary (Hunter and Schmidt, 1982).

The material reviewed above makes it clear that the financial gain derived from improved personnel selection is dependent on the selection ratio, the criterion-related validity of the selection procedure and the financial value of improved work performance. Using this approach it is possible to apply a simple formula to enable financial gain to be estimated for any combination of the relevant variables. A more detailed discussion of the estimation of the financial utility of personnel selection, including the relevant formulae, may be found in various sources, including Boudreau (1989) and Cooper and Robertson (1995).

THE EFFECTIVENESS OF PERSONNEL SELECTION METHODS

The major types of selection method were outlined in an earlier section of this chapter, together with information on their usage. This section concentrates on reviewing the nature of these methods and the research evidence on their validity. The focus of attention is on criterion-related validity, although other forms of validity are discussed when appropriate. It is difficult to give absolute guidance, but validity coefficients of less than 0.2 are unlikely to be of much practical significance, except in special circumstances. Most person-nel specialists would be content with coefficients of 0.3 and above. Validity coefficients above 0.5, for single methods, are rare.

Assessment Centres

An assessment centre is not a place, it is an assessment process involving multiple assessors evaluating groups of candidates on a variety of tasks. Interviews, work-sample tests, group discussions and psychometric tests are often the components of such a centre. Assessment centres have a long history of use for personnel assess-ment, stretching back to pre-Second World War procedures used to assess military officers in Germany (Vernon and Parry, 1949). Sub-sequently, similar techniques were developed and used by the British War Office Selection Board (WOSB; see Vernon and Parry, 1949) and later the British Civil Service Selection Board (CSSB; see Vernon, 1950). The American Office of Strategic Services (OSS) developed procedures derived from WOSB (Mackinnon, 1977; Wiggins, 1973). Feltham (1989) provides a review of these develop-ments.

Modern assessment centres are descendants of the CSSB method and a process devised for managerial assessment in the American Telephone and Telegraph (AT&T) company (Bray and Grant, 1966). The AT&T procedures have a special place in the development of assessment centres, partly because of the systematic follow-up work that was done to assess the predictive validity of the assessments made (Bray and Grant, 1966). The validity evidence for the AT&T procedures was favourable and attracted the attention of assessment specialists in other organizations, who then developed assessment centres, modelled on the AT&T approach, for use in their own organizations. The British CSSBs are still in use today for the selec-tion of new entrants to the British Civil Service and have also had a substantial impact on the design of other assessment centres.

Contemporary assessment centres take place over a period of time varying between half a day and three days. A typical centre might involve twelve candidates, working in groups of six. Candidates are evaluated by trained assessors, probably line managers in the organization. A ratio of two candidates per assessor is likely. Sometimes specialist chartered occupational psychologists might also be part of the assessment team, and psychologists are often involved in the design of centres. All centres make use of job-related work-sample exercises, such as in-trays, leaderless group tasks and individual presentations. Work-sample tests are designed to include the major tasks of the job (see Robertson and Kandola, 1982, for a review). For example, a typical in-tray exercise contains the kind of letters, memoranda, messages, reports, etc. that might normally appear in a jobholder's in-tray. The items will have been developed after a detailed analysis of the job and consideration of the components that are critical for successful performance. More detailed information on the several components of assessment centres may be found in Thornton and Byham (1982) and Woodruffe (1992).

The performance of candidates is assessed on a set of dimensions which should also have been derived from job analysis. 'Dimension' is the traditional term used to describe what would now often be called 'competency', one of the underlying psychological constructs that are thought to determine performance on the assessment tasks. As noted earlier, various generic competency frameworks exist (e.g., Dulewicz, 1989), although most assessment centres use dimensions that are specific to the job(s) in question, rather than those that are generic. These dimensions are the building blocks for assessment centres. They are used to determine which exercises will be most appropriate, and exercises are chosen on the basis of their likely ability to provide information about candidates on the relevant dimensions. Promotion, selection and placement decisions are taken after consideration of the candidates' profiles on these dimensions, and results are typically fed back to candidates in terms of each dimension.

The criterion-related validity of assessment centres could, in principle, be looked at in two different ways: by examining the validity of the component parts of the centre (e.g., the in-tray, psychometric tests or group exercises), or by assessing the validity of the overall scores derived from the centre. With some notable exceptions (e.g., Wollowick and McNamara, 1969), most validation studies have concentrated on the validity of centres as a whole. This makes sense, since the results from the centre as a whole are usually used for decision-making. Meta-analytic reviews of the criterion-related validity for assessment centres (Schmitt, Gooding, Noe and Kirsch, 1984; Gaugler, Rosenthal, Thornton and Bentson, 1987) have revealed favourable results, with uncorrected mean, sample-size-weighted validity coefficients of about 0.3. The clear conclusion from both individual validation studies and meta-analytic reviews is that assessment centres show good levels of criterion-related validity.

Unfortunately, evidence of *construct* validity (in terms of the extent to which assessment centres produce accurate assessments of the dimensions on which they are built) is less convincing. Beginning with a study reported by Sackett and Dreher (1982), a series of investigations in both the UK and USA (see Robertson, Gratton and Sharpley, 1987; Reilly, Henry and Smither, 1990) has revealed problems with this aspect of assessment centres. If assessment centres are in fact measuring specific, stable differences between candidates, the cross-exercise correlations of the same dimension should be large. In other words, the correlation for a particular competency (dimension), such as analytical ability, should be quite high when scores of individual candidates on two different exercises are compared. Of course the correlation would not be perfect, since each specific exercise will have some influence on how each candidate performs. However, the correlations for the same dimension across different exercises should certainly be higher than correlations of different dimensions within the same exercise. For example, the correlation for ratings of analytical ability for a sample of candidates across two different exercises should be greater than the correlation between, say, analytical ability and persuasiveness within the same exercise.

In fact, results show that correlations of different dimensions on the *same* exercise are generally larger than correlations of the same dimension across different exercises! Such results cast doubt on the construct validity of assessment centre scores, and mean that, although there is confidence about the *criterion-related* validity of assessment centres, the source of this validity (i.e., what exactly it is that assessment centres measure) is uncertain. Further research is needed to clarify the extent to which assessment centres are able to provide meaningful and independent scores on specific dimensions.

145

Selection Interviews

When evaluating the role of interviews in personnel selection, it is important to be clear that there are many different types of interview, and that criterion-related validity is not the same for each type. There is consistent evidence that structured interview formats produce better criterion-related validity than unstructured interviews (Weisner and Cronshaw, 1988; Wright, Lichenfels and Pursell, 1989). A recent meta-analytic investigation of the criterion-related validity of interviews was conducted by McDaniel, Whetzel, Schmidt and Maurer (1994). Although they found that the overall mean validity for all types of interview was 0.20 (uncorrected for range restriction or unreliability), they showed that the validity for structured interviews (0.24) was better than the validity for unstructured interviews (0.18). After statistical corrections for range restriction and unreliability were applied to the data, the criterion-related validity coefficients for structured and unstructured interviews were 0.44 and 0.33 respectively.

Structure may be imposed on an interview in a variety of ways. One of the most popular and sensible options is to use job analysis results and information about the competencies that are thought to be important in the job to provide the main components for the interview structure. Questions in the interview can be focused on the key elements of the job and the competencies needed.

The development and use of 'situational interviews' provide a good example of this general approach. A situational interview can be designed in the stages given below.

- Conduct a systematic job analysis.
- Use the results of the job analysis to identify key tasks that are important for overall job success. An integral part of the job analysis, when situational interviews are being developed, is the identification of specific examples of challenging situations that might confront a job holder. The critical incident technique (Flanagan, 1954) is often useful for this and involves asking job holders to recall incidents of particularly good or poor performance.
- Use the results of job analysis to identify the key competencies for job success.

- Develop a set of questions about hypothetical behaviour in the position, based on the challenging situations identified at the job analysis stage. These questions involve asking candidates how they *would* behave in the specific work situation in question.
- Develop a scoring key so that the replies of candidates can be assessed on each of the relevant dimensions. The scoring key needs to be as objective as possible, and may be derived by obtaining sample replies from existing job incumbents who are known to be at different levels of overall job competence.

The questions in this form of situational interview are often written on cards and read to candidates in a predetermined sequence. The situational interview approach was developed by Latham and colleagues (Latham, Saari, Pursell and Campion, 1980). Successful validation studies using situational interviews also have been reported by other investigators (Weekley and Gier, 1987; Robertson, Gratton, and Rout, 1990).

The success of the structured interview compared with other forms of interview has not been explained in any definitive way, and there is still uncertainty about the reasons for its relatively good validity. It seems likely that one important function of structure is to focus the interviewer's attention on particularly salient features, so that candidate attributes that are irrelevant to job success do not intrude and influence decision-making. It also seems probable that opportunities for good candidates to perform well will be increased when questions are job-related and presented in a controlled way. Despite these apparent advantages for structured interviews and the validity evidence in their favour, it has sometimes been argued that they are no more than surrogate tests of general mental ability (Hunter and Hirsh, 1987).

Cognitive Ability Tests

The meta-analytic evidence offers good support for the criterion-related validity of cognitive ability tests in many employment settings.

Several studies based on very large samples have produced positive findings. In fact, the studies' results are quite remarkable in suggesting that general cognitive ability is significantly associated with successful performance in most jobs (see Murphy, 1988, for a review). These findings completely overturn the earlier cautious conclusion (Ghiselli, 1973) that selection methods needed to be checked by a local validation study prior to use in any specific setting. Instead they suggest the wide-ranging conclusion that general cognitive ability tests are useful in almost any setting. Unfortunately, things are not as simple as this!

Two major issues complicate the position in relation to cognitive ability testing. The first is related to the differences in scores that are found amongst different sub-groups. There is clear evidence, from the USA, that members of different ethnic groups produce different scores on tests of general cognitive ability, with black people and Hispanics showing lower average scores (see Gottfredson and Sharf, 1988). When cognitive ability tests are used to select people for jobs, members of some ethnic groups are likely to score less well and hence are less likely to be selected. As noted in an earlier section of this chapter, this imbalance in success rates does not necessarily mean that the tests are unfair (Cleary, 1968), although they will cause adverse impact on a particular sub-group. Unfair tests are those that show differential validity (see the earlier section). The available research on the differential validity of cognitive tests suggests that although there are some differences in validity for different ethnic groups, the differences are so small (differences in validity of about 0.03) that they would be of no practical significance. In other words, there is little evidence of differential validity and, from a technical point of view, there is no reason to be particularly cautious about the widespread use of cognitive testing. On the other hand, the consequences of adverse impact caused by the use of cognitive testing are likely to be socially divisive and damaging.

Three main findings related to cognitive ability testing produce a major problem for selection decision-making. These findings are: the criterion-related validity of cognitive ability tests is good; the scores of some ethnic groups on such tests are consistently low; there is no evidence of practically-important differential validity. When selection decisions are being made with applicants from several ethnic groups, should such tests be included in the selection battery? There is no unequivocal answer to this question. An overriding concern for social justice leads many, including the current author, to recommend caution in the use of such tests when mixed applicant groups are involved. Several schemes exist to allow cognitive tests to be used with minimum adverse impact. For example, it is possible to group candidates into bands based on their test scores and then select from each band, in accordance with sub-group proportions in the applicant pool. This procedure produces no adverse impact, though it does require the selection of candidates from lower-scoring bands and hence the efficiency of selection is compromised.

The other complicating factor for cognitive ability testing becomes apparent when the practical use of such tests is considered. Many American studies have shown general cognitive ability to be linked to effective job performance. The samples for these studies have often been military personnel or civilian blue-collar workers. Perhaps it is not surprising that mental ability turns out to be important for job success in most jobs for samples of this kind. Applicant groups may well be fairly heterogeneous in terms of general cognitive ability, and other factors, such as previous experience, prior job knowledge or qualifications, may be of little relevance to success in these particular jobs. When higher-level jobs are studied, the relevance of general cognitive ability is less clear. In addition, the likelihood of range restriction is increased and the capacity of a cognitive ability test to identify large differences between candidates will be correspondingly reduced. There is no dispute concerning the importance of cognitive ability to performance in a wide range of jobs, and in many settings such tests may well be the most cost-effective and accurate single component in the selection procedure. However, the complications noted above should act as a warning against the unquestioned use of such tests in all settings, particularly in situations where mixed groups of applicants and/or higher level jobs are used.

Personality Scales

Historically, personality inventories have not been amongst the most successful selection procedures (Guion and Gottier, 1965). The initial meta-analytic studies on the criterion-related validity of personality constructs produced fairly poor results. Schmitt *et al.* (1984), for example, reported a criterion-related validity coefficient, for personality scales, of only 0.15. In more recent years evidence has begun to emerge that personality tests may have a valuable role to play in personnel selection. If personality is important for job success, it seems likely that it will be linked most directly with job holders' competencies. In turn, these competencies will help to determine overall job success. The competencies that are associated with overall performance will vary, depending on the nature of the job. This suggests that, while the links between specific personality constructs and specific competencies may be stable, consistent and perhaps quite strong, the links between specific personality and overall job performance will be variable and probably less strong (Robertson, 1993, 1994).

Some researchers have used meta-analytic methods to examine the links between the personality constructs and overall job proficiency (e.g., Barrick and Mount, 1991). This work has shown that there may be some general but rather weak relationships between broad aspects of personality and overall proficiency across most jobs. The correlations revealed in these studies between 'big five' personality scales and overall job proficiency are not sufficiently strong to be of major value for practical personnel selection. For example, Barrick and Mount (1991) showed links between extroversion and overall job proficiency in sales jobs but the mean correlation was only 0.15.

More encouraging findings have emerged from meta-analytic research when the personality constructs used in the original studies have been based on clear hypotheses about what characteristics are needed for overall job success (Tett, Jackson and Rothstein, 1991). As noted above, the clearest links with personality variables and criterion measures are likely to emerge when specific personality constructs are linked to specific competencies, rather than overall job proficiency. Robertson and Kinder (1993) showed that specific personality constructs were indeed associated with specific job competencies, with levels of criterion-related validity from 0.09 up to about 0.3. In that study hypotheses were generated by asking people who were familiar with the personality scales in question to indicate which scales they believed would be associated with specific job competencies. For those aspects of personality expected to be linked to specific competencies, criterion-related validity reached moderate levels; for unrelated personality-competence pairs, validity was much lower.

Other Methods

In addition to interviews, assessment centres and psychological tests, a variety of other personnel selection methods are in common use. Brief descriptions of these methods and indications of their usage have been given in earlier sections of this chapter.

References about job applicants tend to be used a great deal in some countries. In general they are not utilized for the main decision-making process, instead being used at a fairly late stage in the process to confirm candidates' claims and to check that there are no major barriers to making an appointment. This is probably just as well, since evidence on the criterion-related validity of references is not particularly good. The available evidence (e.g., Hunter and Hunter, 1984) shows references to have poor levels of criterion-related validity (less than 0.2). As well as poor levels of criterion-related validity the opportunities for bias in reference reports are obviously quite substantial. Unfortunately, there are few recent, systematic studies to support or refute the possibility of bias of references (see Dobson, 1989).

In contrast to references, work-sample tests have a very good track record for both validity and fairness. The validity evidence for such tests is strong and there is good support for their fairness and acceptability to candidates (Robertson and Kandola, 1982). Work-sample tests have been developed and used for a wide range of occupations, although usage is more widespread in jobs involving practical skills. They have been used in management selection (e.g., in-tray exercises in assessment centres), in studies of clerical work and for practical skills in such diverse areas as dentistry, sewing-machine operating and bricklaying.

Some of these work-sample tests are in 'trainability test' format. In a trainability test the candidate is given a period of learning and then tested on how well this has been assimilated by asking him or her to conduct the tasks involved in the work sample. Validity evidence for this type of work sample is good; the approach is also well received by candidates (Robertson and Downs, 1989). One reservation concerning the use of work-samples is that they are very closely linked to the job in question and may lose validity if and when the demands of the job change. There is some evidence that the validity of work-sample tests does decline over time (Robertson and Downs, 1989), although the reduction may be no greater than that of other selection methods.

Biodata questionnaires may be developed by empirical, rational or mixed procedures. In the empirical approach, correlations between job success criteria and items of biographical data are established by carrying out concurrent validation studies. When purely empirical methods are adopted, there is a risk that the items in the biodata questionnaire that are found to be correlated with job success may have no logical link with the job. For example, in one study known to the author, a history of holidays in Spain was a contra-indication of job success! In another study, living in a certain part of a city with a high percentage of people from a particular ethnic group was associated with a lack of job success. Modern procedures for developing biodata systems require the use of both empirical and logical procedures to identify appropriate items. Any item used for actual selection decisions needs to have a clear empirical link (i.e., it needs to show criterion-related validity) and a clear logical link with the job success criteria. In settings where large numbers of candidates are available, the use of biodata can be an efficient selection procedure. Criterion-related validity for well-developed biodata systems is generally good (Drakeley, 1989; Stokes and Reddy, 1992). There is also growing evidence that life history data (a form of biodata) can provide interesting insights into people's psychological make-up (Stokes and Reddy, 1992).

BEYOND THE TRADITIONAL APPROACH

As the material presented earlier in this chapter makes clear, research into personnel selection has made significant progress since the mid-1980s. Despite this progress, there are clear limitations to the traditional approach to personnel selection on its own. Some of the difficulties relate to the models that are used and the methods of analysis that are adopted (see Hesketh and Robertson, 1993). Limitations of the traditional models include the failure to make clear distinctions between underlying psychological constructs and the measures that are used to assess them. Personnel selection researchers have tended to focus their attention on investigating the criterion-related validity of their methods. This is undeniably a useful endeavour but needs to be supplemented by an interest in the nature of the constructs that are measured. Although assessment centre scores show clear relationships with criterion measures of job success, the construct validity of the competencies (dimensions) that are assessed in assessment centres is uncertain (see above). This creates operational problems for assessment centre users. It also leaves important theoretical questions unresolved and limits the contribution that personnel selection research makes to our understanding of the psychological factors underlying behaviour at work. Similar difficulties arise with other assessment methods, such as work-sample tests and situational/structured interviews, where research is needed to explore the constructs that are in fact measured by these instruments.

In terms of data analysis and conceptual models, the reliance on linear correlation between variables as the main indicator of criterion-related validity sets a limit on the complexity of the models that can be evaluated. Many relationships between selection measures and job success criteria are likely to be curvilinear. Consider, for example, the relationship between extroversion and customer-relations skills. Very low levels of extroversion are not likely to be linked to successful customer relations, because the level of interaction initiated by the job holder would be too low. On the other hand, extremely high levels of extroversion might, for other reasons, be unlikely to bring empathy with customers in many settings.

Similarly, most validity studies examine the validity of merely a single selection method, whereas most real selection decisions are made with the aid of multiple methods, or at least multiple variables. Consider personality again. An above-average level of extroversion may be linked with good counselling skills, but only when coupled with a reasonably high score on agreeableness. The research that is needed to explore these issues is difficult to conduct and is not likely to emerge over a short time-scale.

Another limitation of the traditional approach is that job success criteria are almost inevitably conceptualized and measured at the individual level, whereas in many settings the co-ordinated efforts of several people are inextricably linked to job success. A major difficulty confronted by personnel selection researchers here is that measures of team effectiveness and commensurate measures of individual effectiveness are not available, nor is there any recognized procedure for developing them. It is clear from everyday experience that the addition of a new person to a previously efficient or inefficient group can make a considerable difference. Surprisingly little scientific work has been done to explore this kind of effect, and there is no substantial body of personnel selection research involving the use of criterion measures that are not measured exclusively at the individual level.

This chapter has concentrated on the central issues in personnel selection. It is important to recognize that personnel selection decisions are not taken in a vacuum; they take place within an organizational setting and they involve real people. A thorough discussion of the social-psychological context of personnel selection is beyond the scope of this chapter, but it is clear that truly comprehensive models of the process need to go beyond merely the examination of single jobs to review their place within broader organizational units and strategic needs.

One of the limitations of the traditional approach to personnel selection is that there is a failure to recognize fully that personnel selection is a complex social process. For example, Herriot (1989b) has shown how the personnel selection process can be seen as a series of episodes involving the applicant and the organization. Viewing the personnel selection process in this way concentrates attention on the actors involved, a perspective that is neglected in the traditional paradigm. This perspective brings into focus issues such as the impact of the assessment process on candidates (Robertson, Iles, Gratton and Sharpley, 1991) and the potential interaction of assessment, selection and organizational culture (Kerr and Slocum, 1987; Ouchi, 1980). Finally, consideration of the links between personnel selection and the nature of the organization itself generates a number of very important areas for examination, such as the strategic goals of the organization, its stage of development and the extent to which labour market conditions should be integrated with human resource management practice (see Snow and Snell, 1993).

SUMMARY

Personnel selection is one of the most firmly established areas of work psychology. After a rather stagnant period leading up to the 1980s, there has been a resurgence of research interest and it is currently one of the most exciting areas of activity, with two central concepts in psychometrics – reliability and validity – and the basic issues that underlie the description and measurement of key individual characteristics – cognitive ability and personality – attracting particular attention.

During the 1980s personnel selection researchers, with the aid of the recently developed technique of meta-analysis, have produced some remarkably clear conclusions about the criterion-related validity of all of the major personnel selection methods. The substantial financial gains that can be obtained from improved personnel selection have also been clarified in recent years. Although work on criterion-related validity has given a new confidence to personnel selection activities, there are still several important issues that must be tackled to give a firmer conceptual base to the practice of personnel selection and to maximize the benefit derived from personnel selection research to our understanding of work behaviour in general.

FURTHER READING

The central issues in personnel selection are best followed up by reference to a general text devoted to the topic (e.g., Smith and Robertson, 1993) or a book of readings (e.g., Herriot, 1989a). Very good examples of meta-analytic articles that focus on the criterion-related validity of specific methods cover assessment centres (Gaugler *et al.*, 1987) and interviews (McDaniel *et al.*, 1994).

REFERENCES

Bandura, A. (1986). *Social Foundations of Thought and Action: A Social Cognitive Theory*. Englewood Cliffs, NJ: Prentice Hall.

Barrick, M. R. and Mount, M. K. (1991). The big five personality dimensions and job performance: A meta-analysis. *Personnel Psychology*, 44, 1–26.

Boam, R. and Sparrow, P. (eds.) (1992). *Designing and Achieving Competency*. London: McGraw-Hill.

Boudreau, J. W. (1989). Selection utility analysis: A review and agenda for future research. In M. Smith and I. T. Robertson (eds.), *Advances in Selection and Assessment*, pp. 227–257. Chichester: Wiley.

Boyatzis, R. E. (1982). *The Competent Manager: A Model for Effective Performance*. New York: Wiley.

Bray, D. W. and Grant, D. L. (1966). The assessment center in the measurement of potential for business management. *Psychological Monographs: General and Applied Whole*, 625, 1–27.

Cattell, R. B. (1965). *The Scientific Analysis of Personality*. Baltimore: Penguin.

Cleary, T. A. (1968). Test bias: Prediction of grades of negro and white students in integrated colleges. *Journal of Educational Measurement*, 5, 115–124.

Cooper, D. and Robertson, I. T. (1995). *The Psychology of Personnel Selection*. London: Routledge.

Costa, P. T. and McCrae, R. R. (1985). *Manual for the NEO Personality Inventory*. Odessa, Fla: Psychological Assessment Resources Inc.

Digman, J. M. (1990). Personality structure: Emergence of the five-factor model. *Annual Review of Psychology*, 41, 417–440.

Dobson, P. (1989). Reference reports. In P. Herriot (ed.), *Assessment and Selection in Organizations*, 455–468. Chichester: Wiley.

Drakeley, R. J. (1989). Biographical data. In P. Herriot (ed.), *Assessment and Selection in Organizations*, 437–453. Chichester: Wiley.

Dulewicz, V. (1989). Assessment centres as the route to competence. *Personnel Management*, November, 56–59.

Eysenck, H. J. and Eysenck, M. J. (1985). *Personality and Individual Differences: A Natural Science Approach*. New York: Plenum Press.

Feltham, R. (1989). Assessment Centres. In P. Herriot (ed.), *Assessment and Selection in Organizations*, pp. 401–419. Chichester: Wiley.

Flanagan, J. C. (1954). The critical incident technique. *Psychological Bulletin*, 51, 327–358.

Gaugler, B., Rosenthal, D. B., Thornton, G. C. and Bentson, C. (1987).

Meta-analysis of assessment center validity. *Journal of Applied Psychology*, 72, 493–511.

Ghiselli, E. E. (1973). The validity of aptitude tests in personnel selection. *Personnel Psychology*, 26, 461–477.

Gottfredson, L. S. and Sharf, J. C. (1988). Fairness in employment testing. *Journal of Vocational Behavior Whole*, 33, 225–447.

Guion, R. M. and Gottier, R. F. (1965). Validity of personality measures in personnel selection. *Personnel Psychology*, 18, 135–164.

Herriot, P. (ed.) (1989a). *Assessment and Selection in Organizations*. Chichester: Wiley.

Herriot, P. (1989b). Selection as a social process. In M. Smith and I. T. Robertson (eds.), *Advances in Selection and Assessment*, pp. 171–187. Chichester: Wiley.

Hesketh, B. and Robertson, I. T. (1993). Validating personnel selection: A process model for research and practice. *International Journal of Selection and Assessment*, 1, 3–17.

Hunter, J. E. and Hirsh, H. R. (1987). Applications of meta-analysis. In C. L. Cooper and I. T. Robertson (eds.), *International Review of Industrial and Organizational Psychology*, 321–357. Chichester: Wiley.

Hunter, J. E. and Hunter, R. F. (1984). Validity and utility of alternative predictors of job performance. *Psychological Bulletin*, 96, 72–98.

Hunter, J. E. and Schmidt, F. L. (1982). Fitting people to jobs: The impact of personnel selection on national productivity. In M. D. Dunnette and E. A. Fleishman (eds.), *Human Performance and Productivity*, pp. 233–284. Hillsdale, NJ: Erlbaum.

Hunter, J. E. and Schmidt, F. L. (1990). *Methods of Meta-Analysis*. Newbury Park: Sage.

Hunter, J. E., Schmidt, F. L. and Jackson, G. B. (1982). *Meta-analysis: Cumulating Research Findings across Studies*. Beverly Hills, Calif.: Sage.

Kerr, J. L. and Slocum, J. W., Jr (1987). Managing corporate culture through reward systems. *Academy of Management Executive*, 1, 99–108.

Kline, P. (1991). *Intelligence: The Psychometric View*. London: Routledge.

Kline, P. (1993). *Personality: The Psychometric View*. London: Routledge.

Latham, G. P., Saari, L. M., Pursell, E. D. and Campion, M. A. (1980). The situational interview. *Journal of Applied Psychology*, 65, 422–427.

Mackinnon, D. W. (1977). From selecting spies to selecting managers. In J. L. Moses and W. C. Byham (eds.), *Applying The Assessment Centre Method*, pp. 13–30. New York: Pergamon Press.

McDaniel, M. A., Whetzel, D. L., Schmidt, F. L. and Maurer, S. D. (1994). The validity of employment interviews: A comprehensive review and meta-analysis. *Journal of Applied Psychology*, 79, 599–616.

Mischel, W. (1993). *Introduction to Personality*, 5th edn. New York: Holt-Saunders.

Moser, K. and Schuler, H. (1989). The nature of psychological measurement. In P. Herriot (ed.), *Assessment and Selection in Organizations*, pp. 281–305. Chichester: Wiley.

Murphy, K. R. (1988). Psychological measurement: Abilities and skills. In C. L. Cooper and I. T. Robertson (eds.), *International Review of Industrial and Organizational Psychology*, pp. 213–243. Chichester: Wiley.

Oskamp, S. (1991). *Attitudes and Opinions*, 2nd edn. Englewood Cliffs, NJ: Prentice Hall.

Ouchi, W. (1980). Markets, hierarchies and clans. *Administrative Science Quarterly*, 20, 129–141.

Pervin, L. A. (1989). Persons, situations, interactions: The history of a controversy and a discussion of situational models. *The Academy of Management Review*, 14, 350–360.

Reilly, R. R., Henry, S. and Smither, J. W. (1990). An examination of the effects of using behavior checklists on the construct validity of assessment center dimensions. *Personnel Psychology*, 43, 71–84.

Robertson, I. T. (1993). Personality assessment and personnel selection. *European Review of Applied Psychology*, 43, 187–194.

Robertson, I. T. (1994). Personality and personnel selection. In C. L. Cooper and D. M. Rousseau (eds.), *Trends in Organizational Behavior*, pp. 75–89. Chichester: Wiley.

Robertson, I. T. and Downs, S. (1989). Work sample tests of trainability: A meta-analysis. *Journal of Applied Psychology*, 74, 402–410.

Robertson, I. T., Gratton, L. and Rout, U. (1990). The validity of situational interviews for administrative jobs. *Journal of Organizational Behavior Management*, 11, 69–76.

Robertson, I. T., Gratton, L. and Sharpley, D. A. (1987). The psychometric properties and design of assessment centres: Dimensions into exercises won't go. *Journal of Occupational Psychology*, 60, 187–195.

Robertson, I. T., Iles, P. A., Gratton, L. and Sharpley, D. A. (1991). The impact of personnel selection methods on candidates. *Human Relations*, 44, 963–982.

Robertson, I. T. and Kandola, R. S. (1982). Work sample tests: Validity, adverse impact and applicant reaction. *Journal of Occupational Psychology*, 55, 171–183.

Robertson, I. T. and Kinder, A. (1993). Personality and job competencies: The criterion-related validity of some personality variables. *Journal of Occupational and Organizational Psychology*, 66, 225–244.

Robertson, I. T. and Makin, P. J. (1986). Management selection in Britain: A survey and critique. *Journal of Occupational Psychology*, 59, 45–57.

Sackett, P. R. and Dreher, G. F. (1982). Constructs and assessment center dimensions: Some troubling empirical findings. *Journal of Applied Psychology*, 67, 401–410.

Schmidt, F. L., Mack, M. J. and Hunter, J. E. (1984). Selection utility in the occupation of U.S. park ranger for three modes of test use. *Journal of Applied Psychology*, 69, 490–497.

Schmitt, N., Gooding, R. Z., Noe, R. A. and Kirsch, M. (1984). Meta-analysis of validity studies published between 1964 and 1982 and the investigation of study characteristics. *Personnel Psychology*, 37, 407–422.

Shackleton, V. J. and Newell, S. (1991). Management selection: A comparative survey of methods used in top British and French companies. *Journal of Occupational Psychology*, 64, 23–36.

Smith, M. and Robertson, I. T. (1993). *Systematic Personnel Selection*. London: Macmillan.

Snow, C. C. and Snell, S. A. (1993). Staffing as strategy. In N. Schmitt and W. Borman (eds.), *Personnel Selection in Organizations*, pp. 448–478. San Francisco: Jossey-Bass.

Stokes, G. S. and Reddy, S. (1992). The use of background data in organizational decisions. In C. L. Cooper and I. T. Robertson (eds.), *International Review of Industrial and Organizational Psychology*, pp. 285–321. Chichester: Wiley.

Tett, R. P., Jackson, D. N. and Rothstein, M. (1991). Personality measures as predictors of job performance: A meta-analytic review. *Personnel Psychology*, 44, 703–742.

Thornton, G. C. and Byham, W. C. (1982). *Assessment Centres and Managerial Performance*. London: Academic Press.

Vernon, P. E. (1950). The validation of civil service selection board procedures. *Occupational Psychology*, 24, 75–95.

Vernon, P. E. (1961). *The Structure of Human Abilities*, 2nd edn. London: Methuen.

Vernon, P. E. and Parry, J. B. (1949). *Personnel Selection in the British Forces*. London: University of London Press.

Weekley, J. A. and Gier, J. A. (1987). Reliability and validity of the situational interview for a sales position. *Journal of Applied Psychology*, 72, 484–487.

Weisner, W. H. and Cronshaw, S. F. (1988). A meta-analytic investigation of the impact of interview format and degree of structure on the validity of the employment interview. *Journal of Occupational Psychology*, 61, 275–290.

Wiggins, J. S. (1973). *Personality and Prediction: Principles of Personality Assessment*. Reading, Mass.: Addison Wesley.

Wollowick, H. B. and McNamara, W. J. (1969). Relationship of the components of an assessment center to management success. *Journal of Applied Psychology*, 53, 348–352.

Woodruffe, C. (1992). *Assessment Centres*. London: IPM.

Wright, P. M., Lichenfels, P. A. and Pursell, E. D. (1989). The structured interview: Additional studies and a meta-analysis. *Journal of Occupational Psychology*, 62, 191–199.

6

Careers in a New Context

Nigel Nicholson

The concept of 'career' is one of the most interesting and challenging in applied psychology, because it is a member of a class of concepts (such as 'role') that link the individual with the social structure. A career is both a property of the lives of individuals and of social systems: organizations, occupations and labour markets.

The field is at a turning point. The context for careers – the landscape within which they are acted out, or 'opportunity structures' in the language of sociology – has entered a period of profound qualitative change. This has created major dilemmas for career management practice and mounts a serious challenge to theory and research. Issues and ideas that have predominated in the past suddenly look at best antiquated and at worst irrelevant.

This chapter reviews the major themes of careers psychology, to argue that the concept of career can become a revitalized focus for scholarship, posing questions of fundamental practical and theoretical importance to scholars and practitioners.

What is a 'career'? The origins of the term, from the same root as 'carriageway' (Nicholson and West, 1989), suggest a continuous path, and in everyday usage 'career' is typically used to denote incremental development, the steady ascent of a hierarchy, the accumulation of expertise in a profession, or movement through positions towards mature stability.

This image fails to accommodate the increasing numbers of people who experience incoherent sequences of jobs, sudden or late changes in vocational objectives, stagnated or reversed development. For many, the idealized model of the continuous career is no longer a reasonable expectation. As Goffee and Scase (1992) have forcefully argued, since the 1980s we have seen a steady dismantling of the old psychological contract embodied in the corporate career. The employer offered the prospect of job security and advancement, linked with incremental increases in authority, status and pay, in exchange for the employee's achievement motivation and organizational commitment. These assumptions and traditional career pathways are being swept away in an era of economic, technological and cultural change, as many organizations try to adapt by changing their structures and revising their employment contracts (Handy, 1989). The jargon of these developments is becoming pervasive: delayering, downsizing, casualization, outsourcing, joint ventures, mergers, network and team-based structures, performance measurement, and competencies.

Although the scale and scope of changes in organizational forms and labour markets are profound, it should also be noted that many traditional forms are likely to continue to persist alongside the new. Many large organizations, for example, continue to want to nurture and grow their own talent. The net effect is therefore to create a context of increasing diversity of career experience.

Clearly we need a definition of 'career' that does not solely apply to a minority of people. For this purpose, the formulation adopted by Arthur and colleagues is helpful: 'the evolving sequence of a person's work experiences over time' (Arthur, Hall and Lawrence, 1989, p. 8).

THE PSYCHOLOGY OF CAREER DEVELOPMENT

Psychological approaches to the study of careers have historically been largely concerned with two themes, which we shall consider in turn: career choice and life-span development.

Career Choice

The question that has absorbed attention here is how individuals select career entry points. Feldman (1988) distinguishes 'content' from 'process' approaches in the career-decision-making literature. Content approaches, originating in counselling and psychometric practice, have sought to classify and measure typical patterns of occupational interest, especially at adolescence, and relate these to particular career choices. Process approaches are concerned with explaining how choices are made and the factors that may bias or influence choice. Content approaches have predominated until recently, since when process analysis has become more popular, largely under the influence of the contextual changes outlined above.

The 'content' approach to career choice takes the position that psychological profile is a prime determinant of choice. This view has spawned a rich array of psychometric tools, such as occupational interest aptitude and attainment measures (see Chapter 5). These have been used in vocational guidance practice to help individuals make informed choices on the basis of self-knowledge, and in employment to help managers identify appropriate candidates for positions. They have proved powerful and enduring tools for these purposes, but have contributed relatively little to our more general understanding of careers.

A more theoretically rich content approach has been taken by two groups of scholars, whose work remains among the most cited and replicated in the literature. First is Holland's (1973) taxonomy, which measures career orientations on the dimensions Realistic, Investigative, Artistic, Social, Enterprising, and Conventional. These six factors are modelled diagrammatically as a hexagon to reflect which patterns of interest tend to recur. Commonly linked interests, such as Social and Enterprising, are in adjacent positions on the hexagon. Infrequent conjunctions, such as Conventional and Artistic, are on opposite sides of the hexagon.

Much research effort has been devoted to testing this psychometric model and its measurement methods, with generally confirmatory results. The power of the method lies in matching the profiles of individuals with occupations, the latter detailed in a directory of job titles with empirically derived matching codes. This enables individuals and career counsellors to identify families of occupations where there would be a good fit, or congruence, with interests. The two main theoretical propositions in this work are that individuals in congruent roles are more satisfied and less likely to change environments, and that individuals in incongruent positions will be influenced by their work environment towards congruence, i.e. the interests of people who stay in incongruent environments tend to shift towards the local environmental norm. Assouline and Meier's (1987) meta-analysis of forty-one studies found general support for the first hypothesis, but there has been very little research on the second. An exception was Gottfredson's (1979) longitudinal study of a large sample of white males, which found incongruence declined due to changes in aspirations and job shifts by age 30.

The second body of influential work in this taxonomic content tradition is the Minnesota Studies in Vocational Rehabilitation (Dawis and Lofquist, 1984). The focus here is on work adjustment, indexed by length of job tenure. Adjustment is predicted by 'satisfactoriness': job performance through the exercise of abilities, and 'satisfaction': the reinforcement of needs and values by the work environment. The theory generates predictions very similar to Holland's, and is equally measurement-based. Abilities, ability requirements, and satisfaction are assessed by standardized test batteries, and satisfactoriness by supervisor rating scales (see also Chapter 8). Research has generally supported predictions of the theory (Rounds, Dawis and Lofquist, 1987), for example that person–organization fit is positively related to satisfaction and length of tenure (Bretz and Judge, 1994), though some questions remain about the robustness of factor structures (Doering, Rhodes and Kaspin, 1988).

These taxonomic approaches can be criticized for neglect of contextual influences on choice, fit, and outcome variables, and for their reliance on monocultural (American) norms. Moreover, as we have seen, the stable order of interests and occupations on which they depend is changing rapidly, in ways that could threaten their reliability. The patterning of occupational interests, even the existence of many job titles, may evolve faster than this approach can encompass in a new context of multi-skilled functions, flexible careers and transient occupations. The world of holes and pegs implied by these models is beginning to look distinctly outmoded. This is not to deny that people's interests form identifiable patterns, as a result of personality and experience, nor that they powerfully influence choices. Rather, it seems likely to become much more difficult in the future to relate individual interests reliably to specific occupations.

The future of the taxonomic fit/misfit approach may lie in other directions, such as how individuals choose types of organization.

Schneider (1987) and others interested in the growing field of organizational demography have argued that processes of selective attraction, selection, socialization and attrition progressively move organizations towards homogeneity in their cultural and demographic profiles. Empirical research has supported this proposition in various ways. For example, in a careful longitudinal study of professionals in a large number of accounting firms, Chatman (1991) found inter-firm differences in the fit between the values of the individual and the organization to be a function of how vigorous were their socialization methods. Initial fit was also a predictor of early adjustment and decisions to stay or quit. Research has also found individual deviation from organizational norms in personality and demography to be predictive of quitting.

Process approaches to career choice in the early days of the field concentrated on stages of decision-making, following the descriptive/normative pattern of life-span approaches (see below). More recent work has departed from these orderly assumptions by showing how the rationality of individual choice is 'bounded'. Job seekers tend to consider only a limited range of criteria and 'satisfice' rather than optimize in their decisions (Power and Aldag, 1985). Applicants make inferences on the basis of various incidentals which sway their decisions (Rynes, Bretz and Gerhart, 1991). Feldman (1988) argues that job seekers are becoming more sophisticated in how they search for information and read signals. In addition, how people consciously *send* signals, the study of impression management, is also becoming of interest. Under conditions of increasing diversity and uncertainty, process approaches to choice look likely to be an important focus for future careers scholarship.

Life-span Development

Super's work has been among the most influential in this area, initially proposing a normative phase sequence of exploration–establishment–maintenance–decline. In his later writings (Super, 1980) he elaborated these ideas in two important ways. His 'life-space life-span career rainbow', a graphic representation of development, depicts an outer 'maxicycle' of growth through the major phases, which include 'minicycles' of less normative individual transitions. Second, the rainbow recognizes the interpenetration of different life spheres, and the changing salience of social roles, such as student, homemaker, worker, citizen and leisurite. Although much cited, there has been relatively little empirical research on the model, though it is well established that people's career concerns do shift over the life-span (Williams and Savickas, 1990) and as function of their non-work roles and attitudes to life (Cherniss, 1991). In a recent review of life-span perspectives Minor (1992) concludes that a cyclical view is more appropriate than a stage view to current circumstances.

Within this literature, the mid-career period has attracted particular attention, with 'the midlife crisis' entering urban folklore. Levinson and colleagues' (Levinson, Darrow, Klein, Levinson and McKee, 1978) classic biographical study of forty middle-aged professional men was especially influential in depicting this as a period of radical self-reassessment, in which 'the dream' of earlier life ambitions is reconciled, often uncomfortably, with the dawning realities of limited remaining time and opportunity. Undoubtedly, this chimes with much adult experience and anecdotal evidence, but has proved less easy to substantiate in systematic research (Rush, Peacock, and Milkovich, 1980).

It is perhaps not surprising that this syndrome, and life-span stage models more generally, suffer from problems of uncertain generalizability. They are mostly founded upon white male, mainly American, middle-class experience. Feminists have rightly questioned the normative content and applicability of most current stage models for failing to encompass the differing life-cycle events common to women and for undervaluing interests such as intimacy and cooperation (Gilligan, 1982).

Moreover, the 'crises', or periods of transformation, typically depicted by stage models may be becoming more indistinct in environments of increasing volatility and uncertainty. Instead of occasionally punctuating extended periods of stability, self-reassessment may be becoming a more recurrent and continual activity for many people. But an enduring insight to be retained from stage theory is that we need to understand how people assess career events and goals within shifting frames of autobiographical meaning. We know far too little about how self-perceived career identity adapts to change, and how it affects career behaviour, such as job search and mobility decisions.

INTERACTIONIST THEMES

It is clear from much of what we have reviewed so far that to advance our understanding about careers requires appreciation of the reciprocal influences between the identity of individuals and their working environments: an interactionist perspective is needed. We shall examine three interrelated research strands which have helped to unravel the complexities of these interactions: the socialization process, the outcomes of socialization, and career mobility.

Socialization Processes

Socialization may be defined as the formal and informal social influence processes through which individuals acquire the skills, values and beliefs necessary for them to function as a member of a group or institution. As already indicated, this is a key process in the differentiation of organizational and occupational cultures: organizations 'grow' different cultures through self-reinforcing selection and socialization. In a comprehensive review Fisher (1986) sees organizational socialization as comprising five types of learning for the individual: preliminary learning, learning to adapt to the organization, learning to function in the workgroup, learning to do the job, and personal learning (e.g., about one's own career interests). One important concept in this area is anticipatory socialization: changes in values and attitudes which occur prior to taking up a role. This process has both long- and short-range effects. The long range is how class and education prepare and propel individuals towards particular occupational strata of adult society. The short range can be seen in recruitment to specific jobs, when candidates infer and take on in advance what they perceive to be appropriate membership orientations, though this can, in practice, fail to achieve a match. Because employers typically 'sell' an idealized image of themselves in the recruitment process, applicants may misperceive real role requirements, and only discover incongruity after they have joined. As we have seen, incongruity is a common cause of early turnover, and the 'realistic job preview', giving candidates firsthand exposure to what they will be doing in their work, has been widely used to counteract this risk (Premack and Wanous, 1985). This is a practical aid to choice and is claimed to deflate unrealistic expectations, vaccinate against early frustration and quitting, increase positive attitudes, and enhance subsequent performance. However, at the same time it tends to reduce the proportion of people who complete the application process.

Much recent attention has focused on what happens to employees during the initial entry period, well-known as a period of disillusionment and turnover, especially among college graduates in their first career jobs (Nicholson and Arnold, 1991). Research has focused upon formal and informal socialization practices, or 'people processing' as they have been called. Van Maanen and Schein (1979), in a classic analytical review, suggested a taxonomy of these processes and their effects, distinguishing those likely to result in creative versus conformist orientations to roles. Unfortunately, there has been little empirical research on the propositions of this model, though there is some supportive evidence (Jones, 1986).

In general research suggests that the impact of formal socialization processes (training, induction and supervision) is outweighed by that of informal processes, mediated by peer and work group relationships (Louis, Posner and Powell, 1983). Moreland and Levine (1983) offer a comprehensive analysis of how these can operate at the level of work-group influence and integration of the newcomer. From a more cognitive perspective, Louis (1980) analyses how individuals make sense of surprise and contrasts, via processes of selective attribution and communication.

The trend in socialization research has been moving away from the traditional view of the individual as a malleable recipient of influence, and towards a more active construction of individuals as agents of their own socialization. For example, varieties of early adjustment have been linked to individual differences in self-efficacy and relevant prior experience (Morrison and Brantner, 1992). 'Impression management' seems to be of particular importance. Judge and Bretz (1994) found that graduate recruits who sought to satisfy their supervisors were more successful in their organizations than those who sought to satisfy their job requirements, though more blatant 'self-promotion' tactics were found to be less effective. This suggests the need to distinguish ingratiation from other tactics of impression management.

Various writers have made the point that socialization not only differs according to which boundaries the individual is crossing – e.g., in and out of the organization, upward through the hierarchy, sideways across functions, and towards or away from the central core of the organization (Schein, 1978) – but also may change its character over the duration of a transition. The sequence of adjustment tasks in adopting a new role has been called the 'transition cycle' (Nicholson, 1990). Different challenges and problems arise at the points of preparation (anticipatory socialization), encounter (entry), adjustment (assimilation and accommodation), and stabilization (performance). One particularly interesting question is at which points in a transition are individuals most inclined to innovate in their approach to their roles: during the early encounter or adjustment period, before the conforming pressures of socialization have taken a grip, or later, when local skills, knowledge and power have been acquired? Gabarro's (1987) case study analysis, albeit of a small number of executives, suggests both. Early innovation when 'taking hold' and later 'reshaping' innovation are separated by a reflective 'immersion' period of low innovation. Further research is needed to document how the adjustment strategies of individuals change over time in different kinds of transition.

In new organizational forms of reduced central decision-making and hierarchy, socializing influences can be expected to become less uniform and more pluralistic, though no less psychologically important. The growing number of individuals who are exposed to several relatively short-term employers may be more inclined to resist socializing influences. A widening variety of outcomes to socialization can thus be expected. These will be considered next.

Career and Socialization Outcomes

Outcomes which have figured in research include satisfaction, adjustment and altered values. Much recent attention has focused on the concept of organizational commitment, meaning identification, loyalty and willingness to dedicate effort towards organizational goals. Meta-analysis of research on the construct has found highly committed individuals to be in jobs which offer a sense of personal autonomy and opportunities for self-expression, and in climates of confirmed expectations and fair treatment (Mathieu and Zajac, 1990). Researchers have also recently shown that the antecedents of commitment differ by career stage (Brooks and Sears, 1991). Team cohesion is particularly important early in a career, task challenge at mid-career, and organizational climate during late career. Meta-analysis has also shown the outcomes of low commitment to differ by career stage: turnover in early career, and poor performance and absenteeism more likely at later stages (Cohen, 1991).

This result implies that the barriers to exit rise with lengthening organizational tenure; quitting becomes less available as a response to low commitment. For this reason researchers have found it helpful to distinguish between affective commitment, meaning identification with the organization, and continuance commitment, meaning accumulated investments in the employment relationship. The former is more predictive of employee performance, the latter of tenure (Meyer, Allen and Gellatly, 1990). Researchers have recently also switched attention to behavioural forms of commitment, especially 'citizenship' or extra-role behaviours. These are discretionary actions on which organizations depend, such as doing a favour for a colleague, which are not part of job requirements. These behaviours are more likely to be enacted by individuals who perceive the employment relationship as equitable (Moorman, 1991). However, the relationship between attitudinal and behavioural commitment may be tenuous. One survey-based investigation failed to find a linkage between commitment attitudes and four types of self-reported behaviours: quality, sacrifice, sharing and presence behaviours (Randall, Fedor, and Longenecker, 1990).

These results also suggest that the construct of organizational commitment, as an integrated and positive bond between the individual and the organization, may be of declining relevance. Arguably, more attention should be paid to commitments as *multiple* (attaching not just to organizations but also to non-work domains, organizational subunits, professional associations, etc.); *segmented* (different for people in the core or on the periphery of organizations), and *transactional* (provisional and conditional upon current circumstances and perceptions). Research suggests that the changing context for careers is yielding these effects, especially among middle management, by threatening distributive justice (expected improvements in pay and satisfaction) and procedural justice (perceived fairness of performance assessment and career decisions) (McFarlin and Sweeney, 1992).

In these circumstances other possible career development outcomes may assume importance, such as changes in personal identity and psychological functioning (Nicholson, 1984). These effects have been demonstrated over the short term, for example, in the case of university graduates' career disillusionment and subsequent reoriented career identities (Nicholson and Arnold, 1991), and over much longer time periods (Brousseau, 1984; Kohn and Schooler, 1983; Mortimer, Lorence and Kumka, 1986). The latter effects Brousseau summarizes as amounting to an 'efficacy-enhancement model'. Prolonged exposure to complex, high autonomy, task-significant jobs enhances intellectual flexibility, self-direction and positive self-concept.

To conclude, research is recognizing that the unambiguous career outcomes of former times, such as satisfaction, organizational commitment, success and performance, are inadequate to comprehend the diversity of current experience and trends. There is a renewed focus upon individual differences in cognitions and expectations about careers, and how orientations are shaped by different kinds of mobility and employment.

Mobility and Change

Change has always been a key focus of careers psychology, since even in the most stable of times the life-cycle of individuals and organizations requires role changes: entry, promotion, entry and exit transitions. The last of these, under the label of labour turnover, has until recently absorbed most research attention, focusing on organizational predictors of intentions to quit and actual turnover. This organization-centred perspective looks increasingly myopic in labour markets where types of move and reasons for movement are becoming more varied. Explanations of mobility are shifting away from a search for causes in the organization and towards the consequences for the person.

Curiously, there has been more emphasis upon the negative than the positive consequences of mobility, especially strain, but the importance of these negative outcomes has been overstated. For most job changes, research indicates that positive outcomes outweigh the negative (Nicholson and West, 1989). Two are of special importance: psychological change as a consequence of adjusting to new circumstances, and role innovation (adapting the job to meet one's abilities and needs). These are significant for, respectively, personal and organizational development (Nicholson, 1984; Nicholson and West, 1988). Geographical relocation, however, seems to impose a wider range of demands upon an individual than moves of other types, with prime causes of strain lying more outside than inside the work domain – problems of family adjustment principal among them (Munton and Forster, 1993). Spouse support has also been indicated as a critical prerequisite for successful regional and international relocations, and its absence as a chief cause of expatriate 'failure' (typically indexed by premature homecoming). Much has also been written about 'culture shock' in international migrations, though research has failed to identify this as a general problem (Furnham, 1990). Much more of an issue may be subsequent repatriation, due especially to unrealistic expectations (Gregersen, 1992; Forster, 1994). Repatriates often find themselves uncomfortably brought down to earth from the rosy images of home and a hero's return which they entertained while away.

Indeed, unrealistic expectations would seem to be implicated in poor adjustment to moves of all kinds. They emerge as a chief cause of dissatisfaction at the career entry stage (Arnold and Mackenzie Davey, 1994), in geographical relocations (Fisher and Shaw, 1994), and in managerial mid-career changes (Nicholson and West, 1988). Inaccurate perceptions and false beliefs about impending role changes seem to stem not from unavailability of information about them, but from the individual's inability to visualize beyond the frame of his or her present circumstances to the frame of the impending change's demands and opportunities. In an ethnographic study

Hill's (1992) sample of sales staff making their first move up into management exhibited profound misapprehensions of the requirements of their former bosses' roles, despite their daily visibility. Her study narrates how lengthy and difficult was the comprehensive identity-transformation the new managers underwent to achieve competence and fulfilment in their roles.

The other side to the study of change is immobility. In their longitudinal study of a large sample of UK managers Nicholson and West (1988) found significant declines in job fulfilment for the immobile subset, even over as short a period as eighteen months. In the same study, however, the distinction was drawn between two kinds of 'plateaued' people – those who describe themselves as merely immobile, and those describing themselves as 'stuck'. Only the latter group experienced significant career dissatisfaction. Defining who is plateaued is problematic. Comparing subjective with objective measures may yield different results; Chao (1990) found that the former but not the latter related to dissatisfaction. In a study of 4,000 managers in a single corporation Nicholson (1994), focusing on the objective measure of age-grade norms, found that fast upward movers (i.e., ahead of their age-grade norm) were more career satisfied than those around the norm, but the slow upward-movers (behind their age-grade norm) were no more dissatisfied than the norm. However, for almost all the sample, aspirations for mobility outstripped expectations, not just for promotional moves but lateral moves as well. This finding has been confirmed across many other companies in the author's unpublished survey archive of around 40,000 respondents.

In the future the notion of being plateaued seems likely to change its meaning. Curtailed expectations of promotion in flattened organizational hierarchies, coupled with lower employment security, are likely to shift attention away from hierarchical success criteria, and towards other kinds of mobility, such as functional change, and their outcomes, such as multiskilling and personal development. The current popularity of notions such as the 'learning organization' and 'the flexible firm' can be linked with these ideas. The imaginative and strategic use of mobility seems likely to be a theme of increasing importance for organizations which seek a competitive edge in a climate of career disillusionment.

ORGANIZATIONAL PERSPECTIVES

We have already touched upon a number of organizational themes. Two are of particular importance: career systems and contractual relations.

Career Systems

Large organizations have traditionally sought to create and manage their internal labour markets to stimulate effective performance at all levels, to identify future leaders and to meet employees' aspirations. They have done so in different ways, as a function of their structural design, strategic purposes and cultural norms. Gunz (1989), in an empirical study of large companies in contrasting sectors, provides an analysis of organizational designs as 'climbing frames': they permit and encourage certain movement patterns more than others. These patterns he calls 'career logics', which, he argues, fundamentally affect the capabilities of the organization. Sonnenfeld and Peiperl (1988) offer a typology based upon how individuals are allocated to positions. This amounts to a categorization of careers 'cultures' according to how open or sealed off they are to recruitment from the external labour market, and how competitive are their internal labour markets.

Another way of looking at organizational career systems is to examine the prevailing criteria for allocation decisions. The organization's official stated decision-making model may, on close examination, differ from the actual model in operation, as Rosenbaum (1989) has shown in his detailed empirical study of a major corporation. The official model is more often than not depicted as a 'human capital' system, in which career decision-making is continually seeking to optimize the fit between individuals and roles through its allocation procedures. The reality Rosenbaum observed was the 'tournament model'. Individuals enter successive contests with their current cohort for advancement, moving on to new tournaments on winning, and entering a plateau of ineligibility for further contests on losing. Not only do organizations disguise this reality, but Rosenbaum also points out that individuals are often not aware that they have been in a tournament; they do not know they have been a losing candidate in a superior's shortlist for a position, but merely find themselves being passed over when new openings arise. This system may have the merit of efficiency from the organization's point of view, but it also has a number of dysfunctions, such as creating unrealistic expectations, demotivating staff and encouraging political behaviours such as ingratiation tactics.

Other career systems that can be identified according to the advancement they operate include the 'ladder', in which people advance incrementally with age or service, and the 'caste system', where group membership determines career opportunities. The career disadvantages of women and ethnic minorities can be seen as the product of caste systems based on demographic groups. Advantage or disadvantage may also flow from assigned group memberships. The company division or department one joins may determine long-term career opportunities in the organization (Sheridan, Slocum, Buda and Thompson, 1990). 'Fast track' systems are typically claimed by companies to operate according to the human capital model, but in many cases they may be seen in reality as tournaments to enter a caste system (Thompson, Kirkham and Dixon, 1985). This example also illustrates how a number of career criteria may co-exist within a single organization (Nicholson, 1994); advancement is governed by one set of criteria for part of a career (e.g., the ladder during the first years in an organization) and by others at subsequent stages.

One classic study has illustrated various features of career management. Bray and colleagues conducted an ambitious twenty-year longitudinal study in the American company AT&T (see Howard and Bray, 1988), and demonstrated the success of assessment centre measures in predicting subsequent career outcomes. This would seem to show that the human capital model can operate successfully, though there was also evidence of structurally constrained opportunities in the firm. The results of the study are also of particular interest for showing how managers' career and other attitudes develop as a function of their age and formative sociocultural environment.

This study can be seen as depicting the apotheosis of paternalistic career management systems, where an array of sophisticated human resource assessment methods are deployed to control individual and organizational effectiveness. As has been noted, much of the careers literature has been constructed around the study of managers in large companies. In reality many small and medium-sized companies have typically lacked career systems of any kind, or more accurately their career management systems are haphazard and extemporized. In organizations today one can discern two parallel trends: large companies retreating from comprehensive paternalism, and smaller companies introducing human resources management techniques to improve their performance management. In both cases career management constitutes a serious challenge: what can be offered to replace former guarantees of security and advancement?

One technique attracting much attention in recent times is mentoring: the nomination of an experienced manager, without line responsibility for the person, to act as a coach, sponsor, adviser, broker and pathfinder. Kram's definitive work on this topic (1985) points out that mentoring confers benefits on the mentor as well as the mentored. She observes that different kinds of mentoring are needed by individuals (e.g., the high flier versus an employee lost in the crowd) and that effective mentoring can be enhanced by an understanding of the distinctive phases of the developing mentor relationship. Research generally confirms the benefits of mentoring (Fagenson, 1989), for example in relation to career commitment (Colarelli and Bishop, 1990), but not equally across employee populations: most benefits accrue for individuals of highest socio-economic status (Whitely, Dougherty, and Dreher, 1991), and most difficulties arise in cross-gender mentoring relations (Ragins and McFarlin, 1990).

One can see the benefits of mentoring in a climate of increasing uncertainty and change, so long as mentors are able to look beyond the immediate organizational context to support the individual's interests. But herein lies a contradiction, since mentors who are company-experienced senior figures are the products of past career systems and little acquainted with the external labour market. The mentoring system can be seen as an extension of hierarchical paternalism, albeit often dressed up in the language of 'empowerment'. The emerging new language of careers is of more genuine self-management, supported by information and resource systems (Herriot and Pemberton, 1995b). Some forms of mentoring can contribute to these supports. Already, many individuals informally seek the good counsel of people outside their employing organization for career support and advice. Access via professional and educational bodies whose networks encompass multiple organizations and sectors is likely to figure with increasing importance in the future of career management, especially among the self-employed and highly mobile.

Meanwhile, organizations face the challenge of how to recast their internal career management systems to meet the new contingencies of changing expectations and opportunity structures. Attention to the changing nature of the psychological contract is necessary.

Contractual Relations

The 'psychological contract' in employment denotes the informal and largely unwritten expectations of employees and employers about their mutual rights and obligations, and about expected inducements and contributions. The psychological contract is a focal point of strain at the centre of the new context for careers, and perceived violations of it are common causes of career dissatisfaction and turnover. Evidence suggests that these consequences are more linked with perceived unfairness in how opportunities are allocated than with unequal opportunities *per se* (Herriot, Gibbons, Pemberton, and Jackson, 1994). This implies that people may be able to adjust to reduced career opportunities, so long as they believe access to them and resourcing for them are equitably managed.

Rousseau (see Rousseau and Parkes, 1993) has empirically distinguished two kinds of beliefs about employment obligations: transactional – the belief that hard work will be rewarded with high pay; and relational – the belief that organizations will trade job security in exchange for mutual loyalty, support and career rewards. Her studies find high agreement about what constitutes a fair contract, and that employees with longer tenure are more likely to be in relational contracts. One inference to be drawn from these results and current labour market trends is that decreasing numbers of employees will find themselves in relational contracts, whereas the bulk of employees will have more casualized relations with many more of their functions outsourced (Mirvis and Hall, 1994).

There is increasing recognition in the literature about how formal and informal (psychological) contracts are likely to have to adapt to meet the altered realities of the employment context (see Herriot and Pemberton, 1995a, 1995b). The contract is likely to become increasingly explicit: people hired for specific tasks with no long-term commitment. Employability will become a substitute for employment security; that is, the focus will be on training for possible futures beyond the organization and making available of placement assistance at the point of departure. Many employees may prefer this kind of contract to the traditional paternalistic model, especially those groups whom it disadvantaged, such as women. Evidence from the large female sub-sample (over 700 managers and professionals) in the Nicholson and West (1988) study of managerial job change supports this latter point. The women's career patterns and preferences were much more flexible than the men's, and less fixated on traditional paths and rewards.

This also reinforces the point that careers research and theory has been predominantly concerned with male experience, and almost exclusively focused on managerial and professional groups. Issues specific to women's career development will not be discussed here (see Chapter 10) except to raise the question about whether we are likely to see a convergence in male and female career experience (Goffee and Nicholson, 1995). Even if the persistent disadvantages faced by women do not seem to be disappearing (Stroh, Brett and Reilly, 1992), we can expect to see increasing numbers of male employees encountering the kinds of uncertainty and change that women have been taking for granted for some time. Trends are also likely to be complicated by the increasing numbers of dual-career couples. Of particular interest for future research here are the consequences of partners facing different career developmental issues at the same time (Sekaran and Hall, 1989).

The literature is also relatively silent on the career development of ethnic minorities, though this is an emerging area of interest (Thomas and Alderfer, 1989), especially in the USA, where compliance with formal aspects of the career contract exerts a considerable influence over human resource management policies and practice, as it does in relation to women. Predictably perhaps, research finds restricted mobility channels for minorities, partially mitigated by education (Hachen, 1990). Attention has also been drawn to the distinctive characteristics of black people's career development, including the special requirements of mentoring relationships. Perhaps the most theoretically interesting questions in this area are those to do with racial identity. Research has shown that major shifts in racial identification result from critical experiences, such as challenging encounters (Evans and Herr, 1994), but also that the career aspirations of black employees are unrelated to their racial identity attitudes or their perceptions of local discrimination.

The greatest gap in the field, however, has probably been in the area of blue-collar careers. The literature seems implicitly to have assumed that this is a meaningless formulation, in effect because blue-collar workers do not have careers. Not only is this incorrect on generally accepted definitions of career (see above), but it also ignores the fact that these employees accumulate skills through their work and care a great deal about the meaning of their work experience (Thomas, 1989). In a rare interview study on the subject, Rubin (1976) found many manual workers feel stuck in dead-end jobs which do not fulfil their desires for self-expression. Having escaped into their jobs from childhood worlds bounded by frustration and insecurity, they find themselves frustrated by flat structures of labour which displace their energies towards a number of non-work activities. It is interesting to speculate whether these observations are the portrait of the passing world of a dwindling employee proportion who can be classified as 'blue-collar', or an image of the future of many white-collar jobs, including some in management and professions, which are set to become increasingly casualized, insecure and plateaued.

THE FUTURE OF THE FIELD

We have already identified a number of new issues for future research, and some fresh approaches to topics of traditional interest, which are moving to meet the challenge of the radical new context for careers. From these, four themes can be extracted for the future development of theory and research:

1. *Identity.* In labour markets of increasing uncertainty, diversity and change, the individual employee becomes the locus for integration of career experience, rather than the structure of

occupations and organizations. Systematic investigation is needed into the consequences of new career patterns for aspects of personal identity, such as personality integration, self-esteem and self-efficacy. In parallel, applied research is needed on how interventions and resources, such as education, self-help materials and human resource policies, can mediate these outcomes.

2. *Life-span development.* The new context is dissolving the generalizability of normative career-stage models, yet it remains true that career events have different meaning according to one's age and circumstances. These patterns need to be charted for various social and demographic groups, such as women and minorities, and over time, to appreciate how they are changing historically. This will enable career systems and interventions to be designed and implemented more effectively.

3. *Transitions.* If careers are becoming more fragmented, changeful and unpredictable, then the focus of attention falls on the kinds of role-changes that people experience, the building blocks of careers. In particular, we need to know more about how individuals differ in their assimilation of these changes, and the interdependent influence of affect and cognition, for example, feelings of strain and expectations about the future. Such knowledge can help identify which adjustment strategies are most likely to aid personal development.

4. *Contracts.* The reconstitution of the psychological contract between individuals and organizations is currently more the subject of commentary than of research. What kinds of new deals are evolving, and how these differ across occupations, job levels and organizational types needs to be documented. Additionally, research can examine what kinds of contracts are sustainable under which circumstances, and what balance between organizational control and individual self-determination in career decision-making is optimal and achievable.

One may conclude that the current context of environmental change offers the field the opportunity of major renewal. People's careers have always been of the utmost importance to their sense of self and place in society, though the nature of what a career means is changing drastically. This presents a challenge of major social importance and of special interest to psychology.

SUMMARY

The field of careers is in a state of upheaval due to a revolution in its context affecting the structure of organizations, occupations and the employment contract. This represents both a threat and an opportunity to scholarship and practice. Many areas of previous interest, and much descriptive theorizing, are becoming rapidly outdated, while in many others fresh and important issues can emerge for more durable insights to be developed. These have been reviewed under three main headings which segment the field. First, the psychology of career choice and development seems to be shifting attention more to process than content issues, to organizational rather than occupational choice, and to be exploring the different experiences of particular social groups. Second, interactionist approaches are beginning to examine different kinds of commitment, to pay attention to a wider range of socialization outcomes, and to devote more attention to people's experience of mobility and change. Third, organizational research faces the challenge of what new kinds of career system and contractual relationship are evolving. Four main themes for fruitful theoretical development can be identified from this overview: the effects of career experience on identity, the life-long career patterns of contrasting social groups, how people adjust to transitions and what kinds of new contractual relations are operable.

FURTHER READING

The most complete and recent collection of academic writings is *The Handbook of Career Theory* (see Arthur, Hall and Lawrence, 1989). Feldman's *Managing Careers in Organizations* (1988) presents an excellent overview of the literature from a managerial perspective, as does Herriot's entertaining yet scholarly treatment in *The Career Management Challenge* (1992). Various approaches to the study of transitions can be found in Fisher and Cooper's edited collection

(1990), and ideas around the 'boundaryless' future of careers are explored in a special issue of the *Journal of Organizational Behavior* (vol. 15, no. 4, 1994). Finally, many of the topics discussed in this chapter are the subject of short informative essays for newcomers to the field in Blackwell's *Encyclopedic Dictionary of Organizational Behavior* (Nicholson, 1995).

REFERENCES

Arnold, J. and Mackenzie Davey, K. (1994). Graduate experiences of organizational career management. *International Journal of Career Management*, 6, 14–18.

Arthur, M. B., Hall, D. T. and Lawrence, B. S. (1989). Generating new directions in career theory: The case for a transdisciplinary approach. In M. B. Arthur, D. T. Hall and B. S. Lawrence (eds.), *The Handbook of Career Theory*, pp. 7–25. Cambridge: Cambridge University Press.

Assouline, M. and Meier, E. I. (1987). Meta-analysis of the relationship between congruence and well-being measures. *Journal of Vocational Behavior*, 31, 319–332.

Bretz, R. D. and Judge, T. A. (1994). Person–organization fit and the Theory of Work Adjustment: Implications for satisfaction, tenure and career success. *Journal of Vocational Behavior*, 44, 32–54.

Brooks, J. L. and Sears, A. (1991). Predictors of organizational commitment: Variations across career stages. *Journal of Vocational Behavior*, 38, 53–64.

Brousseau, K. R. (1984). Job–person dynamics and career development. In G. R. Ferris and K. M. Rowland (eds.), *Research in Personnel and Human Resources Management*, vol. 2, pp. 125–154. Greenwich, Conn.: JAI Press.

Chao, G. T. (1990). Exploration of the conceptualization and measurement of career plateau: A comparative analysis. *Journal of Management*, 16, 181–193.

Chatman, J. A. (1991). Matching people and organizations: Selection and socialization in public accounting firms. *Administrative Science Quarterly*, 36, 459–484.

Cherniss, C. (1991). Career commitment in human service professionals: A biographical study. *Human Relations*, 44, 419–437.

Cohen, A. (1991). Career state as a moderator of the relationships between organizational commitment and its outcomes: A meta-analysis. *Journal of Occupational Psychology*, 64, 253–268.

Colarelli, S. M. and Bishop, R. C. (1990). Career commitment: Function, correlates, and management. *Group and Organization Studies*, 15, 158–176.

Dawis, R. V. and Lofquist, L. H. (1984). *A Psychological Theory of Work Adjustment*. Minneapolis: University of Minnesota Press.

Doering, M., Rhodes, S. R. and Kaspin, J. (1988). Factor structure comparison of occupational needs and reinforcers. *Journal of Vocational Behavior*, 32, 127–138.

Evans, K. M. and Herr, E. L. (1994). The influence of racial identity and the perceptions of discrimination on the career aspirations of African American men and women. *Journal of Vocational Behavior*, 44, 173–184.

Fagenson, E. A. (1989). The mentor advantage: Perceived career/job experiences of proteges versus non-proteges. *Journal of Organizational Behavior*, 10, 309–320.

Feldman, D. C. (1988). *Managing Careers in Organizations*. Glenview, Ill.: Scott Foresman.

Fisher, C. D. (1986). Organizational socialization: An integrative review. In G. R. Ferris and K. M. Rowland (eds.), *Research in Personnel and Human Resources Management*, vol. 4, pp.101–145. Greenwich, Conn.: JAI Press.

Fisher, S. and Cooper, C. L. (eds.) (1990). *On the Move: The Psychology of Change and Transitions*. Chichester: Wiley.

Fisher, C. D. and Shaw, J. B. (1994). Relocation attitudes and adjustment: A longitudinal study. *Journal of Organizational Behavior*, 15, 209–224.

Forster, N. (1994). The forgotten employees? The experiences of expatriate staff returning to the UK. *International Journal of Human Resources Management*, 5, 405–425.

Furnham, A. (1990). *Expatriate stress: The problems of living abroad*. In S. Fisher and C. L. Cooper (eds.), *On the Move: The Psychology of Change and Transition*, pp. 275–301. Chichester: Wiley.

Gabarro, J. J. (1987). *The Dynamics of Taking Charge*. Cambridge, Mass.: Harvard Business School Press.

Gilligan, C. (1982). *In a Different Voice: Psychological Theory and Women's Development*. Cambridge, Mass.: Harvard University Press.

Goffee, R. and Nicholson, N. (1995). Career development in male and female managers: Convergence or collapse? In M. J. Davidson and R. Burke (eds.), *Women in Management: Current Research Issues*, pp. 80–92. London: Chapman.

Goffee, R. and Scase, R. (1992). Organizational change and the corporate career: The restructuring of managers' job aspirations. *Human Relations*, 45, 363–385.

Gottfredson, L. S. (1979). Aspiration-job match: Age trends in a large, nationally representative sample of young, white men. *Journal of Counselling Psychology*, 26, 319–328.

Gregersen, H. B. (1992). Commitment to a parent company and a local work unit during repatriation. *Personnel Psychology*, 45, 29–54.

Gunz, H. (1989). *Careers and Corporate Cultures*. Oxford: Blackwell.

Hachen, D. S. (1990). Three models of job mobility in labor markets. *Work and Occupation*, 17, 320–354.

Handy, C. (1989). *The Age of Unreason*. London: Hutchinson.

Herriot, P. (1992). *The Career Management Challenge*. London: Sage.

Herriot, P., Gibbons, P., Pemberton, C. and Jackson, P. (1994). An empirical model of managerial careers in organisations. *British Journal of Management*, 5, 113–121.

Herriot, P. and Pemberton, C. (1995a). Contracting careers. *Human Relations*, in press.

Herriot, P. and Pemberton, C. (1995b). *New Deals: The Revolution in Managerial Careers*. Chichester: Wiley.

Hill, L. A. (1992). *On Becoming a Manager*. Cambridge, Mass.: Harvard Business School Press.

Holland, J. L. (1973). *Making Vocational Choices*. Englewood Cliffs, NJ: Prentice Hall.

Howard, A. and Bray, D. W. (1988). *Managerial Lives In Transition: Advancing Age and Changing Times*. New York: Guildford.

Jones, G. R. (1986). Socialization tactics, self-efficacy, and newcomers' adjustments to organizations. *Academy of Management Review*, 8, 262–379.

Judge, T. A. and Bretz, R. D. (1994). Political influence behavior and career success. *Journal of Management*, 20, 43–65.

Kohn, M. L. and Schooler, C. (1983). *Work and Personality*. Norwood, NJ: Ablex.

Kram, K. (1985). *Mentoring at Work: Developmental Relationships in Organizational Life*. Glenview, Ill.: Scott Foresman.

Levinson, H., Darrow, C. N., Klein, E. B., Levinson, M. H. and McKee, B. (1978). *The Seasons of a Man's Life*. New York: Knopf.

Louis, M. R. (1980). Surprise and sense-making: What newcomers experience in entering unfamiliar organizational settings. *Administrative Science Quarterly*, 5, 329–340.

Louis, M. R., Posner, B. Z. and Powell, G. N. (1983). The availability and helpfulness of socialization practices. *Personnel Psychology*, 36, 857–866.

Mathieu, J. and Zajac, D. (1990). A review and meta-analysis of the antecedents, correlates, and consequences of organizational commitment. *Psychological Bulletin*, 108, 171–194.

McFarlin, D. B. and Sweeney, P. D. (1992). Distributive and procedural justice as predictors of satisfaction with personal and organizational outcomes. *Academy of Management Journal*, 35, 626–637.

Meyer, J., Allen, N. and Gellatly, I. (1990). Affective and continuance commitment to the organization: Analysis of measures and analysis of concurrent and time-lagged relations. *Journal of Applied Psychology*, 75, 710–720.

Minor, C. W. (1992). Career development: Theories and models. In D. M. Montross and C. J. Shinkman (eds.), *Career Development: Theory and Practice*. New York: Charles Thomas.

Mirvis, P. H. and Hall, D. T. (1994). Psychological success and the boundaryless career. *Journal of Organizational Behavior*, 15, 365–380.

Moorman, R. M. (1991). The relationship between organizational justice and organizational citizenship behaviors: Do fairness perceptions influence employee citizenship? *Journal of Applied Psychology*, 76, 845–855.

Moreland, R. L. and Levine, J. M. (1983). Socialization in small groups: Temporal change in individual group relations. *Advances in Experimental Social Psychology*, 15, 137–192.

Morrison, R. F. and Brantner, T. M. (1992). What enhances or inhibits learning a new job? A basic career issue. *Journal of Applied Psychology*, 77, 926–940.

Mortimer, J. T., Lorence, J. and Kumka, D. S. (1986). *Work, Family and Personality*. New York: Ablex.

Munton, A. H. and Forster, N. (1993). *Job Relocation: Managing People on the Move*. Chichester: Wiley.

Nicholson, N. (1984). A theory of work role transitions. *Administrative Science Quarterly*, 29, 172–191.

Nicholson, N. (1990). The Transition Cycle: Causes, outcomes, processes and forms. In S. Fisher and C. L. Cooper (eds.), *On the Move: The Psychology of Change and Transitions*, pp. 83–108. Chichester: Wiley.

Nicholson, N. (1994). Purgatory or place of safety? The managerial plateau and organizational age-grading. *Human Relations*, 46, 1369–1389.

Nicholson, N. (ed.) (1995). *Encylopedic Dictionary of Organizational Behavior*. Oxford: Blackwell.

Nicholson, N. and Arnold, J. (1991). From expectation to experience: Graduates entering a large corporation. *Journal of Organizational Behavior*, 12, 413–429.

Nicholson, N. and West, M. A. (1988). *Managerial Job Change*. Cambridge: Cambridge University Press.

Nicholson, N. and West, M. A. (1989). Transitions, work histories, and careers. In M. B. Arthur, D. T. Hall and B. S. Lawrence (eds.), *The*

Handbook of Career Theory, pp. 181–201. Cambridge: Cambridge University Press.

Power, D. J. and Aldag, R. J. (1985). Soelberg's job search and choice model: A clarification, review, and critique. *Academy of Management Review*, 10, 48–58.

Premack, S. and Wanous, J. P. (1985). A meta-analysis of realistic job preview experiments. *Journal of Applied Psychology*, 70, 706–719.

Ragins, B. R. and McFarlin, D. B. (1990). Perceptions of mentor roles in cross-gender mentoring relationships. *Journal of Vocational Behavior*, 27, 321–339.

Randall, D. M., Fedor, D. B. and Longenecker, C. O. (1990). The behavioral expression of organizational commitment. *Journal of Vocational Behavior*, 36, 210–224.

Rounds, J. B., Dawis, R. V. and Lofquist, L. H. (1987). Measurement of person–environment fit and predictions of satisfaction in the Theory of Work Adjustment. *Journal of Vocational Behavior*, 31, 297–318.

Rosenbaum, J. E. (1989). Organizational career systems and employee misperceptions. In M. B. Arthur, D. T. Hall, and B. S. Lawrence (eds.), *The Handbook of Career Theory*, pp. 329–353. Cambridge: Cambridge University Press.

Rousseau, D. M. and Parkes, J. M. (1993). The contracts of individuals and organizations. In L. L. Cummings and B. M. Staw (eds.), *Research in Organizational Behavior*, vol. 15, pp. 1–43. Greenwich, Conn.: JAI Press.

Rubin, L. (1976). *Worlds of Pain*. New York: Harper and Row.

Rush, J. C., Peacock, A. C. and Milkovich, G. T. (1980). Career stages: A partial test of Levinson's model of life/career stages. *Journal of Vocational Behavior*, 16, 347–359.

Rynes, S., Bretz, R. and Gerhart, B. (1991). The importance of recruitment in job choice: A different way of looking. *Personnel Psychology*, 44, 13–35.

Schein, E. H. (1978). *Career Dynamics: Matching Individual and Organizational Needs*. Reading, Mass.: Addison-Wesley.

Schneider, B. W. (1987). The people make the place. *Personnel Psychology*, 40, 437–453.

Sekaran, U. and Hall, D. T. (1989). Asynchronism in dual-career and family linkages. In M. B. Arthur, D. T. Hall and B. S. Lawrence (eds.), *The Handbook of Career Theory*, pp. 159–180. Cambridge: Cambridge University Press.

Sheridan, J. E., Slocum, J. W., Buda, R. and Thompson, R. C. (1990). Effects of corporate sponsorship and departmental power on career tournaments. *Academy of Management Journal*, 4, 578–602.

Sonnenfeld, J. A. and Peiperl, M. A. (1988). Staffing policy as a strategic response: A typology of career systems. *Academy of Management Review*, 13, 588–600.

Stroh, L. K., Brett, J. M. and Reilly, A. H. (1992). All the right stuff: A comparison of female and male managers' career progression. *Journal of Applied Psychology*, 77, 251–260.

Super, D. E. (1980). A life-span, life-space approach to career development. *Journal of Vocational Behavior*, 16, 282–298.

Thomas, R. J. (1989). Blue-collar careers: Meaning and choice in a world of constraints. In M. B. Arthur, D. T. Hall and B. S. Lawrence (eds.), *The Handbook of Career Theory*, pp. 354–379. Cambridge: Cambridge University Press.

Thomas, D. A. and Alderfer, C. P. (1989). The influence of race on career dynamics: Theory and research on minority career experiences. In M. B. Arthur, D. T. Hall and B. S. Lawrence (eds.), *The Handbook of Career Theory*, pp. 133–158. Cambridge: Cambridge University Press.

Thompson, P. H., Kirkham, K. L. and Dixon, J. (1985). Warning: The fast track may be hazardous to organizational health. *Organizational Dynamics*, 13, 21–33.

Van Maanen, J. and Schein, E. H. (1979). Toward a theory of organizational socialization. In B. M. Staw (ed.), *Research in Organizational Behavior*, vol. 1, pp. 209–264. Greenwich, Conn.: JAI Press.

Whitely, W., Dougherty, T. W. and Dreher, G. F. (1991). Relationship of career mentoring and socioeconomic origin to managers' and professionals' early career progress. *Academy of Management Journal*, 34, 331–351.

Williams, C. P. and Savickas, M. L. (1990). Developmental tasks of career commitment. *Journal of Vocational Behavior*, 36, 166–175.

7

Sources and Management of Excessive Job Stress and Burnout

Michael P. O'Driscoll and Cary L. Cooper

Since the mid-1950s occupational stress has been a topic of substantial interest to organizational researchers and managers, as well as society at large. Hundreds of books, research papers and popular journal articles have been devoted to this topic, many of them focusing on the presumed causes of stress, but also discussing various ways in which stress can be eliminated or its consequences controlled. Along with job satisfaction and leadership, work-related stress is currently one of the most frequently researched areas by organizational psychologists (Barley and Knight, 1992).

Reasons for this interest vary, but a common view is that stress arising from work conditions is pervasive and significant in its impact both on individual employees and on the organizations in which they work. It is also believed that management of job stress is a key factor for enhancing individual performance on the job, and hence increasing organizational effectiveness and efficiency. Summarizing these viewpoints, Sethi and Schuler (1984) outlined four major reasons why job stress and coping have become prominent issues:

- concern for individual employee health and well-being (e.g., coronary heart disease, high blood pressure, job-related accidents)
- the financial impact on organizations (including days lost due to stress-related illness and injury)
- organizational effectiveness
- legal obligations on employers to provide safe and healthy working environments.

The costs of occupational stress to business and industry in monetary terms have become increasingly well documented. Annually, US industry loses approximately 550 million working days due to absenteeism. It is estimated (Elkin and Rosch, 1990) that 54 per cent of these absences are in some way stress-related. Recent figures released by the Confederation of British Industry (Sigman, 1992) calculate that in the UK, 360 million working days are lost annually through sickness, at a cost to organizations of £8 billion. Again it is estimated (UK Health and Safety Executive) that at least half of these lost days relate to stress-related absence.

It is evident that researchers and organizations alike recognize the pervasiveness and potential seriousness of stress in the workplace. While some degree of stress is probably desirable, since it may stimulate people to perform at higher levels, excessive stress can lead to a variety of psychological and possibly physical health problems (Fletcher, 1988), as well as impeding work productivity, causing accidents and increasing absenteeism and turnover (Ganster and Schaubroeck, 1991). Psychologists are especially concerned with determining what is an 'excessive' stress level, understanding the work conditions which produce excessive stress, and developing methods for alleviating (even eliminating) such stress.

WHAT IS STRESS?

Early references to stress were made by Sir William Osler in 1910, who noted that some medical patients were subjected to stress and strain, and by the physiologist Cannon (1935), who spoke of individuals being 'under stress' when they experienced extreme physical conditions (such as heat or cold). However, these early uses of the term were somewhat vague and ill-defined, and did not clearly differentiate between the subjective experiences of individuals and the environmental conditions producing those experiences. Selye (1936) offered a perspective that has served as a stimulus for much research in this field, defining stress as a non-specific outcome (either physical or psychological) of any demand made upon the organism. He also described the response that an organism makes to an environmental demand as the General Adaptation Syndrome or stress response.

The early 1950s saw the initiation of an influential line of research on stress and coping by Lazarus and his associates. Their work began with an experimental study of the impact of psychological stress on task performance (Lazarus, Deese and Osler, 1952), and has since led to the development of a comprehensive model of the stress process. McGrath (1976) extended these earlier ideas by conceptualizing stress as due to 'environmental demands exceeding a person's resources and capacity, when the outcomes are important for the person'. This recognition of the interaction between the individual and the environment has been formalized in the person–environment (P–E) fit model of stress developed over the past twenty years by French and his colleagues (see French, Caplan and Harrison, 1982). In their view, 'strain can result from the mismatch between the person and the environment on dimensions important to the well–being of the individual' (p. 58). Lack of person–environment fit or correspondence may occur in conditions of underdemand (e.g., a monotonous, repetitive task), as well as overdemand (e.g., a task which is too complex for the individual). French *et al.* (1982) have described the relationship between misfit and strain as a U-shaped curve (see Figure 7.1). According to the P–E fit model, for each individual there are optimal levels of environmental demands for that person's capabilities. When these optimal levels are reached, strain will be minimal; if there is either too little or too much demand, strain increases.

Today there is widespread acceptance of the notion that stress is jointly determined by environmental factors and characteristics of the person. Nevertheless, there are certain difficulties with the person–environment fit approach and with research based on this model. These problems have been described in detail by Edwards and Cooper (1990), who note that different versions of P–E fit are frequently confounded, and that the notion of fit itself has been operationalized in at least three distinct ways, by discrepancy (strain increases as E deviates from P), interactive (strain occurs where E is combined in certain ways with P) and proportional techniques (strain increases as the proportion of E to P becomes lower).

As mentioned above, another major approach to the study of

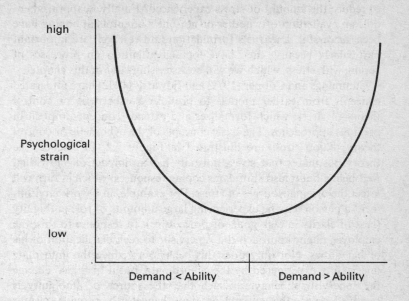

Fig. 7.1 Person–environment fit model of psychological strain (adapted from French, Caplan and Harrison, 1982, p. 29, with permission from J. Wiley and Sons).

stress is reflected in research conducted since the mid-1950s by Lazarus and his colleagues (see Lazarus and Folkman, 1984). In a similar vein to French *et al.* (1982), Lazarus has argued that stress arises when environmental demands or constraints are judged by the individual to exceed his or her resources or capacities. However, the critical variable in Lazarus's model is *cognitive appraisal*, of which there are three types: primary, secondary and reappraisal. Primary appraisal is said to occur when the person evaluates an environmental demand or event in terms of its significance for his or her well-being. That is, does the environment threaten one's well-being (physical or emotional)? This is thought to be followed by secondary appraisal, during which the person assesses how he or she can deal with the situation; that is, what coping strategies or behaviours can be utilized to reduce the amount of stress experienced? Finally, reappraisal entails an evaluation of whether or not one's attempts at coping have been successful. Lazarus's formulation and research are important particularly because they have focused attention on processes of coping with stress, which we will be discussing later in this chapter.

Cummings and Cooper (1979) and Edwards (1992) have integrated concepts from earlier models to propose a cybernetic or control theory of stress, which formalizes and extends concepts implicit in previous approaches. The basic concepts of the cybernetic or control theory of job stress are illustrated in Figure 7.2. In essence, the theory postulates that stress not only has an impact on individual well-being, but it also stimulates coping responses, which in turn will affect the original sources of stress. For example, in a work environment a person may be experiencing large amounts of role ambiguity (lack of clarity in task goals or procedures). In response to this, the employee might approach the supervisor to seek clarification of his or her duties. Not only does this behaviour reduce the immediate uncertainty experienced by the subordinate, but it may also change the supervisor's behaviour such that the source of ambiguity is removed (e.g., the supervisor may henceforth provide clearer instructions or more direction for the subordinate).

Each of the above approaches has contributed to our understanding of work-related stress, and has stimulated research into its causes and consequences. Nevertheless, as mentioned earlier, there is still considerable confusion over the actual meaning of 'stress', which is reflected in the variety of ways in which the term has been defined. Before proceeding to discuss the major findings in this field of research, we offer a working definition of relevant concepts. These are presented in summary form in Figure 7.3.

Beehr and Franz (1987) have commented that stress 'has commonly been defined in one of three ways: as an environmental stimulus often described as a force applied to the individual, as an individual's psychological or physical response to such an environmental force, or as the interaction between these two events' (p. 6). They also observe that there is agreement among researchers that the term *stressor* refers to the environmental stimulus or event, and that the term *strain* refers to the person's response to the stimulus or event. Stressors, therefore, are the antecedents and strain is the consequence

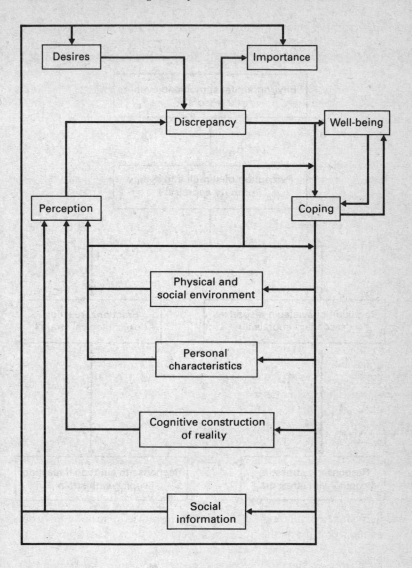

Fig. 7.2 Cybernetic model of the stress-coping process (Edwards, 1992, p. 248; used with permission from Dr J. R. Edwards and J. Wiley and Sons).

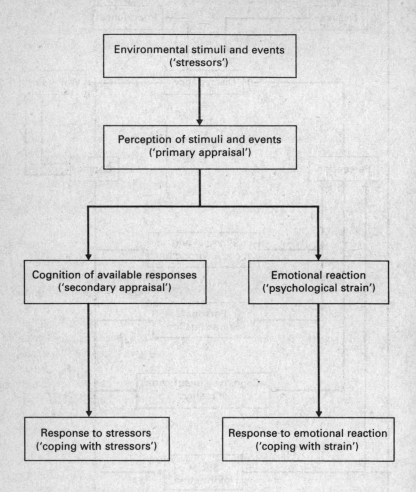

Fig. 7.3 Variables in the stress-coping process.

of a stressful transaction. We agree with Beehr's suggestion (Beehr, 1987; Beehr and Franz, 1987) that the term *stress* be used not to describe specific elements of the transaction between the individual and his or her environment, but merely to denote the general area of investigation which focuses on stressors, strains and coping responses.

MEASURES OF JOB-RELATED STRAIN

In this section we will briefly outline more commonly used approaches to measuring stress in work environments. Our focus here is on strain itself (both physical and psychological), not the factors (or stressors) which induce strain. These factors will be discussed later in this chapter.

Self-Reported Strain

Many studies of stress in the workplace have utilized self-reports to gauge the extent of psychological strain experienced by employees, although some have also collected physiological data relating to physical health problems.

One example of a questionnaire designed to measure levels of psychological stress in work settings is the Crown Crisp Experiential Index, which consists of six scales (depression, anxiety, hysteria, obsessionality, phobic anxiety and somatic anxiety) (CCEI; Crown and Crisp, 1979). For example, Cooper and his colleagues have used this instrument in a series of studies of mental health in various occupational samples (see Cooper and Kelly, 1993; Cooper and Roden, 1985; Cooper, Watts, Baglioni and Kelly, 1988; Sutherland and Cooper, 1992).

Another self-report measure of psychological strain which has been frequently utilized is the General Health Questionnaire (GHQ; Goldberg, 1978), which was developed to detect minor psychological disturbance in 'normal' populations and focuses on issues such as ability to concentrate on tasks, losing sleep because of worries, feeling constantly under strain, ability to enjoy daily activities, and feeling unhappy and depressed.

A final illustration of the questionnaire approach to measuring job strain is the instrument developed by Warr (1987, 1990). His index of affective well-being taps two core bipolar dimensions (anxiety–comfort and depression–enthusiasm); see Chapter 8.

Physiological Measures of Strain

Physiological indicators such as elevated heart rate, blood pressure, serum cholesterol and urinary catecholamines are becoming more common in research on stress. Frequently, these measures are collected concurrently with other indices of strain, such as self-reports (Hendrix, Ovalle and Troxler, 1985). It is then possible to examine the correlation between independent measures to determine their convergent validity. Unfortunately, however, to date evidence for the correspondence between self-reports and physiological indices has been inconsistent (Pennebaker and Watson, 1988), and further empirical research is needed to confirm their comparability.

Studies exploring physiological components of strain have typically focused on one or more of the following indicators (Fried, Rowland and Ferris, 1984): cardiovascular symptoms (especially increased heart rate and blood pressure), biochemical reactions (such as blood cholesterol and urinary catecholamines) and gastrointestinal symptoms (particularly peptic ulcers). There is mounting evidence that intense and frequently occurring stressors in the workplace, arising from either excessive physical demands or psychological pressures, can influence these physiological reactions. Given this, tapping into physiological responses holds promise as a viable complementary method of assessing workplace stress among employees.

Physiological assessments offer several advantages over self-reports. They are not subject to the potential biases of self-reports, since they do not rely upon a person's recall and subjective description of strain. Also, with the use of appropriate technology, they may enable more precise discriminations to be made between levels of strain experienced by different individuals.

SOURCES OF STRAIN

Extensive research has been conducted to determine the factors which produce job-related psychological strain among employees, and substantial knowledge about these factors has now been accumulated. Determinants of strain generally can be classified into three major categories: job-specific sources, organizational sources and individual (personal) sources. Within these categories, a further differentiation has been made by Cooper and Cartwright (1994), who outlined six primary work-related stressors: intrinsic characteristics of the job; roles in the organization; relationships at work; career development; organizational structure and climate; home–work interface.

Intrinsic Job Characteristics

These stressors are associated with the performance of specific tasks that comprise an individual's job, and hence are sometimes called 'task content' factors (Kahn and Byosiere, 1992). They include variables such as the level of job complexity, the variety of tasks performed, the amount of discretion and control individuals have over the pace and scheduling of their work, and even the physical environment in which the job is performed. Numerous studies have demonstrated that lack of variety, monotonous work and an absence of discretion and control are consistent predictors of job-related strain (see Beehr and Bhagat, 1985; Cooper, 1987; Kahn and Byosiere, 1992). Similarly, poor working conditions (for instance, excessive heat, noise or temperature) can have serious detrimental effects on employee psychological well-being and physical health (Cooper, 1987).

Shiftwork is another aspect of the job which has been explored by stress researchers. Principal themes have been illustrated in Chapter 2. There is considerable variation in reactions to shiftwork, with some workers adapting more readily than others to changes in their work hours (e.g., Monk and Tepas, 1985).

Finally, the amount of work that has to be carried out is a significant stressor for many people. Both overload and underload can generate psychological strain. For example, Cooper, Davidson and

Robinson (1982) found that work overload was a potent source of strain for British police officers. On the other hand, work which is repetitive, routine and provides little challenge for the individual can also be stressful if undertaken over long periods. Some machine-paced assembly lines are a clear example of this type of underload, and have been linked with high levels of strain (Cox, 1985; Smith, 1985).

Organizational Roles

Around the same time that French and his colleagues were developing their person–environment fit model, Kahn and his colleagues (Kahn, Wolfe, Quinn and Snoek, 1964) carried out important investigations into role overload as major determinants of job-related strain.

As defined by Kahn and his colleagues, role *ambiguity* refers to unpredictability of the consequences of one's role performance. Later researchers have extended the definition to include a lack of information needed to perform the role, and the typical measure of this construct assesses both unpredictability of consequences and information deficiency regarding expected role behaviours (Pearce, 1981). Numerous studies have demonstrated a consistent link between substantial role ambiguity in the job and high levels of psychological strain (see, for example, Jackson, 1983; Schaubroeck, Cotton and Jennings, 1989; O'Driscoll and Beehr, 1994).

Similarly, role *conflict*, which reflects incompatible demands on the person (either within a single role or between multiple roles occupied by the individual), can induce negative emotional reactions due to perceived inability to be effective on the job (Schaubroeck *et al.*, 1989). Several studies have confirmed this detrimental effect of role conflict on both self-reported strain (O'Driscoll and Beehr, 1994) and physiological indicators of strain (see Kahn and Byosiere, 1992). Typically, however, the association between role conflict and psychological strain is not as strong as that between ambiguity and strain (Jackson and Schuler, 1985).

A third role variable is *overload*, which refers to the number of different roles a person has to fulfil. Not only can role overload lead to excessive demands on an individual's time, but it also may create uncertainty about one's ability to perform these roles adequately. Along with role ambiguity and conflict, overload has been shown to be a major correlate of job-related strain in numerous studies (Cooper, 1987).

One potential explanation for the negative effects of these role variables on employee physical and psychological well-being is that they induce uncertainty, which in itself is psychologically uncomfortable and, if persistent and at high levels, can create emotional distress. Beehr (1985, 1987; Beehr and Bhagat, 1985) has adapted the expectancy theory of motivation to explain the diverse forms of uncertainty which may arise from role stressors. Specifically, ambiguity, conflict and overload may be linked with reduced effort-to-performance expectancy ($E \rightarrow P$) because they create uncertainty among employees that their efforts will lead to satisfactory job performance, and also with performance-to-outcome expectancy ($P \rightarrow O$) because employees are unsure of the link between successful job performance and subsequent rewards.

Work Relationships

Both the quality of interpersonal relationships and lack of social support from others at work have been explored as possible sources of psychological strain (Cooper, 1987). As we shall see shortly, there has been considerable debate over the role of social support as a moderator (or 'buffer') of the impact of stressful work environments. Nevertheless, it is clear that negative interpersonal relations and the absence of support from peers, colleagues or superiors can be a significant stressor for many employees (Motowidlo, Packard and Manning, 1986). Conversely, having access to social support from other people in the organization can directly alleviate psychological strain (Beehr and McGrath, 1992).

Career Development

Career development has been less explored as a potential source of strain among employees, although work attitude surveys have illustrated that concerns about promotion opportunities represent one of the primary sources of job dissatisfaction (Rabinowitz, Falkenbach, Travers, Valentine and Weener, 1983). There is also substantial evidence that, despite changes in societal attitudes concerning equal employment opportunities, women and minority groups still encounter organizational barriers to their career development (see, for example, Burke, 1993), which will tend to lead to higher levels of psychological strain for these groups of employees. Although many organizations are making efforts to enhance career development opportunities, for women in particular (Davidson and Cooper, 1993), progress in this area has not been dramatic; see also Chapter 10.

An aspect of many people's careers is unemployment or threat of unemployment. With the increasing occurrence of downsizing in industries around the world, and attempts to reduce the number of levels of management within organizations, many individuals, especially those occupying middle-level managerial positions, face the threat of losing their jobs (Kozlowski, Chao, Smith and Hedlung, 1993). In fact, job insecurity may be one of the single most salient sources of stress for employees today. Not only does unemployment affect current and future income, but in addition it challenges a person's general self-esteem, which is closely linked with job status.

Organizational Structure and Climate

Psychological strain which may be attributed to organizational factors is often due to the culture and management style adopted within an organization (Cooper and Cartwright, 1994). Hierarchical, bureaucratic organizational structures frequently allow little employee participation in decisions affecting their work and lack adequate communication, especially between managerial and non-managerial levels. These factors contribute to employee strain.

Formalization of procedures has exhibited inconsistent effects, depending on the group studied. Organ and Greene (1981), for example, found that increased formalization reduced role ambiguity among scientists, but increased levels of role conflict, whereas Podsakoff, Williams and Todor (1986) observed negative relationships between formalization and both ambiguity and conflict. Overall, it would seem that clearly outlined formal work procedures may have positive benefits for employees (O'Driscoll, 1987).

The 'politics' which inevitably occur in work organizations can also have a substantial impact on employee strain. Although there have been few direct assessments of these effects, studies of organizational climate (e.g., Guzley, 1992; O'Driscoll and Evans, 1988) have indicated that the content and nature of communication processes within organizations significantly predict employee reactions to their job and the organization as a whole. A climate which is characterized by communications which focus on negative attributions about other personnel, cynicism regarding leadership and management of the organization, and attempts by employees to further their own interests at the expense of others will induce feelings of unsupportiveness and mistrust, which in themselves can increase the stressfulness of work conditions.

The Home–Work Interface

Managing the interface between the job and roles and responsibilities outside of the job is another potential source of strain (Cooper and Cartwright, 1994). Sometimes referred to as *work/nonwork conflict*, this issue has received considerable attention from researchers in recent years. Changes in family structures, increased participation by women in the workforce, along with technological changes (such as portable computers and cellular phones) that enable job tasks to be performed outside of the actual work setting itself, have blurred the boundaries between the job and life off the job, and create the potential for additional conflict to occur between job and off-job roles. This interrole conflict has consistently been linked with increased psychological strain (Frone, Russell and Cooper, 1992; O'Driscoll, Ilgen and Hildreth, 1992), and is especially prevalent among women and dual-career couples (Greenhaus, Parasuraman, Granrose, Rabinowitz and Beutell, 1989).

BURNOUT

The phenomenon known as job 'burnout' was first labelled as such in 1974 by Freudenberger, from his observations and reflections on the extreme strain often experienced by workers in the helping professions, such as social work, nursing, teaching and police work. Since then there have been many studies of burnout, primarily among human service professionals, but also increasingly in other areas of employment.

Recently published reviews of the burnout literature (Cordes and Dougherty, 1993; Lee and Ashforth, 1993) have examined theoretical models of the burnout process, along with antecedents and consequences of this type of job stress. Burnout is a chronic affective response to very extreme demands from the work environment (Ganster and Schaubroeck, 1991), especially pressures and conflicts arising from direct contact with and care of other people. While other stressors in the work context may also contribute to this stress response, high levels of contact with people, particularly in terms of dealing with crises or problems experienced by these individuals, have greatest impact on the development of burnout (Cordes and Dougherty, 1993).

Most researchers have adopted the conceptualization of burnout proposed by Maslach and her associates (Maslach, 1982; Maslach and Jackson, 1981), who define burnout as having three components: (1) emotional exhaustion, (2) depersonalization of others in the work context, and (3) feelings of low personal accomplishment on the job. In Maslach's model of burnout, *emotional exhaustion* is characterized by a depletion of emotional (and, ultimately, physical) energy and a feeling that one's emotional resources are inadequate to deal with the situation. In other words, a combination of emotional exhaustion, physical fatigue and mental 'weariness' can result. This in turn leads to a tendency towards *depersonalization* of individuals in the work setting (e.g., clients or patients), a tendency to treat them as objects rather than people. While this may help to reduce intense emotional arousal that might interfere with functioning in crisis situations, excessive detachment from others can produce a callous and cynical approach to their welfare (Jackson, Schwab and Schuler, 1986). The third component of burnout is *diminished personal accom-*

plishment, characterized by a tendency to evaluate one's behaviour and performance negatively. As a result, the person experiences greater feelings of incompetence on the job and an inability to achieve performance goals.

Burnout has most often been measured via the Maslach Burnout Inventory (MBI; Maslach and Jackson, 1981), which is a twenty-two-item questionnaire assessing both the frequency and the intensity of each of the above three factors. Research has typically found a high correlation between the intensity and frequency of responses (Cordes and Dougherty, 1993); a more recent version of the MBI (Maslach and Jackson, 1986) therefore includes only the frequency scale. Nevertheless, some investigators (e.g., Jackson, Turner and Brief, 1987) have measured intensity only.

Although burnout is conceptualized as a combination of emotional exhaustion, depersonalization and diminished personal accomplishment, in Maslach's formulation the key element is emotional exhaustion, which precedes the two other responses. There is some empirical support for the notion that emotional exhaustion generates depersonalization and diminished personal accomplishment (Leiter and Maslach, 1988), although Golembicwski has argued for an alternative sequence of events, in which depersonalization is a precursor to low personal accomplishment, which in turn results in emotional exhaustion (Golembiewski and Munzenrider, 1988). Debate on this issue continues, with many studies of phase models of burnout being constrained by the use of cross-sectional research designs which limit conclusions about causal sequencing.

Antecedents

Antecedents of burnout have also been the subject of considerable research. As noted above, certain occupational groups are more prone to burnout development, given the nature and intensity of their work. In particular, 'frequent face-to-face interactions that are intense or emotionally charged will likely be more demanding and can be expected to be associated with higher levels of emotional exhaustion' (Cordes and Dougherty, 1993, p. 642). Along with the effects of role conflict, ambiguity and overload, which we discussed earlier as determinants of job stress in general, frequency, duration and intensity of contact with clients (or patients) have been found to affect burnout levels in the human service professions (Cordes and Dougherty, 1993). Sustained uncomfortable or unpleasant interactions with one's co-workers or supervisors are also likely to induce burnout (Leiter and Maslach, 1988).

Most research has focused on personal attributes or role characteristics as determinants of burnout, but there is evidence that wider organizational variables may also play a role in burnout development. For example, lack of organizational support and recognition of employee contributions may contribute to emotional exhaustion and reduced personal accomplishment (Shinn, Rosario, Morch and Chestnut, 1984). Poor organizational communication and feedback on job performance may also increase job stress and burnout among employees (Matteson and Ivancevich, 1987). On the other hand, involvement in decision-making relevant to one's job performance and development of an organizational climate that fosters trust and co-operation may promote feelings of personal accomplishment and have an ameliorating effect on burnout.

Consequences

Consequences of burnout are similar in nature to those of job stress in general, although they are frequently experienced more intensely. Cordes and Dougherty (1993) have categorized burnout outcomes as: physical and emotional; interpersonal; attitudinal; and behavioural. Among the physical and emotional consequences they discuss various psychological problems (including depression, helplessness and anxiety), as well as physical ill-health (such as fatigue, insomnia and gastrointestinal disorders). Several of these outcomes are now well established in the research literature.

Interpersonal effects of burnout relate particularly to the person's relationships with clients and co-workers, but also include relations with family members and other people outside of the job environment. For instance, Burke and Deszca (1986) observed that police officers suffering from burnout experienced a severe negative impact of their job demands on their off-job lives. Other writers (e.g, Jackson and Schuler, 1983) have noted changes in the nature and frequency of client and co-worker interpersonal interactions.

Attitudinal consequences of burnout have probably been the most systematically explored, with several studies demonstrating increased negative attitudes towards clients, co-workers, the job itself and the organization (Cordes and Dougherty, 1993). Lowered commitment to the job and organization has been demonstrated (Jackson, Turner and Brief, 1987; Leiter and Maslach, 1988), and Shirom (1986), in one of the few longitudinal studies in this field, found that burnout among teachers led to increased levels of job dissatisfaction and intention to leave the profession.

Under behavioural consequences, Cordes and Dougherty (1993) discuss increases in absenteeism and turnover, and reductions in job performance, as primary outcomes of burnout. Little research has been conducted to determine the specific areas of job performance that are most affected by burnout. It might be surmised, however, that interpersonal dimensions of the job would be most likely to deteriorate with the development of burnout among employees.

MODERATORS OF THE STRESSOR–STRAIN RELATIONSHIP

Along with research on sources of psychological strain, attention has also been given to variables which might moderate the impact of the factors discussed above on the amount of strain experienced by employees. In essence, research along these lines has searched for variables which might protect or buffer the individual from the negative effects of stressful work conditions. These potential moderators can be grouped into three categories: individual (personal) variables, job-related variables and organizational variables.

Potential Personal Moderators

As individuals can respond differently to stressful circumstances, job stress researchers have examined individual difference variables as possible moderators of the relationship between work-related stressors and psychological strain. A number of studies have focused on personality differences.

One personality variable which has received considerable attention is the behavioural style known as *Type A behaviour*, which is characterized as aggressive, ambitious, hard-driving, impatient, seeking to control and expressing time urgency (Cooper and Bramwell, 1992). Since its original investigation as a possible risk factor for coronary disorders (Rosenman, Friedman, Straus, Wurm, Kositchek, Hahn and Werthessen, 1964), several studies have shown that persons demonstrating Type A characteristics report higher levels of strain and are more likely to experience negative effects from job demands than do their Type B counterparts (Ganster and Schaubroeck, 1991; Haskins, Baglioni and Cooper, 1990). For instance, Froggatt and Cotton (1987) illustrated that Type A individuals create more strain for themselves by increasing the volume of their workload. Nevertheless, there is still debate about the mechanism by which the Type A behaviour style affects levels of psychological strain. While it is possible that Type A people subject themselves to more stressful work conditions (as suggested by Froggatt and Cotton's findings), it is also feasible that they appraise events as being more stressful than do Type B individuals, or that they utilize different methods for coping with strain. Further evidence is needed to establish the precise mechanism by which this variable moderates the relationship between job-related stressors and the experience of strain.

Another individual difference variable which may have a significant moderating effect on the stressor–strain relationship is a person's perceived *locus of control*. Kahn and Byosiere (1992) have noted that locus of control is an enduring individual characteristic which differentiates between people who assume that what happens to them is mostly under their personal control and people who believe that life events and occurrences are mostly determined by factors beyond their control. It would seem plausible to suggest that this variable might moderate the influence of stressors on individual well-being, and that individuals who believe they have control over life events will respond differently when exposed to work stressors than will those whose beliefs reflect predominantly external control. In particular, Ganster and Schaubroeck (1991) have reasoned that people with internal control beliefs will tend to adopt more active coping strategies when confronting stressors.

However, empirical research has not consistently demonstrated the moderating effects of locus of control. Kahn and Byosiere (1992) reviewed four studies that had considered this issue, three of which found a significant moderating influence for this variable. Other studies supporting this influence have been discussed by Ganster and Schaubroeck (1991). Sullivan and Bhagat (1992), on the other hand, present findings which suggest that the effects of control may vary between situations and types of stressor. We would also comment that it is important to distinguish between perceptions of 'personal' control and perceived 'situational' control, which refers to the extent to which a person has control over specific aspects of his or her work environment (see below).

A further variable that may be categorized under 'personal factors' is *hardiness*, which is defined as comprising a belief in personal control over life events, a commitment to internal control, challenge-seeking and high psychological or emotional resilience. This concept was introduced by Kobasa (see Kobasa, Maddi and Zola, 1983), who suggested that hardiness protects the individual from the impact of stressful experiences. While there has been limited research on this construct in work settings, Kobasa and colleagues observed that hardiness did act as a buffer in the stressor–strain relationship for male executives. In contrast, in a study by Manning, Williams and Wolfe (1988) hardiness exhibited direct effects only on the amount of strain experienced, and showed no moderating influence. As with locus of control, further research is needed before definitive conclusions can be drawn about the role of this variable.

Job-related Moderators

Although there are potentially many features of the job itself which may act as moderators of the association between work-related stressors and psychological strain, one which has received particular attention is *situational control*. As noted above, this refers to the extent to which individuals believe they can exert control over specific aspects of their job, such as the pace of work, procedures for task completion, scheduling of tasks and so on.

Much of the research on this issue stems from the work of Karasek and his associates (see Karasek, 1979), who proposed that strain develops from the combined influence of job demands (workload) and the extent of control over important decisions in the workplace (decision latitude). Where individuals have the capacity to influence decisions relevant to the completion of their job tasks, the level of strain due to a high workload is likely to be diminished. In other words, decision latitude ('situational control' in the preceding paragraph) is predicted by Karasek to serve as a moderator of the impact of job demands on psychological strain.

Other investigators have likewise suggested that greater control over the work environment alleviates the negative consequences of job demands (Murphy, 1988). For instance, Jackson (1983) conducted an evaluation of participative decision-making in an outpatient hospital setting, observing that increased participation led to more perceived influence and lower emotional distress. Pierce and Newstrom (1983) observed that having flexible work schedules (flexitime) also produced positive benefits for employees, including reductions in psychological stress symptoms. Finally, having greater autonomy in choosing how to complete job tasks has been associated with lower levels of strain. Wall and Clegg (1981), for example, conducted a longitudinal study of the effects of job redesign in which increases in work group autonomy were linked with significant improvements in employee mental health. The implication of these and other findings is that control over important aspects of the work environment may be a critical factor in reducing psychological strain due to work-related stressors; related themes are examined in Chapter 12.

Organizational Moderators

Earlier we mentioned that the structure and climate of an organization can influence the degree of strain experienced by employees. In addition, however, some features of an organization, such as its internal social environment, may also function as moderators of stress. Given the recognized importance of social relationships in the workplace, numerous studies have been conducted on the degree of *social support* which employees encounter, and there is some evidence that this variable may offset many of the negative effects of stressful environments (Cooper, 1987).

The direct (or main) effect of social support on psychological strain has been extensively researched, and there is consistent evidence that employees with greater access to support from others (their boss, colleagues, even subordinates) experience lower levels of strain (Beehr, 1985; Kahn and Byosiere, 1992). There have also been efforts to demonstrate a 'buffering' effect of support. That is, where an individual is faced with potentially stressful demands, conflicts and problems in the job, having support from others may reduce the impact of these pressures on that person's mental health or wellbeing. In short, social support may be thought to buffer or protect the individual from the negative consequences of work-related stressors.

Unfortunately, evidence for the mollifying influence of social support in work situations is very mixed (see a review by Beehr, King and King, 1990). Some investigations have indeed reported buffering effects, over and above any direct effect of support, whereas others have found no evidence of buffering. Yet other studies have obtained a 'reverse' buffering effect, in which the presence of social support exacerbates the amount of strain experienced by employees (Ganster, Fusilier and Mayes, 1986).

The type of buffering which occurs may depend on the nature of support provided to an individual. Practical and emotional support which assists the individual to cope with difficult and stressful circumstances may have a mitigating influence on psychological strain. In contrast, where collegial communication reinforces and confirms the difficulties and problems a person is experiencing in the work situation, it is likely that this would serve to increase, rather than reduce, the degree of strain reported. Recent studies (e.g., Fenlason and Beehr, 1994) have focused on the conditions under which different buffering effects of social support will be observed.

MANAGING EXCESSIVE STRESS

So far we have examined the nature of job-related stressors and the factors that can affect the degree of psychological strain that employees experience as a result of stressful work environments. For the remainder of this chapter we turn our attention to how people and organizations can deal with job-related strain, beginning first with individual coping strategies, then examining organization-level interventions.

Dewe, Cox and Ferguson (1993) have defined *coping* as 'cognitions and behaviours adopted by the individual following the recognition of a stressful encounter, that are in some way designed to deal with that encounter or its consequences' (p. 7). In essence, coping refers to the cognitive, behavioural and physiological responses that individuals engage in to (1) eliminate or reduce stressors in their environment, (2) alter their appraisal of the potential harmfulness of these stressors or (3) minimize the extent of strain that they will experience as a result of these stressors.

The coping process is a transaction between the individual and his or her environment, consisting of the following steps (Sethi and Schuler, 1984): primary appraisal (perception that a 'threat' to one's well-being has occurred); secondary appraisal (evaluation of what can be done to cope with the situation); selection of a coping response; implementation of that response; and, finally, evaluation of whether the response was effective in reducing the stressor or enabling the person to deal with it.

Appraisal represents a key element in the coping process (see Figure 7.3). Together, primary and secondary appraisals aim to determine the significance of an event or occurrence for the individual and what, if anything, can be done to minimize its impact (Lazarus and Folkman, 1984). This can be achieved in several ways, including self-appraisal using standardized instruments (for example, the Occupational Stress Indicator; Cooper, Sloan and Williams, 1988), or via employee counselling (Berridge and Cooper, 1993).

Research has uncovered a variety of responses that people engage in when confronted by work-related stressors. Lazarus and Folkman's (1984) typology of problem-focused versus emotion-focused strategies has served as a popular framework for understanding the diversity of these stress-coping behaviours. Problem-focused strategies concentrate on direct action to remove the stressor or to reduce its impact, while emotion-focused behaviours are those that attempt to minimize the psychological (emotional) effects of a stressor on the individual.

Edwards (1992) has described some of the primary mechanisms utilized by individuals to cope with job-related demands and pressures. In keeping with Lazarus and Folkman's notion of problem-focused coping, one important mechanism includes attempts to change the objective situation, to alter social information (for example, by de-emphasizing negative information) or to cognitively reconstruct reality (by distortion, repression or denial of undesirable aspects of the situation). A second mechanism involves the adjustment of desires to conform with perceptions (hence reducing any discrepancy between what one wants and what is available). This may be thought of as changing one's expectations. Thirdly, a person may downplay the importance of the discrepancy between desires and perceptions, making it less central to his or her well-being. This entails a cognitive reappraisal of the importance of an event. Finally, individuals may endeavour to enhance their overall physical and psychological well-being via regular exercise, diet or use of relaxation techniques, in order to avoid the negative effects of stressful work conditions. This final strategy is a form of proactive coping, whereas the three previous approaches represent strategies to cope with stressors as they arise.

Many instruments have been developed for studying coping processes (see reviews by Dewe *et al.*, 1993). The Lazarus and Folkman (1984) Ways of Coping questionnaire taps the extent to which a person uses problem-focused and emotion-focused coping behaviours, and is essentially a means of categorizing specific coping behaviours, such as planning and problem-solving, escape/avoidance, distancing oneself from the source of stress, and altering one's emotional response to stressful situations. The number of coping dimensions assessed by different methods varies from one or two to as many as twenty-eight, although several instruments (such as the Health and Daily Living Form; Billings and Moos, 1981) are based upon the Lazarus and Folkman typology.

While there are numerous ways of gauging how people cope with job-related stress, research on stress-coping has been plagued by conceptual and methodological difficulties which have impeded progress towards a complete understanding of the role of coping behaviours. A major concern is that many existing measures of coping were constructed from the investigator's assumptions about coping mechanisms and therefore may not assess how people actually respond in stressful situations (Dewe *et al.*, 1993; O'Driscoll and Cooper, 1994). This criticism has been levelled in particular at instruments that provide a predetermined list of coping responses and ask people to select those which they would use to counter stressors in their work environment. Under these circumstances, the relevance (to the respondent) of the coping responses provided is sometimes questionable.

There are also questions about whether individuals have preferred styles of coping which are stable across time and situations, or whether they adopt specific strategies in response to different stressful situations (Terry, 1994). Attempts to delineate global coping styles have been criticized as lacking a target or focus for coping behaviours (Edwards, 1988). In response to this criticism some studies have attempted to explore the relationship between coping behaviours and specific stressors (e.g., Firth-Cozens and Morrison, 1989; Wiersma, 1994). For instance, Firth-Cozens and Morrison (1989) found that pre-registration doctors identified dealing with death, senior doctors, personal mistakes and overload as major stressors; problem solving and asking for help were the behaviours most frequently initiated to deal with those stressors. Wiersma (1994) used critical incident analysis to identify sources of work–home role conflicts among dual-career couples, and linked these to specific coping behaviours. Conflict due to role overload was handled most often by obtaining support from non-family members, dividing tasks among family members, setting priorities, and cognitive reappraisal of the situation.

Some of the above strategies can be clearly categorized into the Lazarus and Folkman typology. Because they deal with the actual source of strain, problem-focused approaches could be more helpful in the long term than emotion-focused coping, which may have no direct effect on the environment with which the person has to cope.

However, there is no clear consensus on which modes of coping are consistently effective for particular stressors.

One final issue relevant to the consideration of individual coping responses is that there are many situations in which the individual has little control or influence over environmental variables. For example, in assembly-line operations the pace of work is normally determined by machine technology, and workers themselves have little control over this process (Smith, 1985). Pressures and demands which may arise in environments like these cannot be countered directly by individual action alone. In such situations, unless organizations modify work technologies and processes, there is little likelihood of reduction in the amount of psychological strain which employees experience as a result of aversive work environments.

ORGANIZATIONAL STRESS-MANAGEMENT INTERVENTIONS

Ivancevich, Matteson, Freedman and Phillips (1990) have pointed out that efforts to deal with work-related strain can target three different components of the stress cycle. Interventions can attempt to (1) reduce the number or intensity of stressors experienced by employees, (2) help employees modify their appraisal of the stressfulness of the situation or (3) help employees in coping more effectively with stressors and their consequences. A parallel description of approaches to stress management has been offered by Murphy (1988), who identified three levels of intervention: primary (reduction of stressors); secondary (stress-management training); and tertiary (employee assistance programmes, EAPs).

Most stress-management programmes focus attention predominantly on the individual (Murphy's secondary and tertiary levels), either assisting employees to reappraise the stressfulness of their work conditions or helping them to cope with job-related stressors. There is more concern in organizations with modifying employee cognitive appraisals of stressors and their consequences than with eliminating or reducing the actual stressors themselves (Kahn and Byosiere, 1992). Hence there is a predominance of programmes that offer training and counselling for employees experiencing strain,

213

rather than interventions that change the nature of the work, career structure or management styles.

Evidence for the efficacy of secondary interventions, in particular, is sparse and inconsistent (Cooper and Cartwright, 1994; Kahn and Byosiere, 1992). Stress-management training is often generic in nature, rather than targeting specific work-related stressors (Cooper and Payne, 1992), and there may be little preliminary diagnosis of the needs of employees or the organization (Ivancevich and Matteson, 1987). Employee assistance programmes, which typically revolve around counselling and support services for employees, have shown somewhat more promise as an approach to dealing with stressors (Berridge and Cooper, 1993), although again empirical evidence on their effectiveness is somewhat limited. Training or counselling employees to tolerate or cope with poorly designed jobs or organizations may yield short-term gains, but these approaches have questionable benefits for long-term mental health and well-being.

Despite the predominance of individual-level stress-management interventions, Elkin and Rosch (1990) have summarized a range of other strategies which entail changes at the broader organization level. These strategies include: redesigning tasks, redesigning the physical work environment, role definition and clarification, establishing more flexible work schedules, participative management, employee-centred career development programmes, providing feedback and social support for employees, and more equitable reward systems. Many of these approaches are directed towards increasing worker autonomy, participation and control, which we discussed earlier as potential moderators of the stressor–strain relationship. These approaches might be regarded as preventive measures (fitting into Murphy's category of primary interventions), rather than as treatments to reduce strain once it has developed.

Nevertheless, only a small handful of studies have been published that have assessed changes at the organization level. For instance, Ivancevich *et al.* (1990) found only four evaluations where organization-level interventions had been targeted. As discussed earlier in the chapter, Jackson (1983) examined the introduction of participative decision-making, Pierce and Newstrom (1983) studied the effects of more flexible work schedules, and Wall and Clegg (1981) investigated changes in work design that increased levels of autonomy. The fourth study was conducted by Murphy and Hurrell (1987), who explored the effects of introducing an employee representative committee whose function was to develop recommendations on stress management from surveys of employees.

In all of the above studies reductions in employee strain were observed as a result of the intervention. More recently, Burke (1993) summarized research on several organizational-level stress-management programmes, including (in addition to those reviewed by Ivancevich and his associates): goal setting (to enhance role definition and clarity), use of problem-solving to resolve work-related difficulties, reducing the amount of conflict between job demands and family responsibilities, and increasing communication and information-sharing between management and employees. With the exception of problem-solving groups, the above interventions appeared to yield positive benefits for employees. Burke suggested that the problem-solving groups investigated were not implemented as planned, which may have undermined their potential beneficial effects.

Overall, it would appear that there has been little systematic use of organizational interventions that might bring about significant reductions in psychological strain among employees. From a managerial standpoint, it may be more convenient to target stress-management interventions on individual perceptions and behaviours than on organizational or job redesign. Not only would programmes such as stress-management training and EAPs be viewed as less costly and more readily implemented than long-term restructuring or major changes in work practices, but they may also serve to deflect management from accepting responsibility for excessive strain experienced by their employees.

However, as noted by Burke (1993), among others, removal or reduction of stressors is 'the most direct way to reduce stress since it deals with the source' (p. 85). There is mounting evidence that job redesign interventions (especially those which increase employee control and autonomy), adoption of more consultative or participative management styles, development of clearer role descriptions, and utilization of more effective goal-setting and performance feedback systems can all enhance employee well-being and alleviate work-related strain. While these approaches may entail immediate costs for the organization and require greater commitment and effort from management, research suggests that these will be offset by long-term benefits not only for individual employees but also for the organization as a whole.

SUMMARY

Work-related stress is pervasive and costly, for organizations and individuals, so there has been considerable investigation of how stress is manifested and methods for coping with it, along with possible environmental changes which might remove (or at least reduce the impact of) work stressors. In this chapter we have discussed forms of strain in the workplace, especially burnout, and outlined how levels of strain might be assessed – for example, using questionnaires or physiological measures. Following this, we reviewed major sources of strain, including features intrinsic to the job, employees' roles in the organization, relationships at work, career development, the structure and climate of organization, and the interface between home and work. We also examined some of the factors which moderate (or buffer) the stressor–strain relationship, such as personal control and social support.

Many studies have been conducted on the management of excessive levels of stress. By and large these have concentrated on individual coping strategies, especially through Lazarus and Folkman's (1984) typology of problem-focused versus emotion-focused coping. There is increasing recognition, however, that some environmental factors cannot be influenced by individuals acting alone, and that greater attention must be given to organizational interventions. Ultimately, responsibility for stress management must be shared by all constituents of an organization. Individuals need to assume personal responsibility for their appraisal of situations and for the behaviour they engage in to cope with the demands and pressures that are an inevitable part of worklife. There is also an onus on management to design jobs and organizations in ways that enhance, rather than detract from, employee physical and mental health. A collaborative approach to dealing with sources of excessive stress will result in work environments that are both more productive for organizations and more 'healthy' for the people who work within them.

FURTHER READING

In addition to references cited throughout this chapter, recent reviews have been provided by Keita and Hurrell (1994) and Murphy (1995). The first of these covers the field broadly, and the second deals specifically with procedures for managing excessive stress in organizations.

REFERENCES

Barley, S. and Knight, D. (1992). Toward a cultural theory of stress complaints. *Research in Organizational Behavior*, 14, 1–48.

Beehr, T. (1985). Organizational stress and employee effectiveness: A job characteristics approach. In T. A. Beehr and R. S. Bhagat (eds.), *Human Stress and Cognition in Organizations: An Integrated Perspective*, pp. 375–398. New York: Wiley.

Beehr, T. (1987). The themes of social-psychological stress in work organizations: From roles to goals. In A. W. Riley and S. J. Zaccaro (eds.), *Occupational Stress and Organizational Effectiveness*, pp. 71–101. New York: Praeger.

Beehr, T. and Bhagat, R. (1985). Introduction to human stress and cognition in organizations. In T. A. Beehr and R. S. Bhagat (eds.), *Human Stress and Cognition in Organizations: An Integrated Perspective*, pp. 3–19. New York: Wiley.

Beehr, T. and Franz, T. (1987). The current debate about the meaning of job stress. *Journal of Organizational Behavior Management*, 8, 5–18.

Beehr, T., King, L. and King, D. (1990). Social support and occupational stress: Talking to supervisors. *Journal of Vocational Behavior*, 36, 61–81.

Beehr, T. and McGrath, J. (1992). Social support, occupational stress and anxiety. *Anxiety, Stress and Coping*, 5, 7–20.

Berridge, J. and Cooper, C. (1993). Stress and coping in US organizations: The role of the Employee Assistance Programme. *Work and Stress*, 7, 89–102.

Billings, A. G. and Moos, R. H. (1981). The role of coping responses and social resources in attenuating the stress of life events. *Journal of Behavioral Medicine*, 4, 139–157.

Burke, R. (1993). Organizational-level interventions to reduce occupational stressors. *Work and Stress*, 7, 77–87.

Burke, R. and Deszca, E. (1986). Correlates of psychological burnout phases among police officers. *Human Relations*, 39, 487–502.

Cannon, W. (1935). Stresses and strains of homeostasis. *American Journal of Medical Science*, 189, 1–14.

Cooper, C. (1987). The experience and management of stress: Job and organizational determinants. In A. W. Riley and S. J. Zaccaro (eds.), *Occupational Stress and Organizational Effectiveness*, pp. 53–69. New York: Praeger.

Cooper, C. and Bramwell, R. (1992). A comparative analysis of occupational stress in managerial and shopfloor workers in the brewing industry: Mental health, job satisfaction and sickness. *Work and Stress*, 6, 127–138.

Cooper, C. and Cartwright, S. (1994). Healthy mind; healthy organization – A proactive approach to occupational stress. *Human Relations*, 47, 455–471.

Cooper, C., Davidson, M. and Robinson, P. (1982). Stress in the police service. *Journal of Occupational Medicine*, 24, 30–36.

Cooper, C. and Kelly, M. (1993). Occupational stress in head teachers: A national UK study. *British Journal of Educational Psychology*, 63, 130–143.

Cooper, C. and Payne, R. (1992). International perspectives on research into work, well-being and stress management. In J. Quick, L. Murphy and J. Hurrell (eds.), *Stress and Well-being at Work: Assessments and Interventions for Occupational Mental Health,* pp. 348–368. Washington, DC: American Psychological Association.

Cooper, C. and Roden, J. (1985). Mental health and satisfaction among tax officers. *Social Science and Medicine*, 21, 747–751.

Cooper, C. L., Sloan, S. and Williams, S. (1988). *Occupational Stress Indicator: The Manual.* Windsor: NFER Nelson.

Cooper, C., Watts, J., Baglioni, A. and Kelly, M. (1988). Occupational stress among general practice dentists. *Journal of Occupational Psychology*, 61, 163–174.

Cordes, C. and Dougherty, T. (1993). A review and integration of research on job burnout. *Academy of Management Review*, 18, 621–656.

Cox, T. (1985). Repetitive work: Occupational stress and health. In C. L. Cooper and M. J. Smith (eds.), *Job Stress and Blue Collar Work*, pp. 85–112. Chichester: Wiley.

Crown, S. and Crisp, A. (1979). *Manual of the Crown-Crisp Experiential Index*. London: Hodder & Stoughton.

Cummings, T. G. and Cooper, C. L. (1979). A cybernetic framework for studying occupational stress. *Human Relations*, 32, 5, 395–418.

Davidson, M. and Cooper, C. (1993). Issues for the 1990's: Positive approaches to helping women into management. *Business and the Contemporary World*, 5 (3), 157–170.

Dewe, P., Cox, T. and Ferguson, E. (1993). Individual strategies for coping with stress at work: A review. *Work and Stress*, 7, 5–15.

Edwards, J. (1988). The determinants and consequences of coping with stress. In C. L. Cooper and R. Payne (eds.), *Causes, Coping and Consequences of Stress at Work*, pp. 233–263. New York: Wiley.

Edwards, J. (1992). A cybernetic theory of stress, coping and well-being in organizations. *Academy of Management Review*, 17, 238–274.

Edwards, J. and Cooper, C. (1990). The person–environment fit approach to stress: Recurring problems and some suggested solutions. *Journal of Organizational Behavior*, 11, 293–307.

Elkin, A. and Rosch, P. (1990). Promoting mental health at the workplace: The prevention side of stress management. *Occupational Medicine: State of the Art Review*, 5, 739–754.

Fenlason, K. and Beehr, T. (1994). Social support and occupational stress: Effects of talking to others. *Journal of Organizational Behavior*, 15, 157–175.

Firth-Cozens, J. and Morrison, L. (1989). Sources of stress and ways of coping in junior house officers. *Stress Medicine*, 5, 121–126.

Fletcher, B. (1988). The epidemiology of occupational stress. In C. L. Cooper and R. Payne (eds.), *Causes, Coping and Consequences of Stress at Work*, pp. 3–50. New York: Wiley.

French, J., Caplan, R. and Harrison, V. (1982). *The Mechanisms of Job Stress and Strain*. Chichester: Wiley.

Fried, Y., Rowland, K. and Ferris, G. (1984). The physiological measurement of work stress: A critique. *Personnel Psychology*, 37, 583–614.

Froggatt, K. and Cotton, J. (1987). The impact of Type A behavior pattern on role overload-induced stress and performance attributions. *Journal of Management*, 13, 87–98.

Frone, M., Russell, M. and Cooper, L. (1992). Antecedents and outcomes of work–family conflict: Testing a model of the work–family interface. *Journal of Applied Psychology*, 77, 65–78.

Ganster, D., Fusilier, M. and Mayes, B. (1986). Role of social support in the experience of stress at work. *Journal of Applied Psychology*, 71, 102–110.

Ganster, D. and Schaubroeck, J. (1991). Work stress and employee health. *Journal of Management*, 17, 235–271.

Goldberg, D. (1978). *Manual of the General Health Questionnaire*. London: Oxford University Press.

Golembiewski, R. and Munzenrider, R. (1988). *Phases of burnout: Developments in Concepts and Applications*. New York: Praeger.

Greenhaus, J., Parasuraman, S., Granrose, C., Rabinowitz, S. and Beutell,

N. (1989). Sources of work–family conflict among dual-career couples. *Journal of Vocational Behavior*, 34, 133–153.

Guzley, R. (1992). Organizational climate and communication climate: Predictors of commitment to the organization. *Management Communication Quarterly*, 5, 379–402.

Haskins, M., Baglioni, A. and Cooper, C. (1990). An investigation of the sources, moderators and psychological symptoms of stress among audit seniors. *Contemporary Accounting Research*, 6, 361–385.

Hendrix, W., Ovalle, N. and Troxler, R. (1985). Behavioral and physiological consequences of stress and its antecedent factors. *Journal of Applied Psychology*, 70, 188–201.

Ivancevich, J. and Matteson, M. (1987). Organizational level stress management interventions: A review and recommendations. *Journal of Organizational Behavior Management*, 8, 229–248.

Ivancevich, J., Matteson, M., Freedman, S. and Phillips, J. (1990). Worksite stress management interventions. *American Psychologist*, 45, 252–261.

Jackson, S. (1983). Participation in decision making as a strategy for reducing job-related strain. *Journal of Applied Psychology*, 68, 3–19.

Jackson, S. and Schuler, R. (1983). Preventing employee burnout. *Personnel*, 60 (2), 58–68.

Jackson, S. and Schuler, R. (1985). A meta-analysis and conceptual critique of research on role ambiguity and role conflict in work settings. *Organizational Behavior and Human Decision Processes*, 36, 16–78.

Jackson, S., Schwab, R. and Schuler, R. (1986). Toward an understanding of the burnout phenomenon. *Journal of Applied Psychology*, 71, 63–640.

Jackson, S., Turner, J. and Brief, A. (1987). Correlates of burnout among public service lawyers. *Journal of Occupational Behaviour*, 8, 339–349.

Kahn, R. and Byosiere, P. (1992). Stress in organizations. In M. Dunnette and L. Hough (eds.), *Handbook of Industrial and Organizational Psychology* (2nd edn), vol. 3, pp. 571–650. Palo Alto, Calif.: Consulting Psychologists Press.

Kahn, R., Wolfe, D., Quinn, R. and Snoek, J. (1964). *Organizational Stress: Studies in Role Conflict and Ambiguity*. New York: Wiley.

Karasek, R. (1979). Job demands, job decision latitude, and mental strain: Implications for job redesign. *Administrative Science Quarterly*, 24, 285–308.

Keita, G. and Hurrell, J. (eds.) (1994). *Job Stress in a Changing Workforce*. Washington DC: American Psychological Association.

Kobasa, S., Maddi, S. and Zola, M. (1983). Type A and hardiness. *Journal of Behavioral Medicine*, 6, 41–51.

Kozlowski, S. W. J., Chao, G. T., Smith, E. M. and Hedlung, J. (1993).

Organizational downsizing: Strategies, interventions and research implications. In C. L. Cooper and I. T. Robertson (eds.), *International Review of Industrial and Organizational Psychology,* vol. 8, pp. 263–332. Chichester: Wiley.

Lazarus, R., Deese, J. and Osler, S. (1952). The effects of psychological stress on performance. *Psychological Bulletin,* 48, 293–315.

Lazarus, R. and Folkman, S. (1984). *Stress, Appraisal and Coping.* New York: Springer Publications.

Lee, R. and Ashforth, B. (1993). A further examination of managerial burnout: Toward an integrated model. *Journal of Organizational Behavior,* 14, 3–20.

Leiter, M. and Maslach, C. (1988). The impact of interpersonal environment on burnout and organizational commitment. *Journal of Organizational Behavior,* 9, 297–308.

Manning, M., Williams, R. and Wolfe, D. (1988). Hardiness and the relationship between stressors and outcomes. *Work and Stress,* 2, 205–216.

Maslach, C. (1982). *Burnout: The cost of caring.* Englewood Cliffs, NJ: Prentice Hall.

Maslach, C. and Jackson, S. (1981, 2nd edn 1986). *The Maslach Burnout Inventory.* Palo Alto, Calif.: Consulting Psychologists Press.

Matteson, M. and Ivancevich, J. (1987). *Controlling Work Stress: Effective Human Resource and Management Strategies.* San Francisco: Jossey-Bass.

McGrath, J. (1976). Stress and behavior in organizations. In M. Dunnette, (ed.), *Handbook of Industrial and Organizational Psychology,* pp. 1351–1395. Chicago: Rand McNally.

Monk, T. and Tepas, D. (1985). Shift work. In C. L. Cooper and M. J. Smith (eds.), *Job Stress and Blue Collar Work,* pp. 65–84. Chichester: Wiley.

Motowidlo, S., Packard, J. and Manning, M. (1986). Occupational stress: Its causes and consequences for job performance. *Journal of Applied Psychology,* 71, 618–629.

Murphy, K. (1995). Occupational stress management: Current states and future directions. In C. Cooper and D. Rousseau (eds.) *Trends in Organizational Behavior,* vol. 2, pp. 1–14. Chichester: Wiley.

Murphy, L. (1988). Workplace interventions for stress reduction and prevention. In C. L. Cooper and R. Payne (eds.), *Causes, Coping and Consequences of Stress at Work,* pp. 301–339. New York: Wiley.

Murphy, L. and Hurrell, J. (1987). Stress management in the process of organizational stress reduction. *Journal of Managerial Psychology,* 2, 18–23.

O'Driscoll, M. (1987). Attitudes to the job and the organization among new recruits: Influence of perceived job characteristics and organizational structure. *Applied Psychology: An International Review*, 36, 133–145.

O'Driscoll, M. and Beehr, T. (1994). Supervisor behaviors, role stressors and uncertainty as predictors of personal outcomes for subordinates. *Journal of Organizational Behavior*, 15, 141–155.

O'Driscoll, M. and Cooper, C. (1994). Coping with work-related stress: A critique of existing measures and proposal for an alternative methodology. *Journal of Occupational and Organizational Psychology*, 67, 343–354.

O'Driscoll, M. and Evans, R. (1988). Organizational factors and perceptions of climate in three psychiatric units. *Human Relations*, 41, 371–388.

O'Driscoll, M., Ilgen, D. and Hildreth, K. (1992). Time devoted to job and off-job activities, interrole conflict and affective experiences. *Journal of Applied Psychology*, 77, 272–279.

Organ, D. and Greene, C. (1981). The effects of formalization on professional involvement: A compensatory process approach. *Administrative Science Quarterly*, 26, 237–252.

Pearce, J. (1981). Bringing some clarity to role ambiguity research. *Academy of Management Review*, 6, 665–674.

Pennebaker, J. and Watson, D. (1988). Self-reports and physiological measures in the workplace. In J. Hurrell, L. Murphy, S. Sauter and C. Cooper (eds.), *Occupational Stress: Issues and Developments in Research*, pp. 184–199. New York: Taylor & Francis.

Pierce, J. and Newstrom, J. (1983). The design of flexible work schedules and employee responses: Relationships and processes. *Journal of Occupational Behaviour*, 4, 247–262.

Podsakoff, P., Williams, L. and Todor, W. (1986). Effects of organizational formalization on alienation among professionals and nonprofessionals. *Academy of Management Journal*, 29, 820–831.

Rabinowitz, W., Falkenbach, K., Travers, J., Valentine, C. and Weener, P. (1983). Worker motivation: Unsolved problem or untapped resource. *California Management Review*, 25 (2), 48–53.

Rosenman, R., Friedman, M., Straus, R., Wurm, M., Kositchek, R., Hahn, W. and Werthessen, N. (1964). A predictive study of coronary heart disease. *Journal of the American Medical Association*, 232, 872–877.

Schaubroeck, J., Cotton, J. and Jennings, K. (1989). Antecedents and consequences of role stress: A covariance structure analysis. *Journal of Organizational Behavior*, 10, 35–58.

Selye, H. (1936). A syndrome produced by diverse noxious agents. *Nature*, 138, 32.

Sethi, A. and Schuler, R. (1984). *Handbook of Organizational Stress Coping Strategies*. Cambridge, Mass.: Ballinger.

Shinn, M., Rosario, M., Morch, H. and Chestnut, D. (1984). Coping with job stress and burnout in the human services. *Journal of Personality and Social Psychology*, 46, 864–876.

Shirom, A. (1986, July). Does stress lead to affective strain, or vice versa? A structural regression test. Paper presented at Twenty-First Congress of the International Association of Applied Psychology, Jerusalem.

Sigman, A. (1992). The state of corporate health care. *Personnel Management*, February, 24–31.

Smith, M. (1985). Machine-paced work and stress. In C. L. Cooper and M. J. Smith (eds.), *Job Stress and Blue Collar Work*, pp. 51–64. Chichester: Wiley.

Sullivan, S. and Bhagat, R. (1992). Organizational stress, job satisfaction and job performance: Where do we go from here? *Journal of Management*, 18, 353–374.

Sutherland, V. and Cooper, C. (1992). Job stress, satisfaction and mental health among general practitioners before and after introduction of a new contract. *British Medical Journal*, 304, 1545–1548.

Terry, D. (1994). Determinants of coping: The role of stable and situational factors. *Journal of Personality and Social Psychology*, 66, 895–910.

Wall, T. and Clegg, C. (1981). A longitudinal study of work group design. *Journal of Occupational Behaviour*, 2, 31–49.

Warr, P. (1987). *Work, Unemployment and Mental Health*. Oxford: Oxford University Press.

Warr, P. (1990). The measurement of well-being and other aspects of mental health. *Journal of Occupational Psychology*, 63, 193–210.

Wiersma, U. (1994). A taxonomy of behavioural strategies for coping with work–home role conflict. *Human Relations*, 47, 211–221.

8

Employee Well-being

Peter Warr

The outcome variables examined by psychologists in work settings are of two general kinds, concerned with aspects of performance or of employee well-being. This chapter provides an overview in respect of the second of those outcomes. What are the principal types of employee well-being, what are their main determinants, how are they related to performance, and how can they be measured?

Studies of well-being examine people's feelings, about themselves and the settings in which they live and work. It is important to distinguish between specific forms of well-being and feelings about one's life that are more general. The specific form of primary concern in this book is 'job-specific' well-being, people's feelings about themselves in relation to their job. 'Context-free' well-being has a much broader focus, covering feelings irrespective of any particular setting. Of intermediate scope is 'non-job' well-being, that experienced on average in all settings apart from one's job. These distinctions will be used throughout the chapter.

PRINCIPAL AXES OF WELL-BEING

Well-being of all kinds is often viewed along a single dimension, roughly from feeling bad to feeling good. Such a dimension can, of course, capture important feelings, but it is preferable to think in terms of a two-dimensional framework of the kind set out in Figure 8.1. This has been substantiated in many investigations (e.g., Matthews, Jones and Chamberlain, 1990; Watson, Clark and Tellegen, 1988), which have pointed to the importance of two independent dimensions of feeling, here labelled as 'pleasure' and 'arousal'.

We may describe a person's well-being in terms of its location

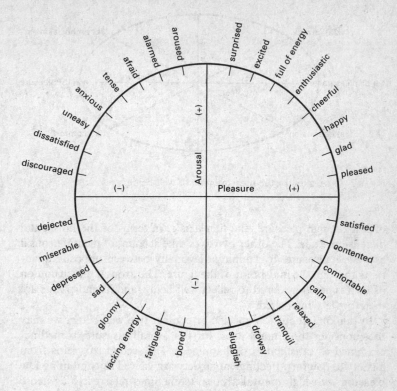

Fig. 8.1 A two-dimensional view of well-being.

relative to those two dimensions (representing the *content* of feelings) and its distance from the mid-point of the figure (such that a more distant location indicates a greater *intensity*). A particular degree of pleasure or displeasure may be accompanied by high or low levels of mental arousal, and a particular quantity of mental arousal (sometimes referred to as 'activation') may be either pleasurable or unpleasurable. A person's well-being may thus be described in terms of those two dimensions.

Within this framework, three principal axes of measurement are illustrated in Figure 8.2. In view of the central importance of feelings

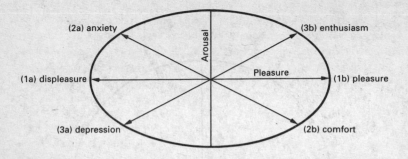

Fig. 8.2 Three axes for the measurement of well-being.

of low or high pleasure, the first axis is in terms of the horizontal dimension alone. The other two axes take account of mental arousal as well as pleasure, by running diagonally between opposite quadrants through the mid-point of the figure. The arousal dimension on its own is not considered to reflect well-being, and its end-points are therefore left unlabelled.

In thinking about job-specific or context-free well-being, we may thus consider three main axes. First is overall pleasure, sometimes examined as satisfaction or happiness. The second axis runs from anxiety to comfort. Feelings of anxiety are viewed as combining low pleasure with high mental arousal (sometimes referred to as 'tense arousal'), whereas comfort is illustrated as low-arousal pleasure. Third is the axis from depression to enthusiasm. Feelings of enthusiasm are in the top-right quadrant, and depression and sadness (low pleasure and low arousal) are at the other end of the axis. A person may be characterized in terms of his or her location on each of the axes, which are, of course, intercorrelated because of the central importance of feelings of pleasure (the horizontal dimension).

Job-specific and Context-free Well-being

What is known about the association between a person's job-specific well-being and his or her more general well-being? This has frequently been investigated in terms of the statistical relationship between overall job satisfaction and overall life satisfaction; the correlation coefficient is on average found to be about +0.35 (Tait, Padgett and Baldwin, 1989). Some overlap is, of course, in part logically necessary, since feelings about a job are themselves one component of wider life satisfaction; it appears that no studies have asked separately about 'non-job' satisfaction in relation to job-specific feelings.

Research has sought to identify the pattern of causality in this relationship: does job satisfaction cause life satisfaction, or vice versa? A longitudinal investigation by Judge and Watanabe (1993) indicated that the pattern was one of mutual causation, but that the effect from life satisfaction to job satisfaction was greater than in the other direction (see also Judge and Locke, 1993). A person's overall well-being has strong influence on his or her job-specific well-being, and job well-being also affects wider feelings.

These overlaps have been examined in terms of the 'spillover' from job to home and from home to work. For example, in a study of male employees Piotrkowski (1978) described cases of positive spillover, where a husband enjoyed his work and experienced feelings of self-enhancement from the working day; such a person came home cheerful and both emotionally and interpersonally available to his family. On the other hand, some husbands were tired, irritable and emotionally non-responsive after a day's work, and family members had to work hard to engage them in domestic and social activities. Taking the reverse perspective, Crouter (1984) focused particularly on family-to-work spillover. She showed that both positive and negative influences from family experience were widespread, particularly for mothers of young children.

It is thus likely that the relations between job-specific and context-free well-being will vary between individuals, within the framework of an overall positive and reciprocal association. For example, Bamundo and Kopelman (1980) found that the association was stronger for high-income, more educated and self-employed individuals. Examining findings reported over a period of some forty years, Tait *et al.* (1989) looked specifically at differences between men and women. Prior to 1974 the correlation between job satisfaction and life satisfaction for women was quite low (+0.16), but thereafter it increased to the level found for men (+0.31). This increase may be due to a greater centrality of paid employment to women in more recent years; see Chapter 10.

Differences between employees with relatively high or low personal involvement in their paid work have been studied by Steiner and Truxillo (1989). They hypothesized that job satisfaction and life satisfaction would be more strongly intercorrelated among those people with higher work involvement than among others. Such a pattern was found.

So far, three forms of well-being have been identified as important for this chapter (job-specific, context-free and non-job) and three measurement axes have been defined for each. In relation to the most commonly studied axis (number 1 in Figure 8.2), the association between job and life satisfaction has been shown to be bidirectional.

Components of Job Satisfaction

The nature and degree of people's satisfaction with their jobs have been examined in many thousand research investigations. In some cases, especially in nationwide surveys, a single question has been asked, such as 'All in all, how satisfied would you say you are with your job?' However, in most settings multiple-item questionnaires have been used to obtain more reliable estimates. Several of those are illustrated at the end of the chapter.

Just as the focus of job-specific satisfaction is narrower than that of context-free satisfaction, so may we identify within job satisfaction itself several levels of specificity. The most general construct is 'overall job satisfaction', the extent to which a person is satisfied with his or her job as a whole. More focused 'facet-specific' satisfactions concern different aspects of a job, such as one's pay, colleagues, supervisors, working conditions, job security, promotion prospects, the company and the nature of the work undertaken. Different facet-specific satisfactions tend to be positively intercorrelated, and satisfaction with one (the nature of the work undertaken) is particularly closely associated with other facet-specific satisfactions and with overall job satisfaction.

At an intermediate level of abstractness is the distinction between 'intrinsic' and 'extrinsic' job satisfaction. 'Intrinsic' satisfaction covers satisfaction with features inherent in the conduct of the job itself: opportunity for personal control or the utilization of skills, amount of task variety, and so on. 'Extrinsic' job satisfaction concerns aspects of a job that form the background to work activities themselves: satisfaction with pay, working conditions, job security, industrial relations procedures, etc. Intrinsic and extrinsic satisfaction scores are positively intercorrelated, but the conceptual distinction between them is sometimes important; that will be illustrated later.

ENVIRONMENTAL DETERMINANTS OF WELL-BEING

Much psychological research has investigated links between specific aspects of a person's work environment and his or her well-being, usually that which is job-specific rather than context-free. Studies of particular job characteristics and the reactions of employees are illustrated in Chapters 7, 12 and 13.

Job features which may affect one or more of the three axes of job-related well-being have been classified by Warr (1987, 1994) in terms of nine main groups, as follows. In each case below, a principal label is accompanied by other terms which are common in the literature.

1. *Opportunity for personal control*: employee discretion, decision latitude, autonomy, absence of close supervision, self-determination, participation in decision-making.

2. *Opportunity for skill use*: skill utilization, utilization of valued abilities, required skills.

3. *Externally generated goals*: job demands, task demands, quantitative or qualitative workload, attentional demand, demands relative to resources, role responsibility, conflicting demands, role conflict, normative requirements.

4. *Variety*: variation in job content and location, non-repetitive work, skill variety.

5. *Environmental clarity*: (a) information about the consequences of behaviour, task feedback; (b) information about the

future, absence of job future ambiguity, absence of job insecurity; (c) information about required behaviour, low role ambiguity.

6. *Availability of money*: income level, amount of pay, financial resources.

7. *Physical security*: absence of danger, good working conditions, ergonomically adequate equipment, safe levels of temperature and noise.

8. *Opportunity for interpersonal contact*: (a) quantity of interaction, contact with others, social density, adequate privacy; (b) quality of interaction, good relationships with others, social support, good communications.

9. *Valued social position*: (a) wider evaluations of status in society, social rank, occupational prestige; (b) more localized evaluations of in-company status or job importance; (c) personal evaluations of task significance, valued role incumbency, meaningfulness of job, self-respect from job.

Specific variables within each of those groups have been shown to be significantly associated with the three axes of job-specific well-being described above (e.g., Warr, 1987). Some job characteristics are more predictive of one form of well-being than others. For example, a very high level of job demands (group 3 above) is more strongly associated with low well-being on axis two (anxiety) than on axis three (depression); however, for very low opportunity for personal control (group 1, above) the opposite is the case (Warr, 1990a). Although most research has been cross-sectional, correlating job features and well-being at a single point in time, causal interpretation has been supported by longitudinal studies showing that changes in job conditions lead to predicted changes in well-being (e.g., Martin and Wall, 1989). There is no doubt that job features can have a strong impact on job-specific well-being.

In a similar manner, features in a person's non-job environment (family, social and spare-time activities) can influence well-being. A question of importance here concerns the relationship between job features and *context-free* well-being: do jobs have a wider impact upon the feelings of employees outside their work? The strong correlation between job satisfaction and life satisfaction (above) suggests that they do, and some research has examined the association between specific job features and context-free well-being. Significant linkages of that kind have been demonstrated (e.g., Martin and Wall, 1989).

Is that association of job features with context-free well-being direct or indirect? Job characteristics might influence both job-specific and context-free well-being directly; or a job might have its direct effect only on job-specific feelings, and these might subsequently spill over into wider well-being. This question has been addressed through techniques of statistical path analysis, and it appears that the major path is through job well-being itself (Kelloway and Barling, 1991). The effect of a job on wider forms of well-being is principally indirect, being mediated by its previous impact on job-specific well-being.

A MODEL OF WELL-BEING AND ITS DETERMINANTS

The pattern of findings outlined so far may be viewed in terms of the schematic model shown in Figure 8.3. At the centre of the diagram are two boxes containing titles of the three axes of job-specific and context-free well-being. The double-headed arrow between those boxes represents the bidirectional causality identified earlier: feelings at work and feelings outside work influence each other in a mutual fashion. At the bottom of the figure are characteristics of job and non-job environments. These are suggested, by the two upward-pointing arrows, to bear upon job-specific and context-free well-being, directly in their own domain but also indirectly influencing the other form of well-being, as shown by the horizontal arrow between the two upper boxes.

As summarized earlier, all these relationships have been supported in studies of people at work. Research has traditionally been restricted to the four lower boxes of the diagram, in that, for instance, determinants of job satisfaction have been sought in the characteristics of a person's job. As indicated earlier and in other chapters, this influence from job features has frequently been demonstrated.

However, the environment is only one of the factors affecting how

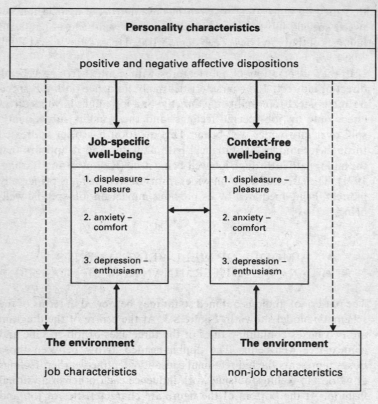

Fig. 8.3 Principal aspects of well-being, with determinants in the person and the environment.

we feel. It is also essential to include in the model certain personality dispositions, which can themselves influence the level of an individual's well-being. This is indicated by the box at the top of Figure 8.3.

PERSONALITY DETERMINANTS OF WELL-BEING

Recent research has examined the nature and consequences of two main 'affective dispositions', typically referred to as personality traits of 'negative affectivity' and 'positive affectivity'. These reflect pervasive individual differences in emotional style and feelings about oneself, and both traits have a general influence on a person's affective (emotional) responses to features and events in the environment. Scores on measures of the two dispositions are only moderately (negatively) correlated with each other (about -0.25; Cropanzano, James and Konovsky, 1993; Elliott, Chartrand and Harkins, 1994; George, 1989; Watson and Pennebaker, 1989; Watson and Slack, 1993).

Watson and Clark (1984) illustrate how the personality trait of negative affectivity (NA) embraces a broad range of aversive emotional states, such that people with high negative affectivity are more likely than others to experience raised levels of distress and dissatisfaction in any circumstances. High-NA individuals tend to focus on the negative side of themselves and the world in general; they scan the environment for impending trouble, and they experience anxiety about what they see. On the other hand, low-NA individuals are more likely to feel secure and be satisfied with their environments. Questionnaire items representing high negative affectivity include self-descriptions as nervous, worrying and overly sensitive (e.g., Levin and Stokes, 1989; Watson and Slack, 1993).

On the other hand, the trait of positive affectivity (PA) is seen in high levels of energy, excitement and enthusiasm. High-PA individuals tend to lead more active lives than low-PA people and to view their environments in a positive fashion. Questionnaire items to tap dispositional positive affectivity cover feelings of happiness, enthusiasm, energy and interest in life.

In general, personality 'traits' are liable to be reflected in a person's 'state' when he or she is in a trait-relevant situation. Affective well-being experienced at one point in time is a form of 'state', and well-being axes two and three in Figure 8.2 are in practice state measures of trait negative affectivity and trait positive affectivity respectively; the content of the constructs remains the same between trait and state, but the time-frame is different. This means that persons with high trait negative affectivity (NA) are expected to be in a more anxious state than others when in work situations (that is, to exhibit lower job-specific well-being on axis two in Figure 8.2), and that individuals with high trait positive affectivity (PA) are likely to have raised job-related scores on axis three. Are these expectations supported by research findings?

Personality Dispositions and Job-specific Well-being

Consider first studies of job-specific well-being. It is clear that trait negative affectivity (NA) is significantly predictive of low job well-being on axis two (from anxious to comfortable). For example, Brief, Burke, George, Robinson and Webster (1988) measured trait NA through an established personality scale and negative affect at work during the past week by a separate questionnaire, finding a correlation of +0.57. George (1989) recorded a value of +0.34, using a more comprehensive measure of personality. Elliott *et al.* (1994) reported a median correlation of +0.45 between trait NA and reports of recent emotional distress at work.

Studies of positive affectivity (PA) and the third axis of job-related well-being (from depressed to enthusiastic) also show that trait PA is significantly associated with short-term feelings of that kind in a job setting (e.g., George, 1989). However, this trait–state effect is specific to its own axis of well-being (either two or three in Figure 8.2). For example, George (1989) found that, although the correlation between trait negative affectivity and job well-being on axis two (the relevant axis, from anxiety to comfort) was +0.34, the coefficient was only −0.03 for axis three (from depression to enthusiasm).

Several investigations have examined people's overall job satisfaction (axis one) as a function of these dispositional measures. In keeping with its intermediate position as the horizontal axis in Figure 8.2, this form of job-related well-being is expected to be moderately positively correlated with trait PA and moderately negatively correlated with negative affectivity. Median values are in fact +0.31 from four studies of positive affectivity, and −0.26 from seven studies of negative affectivity (Agho, Mueller, and Price, 1993; Brief *et al.*, 1988; Chen and Spector, 1991; Cropanzano *et al.*, 1993; Levin and Stokes, 1989; Schaubroeck, Ganster, and Fox, 1992; Watson and Slack, 1993). However, it has also been found that this association varies between intrinsic and extrinsic satisfactions. In research into specific facet satisfactions, Judge and Locke (1993) and Watson and

Slack (1993) reported that trait PA and trait NA were more highly associated with (intrinsic) satisfaction with the nature of work undertaken (medians of $+0.39$ and -0.35 respectively) than with (extrinsic) satisfactions with pay, promotion, supervision or co-workers (medians of $+0.18$ and -0.24 for PA and NA respectively) (see also Necowitz and Roznowski, 1994).

There is thus sound empirical support for the vertical arrow in Figure 8.3 from affective dispositions to job-specific well-being, especially its more intrinsic aspects. Furthermore, some studies have examined together that downward arrow to well-being and also the one upward from job characteristics, finding in multivariate analyses that both sets of features contribute significantly to job well-being (e.g., Agho *et al.*, 1993; Watson and Slack, 1993). Levin and Stokes (1989) showed that the impact of job characteristics was stronger than that of trait negative affectivity.

People's feelings about their work are thus a function both of that work itself and also of their own personality. In modifying aspects of a job in order to influence well-being, variations in employees' cross-situational dispositions will therefore limit the magnitude of resulting changes in well-being; job redesign is important in enhancing well-being, but its impact will be tempered by employees' continuing dispositions. However, systematic information is lacking about the relative importance of the two influences after experimental interventions to change the design of jobs.

The importance of these cross-situational affective dispositions suggests that job satisfaction and other indicators of job-related well-being should be relatively stable across time. That is indeed the case. For example, Staw and Ross (1985) showed that, for people remaining with the same employer across either two or five years, test–retest correlations for overall job satisfaction were $+0.47$ and $+0.37$ respectively. For employees who changed both their occupation and their employer over those periods, correlations remained as high as $+0.33$ and $+0.19$ respectively.

This long-term stability of job satisfaction was further examined by Arvey, Bouchard, Segal and Abraham (1989), who raised the question whether variations in satisfaction might in part be inherited. They reported data from thirty-four pairs of monozygotic twins who had been reared apart. Those individuals completed the short form of the Minnesota Satisfaction Questionnaire (see later), and statistical analyses were applied to determine how far their genetic similarity could account for the pattern of responses. The investigators concluded that approximately 30 per cent of variance in overall job satisfaction was attributable to genetic factors. This conclusion was supported in a much larger investigation, with more than 2,200 pairs of monozygotic and dizygotic twins, carried out by Arvey, McCall, Bouchard, Taubman and Cavanaugh (1994). The precise magnitude of the effect of heredity is open to dispute (for a range of methodological reasons; see Cropanzano and James, 1990), but some genetic influence on job satisfaction appears to occur through inherited aspects of broader personality dispositions.

Personality Dispositions and Context-free Well-being

What about the relationship between personality and wider forms of well-being (the right-hand side of Figure 8.3)? Although specifically *non-job* feelings have rarely been investigated, associations of the kind illustrated in the previous section have often been demonstrated for *context-free* well-being. For example, Costa and McCrae (1980) examined the two continuing affective dispositions in terms of trait neuroticism and extroversion. They found significant correlations between trait neuroticism and recent negative affect, and between trait extroversion and reports of recent positive affect. (However, as with job-specific well-being, above, the correlations were negligible between each aspect of personality and the *other* index of recent affect.) Furthermore, that pattern was also found in predictions from the two personality dispositions measured ten years previously.

In the case of both job-specific and context-free well-being, research has so far emphasized these two aspects of personality. Trait negative affectivity and trait positive affectivity, as studied in relation to job-related well-being (see above), are highly correlated with neuroticism and extroversion respectively. There is no doubt that these two traits are reflected in transient states in particular situations. However, we do not know whether other aspects of personality might be similarly associated with differences in well-being.

Personality Dispositions and the Environment

The relationships in Figure 8.3 between well-being, environmental features and personality are thus supported by the findings from research. Continuous lines in that diagram, representing probable causal influences, have been discussed so far, but two dotted lines are also shown: from personality to job characteristics and to non-job characteristics. Those lines are dotted rather than continuous to indicate that they should be interpreted not causally but primarily in terms of an influence upon the way environmental features are *perceived*.

This effect has been investigated mainly in respect of trait negative (rather than positive) affectivity. Consistent with the fact that high-NA people are typically anxious and prone to scan their environments for potentially threatening features, it has been shown that negative affectivity is associated with perceptions of more stressful characteristics in jobs and elsewhere (e.g., Brief *et al.*, 1988; Burke, Brief and George, 1993; Chen and Spector, 1991; Elliott *et al.*, 1994; Levin and Stokes, 1989).

The dotted lincs in Figure 8.3 also point to another possibility. It may be that personality has a causal impact on behaviour, which in turn affects well-being. For instance, positive affectivity might influence the settings that a person enters or within which he or she remains. Alternatively, people with high negative affectivity might generate more stress in their environment than do low-NA individuals. More research across time is needed to explore these possible sequential forms of influence from personality to well-being.

WELL-BEING AND PERFORMANCE

So far the chapter has described three axes of job-specific well-being (job satisfaction, job-related feelings ranging from anxiety to comfort, and job-related feelings from depression to enthusiasm) and explored their origins in the characteristics of a job and an individual's personality. What about their associations with job performance? It is sometimes suggested that employees with greater well-being will be the higher performers.

Even if such an association were found, the direction of causality would remain unclear. It would not necessarily be the case that (say) high job satisfaction causes high performance. The opposite might be true: high performers might be more satisfied as a result of their effective work. Alternatively, a third factor (or several of them) might bring about both high performance and high satisfaction. For instance, particular equipment characteristics or managerial behaviour might enhance both performance and satisfaction. Note also that job performance is determined by a range of different factors (organizational policies, management practices, group pressures, individual abilities, etc.), so that the maximum possible correlation with well-being alone is expected to be much less than +1.00.

Recognizing the causal ambiguity of correlations, let us review what is known in respect of the three axes of job-related well-being. Iaffaldano and Muchinsky (1985) provided a meta-analysis of previous studies of job performance (usually supervisor ratings) and job satisfaction (axis one in Figure 8.2). They found that multiple-item measures of overall job satisfaction were significantly positively associated with performance (the average coefficient was +0.25). Stronger associations with good performance were found for intrinsic satisfaction than for extrinsic satisfaction.

Petty, McGee and Cavender (1984) reported very similar findings for overall job satisfaction (the average correlation was +0.23), but also noted that the association of satisfaction with performance was stronger for managerial and professional employees than for others (average correlations of +0.31 and +0.15 respectively). A median correlation of +0.25 was recorded by Shore and Martin (1989), and that value has also been found for teachers' overall job satisfaction in relation to the amount of additional (unpaid) time they devoted to work-related activities (Gechman and Wiener, 1975).

Ostroff (1992) examined this association at the level of entire organizations, predicting that those with more satisfied employees will be more productive than others. In a study of 298 schools, standardized measures of academic performance, administrative efficiency and student behaviour were found to be significantly associated with teachers' overall job satisfaction (an average coefficient of +0.28). This pattern was retained after statistical controls were introduced for differences between the schools in student characteristics and the resources available.

What about axis two, from feelings of job-related anxiety to comfort? It seems likely that employees who report more anxiety and strain might be experiencing difficulty in coping with job demands and thus performing relatively less effectively; a negative association between job-related tension and job performance is thus probable. Very few investigations have examined this question, but the expectation does appear to be supported. Jamal (1984) found that higher levels of job-related tension were associated with lower supervisory ratings (a median correlation of −0.35). Spector, Dwyer and Jex (1988) reported a correlation of −0.18.

An alternative hypothesis is in terms of a possible optimal amount of challenge, with lower performances occurring either side of that optimum. It may be the case that the relationship between job tension and performance is one of an inverted-U, such that moderate demands are linked to raised but manageable tension and also to high performance, but that both lower and higher levels of tension (and of job demands) are accompanied by lower performance. Anderson (1976) suggested that this was the case in data from a sample of small-business owners, but the possibility remains in need of more substantial examination.

The third axis of job-specific well-being in Figure 8.2 ranges from depression to enthusiasm. It appears likely that employees with positive feelings of this active kind will be among the more productive, with the association being caused in multiple ways as illustrated above. However, this form of well-being has rarely been investigated. Limited support comes from George's (1991) finding of a correlation of +0.26 with supervisors' ratings of salespeople's helpful customer behaviour; however, the correlation with actual sales performance was only +0.10.

Another index of employee performance is in terms of absenteeism (or its converse, attendance at work). Such behaviour is determined by a range of factors. In addition to sickness itself, social and family pressures can affect decisions to attend (e.g., Brooke and Price, 1989; Nicholson, 1977). Organizational influences include specific policies to encourage attendance, support from a supervisor (Tharenou, 1993), and more broadly the 'absence culture' in which a person works (Martocchio, 1994; Nicholson and Johns, 1985) – norms and sanctions (informal as well as formal) about reasonable levels of absence. Although employee well-being at work might be expected to relate to absenteeism, other factors are clearly also important.

Absenteeism is conventionally measured in two ways, through the Time-Lost Index and the Frequency Index. The Time-Lost Index is computed as the total duration of absence during a specified period, perhaps expressed as a proportion of the total time examined; and the Frequency Index is the number of separate incidents of absence in a specified period, regardless of their duration. The Time-Lost Index, which gives greater emphasis to long periods of absence, is considered primarily to represent *involuntary* responses to incapacitating sickness. On the other hand, the Frequency Index, in which a single day's absence is given the weight of, say, a three-month absence, is widely thought to describe *voluntary* choices to take time off work for brief periods of time.

How do the three aspects of job-specific well-being correlate with these two indices of absenteeism? We might expect the Frequency Index (with its emphasis on possibly voluntary behaviour) to be more predicted by well-being, but, as with job performance (above), the causes underlying any observed association would be complex and multi-directional.

In a meta-analysis of previous studies, Farrell and Stamm (1988) found that overall job satisfaction (the first axis in Figure 8.2) on average correlated only -0.10 with the Frequency Index and -0.13 with Total Time Lost. Hackett (1989) obtained similar findings, but showed that job satisfaction is more associated with absence frequency for women than for men; he suggested that this difference might arise from many women's greater family responsibilities.

The average correlations of job-related anxiety (axis two) with the Frequency Index and the Time-Lost Index were $+0.11$ and $+0.18$ respectively in Farrell and Stamm's (1988) analysis. The Frequency Index of absenteeism was also examined by Jamal (1984) and Spector *et al.* (1988), who reported correlations with job-related anxiety of $+0.25$ (median value) and $+0.15$ respectively.

The third axis of job-related well-being ranges from feelings of depression to enthusiasm. It might be expected that higher well-being on this axis will be accompanied by less time off work. George (1989) examined positive feelings of this kind and observed a correlation of -0.28 with the number of single-day absences (thought to indicate voluntary time off work). In the review by Farrell and Stamm (1988), measures of job involvement (emphasizing active interest in one's role, as in positive forms of axis three) were on average correlated -0.28 with the Frequency Index of absenteeism.

THE MEASUREMENT OF JOB-RELATED WELL-BEING

The findings summarized in this chapter have usually been obtained in studies which ask employees to respond to interview or questionnaire items about their well-being. Several illustrative scales of well-being are presented below in terms of the three axes set out in Figure 8.2. In all cases responses are given a numerical value and either summed or averaged.

Axis One: Job Satisfaction

In this section are three scales to tap overall job satisfaction and two that examine facet-specific satisfactions.

1.1 Minnesota Satisfaction Questionnaire
Weiss, Dawis, England, and Lofquist (1967) presented a twenty-item scale of General Satisfaction. Responses to each item (scored from one to five respectively) range through: very dissatisfied, dissatisfied, I can't decide whether I am satisfied or not, satisfied, very satisfied. Items were allocated through factor analysis to sub-scales of Intrinsic and Extrinsic Satisfaction. Subsequent analyses have suggested a slight modification to the original allocation (R. V. Dawis, personal communication, 1990), and appropriate sub-scales are indicated as I or E below. Three scores may thus be derived for overall, intrinsic and extrinsic job satisfaction.

Items are preceded by 'In my present job, this is how I feel about . . .', and are as follows: being able to keep busy all the time (I); the chance to work alone on the job (I); the chance to do different things from time to time (I); the chance to be 'somebody' in the community

(I); the way my boss handles his/her workers (E); the competence of my supervisor in making decisions (E); being able to do things that don't go against my conscience (I); the way my job provides for steady employment (E); the chance to do things for other people (I); the chance to tell people what to do (I); the chance to do something that makes use of my abilities (I); the way company policies are put into practice (E); my pay and the amount of work I do (E); the chances for advancement in this job (E); the freedom to use my own judgement (I); the chance to try my own methods of doing the job (I); the working conditions (E); the way my co-workers get along with each other (E); the praise I get for doing a good job (E); the feeling of accomplishment I get from the job (I).

1.2 Overall job satisfaction

Warr, Cook and Wall (1979) presented information about a fifteen-item inventory, covering principal aspects of most jobs. This has been modified slightly in the light of subsequent experience, and now covers seventeen issues. These are categorized as intrinsic or extrinsic (I or E) in the manner shown here: the physical work conditions (E), the freedom to choose your own method of working (I), your fellow workers (E), the recognition you get for good work (I), your immediate boss (E), the amount of responsibility you are given (I), your pay (E), the opportunity to use your abilities (I), relations between management and workers (E), your opportunity to learn new things (I), your chance of promotion or progression (E), the way the organization is managed (E), the attention paid to suggestions you make (I), your hours of work (E), the amount of variety in your job (I), your job security (E), the training you receive (E).

The questionnaire is usually labelled 'Feelings about your Job', with an introduction of this kind: 'The following statements describe aspects of your job. Please tick the answer which best indicates how satisfied or dissatisfied you are with each one.' Responses (scored 1 to 7 respectively) are: extremely dissatisfied, very dissatisfied, moderately dissatisfied, not sure, moderately satisfied, very satisfied, extremely satisfied.

1.3 Job In General Scale

The previous two measures examine overall satisfaction by asking the same question about a wide variety of job features. The alternative multi-item procedure, asking several different questions about a person's job as a whole, has been adopted by Ironson, Smith, Brannick, Gibson and Paul (1989).

Employees are asked, 'Think about your job in general. All in all, what is it like most of the time?', with responses in terms of eighteen evaluative items. These are (with 'R' indicating that an item is reverse-scored): pleasant, bad (R); ideal, waste of time (R); good, undesirable (R); worthwhile, worse than most (R); acceptable, superior, better than most, disagreeable (R); makes me content, inadequate (R); excellent, rotten (R); enjoyable, poor (R). Responses are yes, uncertain and no. These are scored as 3, 1 and 0 respectively, on the grounds that an uncertain response more indicates dissatisfaction than satisfaction and should not have a truly intermediate value (as would be the case with scores of 3, 2 and 1). A total score is calculated.

The Job In General Scale is copyrighted by Bowling Green University, 1990. The complete forms, scoring key, instructions and norms can be obtained from Dr Patricia C. Smith, Department of Psychology, Bowling Green State University, Bowling Green, Ohio 43403, USA. If you plan to use the scale, please contact her for permission and up-to-date information.

1.4 Facet-specific Job Satisfaction

Quinn and Staines (1979) created a thirty-three-item scale to tap employees' evaluations of six job features. Responses, scored from one to four, are: not at all true, a little true, somewhat true, very true. Two short forms are also offered, with eighteen and seven items; these are indicated as (A) (eighteen items) and (B) (seven items) below. In administration, the items are intermingled, rather than being under the headings shown here.

COMFORT: I have enough time to get the job done (A); the hours are good (A); travel to and from work is convenient (A); the physical surroundings are pleasant (A, B); I can forget about my personal problems; I am free of conflicting demands from other people (A, B); I am not asked to do excessive amounts of work.

CHALLENGE: The work is interesting; I have the opportunity to develop my own special abilities (A); I can see the results of my work; I am given the chance to do the things I do best (A, B); I am given a lot of freedom to decide how I do my own work; the problems I am expected to solve are hard enough (A).

FINANCIAL REWARDS: the pay is good; the job security is good (A); my fringe benefits are good (A, B).

RELATIONS WITH CO-WORKERS: the people I work with are friendly; I am given a lot of chances to make friends (A); the people I work with take a personal interest in me (A, B).

RESOURCE ADEQUACY: I have enough information to get the job done; I receive enough help and equipment to get the job done (A); I have enough authority to do my job (A); my supervisor is competent; my responsibilities are clearly defined; the people I work with are competent; my supervisor is very concerned about the welfare of those working for him/her; my supervisor is successful in getting people to work together (A, B); my supervisor is helpful to me in getting the job done (A); the people I work with are helpful to me in getting the job done; my supervisor is friendly.

PROMOTIONS: promotions are handled fairly (A, B); the chances for promotion are good (A); my employer is concerned about giving everybody a chance to get ahead.

1.5 Job Descriptive Index

This five-facet measure (Smith, Kendall and Hulin, 1969) has recently been modified as shown below. Respondents are asked to consider each aspect of their job separately and to indicate 'how well does each of the following words or phrases describe' it. Responses and scoring are as for the Job In General Scale (1.3 above). Total scores are calculated in each case, with the values for Present Pay and Opportunities for Promotion doubled, since they contain only half the number of items in other scales. In the list below, 'R' indicates that an item is reverse-scored.

WORK ON YOUR PRESENT JOB: fascinating, routine (R), satisfying, boring (R), good, creative, respected, uncomfortable (R), pleasant, useful, tiring (R), healthful, challenging, too much to do (R), frustrating (R), simple (R), repetitive (R), gives sense of accomplishment.

PRESENT PAY: income adequate for normal expenses, fair, barely live on income (R), bad (R), income provides luxuries, insecure (R), less than I deserve (R), well paid, underpaid (R).

OPPORTUNITIES FOR PROMOTION: good opportunities for promotion, opportunities somewhat limited (R), promotion on ability, dead-end job (R), good chance of promotion, unfair promotion policy (R), infrequent promotions (R), regular promotions, fairly good chance of promotion.

SUPERVISION: asks my advice, hard to please (R), impolite (R), praises good work, tactful, influential, up-to-date, doesn't supervise enough (R), has favourites (R), tells me where I stand, annoying (R), stubborn (R), knows job well, bad (R), intelligent, poor planner (R), around when needed, lazy (R).

PEOPLE ON YOUR PRESENT JOB: stimulating, boring (R), slow (R), helpful, stupid (R), responsible, fast, intelligent, easy to make enemies (R), talk too much (R), smart, lazy (R), unpleasant (R), gossipy (R), active, narrow interests (R), loyal, stubborn (R).

The Job Descriptive Index is copyrighted by Bowling Green University, 1990. The complete forms, scoring key, instructions and norms can be obtained from Dr Patricia C. Smith, Department of Psychology, Bowling Green State University, Bowling Green, Ohio 43403, USA. If you plan to use the Index, please contact her for permission and up-to-date information.

Axis Two: Anxiety to Comfort

The second axis of well-being shown in Figure 8.2 extends from feelings of anxiety to comfort. It has most often been examined in its negative form, emphasizing low well-being.

2.1 Job-induced tension
Within a broader examination of job-related affect, House and Rizzo (1972) developed a seven-item scale to tap job-induced tension. Respondents indicate whether each statement is considered to be true or false, scored 2 or 1 respectively.

The items are: I work under a great deal of tension; my job tends directly to affect my health; I have felt fidgety or nervous as a result of my job; if I had a different job, my health would probably improve; problems associated with my job have kept me awake at night; I have felt nervous before attending meetings; I often 'take my job home', in that I think about it when doing other things.

2.2 Job-related anxiety

Caplan, Cobb, French, Van Harrison, and Pinneau (1975) measured both job-related anxiety and depression in a single section of their questionnaire; the depression items are shown as 3.2, below. Responses are scored from 1 to 4: never or a little of the time, some of the time, a good part of the time, most of the time.

Anxiety items (preceded by 'When you think about yourself and your job nowadays, how much of the time do you feel this way?') were: I feel nervous; I feel jittery; I feel calm (reverse-scored); I feel fidgety.

2.3 Job-related anxiety–comfort

Scales designed specifically to examine axes two and three in Figure 8.2 have been developed by Warr (1990b). Items are preceded by: 'Thinking of the past few weeks, how much of the time has your job made you feel each of the following?' Responses are: never, occasionally, some of the time, much of the time, most of the time, all of the time; these are scored from 1 to 6 respectively. Items covering both aspects of well-being (see 3.3, below, for axis three) are usually intermixed randomly in a single presentation.

In the light of subsequent experience (e.g., Sevastos, Smith and Cordery, 1992), two items tapping anxiety–comfort have been changed. The revised scale is: tense, anxious, worried, calm, comfortable, relaxed. In order that a high score indicates high well-being, the first three items should be reverse-scored.

2.4 Job-related negative affect

Watson *et al.* (1988) have described brief measures of positive and negative affect, which may be applied with different focal time periods and settings. In addition to context-free uses, these may be directed at 'how you have felt at work during the past few weeks', with a request that people indicate the extent to which each item describes their feelings. Responses are: very slightly or not at all, a little, moderately, quite a bit, extremely; these are scored from 1 to 5.

Ten items cover each of positive and negative affect, mixed together in application. Negative affect is described as 'a general dimension of subjective distress and unpleasant engagement' (p. 1063), and is tapped as follows: distressed, upset, hostile, irritable, scared, afraid, ashamed, guilty, nervous, jittery. The positive affect items appear as 3.4 below.

Axis Three: Depression to Enthusiasm

The third axis in Figure 8.2 covers feelings that extend from low mental arousal and pleasure to high levels of both. In practice, research attention has mainly been on low well-being.

3.1 Depressed mood at work
Quinn and Shepard (1974) obtained responses through a ten-item scale, asking employees to 'check how you feel when you think about yourself and your job'. Responses were: never, rarely, sometimes, often; these were scored from 1 to 4, with four items reverse-scored (indicated below as 'R'). Note that a high score thus indicates low depression at work.

Items are: I feel downhearted and blue (R); I get tired for no reason (R); I find myself restless and can't keep still (R); My mind is as clear as it used to be; I find it easy to do the things that I used to do; I feel hopeful about the future; I find it easy to make decisions; I am more irritable than usual (R); I still enjoy the things I used to; I feel that I am useful and needed.

3.2 Job-related depression
The six items tapping job-related depression in the study by Caplan *et al.* (1975) (see 2.2, above) are: I feel sad; I feel unhappy; I feel good (R); I feel depressed; I feel blue; I feel cheerful (R).

3.3 Job-related depression–enthusiasm
Within Warr's (1990b) affective well-being scale (see 2.3, above) six items tap the third axis. After recent modification, these are:

depressed, gloomy, miserable, motivated, enthusiastic, optimistic. Responses to the first three are reverse-scored, so that high values indicate positive well-being.

3.4 Job-related positive affect

Positive affect at work has been measured by ten items in the scale devised by Watson *et al.* (1988). The construct is described as reflecting 'the extent to which a person feels enthusiastic, active and alert' (p. 1063), and is covered by: attentive, interested, alert, excited, enthusiastic, inspired, proud, determined, strong, active. In application of the scale, these items are mixed with those in 2.4, above.

SUMMARY

In thinking about a person's well-being it is important to distinguish between those feelings that are job-specific and those that are non-job or context-free. Three principal axes for the measurement of all forms of well-being range from displeasure to pleasure, from anxiety to comfort, and from depression to enthusiasm. These axes are significantly intercorrelated, but have partially different causes and outcomes.

Employee well-being is associated in systematic ways with particular features of a job, but it is also influenced by stable personality dispositions. These are usually examined in terms of trait negative affectivity and trait positive affectivity. Changes to job characteristics can yield changes to job-specific well-being, but these are limited by the cross-situational stability of the two traits.

Research into well-being and job performance has demonstrated that significant associations exist between them. However, other organizational and individual factors have substantial impact on job performance, and a large contribution from well-being should not be expected. Furthermore, the causal pattern is likely to be complex, with mutual impact between performance and well-being as well as influences on both from other variables.

FURTHER READING

More extended treatments of components and causes of well-being have been provided by Warr (1987, 1994). Reviews focused specifically on job satisfaction are in the book edited by Cranny, Smith and Stone (1992) and the chapter by Arvey, Carter and Buerkley (1991). Many other relevant papers have been cited in the text.

ACKNOWLEDGEMENTS

The Minnesota Satisfaction Questionnaire is used with permission from Dr R. V. Dawis; The Job In General Scale and the Job Descriptive Index are used with permission from Dr P. C. Smith; the Facet-Specific Satisfaction and Depressed Mood at Work scales are used with permission from Institute for Social Research, University of Michigan; the Job-induced Tension scale is used with permission from Dr R. J. House; the Job-related Anxiety and Job-related Depression scales are used with permission from US National Institute for Occupational Safety and Health; the Job-related Negative Affect and Job-related Positive Affect scales are used with permission from Dr D. Watson and the American Psychological Association.

REFERENCES

Agho, A. O., Mueller, C. W. and Price, J. L. (1993). Determinants of employee job satisfaction: An empirical test of a causal model. *Human Relations*, 46, 1007–1027.

Anderson, C. R. (1976). Coping behaviors as intervening mechanisms in the inverted-U stress–performance relationship. *Journal of Applied Psychology*, 61, 30–34.

Arvey, R. D., Bouchard, T. J., Segal, N. L. and Abraham, L. M. (1989). Job satisfaction: Environmental and genetic components. *Journal of Applied Psychology*, 74, 187–192.

Arvey, R. D., Carter, G. W. and Buerkley, D. K. (1991). Job satisfaction: Dispositional and situational influences. In C. L. Cooper and I. T. Robertson (eds.), *International Review of Industrial and Organizational Psychology*, vol. 6, pp. 359–383. Chichester: Wiley.

Arvey, R. D., McCall, B. P., Bouchard, T. J., Taubman, P. and Cavanaugh, M. A. (1994). Genetic influences on job satisfaction and work values. *Personality and Individual Differences*, 17, 21–33.

Bamundo, P. J. and Kopelman, R. E. (1980). The moderating effects of occupation, age, and urbanization on the relationship between job satisfaction and life satisfaction. *Journal of Vocational Behavior*, 17, 106–123.

Brief, A. P., Burke, M. J., George, J. M., Robinson, B. S. and Webster, J. (1988). Should negative affectivity remain an unmeasured variable in the study of job stress? *Journal of Applied Psychology*, 73, 193–198.

Brooke, P. P. and Price, J. L. (1989). The determinants of absenteeism: An empirical test of a causal model. *Journal of Occupational Psychology*, 62, 1–19.

Burke, M. J., Brief, A. P. and George, J. M. (1993). The role of negative affectivity in understanding relations between self-reports of stressors and strains: A comment on the applied psychology literature. *Journal of Applied Psychology*, 78, 402–412.

Caplan, R. D., Cobb, S., French, J. R. P., Van Harrison, R. and Pinneau, S. R. (1975). *Job Demands and Worker Health*. Washington, DC: National Institute for Occupational Safety and Health.

Chen, P. Y. and Spector, P. E. (1991). Negative affectivity as the underlying cause of correlations between stressors and strains. *Journal of Applied Psychology*, 76, 398–407.

Costa, P. T. and McCrae, R. R. (1980). Influence of extroversion and neuroticism on subjective well-being: Happy and unhappy people. *Journal of Personality and Social Psychology*, 38, 668–678.

Cranny, C. J., Smith, P. C. and Stone, E. F. (1992). *Job Satisfaction: How People Feel about their Jobs and How it Affects their Performance*. New York: Lexington Books.

Cropanzano, R. and James, K. (1990). Some methodological considerations for the behavioral genetic analysis of work attitudes. *Journal of Applied Psychology*, 75, 433–439.

Cropanzano, R., James, K. and Konovsky, M. A. (1993). Dispositional affectivity as a predictor of work attitudes and job performance. *Journal of Organizational Behavior*, 14, 595–606.

Crouter, A. C. (1984). Spillover from family to work: The neglected side of the work–family interface. *Human Relations*, 37, 425–442.

Elliott, T. R., Chartrand, J. M. and Harkins, S. W. (1994). Negative affectivity, emotional distress, and the cognitive appraisal of occupational stress. *Journal of Vocational Behavior*, 45, 185–201.

Farrell, D. and Stamm, C. L. (1988). Meta-analysis of the correlates of employee absence. *Human Relations*, 41, 211–227.

Gechman, A. S. and Wiener, Y. (1975). Job involvement and satisfaction as related to mental health and personal time devoted to work. *Journal of Applied Psychology*, 60, 521–523.

George, J. M. (1989). Mood and absence. *Journal of Applied Psychology*, 74, 317–324.

George, J. M. (1991). State or trait: Effects of positive mood on prosocial behaviors at work. *Journal of Applied Psychology*, 76, 299–307.

Hackett, R. D. (1989). Work attitudes and employee absenteeism: A synthesis of the literature. *Journal of Occupational Psychology*, 62, 235–248.

House, R. J. and Rizzo, J. R. (1972). Role conflict and ambiguity as critical variables in a model of organizational behavior. *Organizational Behavior and Human Performance*, 7, 467–505.

Iaffaldano, M. T. and Muchinsky, P. M. (1985). Job satisfaction and job performance: A meta-analysis. *Psychological Bulletin*, 97, 251–273.

Ironson, G. H., Smith, P. C., Brannick, M. T., Gibson, W. M. and Paul, K. B. (1989). Construction of a job in general scale: A comparison of global, composite, and specific measures. *Journal of Applied Psychology*, 74, 193–200.

Jamal, M. (1984). Job stress and job performance controversy: An empirical assessment. *Organizational Behavior and Human Performance*, 33, 1–21.

Judge, T. A. and Locke, E. A. (1993). Effect of dysfunctional thought processes on subjective well-being and job satisfaction. *Journal of Applied Psychology*, 78, 475–490.

Judge, T. A. and Watanabe, S. (1993). Another look at the job satisfaction–life satisfaction relationship. *Journal of Applied Psychology*, 78, 939–948.

Kelloway, E. K. and Barling, J. (1991). Job characteristics, role stress and mental health. *Journal of Occupational Psychology*, 64, 291–304.

Levin, I. and Stokes, J. P. (1989). Dispositional approach to job satisfaction: Role of negative affectivity. *Journal of Applied Psychology*, 74, 752–758.

Martin, R. and Wall, T. D. (1989). Attentional demand and cost responsibility as stressors in shopfloor jobs. *Academy of Management Journal*, 32, 69–86.

Martocchio, J. J. (1994). The effects of absence culture on individual absence. *Human Relations*, 47, 243–262.

Matthews, G., Jones, D. M. and Chamberlain, A. G. (1990). Defining the measurement of mood: The UWIST mood adjective checklist. *British Journal of Psychology*, 81, 17–42.

Necowitz, L. B. and Roznowski, M. (1994). Negative affectivity and job satisfaction: Cognitive processes underlying the relationship and effects on employee behaviors. *Journal of Vocational Behavior*, 45, 270–294.

Nicholson, N. (1977). Absence behaviour and attendance motivation: A conceptual synthesis. *Journal of Management Studies*, 14, 231–252.

Nicholson, N. and Johns, G. (1985). The absence culture: Who's in control of absence? *Academy of Management Review*, 10, 397–407.

Ostroff, C. (1992). The relationship between satisfaction, attitudes, and performance: An organizational level analysis. *Journal of Applied Psychology*, 77, 963–974.

Petty, M. M., McGee, G. W. and Cavender, J. W. (1984). A meta-analysis of the relationship between individual job satisfaction and individual performance. *Academy of Management Review*, 9, 712–721.

Piotrkowski, C. S. (1978). *Work and the Family System*. New York: The Free Press.

Quinn, R. P. and Shepard, L. J. (1974). *The 1972–73 Quality of Employment Survey*. Ann Arbor, Mich.: University of Michigan, Institute for Social Research.

Quinn, R. P. and Staines, G. L. (1979). *The 1977 Quality of Employment Survey*. Ann Arbor, Mich.: University of Michigan, Institute for Social Research.

Schaubroeck, J., Ganster, D. C. and Fox, M. L. (1992). Dispositional affect and work-related stress. *Journal of Applied Psychology*, 77, 322–335.

Sevastos, P., Smith, L. and Cordery, J. L. (1992). Evidence on the reliability and construct validity of Warr's (1990) well-being and mental health measures. *Journal of Occupational and Organizational Psychology*, 65, 33–49.

Shore, L. M. and Martin, H. J. (1989). Job satisfaction and organizational commitment in relation to work performance and turnover intentions. *Human Relations*, 42, 625–638.

Smith, P. C., Kendall, L. M. and Hulin, C. L. (1969). *The Measurement of Satisfaction in Work and Retirement*. Chicago: Rand McNally.

Spector, P. E., Dwyer, D. J. and Jex, S. M. (1988). Relation of job stressors to affective, health, and performance outcomes: A comparison of multiple data sources. *Journal of Applied Psychology*, 73, 11–19.

Staw, B. M. and Ross, J. (1985). Stability in the midst of change: A dispositional approach to job attitudes. *Journal of Applied Psychology*, 70, 469–480.

Steiner, D. D. and Truxillo, D. M. (1989). An improved test of the disaggregation hypothesis of job and life satisfaction. *Journal of Occupational Psychology*, 62, 33–39.

Tait, M., Padgett, M. Y. and Baldwin, T. T. (1989). Job and life satisfaction: A re-evaluation of the strength of the relationship and gender effects as a function of the date of the study. *Journal of Applied Psychology*, 74, 502–507.

Tharenou, P. (1993). A test of reciprocal causality for absenteeism. *Journal of Organizational Behavior*, 14, 193–210.

Warr, P. B. (1987). *Work, Unemployment, and Mental Health*. Oxford: Oxford University Press.

Warr, P. B. (1990a). Decision latitude, job demands, and employee well-being. *Work and Stress*, 4, 285–294.

Warr, P. B. (1990b). The measurement of well-being and other aspects of mental health. *Journal of Occupational Psychology*, 63, 193–210.

Warr, P. B. (1994). A conceptual framework for the study of work and mental health. *Work and Stress*, 8, 84–97.

Warr, P. B., Cook, J. and Wall, T. D. (1979). Scales for the measurement of some work attitudes and aspects of psychological well-being. *Journal of Occupational Psychology*, 52, 129–148.

Watson, D. and Clark, L. A. (1984). Negative affectivity: The disposition to experience aversive emotional states. *Psychological Bulletin*, 96, 465–490.

Watson, D., Clark, L. A. and Tellegen, A. (1988). Development and validation of brief measures of positive and negative affect: The PANAS scales. *Journal of Personality and Social Psychology*, 54, 1063–1070.

Watson, D. and Pennebaker, J. W. (1989). Health complaints, stress, and distress: Exploring the central role of negative affectivity. *Psychological Review*, 96, 234–254.

Watson, D. and Slack, A. K. (1993). General factors of affective temperament and their relation to job satisfaction over time. *Organizational Behavior and Human Decision Process*, 54, 181–202.

Weiss, D. J., Dawis, R. V., England, G. W. and Lofquist, L. H. (1967). *Manual for the Minnesota Satisfaction Questionnaire*. Minneapolis: University of Minnesota, Industrial Relations Center.

9

Leadership and Management

David Guest

The idea of leadership continues to fascinate. What sort of people make great leaders? Why are we willing to place our faith in some leaders but not others? How do leaders emerge from the pack? Can an effective leader really turn around an ailing company or football club? And can that same leader do it again in another organization? Issues of leadership are currently fashionable, as any quick glance around airport bookshops will reveal. Is it leadership that will make the difference in industry and commerce? Or is it the more prosaic need for plain old-fashioned good management?

Psychologists have shared some of the fascination with leadership. It has proved a rich territory for research and writing. Many reviewers suggest it has proved rather too rich, resulting in an indigestible mass of disparate ideas, few of which stand up to close scrutiny. This may be a harsh judgement. The field is rich and complex; but like any area of research that is in turmoil, it is exciting and full of possibilities. This chapter will attempt to provide a flavour of some of the main directions of current work. To do so, however, it also needs to touch on some of the more traditional but still robust approaches that provide the cornerstones of thinking and research on leadership.

We will start by examining leadership behaviour. This is very much the traditional area of theory and research. It suggests that leadership is defined by what leaders do. Much research has focused on leadership style, in effect posing two questions: in order to be effective how should leaders behave, and to what extent should their behaviour vary according to the circumstances?

* I would like to acknowledge the help of Jeremy Slaughter in preparing material for this chapter.

Secondly, we will look at the relationship between leadership and management. In so doing, we touch briefly on the debate about management competencies and how they might be acquired. One of the central issues is whether leadership is a distinguishable competence and if so, how important it is. We then explore a topic which has assumed considerable prominence recently, the idea of transformational or charismatic leadership. Whereas much traditional work on leadership behaviour and management has been concerned with 'doing things right' in organizations, transformational leadership is more concerned with shaping the direction and values of the organization, in other words, with 'doing the right things'.

One aspect of the current interest in charisma is that the focus of attention partly shifts from leaders and their behaviour to followers and how they perceive the leader. This finds an echo in the growing influence within psychology of cognitive models and issues of information-processing. Both provide some distinctive insights into the nature of leadership, which we will explore in the third main section. The final section looks more closely at the impact leaders have on organizational performance.

No general definition of leadership will be offered in this chapter because the most appropriate definition depends on which approach to leadership is taken. Broadly speaking, leadership is about influencing the behaviour of others. However, this is also a definition of 'power', so it may be of limited value. Perhaps by the end of this chapter you may be in a position to adopt your own preferred definition.

LEADERSHIP BEHAVIOUR

One obvious starting point in the study of leaders is to explore what they do; so in this section we focus on variations in leader behaviour. Interest in what leaders do rests on the assumption that a leader's behaviour influences the effectiveness of subordinates' behaviour. To test this assumption we need to identify useful dimensions along which to differentiate leadership behaviour. The most widely used approach to this has been to focus on variations in the 'style' of different leaders.

Theories of Leadership Style

Early work by Lewin, Lippit and White (1939) emphasized one main dimension of style along a continuum from participative/democratic to autocratic/authoritarian. While recognizing that a focus on a single dimension of leadership style was over-simple, researchers at the Michigan University Institute for Social Research reported a series of studies comparing high- and low-performing groups which consistently showed that leaders of high-performing groups displayed a more participative and employee-centred style (Likert, 1961, 1967). Likert developed these findings into what he termed 'System 4' leadership, which, in effect, amounted to a sophisticated application of the ideas of 'human relations' theorists, including extensive delegation of decision-making to group members.

Many of the studies reported by Likert and his colleagues were correlational; they reported an association between a participative style and higher satisfaction and performance. But this pattern of association does not establish cause and effect. For example, it is possible that leaders who have high performing groups can afford to be more participative, so that performance influences style rather than vice versa. There have been a few studies that have explored this question through careful research designs (see, for example, Rosen, 1969; Misumi, 1985) and they conclude that both causal interpretations are equally plausible. The longitudinal studies reported by Likert (1961) fail to show a clear link between *changes* in leadership style and subordinate performance; so do later studies testing the application of System 4 management (Marrow, Bowers and Seashore, 1967; Dowling 1975).

Wagner's (1994) meta-analysis of a range of participative approaches in industry, ranging from quality circles to leadership style, indicates that their impact on performance and satisfaction is positive but very modest and not really sufficient to justify serious investment. This finding reflects the dominant current view about the impact of interventions intended to increase the participative style of the supervisor or first line leader.

In parallel with the work at Michigan, a team at Ohio University had proposed a two-dimensional model of leadership style (Fleishman, 1953), based on two distinct dimensions of leadership, which they labelled 'consideration', a focus on concern for staff, and 'initiating structure', a focus on progressing the task. Although this two-dimensional model has sometimes been seen as an either/or approach, in fact it leads to the view that an effective leader needs to focus on both task and people. The best known approach to this is Blake and Mouton's (1964) managerial grid, a major training and organization development programme to improve leadership skills.

Research on the two-dimensional approach suffers from the same deficiencies as that on participative leadership in that it is largely correlational. It broadly confirms that leaders who show 'consideration' have more satisfied subordinates, but the link between the two dimensions and performance has proved to be much less clear-cut. Despite these reservations, many thousands of junior and middle managers have at some stage received training in leadership style on the all-too-rarely tested assumption that it is likely to be of some benefit.

Although research on the two dimensions of leadership style has declined, a variation of the approach has emerged in some cross-cultural studies of leadership. A long-standing Japanese research programme (Misumi, 1985; Misumi and Peterson, 1985) draws heavily on the Ohio approach but re-labels the dimensions Performance (P) and Maintenance (M) styles. The former is more concerned with the task, the latter with relations. The second aspect of Misumi's model is that leadership style can be considered at both a general and a specific level. There is likely to be a dominant general style that reflects the leader's approach. However, the specific leadership behaviours seen as characterizing the style may vary from country to country.

Smith, Misumi, Tayeb, Peterson and Bond (1989) found national differences much in line with Hofstede's (1980) distinction between individualist and collectivist cultures. In the four countries studied, the two dimensions could be identified at a general level, but the specific behaviour that characterized the dimensions varied. In Japan and Hong Kong, the more collectivist cultures, the general preference for reciprocal influence processes between leader and subordinates meant that the distinction between specific behaviours reflecting the two dimensions was blurred. In the more individualist United Kingdom and the United States the specific behaviours associated with the two general dimensions were more clearly differentiated. In particular, supervisors were more willing to exert goal-directed pressure as a distinctive aspect of the Performance style.

Taking the research a step further, Smith, Peterson and Misumi (1994) have shown that different supervisory styles at general and specific level are associated with group effectiveness in the four cultures. Japanese supervisors display a more consistent holistic pattern of behaviour, whatever the situation, while British and American supervisors appear to adjust their style much more to the specific circumstances and events.

The research on national cultural differences is illustrating how the effectiveness of a leadership style may depend on the national context. From a somewhat different perspective, Lawler (1986) has been critical of those who suggest that a participative style has no positive effects, because most studies ignore the extent to which the organizational culture is or is not supportive. This highlights the need to take account of the context in which leadership takes place, a point emphasized in contingency or situational theories of leadership.

Fiedler's Contingency Theory of Leadership

Fiedler (1967) presented a comprehensive contingency theory of leadership. He used a single dimension of leadership style with task-focused leadership at one end and person-focused at the other, and proposed that the appropriate style depended on the context. Specifically, Fiedler suggested that the effective style was a function of three variables: the leader's power position *vis-à-vis* subordinates, the nature of the task and the nature of leader–group relations. As Table 9.1 shows, in conditions that are either very favourable to the leader or unfavourable, a task-centred, structured leadership style is predicted to be most effective. In all other conditions, a considerate person-centred style is expected to get the best results.

Fiedler argued that the style adopted by a leader was a reflection of a relatively stable personality attribute, which he measured through the Least Preferred Co-worker (LPC) scale. Those who rate their least preferred co-worker quite positively on this scale are seen

Table 9.1 Fiedler's Contingency Model

Leader–member relations	Task structure	Leader's position power	Effective leadership style
1 Good	high	strong	low LPC/task-C
2 Good	high	weak	low LPC/task-C
3 Good	low	strong	low LPC/task-C
4 Good	low	weak	high LPC/person-C
5 Poor	high	strong	high LPC/person-C
6 Poor	high	weak	high LPC/person-C
7 Poor	low	strong	high LPC/person-C
8 Poor	low	weak	low LPC/task-C

as socially concerned and likely to adopt a person-centred style, while those who give a low rating are seen as task-centred and likely to adopt a task-centred style. This concept and its measurement have attracted extensive critical attention. One difficulty is that over the years Fiedler seems to have shifted his ground about its meaning. Another is the focus on extreme scores, when most people may fall in the middle of the continuum. There are also questions about the stability of the LPC score and about its relative importance in predicting leadership behaviour and outcomes. In short, it is a concept that has not withstood close scrutiny. Even Fiedler, despite some robust defence (Fiedler, 1977), seems to have lost some of his earlier enthusiasm for the concept.

There has been extensive research on the more general properties of Fiedler's contingency theory. In most cases the research has studied leadership of small groups. Major reviews of the research (see, for example, Peters, Harthe and Pohlmann, 1985) show that there is moderate support for much of the theory when it is tested in laboratory settings, but much less support when explored in workplaces. Indeed, in workplaces there is little or no support for predictions in a number of the eight contingent situations. In practice it has been found to be extremely difficult, especially in work settings, to create the conditions to test the theory adequately. As a result, despite its major influence over a number of years, interest in the theory has now declined.

Other Situational Theories of Leadership

Following Fiedler's original theory, several other situational theories of leadership have been developed. We will look briefly at three that have attracted a significant amount of research or applied attention.

The path-goal theory of leadership, developed by House (1971), is concerned with the actions leaders must take to motivate subordinates to perform well and to achieve satisfaction from their work. Specifically, it proposes that the role of the leader is to increase the personal pay-offs for subordinates from work-goal achievement and to remove or reduce obstacles in the path to this achievement. Leadership may thus involve action to remove barriers, ensure sufficient resources, or provide guidance in the form of training, communication, role clarification and goal-focus. Four leadership styles are identified within this model, labelled supportive, directive, participative and achievement-oriented. The choice of most effective style is suggested to depend on situational variables, including characteristics of the task and the subordinates. The prescriptions are broadly as one might expect. For example, routine tasks are said to call for supportive leadership, while complex and ambiguous tasks are viewed as requiring directive leadership, especially when subordinates are inexperienced in the role.

Research into path-goal leadership theory reports moderate support (Yukl, 1994), but that is based largely on static correlational studies that explore only some elements of the theory. We are therefore not in a position to claim that it is valid. However, it usefully identifies variables to take into account in considering leadership behaviour. In practical terms it implies that leaders should recognize the importance of information and communication; should ensure that obstacles to high performance and high satisfaction are removed from the 'path' of employees, and should ensure that individuals have sufficient clarity about their role and about their work goals.

Hersey and Blanchard's (1982) theory of situational leadership shares some features in common with path-goal theory. It identifies two key dimensions of leadership behaviour, labelled task behaviour and relational behaviour, which are similar to the traditional task- and person-centred styles of leadership. Task behaviour is concerned with defining subordinate roles and responsibilities; relational behaviour is concerned with providing socio-emotional support to members of one's team. The extent to which either is used appropriately is considered to be a function of subordinate maturity, a concept that again has two dimensions. Job maturity reflects the extent to which subordinates possess task-relevant knowledge and skills. Psychological maturity indicates level of self-confidence about undertaking the work. The theory proposes that as subordinate maturity increases from a low base there should be a consistent decline in the requirement for task leadership. Up to a mid-point there should be an increase in the emphasis placed on relational leadership, but thereafter a decrease as subordinates become more competent and confident about undertaking the work.

Despite its plausibility and its success in industry as a packaged approach, Hersey and Blanchard's situational leadership theory has not attracted much research attention. One reason for this is that some of the key concepts (most notably 'maturity') are broadly defined and difficult to operationalize. Another is that it lacks any underlying theoretical rationale. A critical review by Graeff (1983), in addition to highlighting the conceptual problems, observes that the limited research has produced results that are, at best, equivocal. This suggests that while we might take from this approach some of its focus on development of subordinates, we should not treat it as a validated theory of leadership.

Vroom and Yetton (1973) developed a prescriptive decision-making theory to identify the appropriate leadership style in different situations. They focus on how the leader's decision-making affects the quality of a decision and its acceptance by subordinates. These are seen as key intervening variables affecting group performance. Five decision-making procedures are outlined, ranging from autocratic to joint decision-making. The effectiveness of a given decision-making procedure depends on several variables, such as the amount of information possessed by the leader and subordinates, the likelihood of subordinate acceptance of an autocratic decision or involvement in a participative one, and the complexity of the decision. What results is a complex set of flow charts through which it becomes possible to rule out certain decision-making procedures as likely to be ineffective.

Results of tests of this model have been reviewed by Vroom and

Jago (1988). A typical research approach has been to ask leaders about successful and unsuccessful decisions taken in the past and how they arrived at them. The prediction is that those that followed the framework will have been more successful. The review concludes that 62 per cent of those following the framework but only 37 per cent of those that did not were successful, indicating some support for the theory.

Vroom and Jago amended the theory in the light of their findings. Instead of ruling out specified options, they sought to identify a leader's preferred decision-making procedure; they allowed a continuum of responses to their check-list of questions instead of yes/no answers; and they added further situational variables. The result is to make an already extremely complex approach even more complicated and virtually unusable without a computer program. Perhaps not surprisingly, there has been little attempt to research this version of the theory beyond the initial work of Vroom and Jago. The lack of support, the assumptions about rational decision-making and the extreme complexity of the theory make it unattractive to many users.

Overview of Approaches to Leadership Behaviour

So far we have touched on the main approaches to leadership within one of the traditions of psychological research, careful study of small group leadership under controlled conditions and based on theories with varying degrees of complexity. It is a tradition that is now well over fifty years old, which reflects a steady cumulation of knowledge and which still attracts research attention and applied interest. Despite this, it can be argued that for several reasons the approach has largely run out of steam.

The first problem lies in the assumption that there is one best style of leadership behaviour in a given context. The logical basis of this assumption is unclear and it requires most settings to be sufficiently clear and unambiguous to permit diagnosis. Vroom and Jago are unusual in accepting that there is more than one possible acceptable style in many cases. The second problem is that as the theories have become more complex they have become more difficult to test. Vroom and Jago again provide the clearest case of this. However, there is something of a paradox that the so-called situational theories have tended to over-simplify their position by selecting only a small number of contingent variables. At the same time we have become more demanding of our research methodology, and most of the research that is published is still a partial test of a theory based on static correlational analysis.

Finally, research studies of leadership style explain only a small amount of the variation in subordinate performance and satisfaction, and do not specify how much of the variance they should seek to explain. It could be argued that it is unreasonable to expect leaders at supervisory and junior management levels to have much influence on subordinate outcomes. These are much more likely to be shaped by a range of other factors in the wider internal context of the organization, such as the technology or reward system, and in the external context, such as the market conditions. By implication, we need to shift our attention to leadership of organizations, to the factors that shape the organization and in particular to the organizational culture.

LEADERSHIP AND MANAGEMENT

All leaders in formal organizational roles sometimes have to act as managers, but not all managers are leaders. Attempts to characterize the difference between leadership and management have resulted in a number of striking comments. For Bennis and Nanus (1985), for example, the distinction, noted at the start of the chapter, was between doing the right thing and doing things right; leaders set the purpose and the vision for the organization, or perhaps the department, while managers implement it. Two approaches have dominated recent research and writing, both of which have strong links with the past. The first, perhaps emphasizing the management element, is the study of managerial competencies. The second is transformational or charismatic leadership. We will examine each in turn.

Managerial Competencies

Managerial competencies have been very much in fashion in organizations for a number of years. However, as Sparrow (1994) and others have observed, the field has become very messy and muddled. One reason for this is that targets for managerial competence have become a national policy issue in the United Kingdom. More specifically, a system of national vocational qualifications (NVQs), as a framework for the description and development of competence throughout the workforce, has, through the Management Charter Initiative, sought to raise the quality of management. Indeed, all aspects of managerial and related professional work have been subject to a process of extensive job analysis seeking to identify the knowledge and skills required for effective performance. These have then been translated into training programmes through which an appropriate competency might be acquired.

The strand of work on competence that has attracted greater attention among applied psychologists has evolved out of research intended to identify the features that distinguish effective from less effective management. This has focused on the knowledge, skills and attitudes of managers, often based on critical incidents of effective and ineffective behaviour or study of managers judged on various criteria to be more or less effective.

A highly influential study by Boyatzis (1982), using a form of critical incident technique with over 250 managers at various levels and with varying degrees of effectiveness, identified nine core competencies. These ranged from competencies that might be considered close to traits, such as 'self-confidence', defined in terms of belief in one's own ideas, ability to act decisively on them, and general manner and poise, through what might be described as preferences, such as 'efficiency orientation', defined as a concern for getting the work done through goal setting, to something closer to a skill, such as 'management of group processes', which is concerned with building an effective team. It would appear from research on competencies that some importance is still attached to leadership traits.

In the period when research concentrated almost entirely on leadership behaviour (see above) it was quite fashionable to be somewhat scathing of trait approaches to leadership. Some of the criticism can be traced back to a comprehensive and critical early review by Stogdill (1948), which concluded that no consistent pattern of leadership traits had emerged from the research. Why, then, have they come back into fashion? There are three answers to this. One is the failure of the focus on environment and style to provide convincing explanations of variations in leadership effectiveness. A second is the shift of interest from supervisory to senior management leadership, where there may be more scope for personal qualities to influence effectiveness. A third is that the relevant stream of research never stopped and we have become more fully informed and more positive (Stogdill, 1974) about what it can reveal.

One of the theories that has survived the test of time is McClelland's (1985) work on the three motives of need for achievement, need for power and need for affiliation. McClelland and Boyatzis (1982) present evidence to indicate that a high need for power, and more especially what they term 'socialized' power, defined in terms of exercising power for the benefit of others, is likely to be necessary for effective leadership at senior management levels. Miner (1993) has also been interested in management motivation through an exploration of requirements for effectiveness in leadership roles. His research has highlighted the importance of qualities such as a need or desire to exercise power, to compete with peers and to respect authority. Both McClelland and Miner have made extensive use of projective measures of motivation, and there is also a need for research using other methods to test the robustness of their results.

Fiedler has now presented a new theory, the cognitive resource theory (Fiedler and Garcia, 1987; Fiedler, 1995), which, like his earlier contingency theory, seeks to combine trait and situational elements. The question posed is: under what conditions do 'cognitive resources' such as intelligence and experience matter for effective leadership? This question is partly stimulated by the knowledge that something like intelligence is only weakly associated with leadership effectiveness. It is predicted that effective group performance will depend on the interaction between leader intelligence and experience and stress and group support. More specifically, leader intelligence is expected to predict group effectiveness as long as the leader is directive. However, this relationship is predicted to break down under stress; in these circumstances experience and a reversion to habitual behaviour are thought likely to become more important for effective group performance. It can be seen that the theory is complex and generates a host of predictions. With only a few exceptions (see, for example, Vecchio, 1990), it has been tested mainly by Fiedler and his colleagues, often in laboratories or through re-analysis of earlier studies. Both the results and some of the measures used in the studies promise to be as controversial as the Least Preferred Co-worker concept (see above).

In summary, we have touched briefly on the topic of managerial competencies. The search for qualities associated with effective management behaviour has led to the identification of various aspects of 'leadership'. In so doing, the work has restored to prominence research on leadership traits. There is a presumption in much of the research on competencies that the personal qualities revealed are relatively stable. Once they have been uncovered through the initial work comparing more and less effective leaders, the competencies are typically identified in assessment centres, often at the point of selection into an organization (see Chapter 5), and individual effectiveness is measured by degree of career advancement some years later. This shifts the focus of policy away from a concern for training of leaders or manipulation of the environment towards effective staff selection. The key question becomes, do these potential recruits to leadership possess the necessary qualities for leadership effectiveness?

There are limits to this policy perspective. The research indicates that while certain traits may be associated with certain measures of leadership effectiveness, the association is not consistent and the possession of a specific trait cannot be demonstrated always to be either a necessary or a sufficient condition for effective leadership. The measures of traits have been difficult to validate and enthusiasm for them has often been restricted to those who developed them and to a number of consultants.

Another interesting challenge to the work on individual competencies comes from research by, among others, Prahalad and Doz (1987), who have extended the concept of managerial competencies to incorporate the idea of 'organizational' competencies. These are distinctive features of an organization that are thought to provide it with competitive advantage. Such thinking moves beyond Porter's (1985) generic competitive strategies, such as cost-effectiveness or quality, to argue that it is a distinctive feature of the organization that makes the difference. Probably the most cited example is the Sony company's expertise in miniaturization. The important point about this is that it resides in the organization culture and cannot easily be replicated. If this is a key to organizational effectiveness, it requires a degree of adaptiveness on the part of managers who join the organization. They need to display sufficient flexibility to fit in with the distinctive culture and to develop it. Ironically, this returns us to a kind of situational model. Those who can adapt to the organizational culture and work with it are likely to be effective leaders in that culture.

However, there is a prior question: where does the culture come from? What is the source of organizational competencies? As organizations compete ever more fiercely in the marketplace, this has become a vital question and has helped to stimulate interest in transformational or charismatic leadership.

Charismatic and Transformational Leadership

Since the early 1980s there has been a marked growth of interest in the idea of 'charismatic' leadership. This flows from a recognition that if organizations are to thrive, they require, at their head, leaders who can provide a compelling vision that would attract the commitment of the staff, generate support for large-scale organizational change and facilitate the kind of full utilization of human resources that might sustain competitive advantage. This view was implicit in the writing of Peters and Waterman (1982) on organizational excellence; and it is equally apparent in Prahalad and Doz's (1987) approach to organizational competencies.

One of the attractions of charismatic leadership is that it appeals to the emotions. It holds out the prospect of motivation and performance above and beyond the call of duty, willingly given, without apparent expectation of additional economic reward. In principle, therefore, it is of enormous potential benefit to organizations.

Early this century Weber (1947) presented his views on the role of charisma as a source of authority in organizations. For him, charisma was influence and control based on qualities of the person rather than on formal authority or tradition. The fact that charisma has a slightly intangible quality to it has not stopped organizational psychologists from attempting to define and measure it so that it can be studied empirically using traditional psychological methods. House (1977), followed by Bass (1985) and Conger and Kanungo (1994), have developed measures to identify variations in charismatic leadership.

Much of the conceptual and empirical work on charisma has focused on what certain leaders do to become perceived as charismatic. Typically, it is argued, charismatic leaders have a capacity to articulate ideological goals; and they will often lead from the front, setting an example for others to follow. Conger and Kanungo (1987) suggest that they are often likely to stand out by being different, almost rebellious, and by providing an attractive alternative to the status quo. As a result, followers may display liking, trust, obedience and a desire to follow and emulate a charismatic leader.

Bass (1985) has drawn attention to the fact that some charismatic people, for example film stars and rock stars, may attract followers but do not generate the kind of action required of leaders. What is needed is a theory about what aspects of a person or his or her behaviour will change or transform the values, beliefs and behaviour of other people. He has therefore argued for the more broadly defined concept of transformational leadership, building on the ideas of Burns (1978), who presented a contrast between transformational and transactional leadership. By treating these two approaches as potentially complementary, Bass is able to present a model of leadership which contains seven components and provides some sort of integration with traditional models. Four components are concerned with transformational leadership and two with transactional leadership. The four dimensions of transformational leadership are charisma, defined broadly as set out above; inspirational motivation, a symbolic and emotional appeal to specified goals; intellectual stimulation, a challenge to old ways of thinking; and individualized consideration, fair but individual treatment to ensure that everyone has opportunities for development and learning. The transactional leadership components are use of contingent rewards and management by exception. He also identifies *laissez-faire* leadership as a form of non-leadership behaviour.

Bass has made useful progress in clarifying some of the concepts, although most people continue to use charismatic and transformational leadership as interchangeable terms. He has developed a measure of transformational leadership that has been subject to criticism (Yukl, 1994), partly because it looks rather too much like some of the older measures of leadership style. However, research does appear to show that those leaders who are rated as more transformational or charismatic by followers are also rated by them as more effective (Bass and Avolio, 1993).

Attempts to research the subject of this chapter have led to laboratory research, survey research, interviews and case studies. There have also been intriguing studies of key historical figures, including American presidents; biographies and autobiographies of business leaders; and clinical analyses of the dynamics underlying both charismatic leadership and the behaviour of followers (Conger and Kanungo, 1987; Bryman, 1992). These generally support the view that what appears to be transformational leadership is associated with superior performance. In summary, charismatic or transformational leadership is generating a lot of interest in organizations and an increasing amount of research among organizational psychologists. It remains to be seen how well these concepts withstand prolonged critical scrutiny.

LEADERSHIP FROM BELOW

Writing from within a social information-processing perspective, Lord and Maher (1991) define leadership as 'the process of being perceived by others as a leader' (p. 11), thereby emphasizing the role of followers in attributing leadership to individuals. This raises the question of why some people are perceived as leaders while others, perhaps in the same formal role, are not; and it may provide particular insights into charismatic leadership.

Lord and Maher suggest that perceptions of leadership are based first on the fit between beliefs about how a leader ought to act and appear and the way an individual actually behaves; and, secondly, they are also inferred from outcomes of his or her behaviour. To take the first element, social information-processing theory assumes that we all carry around a number of mental 'scripts' about leadership. Research on social categorization by Lord and his colleagues has identified at least eleven domains of leadership – for example in politics, in business and in the media – and within each domain it is possible to identify agreed qualities that reflect perceptions of leadership. These are widely held assumptions about how leaders ought to behave and the qualities they should possess, and they largely reflect our prior socialization. For example, leaders in America are supposed to be intelligent; in most cases they are also expected to be honest and energetic. Those who display these expected characteristics, particularly in leadership roles, are more likely to be characterized as leaders. In short, they 'look the part'. This has important implications for understanding leadership, confirming that individual characteristics and behaviour are important even if they are not linked to any outcomes. The approach also emphasizes the importance of symbolic leadership. If you dress like a leader and possess the trappings of leadership, then in many cases you will be considered to be a leader. However, it may not make you an effective leader.

The second element in social information-processing theory deals with leadership effectiveness. It is concerned with attributions for outcomes. If a unit that you lead is highly successful, there is a strong likelihood that some of the credit will reflect on you as leader, even if you had little influence over the outcomes. One reason for this is that in seeking explanations of success or failure we fall back on the familiar 'scripts' or reasons. Leadership is something we expect to use as a reason in explaining the performance of a team. The same process occurs for failure, and in both cases the 'real' explanation may be less influential than those selected by observers. One side-effect is that some people who do not consider themselves to be leaders and who do not believe that they are displaying leadership may nevertheless sometimes be categorized as leaders, with positive or negative outcomes attributed to them.

Lord and Maher argue that despite the risk of faulty attribution, leaders can still have a real impact on outcomes under two particular sets of circumstances. The first is when they have sufficient discretion. This will be more likely in senior positions and in settings such as small family businesses or growing organizations of the sort Schein (1992) described in his studies of leaders' influence on the emergence of organizational culture. The second concept they use is drawn from 'catastrophe theory'. They suggest that in some circumstances leadership will be exerted but will have little impact; in others, because the organization or team is on the cusp of a curve, major change may result. For example, two successive leaders of a cash-rich organization may be able to invest rashly in new ventures with no discernible impact on the organization; to many observers these leaders may appear bold and adventurous. Suppose that the next leader continues the practice but when the resources have been depleted, the returns from the previous investments are too low, and the business goes bankrupt. The last leader was behaving in the same way as his two predecessors but on the edge of the cusp, or, in terms of the theory, on the edge of 'catastrophe'. All may have been ineffective leaders, but only for the last did the same leadership behaviour have a 'catastrophic' effect. The outcomes were more clearly visible and the attribution process differed accordingly.

Social information-processing approaches to leadership reflect the growing influence of cognitive psychology, and we can expect to see much wider application of this perspective. In contrast to the work on charisma, it is developed out of a more careful research base and through the conventional research methodology of social psychology. Yet it also neatly complements some of the research on charisma, particularly in the area of culture and leadership, where it sheds new light on the perceptions of followers. It also illustrates how we may 'talk up' leaders beyond their actual effectiveness. On the other hand, it is an approach that has been overly restricted to laboratory settings and student samples and it is now time to apply it much more extensively in organizational research.

DOES LEADERSHIP MAKE A DIFFERENCE?

Social information-processing theory helps to explain what has been described as the 'paradox of leadership' (Calder, 1977), the tendency to attribute leadership qualities to those in leadership positions even when formidable constraints severely limit their impact. There are a number of reasons, quite apart from a leader's competence, why those in formal leadership roles might have no impact on subordinate performance. For example, *laissez-faire* leaders do not seek to exert any influence. There are also circumstances in which highly participative group leadership renders the role of formal leader much more that of a resource and support rather than an influence on outcomes.

Kerr and Jermier (1978) have tried to identify other types of circumstance in which leaders will have little impact on outcomes. For example, they propose that where subordinates are highly competent and well qualified, where there is a clear organization structure and a set of formal and well-understood roles and where the task is well defined, predictable and provides good feedback on performance, then there is little need for leadership. These factors serve, in effect, as substitutes for leadership. These can be distinguished from neutralizers, such as legislation, market conditions or staff incompetence, which can prevent leadership from having an impact. Research (Howell and Dorfman, 1981, 1986), while revealing some evidence of substitution, has failed to demonstrate that it has a major effect or that it negates the influence of leadership. In circumstances where leadership has limited impact, the substitutes also have little impact. This implies that it may be more useful, as a first step, to identify key 'neutralizers'.

Much of the research on leadership at supervisory level has not given serious consideration to the expected size of the leadership effect. Indeed, many studies are concerned mainly to compare the impact of different styles in a given setting and to demonstrate that one is superior to another; a comparison group with no leader is not investigated. Where attempts have been made to show that leadership has a significant effect, the aim has usually been to demonstrate, through some form of regression analysis, that leadership explains a significant amount of the variance in the outcome. A successful result is thought to be one that reaches statistical significance. However, it may be more useful to focus on the actual size of the leadership effect. Furthermore, building on the substitutes for leadership theme, the size of an effect may depend on what other variables are taken into account.

A number of studies have addressed the question of how much influence leaders have on organizational performance. An early investigation by Lieberson and O'Connor (1972) explored the influence of chief executives in large American corporations. They did this by examining a number of criteria of corporate performance over several years, identifying any changes associated with changes in chief executive while controlling for other influences. They concluded that leadership explained about 8 per cent of the variation in profits, once other factors had been accounted for. Similarly, Pfeffer and Salancik (1978), in a study of the impact of a change in mayor on city budgets in America, found that these changes accounted for about 10 per cent of variance. Weiner and Mahoney (1981) obtained similar results in a methodologically more sophisticated study of changes in company chief executives over nineteen years.

Thomas (1988), reviewing these studies, notes that a factor such as size of organization inevitably explains a large amount of the variation in performance, and that the results depend in part on what is included in the regression analysis and even what order the items are entered. He also points out that, once the major influences are accounted for, if we look at what explains the remaining variance, then leadership becomes rather more important. In other words, once constraints imposed by size, the general economy and the industry have been taken into account, then leadership becomes a clearly important influence on performance. Fiedler and House (1988) reinforce this, adding that many organizations would be delighted to be able to influence even 10 per cent of the variance in performance. They cite an interesting study of Icelandic trawlers, showing that over a three-year period, the skipper accounted for between a third and half of the variation in size of trawler catch. In other words, leadership does matter.

SUMMARY

This chapter has explored some of the key themes in the psychology of leadership and management. We have considered the long-running stream of research on leadership style and contingency theories, suggesting that, for a number of reasons, they are running out of steam. We have shown how research on competencies has helped to give a new lease of life to trait theories of leadership. The idea of charismatic or transformational leadership holds considerable appeal and attracts burgeoning research but has some way to go to establish full credibility. Social information-processing theory provides new insights and now needs more application in organizational settings.

Finally, studies on the impact of leadership, from a range of disciplinary perspectives, confirm its importance.

The study of leadership and management highlights many of the challenges facing work and organizational psychology. It is widely believed that leadership is a key factor in our lives at work and an important direct or indirect influence on our well-being. Some of the research explains how we arrive at this view. At the same time, it is an enormously complex subject and research has progressed painfully slowly over many years. Indeed, our research methods seem to lag well behind the complexity of the theory. The research is subject to fads and fashions – the rediscovery of charisma and the role of leadership traits are two good examples – so any progress is crab-like. It is also revealing in its need for a variety of levels of analysis and research methods. If, as noted at the outset, this richness seems almost indigestible to some, to others it is a challenge. The amount of research that continues in the field is a testament to the fascination of this challenge and to the importance of the subject for all of us.

FURTHER READING

A good text book is Yukl's (1994) *Leadership in Organizations*. A useful overview of developments in charismatic and transformational leadership is provided by Bryman's (1992) *Charisma and Leadership in Organizations*. For the real enthusiasts, Bass's (1990) latest version of *Bass and Stogdill's Handbook of Leadership* reviews almost all the theory and research on the subject. Those wanting an up-to-date view of current developments in the field might look at the journal *Leadership Quarterly*. Finally, for a lighter account of leadership, there are numerous autobiographies by eminent industrial leaders such as Harvey-Jones (1991) and Iacocca (1985), although the best remain some of the 'classics', such as Sloan's (1964) *My Years With General Motors*.

REFERENCES

Bass, B. (1985). *Leadership and Performance Beyond Expectations*. New York: Free Press.

Bass, B. (1990). *Bass and Stogdill's Handbook of Leadership*, 3rd edn. New York: Free Press.

Bass, B. M. and Avolio, B. J. (1993). Transformational leadership: A response to critiques. In M. M. Chemers and R. Ayman (eds.), *Leadership Theory and Research: Perspectives and Directions*, pp. 49–80. San Francisco: Jossey-Bass.

Bennis, W. G. and Nanus, B. (1985). *Leaders: The Strategies for Taking Charge*. New York: Harper and Row.

Blake, R. R. and Mouton, J. S. (1964). *The Managerial Grid*. Houston: Gulf Publishing.

Boyatzis, R. E. (1982). *The Competent Manager*. New York: Wiley.

Bryman, A. (1992). *Charisma and Leadership in Organizations*. London: Sage.

Burns, J. M. (1978). *Leadership*. New York: Harper and Row.

Calder, B. J. (1977). An attributional theory of leadership. In B. M. Staw and G. .R. Salancik (eds.), *New Directions in Organizational Leadership*, pp. 179–204. Chicago: St Clair.

Conger, J. A. and Kanungo, R. N. (1987). Behavioral dimensions of charismatic leadership. In J. A. Conger and R. N. Kanungo (eds.), *Charismatic Leadership*, pp. 78–97. San Francisco: Jossey-Bass.

Conger, J. A. and Kanungo, R. N. (1994). Charismatic leadership in organizations: Perceived behavioral attributes and their measurement. *Journal of Organizational Behavior*, 15, 439–452.

Dowling, W. F. (1975). At General Motors: System 4 builds performance and profits. *Organizational Dynamics*, 3, 23–38.

Fiedler, F. E. (1967). *A Theory of Leadership Effectiveness*. New York: McGraw-Hill.

Fiedler, F. E. (1977). A rejoinder to Schriesheim and Kerr's premature obituary of the contingency model. In J. G. Hunt and L. L. Larson (eds.), *Leadership: the Cutting Edge*, pp. 45–51. Carbondale, Ill.: Southern Illinois University Press.

Fiedler, F. E. (1995). Cognitive resources and leadership performance. *Applied Psychology: An International Review*, 44, 5–28.

Fiedler, F. E. and Garcia, J. E. (1987). *New Approaches to Effective Leadership: Cognitive Resources and Organizational Performance*. New York: Wiley.

Fiedler, F. E. and House, R. J. (1988). Leadership theory and research: a report of progress. In C. L. Cooper and I. T. Robertson (eds.), *International Review of Industrial and Organizational Psychology 1988*, pp. 73–92. Chichester: Wiley.

Fleishman, E. A. (1953). The description of supervisory behavior. *Personnel Psychology*, 37, 1–6.

Graeff, C. L. (1983). The situational leadership theory; a critical review. *Academy of Management Review*, 8, 285–296.

Harvey-Jones, J. (1991). *Getting It Together*. London: Heinemann.

Hersey, P. and Blanchard, K. H. (1982). *Management of Organizational Behavior*, 4th edn. Englewood Cliffs, NJ: Prentice Hall.

Hofstede, G. (1980). *Culture's Consequences*. Beverly Hills, Calif.: Sage.

House, R. J. (1971). A path-goal theory of leader effectiveness. *Administrative Science Quarterly*, 16, 321–339.

House, R. J. (1977). A 1976 theory of charismatic leadership. In J. G. Hunt and L. L. Larson (eds.), *Leadership: The Cutting Edge*, pp. 189–207. Carbondale, Ill.: Southern Illinois University Press.

Howell, J. P. and Dorfman, P. W. (1981). Substitutes for leadership: Test of a construct. *Academy of Management Journal*, 24, 714–728.

Howell, J. P. and Dorfman, P. W. (1986). Leadership and substitutes for leadership among professional and non-professional workers. *Journal of Applied Behavioral Science*, 22, 29–46.

Iacocca, L. (1985). *Iacocca: An Autobiography*. New York: Bantam Books.

Kerr, S. and Jermier, J. M. (1978). Substitutes for leadership: Their meaning and measurement. *Organizational Behavior and Human Performance*, 22, 375–403.

Lawler, E. E. (1986). *High Involvement Management*. San Francisco: Jossey-Bass.

Lewin, K., Lippit, R. and White, R. (1939). Patterns of aggressive behaviour in experimentally created 'social climates'. *Journal of Social Psychology*, 10, 271–299.

Lieberson, S. and O'Connor, J. F. (1972). Leadership and organizational performance: a study of large corporations. *American Sociological Review*, 37, 117–130.

Likert, R. (1961). *New Patterns of Management*. New York: McGraw-Hill.

Likert, R. (1967). *The Human Organization*. New York: McGraw-Hill.

Lord, R. G. and Maher, K. J. (1991). *Leadership and Information Processing*. Boston, Mass.: Unwin Hyman.

Marrow, A. J., Bowers, D. G. and Seashore, S. E. (1967). *Management by Participation*. New York: Harper and Row.

McClelland, D. C. (1985). *Human Motivation*. Glenview, Ill.: Scott Foresman.

McClelland, D. C. and Boyatzis, R. E. (1982). Leadership motive pattern and long-term success in management. *Journal of Applied Psychology*, 67, 737–743.

Miner, J. B. (1993). *Role Motivation Theories*. London: Routledge.

Misumi, J. (1985). *The Behavioral Science of Leadership: An Interdisciplinary Japanese Research Program*. Ann Arbor, Mich.: University of Michigan Press.

Misumi, J. and Peterson, M. (1985). The performance-maintenance (PM) theory of leadership: Review of a Japanese research program. *Administrative Science Quarterly*, 30, 198–223.

Peters, L. H., Harthe, D. D. and Pohlmann, J. T. (1985). Fiedler's contingency theory of leadership: an application of the meta-analysis procedures of Schmidt and Hunter. *Psychological Bulletin*, 97, 274–285.

Peters, T. and Waterman, R. (1982). *In Search of Excellence*. New York: Harper and Row.

Pfeffer, J. and Salancik, G. R. (1978). *The External Control of Organizations: A Resource Dependence Perspective*. New York: Harper and Row.

Porter, M. (1985). *Competitive Advantage: Creating and Sustaining Superior Performance*. New York: Free Press.

Prahalad, C. K. and Doz, Y. (1987). *The Multinational Mission*. New York: Free Press.

Rosen, N. A. (1969). *Leadership Change and Work Group Dynamics: An Experiment*. Ithaca, NY: Cornell University Press.

Schein, E. A. (1992). *Organizational Culture and Leadership*, 2nd edn. San Francisco: Jossey-Bass.

Sloan, A. (1964). *My Years With General Motors*. New York: Doubleday.

Smith, P. B., Misumi, J., Tayeb, B., Peterson, M. and Bond, M. (1989). On the generality of leadership styles across cultures. *Journal of Occupational Psychology*, 62, 97–109.

Smith, P. B., Peterson, M. F. and Misumi, J. (1994). Event management and work team effectiveness in Japan, Britain and the USA. *Journal of Occupational and Organizational Psychology*, 67, 33–43.

Sparrow, P. R. (1994). Organisational competencies: creating a strategic framework for selection and assessment. In N. Anderson and P. Herriot (eds.), *Handbook of Assessment and Appraisal*, pp. 1–26. London: Wiley.

Stogdill, R. M. (1948). Personal factors associated with leadership: a survey of the literature. *Journal of Psychology*, 25, 35–71.

Stogdill, R. M. (1974). *Handbook of Leadership: A Survey of the Literature*. New York: Free Press.

Thomas, A. B. (1988). Does leadership make a difference to organizational performance? *Administrative Science Quarterly*, 33, 388–400.

Vecchio, R. P. (1990). Theoretical and empirical examination of cognitive resource theory. *Journal of Applied Psychology*, 75, 141–147.

Vroom, V. H. and Jago, A. G. (1988). *The New Leadership: Managing Participation in Organizations*. Englewood Cliffs, NJ: Prentice Hall.

Vroom, V. H. and Yetton, P. W. (1973). *Leadership and Decision-Making*. Pittsburgh: University of Pittsburgh Press.

Wagner, J. (1994). Participation's effect on performance and satisfaction: A reconsideration of research evidence. *Academy of Management Review*, 19, 312–330.

Weber, M. (1947). *The Theory of Social and Economic Organizations*. New York: Free Press.

Weiner, N. and Mahoney, T. H. (1981). A model of corporate performance as a function of environmental, organizational and leadership influence. *Academy of Management Journal*, 24, 453–470.

Yukl, G. (1994). *Leadership in Organizations*, 3rd edn. London: Prentice Hall.

10

Women and Employment

Marilyn J. Davidson

In a recent survey only half of the British women aged between 16 and 35 years reported that bearing children was first on their agenda; the rest gave priority to their careers (Wilkinson, 1994). These contemporary attitudes are in sharp contrast to those of women brought up in the first half of the century, when women were raised to marry, have children and care for husband and home. The aim of this chapter is to examine the changing position of women at work and to highlight some of the major problem areas. The central issues arise from the fact that, despite the increase of labour market participation of women (especially mothers), women's employment is mostly concentrated in a limited number of industrial sectors and certain low-status, low-pay job categories. The effects of legislation on women's rights in the workforce and the barriers to women's advancement will be considered, as will those additional stressors often experienced by working women, particularly if married and with a family. The chapter will also review current and likely future trends in women's employment and positive strategies being initiated through legislative pressure, changing work patterns, new technology, organizations and women themselves.

CHANGES IN WOMEN'S WORK PATTERNS

Due to the rapid demographic, social and economic changes over the past few decades, there has been a large increase in the number of women entering paid employment throughout Western Europe, North America and Australasia (Davidson and Cooper, 1993). In the USA, for example, in 1950 women constituted 33 per cent of the labour force, whereas today they represent 45 per cent of the workforce; 58 per cent of US women are employed outside the home in part-time or full-time employment (US Department of Labor, 1992).

Similar changes have occurred in the United Kingdom. The number of women in employment increased by 16 per cent between 1984 and 1993, while the number of men in work remained about the same. Over this same period the percentage of women of working age who are economically active increased from 66 to 71 per cent, while the figures for men declined from 88 to 86 per cent. Today British women constitute 44 per cent of the workforce (Hammond, 1994; Labour Force Survey, 1993; Sly, 1993).

Throughout the 1980s there has also been a surge in women's participation in the European labour market as a whole. Women now make up 41 per cent of all adults in the European Community who are in work or looking for work (Rubery and Fagan, 1993). Moreover, one of the significant changes in the female labour force has been the influx of married working women aged between 25 and 49 years. Denmark has the highest percentage of married working women at over 80 per cent, followed by the UK at around 65 per cent, and Portugal and France, both around 60 per cent (Davidson and Cooper, 1993). Similar patterns emerge in Australia, where women account for 42 per cent of the workforce (Still, 1993). Furthermore, these rates are predicted to continue increasing, particularly among younger women. In the UK, for example, about three-quarters of women are expected to be working by the year 2001 (Commission of the European Communities, 1990).

This significant continued rise in employment among women has its roots in a number of developments. These include the expansion of service industries, the increase in part-time employment, and changes in life expectancy, economic circumstances (especially in relation to employment and housing) and social expectations (Millar, 1992). In addition, the changing nature of the family means smaller families and households, later marriage, more cohabitation, more extra-marital births, more divorce and more and more people living in one-parent families with dependent children (predominantly headed by women) and dependent elderly relatives (7 per cent of British households).

Since the mid-1970s there has been a swing from employment in traditional industries such as manufacturing towards the personal service sector, an area of employment that is traditionally female and one which offers plenty of flexible employment patterns. Indeed, for several years the UK government has promoted greater labour market flexibility in relation to flexible hours, job sharing, part-time working, home working and self-employment (Watson, 1994). In 1993 38 per cent of all UK workers were either part-time, temporary, self-employed, on a government training scheme or unpaid family business workers – an increase of 1.25 million since 1986. Eighty-five per cent of part-timers and 56 per cent of temporary employees are women. While the proportion of women in employment who are part of the flexible workforce has remained stable at about 50 per cent, the figure for men has risen from 18 per cent in 1981 to 27 per cent in 1993. Women hold 83 per cent of all part-time jobs in the European Union (EU), with 14 per cent of all EU workers being part-timers. Moreover, women are twice as likely to be concentrated in lower-paid jobs in the service industry compared to their full-time counterparts (30 per cent compared to 15 per cent) (Rubery and Fagan, 1994).

While the percentage of female part-time workers belonging to unions is lower than that of full-time workers, at the end of 1992 UK women members of TUC-affiliated trade unions constituted 36 per cent of the total membership. Against a background of falling union membership generally, nine out of the twenty-six unions with over 10,000 women members reported gains in female membership between 1991 and 1992 (Equal Opportunities Review, 1994). However, according to Labour Research (1994), women in the UK are still underrepresented on national executive bodies, on delegations to the annual Trades Union Congress and among full-time officials. With union representation being associated with better pay, job benefits and opportunities, this underrepresentation of women in unions appears likely to continue to act as a major disadvantage for women workers (particularly part-timers).

Life-stages, particularly parenthood, clearly have a much greater influence on women's working lives than on men's. In 1994 64 per cent of UK mothers with children under 16 were economically active compared with 55 per cent in 1984. Among people of working age 63 per cent of mothers worked part-time, and the greatest increase in labour market participation has been among women with children aged under 5, an increase from 37 per cent in 1984 to 52 per cent in 1994. In contrast, employment grew more slowly or even declined among mothers with no educational qualifications, lone mothers, mothers with a youngest child of secondary school age, mothers with three or more children, and black mothers (Sly, 1994). Indeed, it should be noted that despite having higher levels of education and qualifications than white women, 16 per cent of ethnic-minority women are unemployed (this compares with an official 1993 unemployment rate of 8 per cent for British women and 12 per cent for men).

Occupation Segregation by Gender

Throughout Western countries occupational segregation by gender still persists. Table 10.1 illustrates that in the European Union 50 per cent of employed women are found in service or clerical jobs, compared with less than 20 per cent of men. According to Rubery and Fagan (1993), the majority of the new jobs entered by women in the 1980s were in two occupational areas: professional work and clerical work. These authors maintain that while an increasing number of women are entering the lower-level service and clerical jobs (making these job categories even more female-dominated), a smaller proportion of women are gaining access to highly skilled professional jobs (including management).

Similar trends are occurring in Australasia and the USA. In Australia, 55 per cent of female employees in 1992 were concentrated in two major occupational groups: clerks and salespersons. While 20 per cent of Australian female employees were in professional and para-professional occupations, 22 per cent were registered nurses (Australian Bureau of Statistics, 1992). Even in the USA, with the strongest legislation affecting the employment of women, women are most frequently found in the helping professions, and in sales and retail jobs. In 1992 US women held 98 per cent of secretarial, typist and stenographer positions, 79 per cent of administrative support jobs, and 94 per cent of registered nurse positions (US Department of Labor, 1992).

Table 10.1 International Standard Classification of Occupations (ISCO 68) from the European Community Labour Force Survey

Major occupational groups	Female/male share of jobs (%)	Concentration of employment women (%)	men (%)
Professional, technical and related workers Scientists, nurses, teachers, lawyers, artists, etc.	45/55	19	16
Administrative and managerial workers Government administrators plus managers not classified elsewhere	23/77	2	4
Clerical and related workers Clerical supervisors, typists, cashiers, telephonists, etc.	64/36	30	11
Sales workers All sales workers, including managers and working proprietors	49/51	12	9
Service workers All catering and related workers, including managers; personal service workers such as cleaners and hairdressers; the police	66/34	20	7
Agricultural and related workers All agricultural and related workers, including managers and supervisors	34/66	5	7
Production, transport, labourers and related workers Manufacturing and construction workers and supervisors	16/84	12	45
Military	*/100	*	1
All employment (**EC11**)†	41/59	100	100

Source: Rubery and Fagan (1993).

* less than 0.5%.   † no occupational data available for Italy.

There have, however, been some advances in women entering traditionally male dominated jobs, and in all the European Union countries women are increasing their share of professional jobs (i.e., scientists, nurses, teachers, lawyers, artists, etc.). In the UK, for example, in 1994 women accounted for 54 per cent of newly qualified solicitors, which was an increase of nearly 9 per cent over the preceding seven years. There has also been an increase of 10 per cent of women becoming chartered accountants since the mid-1980s and in 1994 they represented 37 per cent of newly qualified accountants (Wilkinson, 1994). Even so, the majority of women in professional jobs are still concentrated in the caring professional and the public sector and occupy the lower managerial positions (Davidson and Cooper, 1993). In the European Union countries fewer than 5 per cent of women are in senior management roles.

There is an increasing trend for women to start their own businesses, with between 15 and 30 per cent of entrepreneurs or business owners in the European Union being female (Davidson and Cooper, 1993). In the USA women-owned small businesses have increased from 5 per cent in 1970 to 35 per cent in 1994, with forecasts of the figure reaching 50 per cent by the year 2000 (Tarr Whelan, 1994). In the UK, with nearly a quarter of all self-employed people being women, this is a figure that has doubled since 1980 (Department of Employment and Equal Opportunities Commission, 1994). While many of these businesses are small, they are undoubtedly growing in size and number. Indeed, it has been suggested that the control and flexibility provided by owning one's own business are often a greater attraction to working women, particularly those with children, than is employment in a hierarchy-driven, male-dominated corporate culture (Marshall, 1994).

In Britain there are approximately 3 million managers at all levels, about a fifth of whom are women. However, of the million or so middle and senior managers, at most 4 per cent are women (Davidson and Burke, 1994). A British Institute of Management (BIM) survey, which covered the careers of 1,882 male and female managers, revealed that women were found less in manufacturing management than men and were more likely to be managers in service organizations (Nicholson and West, 1988). Women managers are also likely to be found in certain areas, such as personnel, office administration and training, and in organizations where there are a higher than average number of other women. However, even in those professions where women outnumber men, such as teaching and personnel, men still dominate the senior positions. For example, in 1994, while 44 per cent of personnel managers were female, only 9.5 per cent of personnel directors were women (Lownes, 1994).

In the United States in 1979 30 per cent of American managers were women. By 1994 this figure had risen to over 44 per cent. Even so, despite affirmative action legislation, American female managers are still finding the 'glass ceiling' difficult to shatter at senior executive level, where women hold only 5 per cent of managerial positions – a percentage that has hardly changed in the last decade (Davidson and Burke, 1994).

All in all, we can conclude that there has been little reduction in the segregation of jobs based on gender over the years. While there have been increases in the number of women entering the professions, positions in middle management and senior executive roles and directorships are still predominantly held by men. Indeed, gender segregation in the workforce has also encouraged the pay differences which still persist between men and women, despite the introduction of sexual discrimination and equal pay legislation. In the European Union countries, while gender pay gaps persist in every member state, the size of the gap varies not only by country but also between manual and non-manual jobs. Women in manual jobs earn between 67 and 84 per cent of men's average pay. The ratio is highest in Denmark, Italy and Greece, where it ranges from 79 to 84 per cent, and lowest in the UK, Luxembourg and Ireland, where it stands between 67 and 70 per cent. The difference in earnings between male and female non-manual workers is even wider. Women in non-manual work receive less than two-thirds of men's average pay in all countries except four (Portugal, Greece, France and Germany) and the ratio is as low as 58 and 55 per cent in the UK and Luxembourg (Rubery, Fagan and Grimshaw, 1994).

BARRIERS TO WOMEN'S ADVANCEMENT

Barriers to women's advancement arise from numerous sources, including sex stereotyping from an early age and the substantial influence of the discontinuous pattern of many women's working lives. These are compounded by barriers within organizations related to their structure and climate, prejudice and discrimination, and attitudinal barriers from both men and women themselves. These in turn may subject women to additional stresses in the workplace, which can be made worse by conflicts between their home and work roles.

Gender Stereotyping and the Education System

Gender stereotyping begins at birth and continues during education and training. The attitudes of teachers, peers and parents can act as limiting agents on females in terms of undermining their ambition and restricting their choice of jobs and careers. This has been reinforced by a lack of female role models in senior positions in education, science, engineering and technology (Department of Employment, 1994). Certainly, the media reinforces these attitudes by depicting women in traditional gender stereotyped roles in advertising, television (particularly in dramas), movies, newspapers and magazines (Lahtinen and Wilson, 1994).

There is still a marked difference between the educational courses taken by males and females within both academic and vocational subjects. In Britain and throughout Europe females' participation in technology, engineering and science education after the age of 16 (and their subsequent occupational participation) shows limited improvement. Nevertheless, research suggests that schoolgirls in Britain are more ambitious, have higher self-esteem and obtain better academic examination results than boys (Balding, 1993).

There have been significant increases in the number of females going into higher education. By 1991 the proportion of women in full-time higher education increased to 48 per cent in first-degree courses and 40 per cent in postgraduate courses, compared to 41 and 32 per cent respectively in 1983. Although men still dominate science undergraduate degree courses (46 per cent of all male undergraduates compared to 26 per cent of all female undergraduates), today in the UK more than 45 per cent of students of business degrees are female (Davidson and Cooper, 1992).

Patterns of Women's Working Lives

Once women are established in the workforce, another barrier that has been linked to their predominance in low-status, low-pay jobs is the fact that, unlike men, the majority of women have discontinuous work patterns, as they withdraw temporarily from the labour market to care for young children.

Even so, recent British statistics show that 63 per cent of women with dependent children were employed in 1993 and the proportion of women returning to work soon after childbirth had doubled since 1983. (The average age for mothers to have a first child has increased to 28 years.) Nearly two-thirds of women in employment who leave to have a baby are again economically active within nine months of childbirth (Labour Force Survey, 1994). Thus, the working lives of mothers are reduced, but not dramatically curtailed.

Many women also report that the career-related dilemma concerning whether to start a family is a major stressor in their lives (Davidson, Cooper and Baldini, 1995). Many say they would benefit greatly from extended maternity-break schemes, as well as more flexible working arrangements such as part-time work, flexitime, job sharing, job splitting, etc. (Ferrario, 1994). More and more organizations are now introducing extended maternity break schemes for their female employees, and the economic losses as well as the losses in terms of talent when women are not encouraged to return to work after childbearing are now beginning to be acknowledged.

Certainly, women are often unfairly penalized by the majority of employers for having a break from the workforce. Inflexible working patterns, poor maternity rights and lack of affordable childcare result in the majority of women with children re-entering the workplace in part-time jobs, often in low-paid, low-status positions with less favourable contractual arrangements than others (Employment Gazette 1994).

It is also often assumed that women are not as geographically mobile as men. However, British research has indicated that women managers, for example, tend to be more mobile and more radical in their job changes compared to men managers. This study (Nicholson and West, 1988) also found that women managers with children made the most rapid job changes compared to childless female managers and male managers generally (as well as being highly motivated regarding success and scoring high on dominance, adjustment and need for growth). However, the investigators reported that many of the women referred to job changes which had been imposed on them because their male partners had to move location for career reasons. Unlike the majority of married male managers, the majority of married women managers are in dual-career partnerships and must deal with the issues associated with the management of two careers and family life. While both men and women in dual-career families have to face these issues, the impact on women's careers is generally much greater than that on men's (Lewis, 1994; White, Cox and Cooper, 1992).

Barriers within Organizations

Barriers within organizations hampering women's development in the workplace fall into two broad categories: structural and attitudinal. Structural barriers include personnel policies, procedures and practices. Attitudinal barriers, on the other hand, relate to women's attitudes and attitudes towards working women generally, particularly those held by employers.

Structural barriers

Although the majority of clearly discriminatory practices within personnel policies and practices have been eliminated, owing largely to antidiscrimination legislation, many forms of indirect discrimination still persist. Examples of indirect discrimination against women include job vacancies that are open only to candidates of certain age groups (which may exclude older women re-entering the labour market), those requiring specific qualifications and job experience, inflexible working arrangements, mobility requirements, and so on (Hansard Society Commission 1990).

Discriminatory personnel practices have also been found to persist within recruitment, promotion appraisal systems and training opportunities (particularly for women in non-traditional female jobs) (Alimo-Metcalfe, 1994). Hirsh and Jackson (1989) make the important point that the majority of organizations still rely on the nonstandardized interview method of selection, despite all the evidence that shows it to be unreliable and more likely to facilitate bias against minority candidates. Some researchers, such as Pearn, Kandola and Mottram (1987), maintain that properly chosen and used psychological tests can help minimize bias in selection. However, others emphasize the dangers and problems of identifying gender bias as assessment techniques become more complex (Alimo-Metcalfe, 1994).

Recent reports have indicated that, among full-time employees, women are more likely (18 per cent) than men (14 per cent) to have received job-related training in the recent past. However, part-time female employees are less likely to have received job-related training than those women working full-time. Employers are also less likely to finance female employees' training outside the workplace compared to male employees', and young men are more likely than young women to have received recent training. Furthermore, employers are often reluctant to retrain women re-entering the workforce after a break, even though they often have many years of working life in front of them. The incidence of training in the recent past among women returning to the labour market was only 9 per cent, compared to 18 per cent for all full-time women employees (Labour Force Survey, 1994).

Attitudinal barriers
Undoubtedly, women's attitudes and behaviour also have a bearing on their position within the workforce. Whether employed full- or part-time, the majority of women work not only for financial rewards, but also because they enjoy their job. In one of the most extensive surveys of British working women's attitudes, over half of the women (52 per cent) stated that they took a job because they enjoyed working, followed by 'financial reasons' (47 per cent), 'for the company of other people' (44 per cent) and 'to earn money of my own' (37 per cent) (Martin and Roberts, 1984). A more recent qualitative investigation reported that the majority of women who worked part-time did so not only as a way of balancing family and work commitments and obtaining some financial independence, but also as a way of gaining self-esteem (Department of Employment, 1992). The Labour Force Survey (1994) found that the majority of women (and men) worked part-time because it fitted into their domestic

needs, and less than 14 per cent worked part-time because they had failed to get a full-time job. However, less than one-third of ethnic-minority women in employment worked part-time compared to 46 per cent of white women. It has been suggested that this may be due to the fact that ethnic-minority families have lower family incomes and rely on two full-time wage earners, as well as ethnic female workers being concentrated in the manufacturing sector, where part-time hours are less available (Department of Employment, 1994a).

In terms of job satisfaction, women who said they were working to earn money to provide basic essentials were the least satisfied, and those who worked because they enjoyed it were the most satisfied (Martin and Roberts, 1984). When job-content variables are controlled, numerous studies have found no differences in job satisfaction between the sexes (e. g., Lefkowitz, 1994). Similarly, research investigating the effect of part-time work on job attitudes also suggests there are no systematic differences in overall levels of satisfaction between part-time and full-time employees (Rotchford and Roberts, 1982). However, in his extensive review of the literature Feldman (1990) concludes that part-time workers may be more dissatisfied with particular aspects of their jobs, such as fringe benefits and pay, compared to full-time workers.

The British Department of Employment survey also investigated the attitudes of both men and women towards their segregation in the workforce (Martin and Roberts, 1984). Not surprisingly, women working in higher occupational levels were least likely to class their work as 'women's work', whereas women working in all-female environments (particularly part-timers) were most likely to think of their jobs as 'women's work'. It is important to note that this study highlighted that working in all-male environments also influences men's attitudes towards women as workers. A higher proportion of men (60 per cent) saw their work as 'men's work', compared to 40 per cent of women who viewed their work as 'women's work' (Martin and Roberts, 1984).

There is also little evidence to suggest that employed women are any less ambitious than men about promotion and attaining leadership positions. Almost half of all the female employees surveyed by Martin and Roberts (1984) said they would like to be considered for promotion and 32 per cent of these were in jobs that respondents viewed as having no promotion prospects.

While women in higher occupational groups are most likely to desire promotion and also enjoy promotional opportunities, an Industrial Society (1994b) survey revealed that a high proportion of female secretaries (39 per cent) who desired promotion also asserted that they had no promotion prospects. In fact, women working in clerical and secretarial jobs have been found to have particularly high job dissatisfaction and frustration over future career development (Silverstone and Towler, 1983; Industrial Society, 1994b).

Lastly, it has been suggested in the past that a major problem for women professionals' career advancement is their fear of responsibility and leadership positions, the alleged 'fear of success syndrome' (e.g., Horner, 1970). However, numerous studies have reported no differences regarding achievement motivation, aspirations towards promotion, or motivation to manage (Davidson and Burke, 1994), and some studies have found women managers to be more ambitious and committed to their careers than their male counterparts (Nicholson and West, 1988; Lahtinen and Wilson, 1994).

Attitudes towards working women
Prejudiced attitudes towards women in paid work are associated with beliefs such as 'a woman's place is in the home', women are suited only for certain types of jobs and women do not make as good leadership or management material as men. Qualitative studies, for example, tend to confirm that the majority of men are ambivalent about married women seeking paid employment, tending to play down the economic pressures for them to work and viewing it as 'the women's choice' (Brannen and Moss, 1990). Studies have shown that compared to their male counterparts women managers are more likely to say that prejudice against them as a group has affected their promotional prospects. Women have also quoted examples of less qualified and less experienced male colleagues achieving considerably faster promotion; having a female boss does not always prevent this (Alban-Metcalfe and Nicholson, 1984; Davidson and Burke, 1994).

Certainly, one of the major barriers preventing women professionals and women managers from shattering the 'glass ceiling' and attaining more senior positions is the continued biased attitude towards women based on the sex-role stereotyping of the managerial position. It is widely felt that the characteristics required for success in traditional male professions are more likely to be held by men in general than by women in general. In other words the tendency is to 'think pilot, think male', 'think surgeon, think male', 'think manager, think male' (Schein, 1994). Examining attitudes towards women managers and women in general by males is particularly important, taking into account a recent survey of 1,500 female managers and 800 male managers carried out by the UK Institute of Management on its members (Institute of Management, 1992). While 74 per cent of women 'strongly agreed' that women managers brought positive skills to the workplace, only one-third of men believed this to be the case. Furthermore, nearly 20 per cent of men maintained they would find it difficult to work for a woman. Their reasons included 'in general, women do not make good managers, although they have much to offer in the workplace'.

In the USA Brenner, Tomkiewicz and Schein (1989) and Schein (1989) carried out fifteen-year follow-up studies on the relationship between sex-role stereotypes and requisite management characteristics. These surveys revealed that, unlike women in the 1970s, American female managers and female management students today do not sex-type managerial positions, but view women and men as equally likely to possess characteristics necessary for managerial success. However, American male management students viewed the management position in the same way today as did US male management students and male managers in the 1970s. All three male groups believed that, compared with women, men were more likely to possess characteristics necessary for managerial success. More recently, Schein and Davidson (1993) confirmed that 'think manager, think male' is a strongly held attitude among British undergraduate male management students. Although the British female undergraduate management sample also sex-typed the managerial position, it was to a lesser extent than their male counterparts. American research confirms that black and ethnic-minority managers (particularly women) are doubly disadvantaged in terms of upward mobility, as they are subjected to both sex and ethnic role stereotyping of the managerial job: 'think manager, think "Caucasian" male' (Bell, 1990; Greenhouse, Parasuraman and Warmley, 1990).

An examination of the specific item ratings in these studies can provide some understanding of how managerial sex-typing can impact negatively on women's managerial opportunities. Characteristics such as 'leadership ability' and 'skilled in business matters' would be considered as very important to effectiveness by most management theorists and practitioners. Yet, according to the results of Schein and Davidson (1993), women are considered less likely than men to possess these characteristics. If this view is held by current managers as well as the students sampled, it is no wonder that so many of the male managers surveyed by the Institute of Management (1992) believed that women do not make good managers. All else being equal, the perceived similarity between the characteristics of successful middle managers and men in general increases the likelihood of a (Caucasian) male rather than a female being selected for, or promoted into, a managerial position. As such, future managers and 'captains of industry' can be expected to view women as less qualified for managerial positions, and make selection, placement and promotion decisions that regularly impair women's advancement. This is despite the fact that there are far more similarities than differences in the way men and women 'manage' (Ferrario, 1994). Moreover, since the mid-1970s research has consistently shown that women are as effective as men as managerial leaders (Bourantas and Papalexandris, 1990; Ferrario, 1994).

Stress at Work

Certain female-dominated jobs, such as secretary, waitress and clinical technician, have been shown to be particularly stressful (Terbourg, 1985). As the topic of occupational stress is treated as a whole in Chapter 7, the focus here will be on those additional pressures faced by working women which are gender-related. While paid employment provides many positive benefits for women, for some (especially the working wife) the excessive pressure and scarcity of free time can adversely affect their ability to cope. In some cases the result may be mental and physical illnesses such as depression, anxiety, high blood pressure and headaches. This, in turn, can sometimes lead to decreased work performance; changed sleeping habits;

293

alcohol, drug and smoking abuse; poor personal relationships with colleagues; and occasional absenteeism (Davidson and Cooper, 1983; 1987; 1992).

In particular, it is 'token women' working in non-traditional jobs, whether blue- or white-collar, who have been found to suffer most from discrimination and prejudice at work. When women comprise less than 15 per cent of a total category in an organization, they can be labelled 'tokens', which means that they tend to be viewed as symbols of their group rather than as individuals. Women working in traditionally male jobs have been shown to have higher self-esteem than homemakers of similar status (Nelson and Quick, 1985). Nevertheless, as a minority group subjected to male-dominated organizational culture and policy making, research indicates that these women face a greater number of work-related pressures than their male counterparts. For example, women managers have been found to have more psychosomatic ill-health symptoms than men managers. The specific problems and pressures which have been observed in female managers include: strains of coping with prejudice and sex stereotyping; overt and indirect discrimination from fellow employees, employers and the organizational structure and climate; lack of role models; feelings of isolation; and burdens of coping with the role of the 'token woman' (Davidson and Cooper, 1987, 1992; Davidson, Cooper, and Baldini, 1995; Devanna, 1987).

Sexual harassment (unwanted conduct of a sexual nature, or other conduct based on sex affecting the dignity of women and men at work; Rubenstein, 1991) is a potential problem for the majority of working women, and victims of sexual harassment often experience negative behavioural, physical, psychological and health-related outcomes. Specific negative effects of sexual harassment can include depression, anger, fear, irritability, anxiety, nausea, headaches, insomnia, tiredness, increased alcohol drinking and smoking, as well as dependence on drugs (Terpstra and Baker, 1991; Wright and Bean, 1993). Earnshaw and Davidson's (1994) study of British women who had taken sexual harassment claims to Industrial Tribunals indicated that over half those interviewed had to seek medical help and were prescribed drugs such as sleeping tablets, anti-depressants, etc. Not surprisingly the victims' relationships with others (particularly other men) can be adversely affected, as can their general attitude towards work in terms of lowered motivation, decreased job satisfaction, lowered confidence to do the job and lowered organizational commitment (Gutek, 1985). One of the most serious negative work-related outcomes as a result of sexual harassment is loss of one's job. Victims of sexual harassment are much more likely than the (male) harasser to be relocated within the company, quit or lose their job. Although research shows that all women are at risk regardless of their appearance or age, certain groups of women appear to be more vulnerable to sexual harassment. These include women working in masculine sex-typed jobs, women in non-senior positions, younger women, and divorced and separated women (Terpstra and Baker, 1991; Earnshaw and Davidson, 1994).

In the USA sexual harassment in employment is treated seriously, having become an economic issue whereby litigation damages have been awarded against companies sanctioning the behaviour of harassers (Terpstra and Baker, 1991). Conversely, in Britain and continental Europe it has been more difficult to get employers or the media to treat the issue as seriously. However, in the late 1980s the European Commission began to show concern about workplace sexual harassment and the lack of management action to stamp it out. They commissioned a research report to determine the extent to which sexual harassment was a problem across the European Community (Rubenstein, 1988). Following the submission of this report, an EC Recommendation and Code of Practice were published, emphasizing the role of both management and unions in combating, and communicating procedures for dealing with, sexual harassment in work settings (Rubenstein, 1991).

Home / Work Conflicts

Besides being subjected to additional pressures at work, the majority of working women, especially those with children, are far more affected by the burdens and pressures of their home and childcare duties than are most employed men. Indeed, women in paid employment who appear most vulnerable to stress-related maladies are those who have acquired a dual role in which they combine paid work with unpaid domestic work in the family (Pugliesi, 1988). Multiple-role strain is a major source of overload for employed women, especially in a society that prescribes certain expectations and behaviours in women's roles that are often contradictory. The conflicts and frustration arising from multiple roles serve to increase the demands on women, potentially leading to fatigue and lower mental health (Repetti, Mathews and Waldron, 1989). The main forms of inter-role conflict for many working women revolve around guilt feelings, lack of emotional and domestic social support from partners, and inadequate childcare facilities. Thus, in families where both partners have full-time jobs a major source of stress is the fact that the number of demands on a partner (particularly the female) often exceeds the time and energy to deal with them (Lewis, 1994).

The *British Social Attitudes Survey* (HMSO, 1991) found that in dual-earner couples (which constitute 60 per cent of the total, compared to only 43 per cent in 1973), where both partners worked full-time, women are still mainly responsible for domestic duties in 67 per cent of households. These findings are also paralleled by American studies, which have shown that in partnerships where both individuals are in employment, women are working at least an extra fifteen hours extra unpaid a week through domestic labour in the home (Swiss and Squires, 1993). Although British research indicates that compared to a decade ago, fathers are spending more time with their children, the majority of men remain attached to their role as male breadwinner, and job segregation based on gender still persists even in the home environment (HMSO, 1991). For example, a recent UK report noted that although 69 per cent of the male and female sample maintained that men ought to do the same jobs around the house as women, in reality 85 per cent of the women did the laundry, 77 per cent did the cooking, 75 per cent the cleaning and 66 per cent the shopping (Ferri, 1993).

British studies have repeatedly shown that many women who want a job are either unable to take one or are restricted to part-time hours because of the severe shortage of childcare facilities. Although pre-school childcare places have become more available, with the number of places in day nurseries and with registered childminders more than doubling between 1985 and 1992, fewer than 50 per cent of children aged between 3 and 5 years have access to childcare provisions (compared to over 90 per cent of French children) (Davidson and Cooper,

1993). The UK Government supports the EC Childcare Recommendation, which places an emphasis on co-operation and partnership between statutory, private, voluntary, employer and employee interests. However, the number of employer-sponsored nurseries, for example, has increased only from 425 in 1992 to 482 in 1994, with only one child in every 250 having access to such a place (Working For Childcare, 1994). While higher-income families can afford the luxuries of nannies and au pairs, the majority of working women with young children (particularly shift-workers and single parents) have to rely on family-based childcare, frequently grandparents (Kozak, 1994).

FUTURE TRENDS AND PROSPECTS

With the advent of changing employment patterns what does the future hold for employed women? What are the changes necessary in order to improve women's position in the workforce?

Of the projected total rise in the British labour force by 2006 of 1.5 million, 1.3 million is accounted for by women. As a consequence, women are projected to make up 46 per cent of the total workforce in 2006, compared with 44 per cent in 1993 (Ellison, 1994). These new jobs are expected to be located in the services sector, where women's level of employment will continue to grow substantially. Wilson (1994) also forecasts that women are likely to increase their share in almost all occupations, particularly in the professional, managerial and associated professional area, where they are currently underrepresented.

However, on a more pessimistic note, most of projected increased employment for women will be in the lower-status, lower-paid, part-time jobs. Even where women are increasing their share in higher-level occupations such as management, Wilson (1994) questions whether this is indicative of a growing equality or rather contributes towards enhanced gender segregation within these particular professions. For example, he cites evidence that the increasing number of females entering their first management positions in hotel and catering are actually receiving below even the average female earnings.

Employment gains for ethnic-minority women are predicted to be much fewer than those for white women. In 1989, whereas 17 per cent of white women were employed in occupational groups forecast to grow, this compared to only 5 per cent of ethnic-minority women. Furthermore, compared with only 11 per cent of white women, 30 per cent of ethnic-minority women were employed in occupations forecast to contract substantially. This, allied with the expected increased proportion of ethnic-minority women in the workforce (particularly qualified workers), has led some to conclude that these women will make up a larger percentage of female unemployment in the future (Wilson, 1994).

It is also evident that larger numbers of people are working at home, remote from their employing organizations. Home-based workers now form about 3 per cent of all employees and self-employed in the workforce, and this figure has doubled between 1981 and 1993 (Labour Force Survey, 1994). Eleven per cent of firms employ such 'teleworkers' working from home, and there are around sixty 'telecottages' in Britain (HMSO, 1995). Working from home with information technology has steadily increased, particularly by women who have young children (especially in rural areas), and over 70 per cent of the 622,000 working at home in 1993 were women. Less than a quarter of homeworkers in Britain are carrying out manufacturing work (compared to one-third a decade ago), and the majority of information technology homeworkers (472,000) are in managerial, professional, technical, clerical and secretarial occupations (Labour Force Survey, 1994).

As computers continue to proliferate throughout the workplace with the increasing application of information technology, there is growing concern that females are much less likely than males to study computer sciences (Brosnan and Davidson, 1994). In 1979 the proportion of females within computer science education peaked at 25 per cent. Since that time, however, the percentage of females taking computer science has steadily declined to 7 per cent in 1990. Moreover, it has been proposed that failure to acquire computer literacy may in future become a 'critical filter' for women, who will therefore not have access to the numerous careers that require computer literacy (Brosnan and Davidson, 1994). Certainly, teachers and employers have to make positive efforts to encourage girls and women to study and train in computer and technical skills in order to eradicate the masculinization of computers.

Recommendations for the Future

In addition to all the moral arguments, it is in the long-term economic interest of governments and work organizations to better accommodate the needs of the increasing numbers of women at work (from all ethnic groups), particularly those with dependent children.

The long-term solution for the elimination of job segregation and inequalities in the workplace for women certainly depends on changes in sex-stereotyped attitudes. Traditional stereotyping starts from birth, and parents, the media, educational establishments and organizations must take on the responsibility for challenging and changing attitudes that inappropriately differentiate men and women.

Evidence is mounting that corporate culture is often too much determined by 'male values' and that competition, confrontation and the 'macho' management style are possibly producing more workplace stress and less productivity (Cartwright and Cooper, 1994). Organizations tend to demand long hours and total commitment, in a period when both partners may be employed. Corporate cultures and management styles which support and reward people (regardless of gender, age, disability or ethnic origin) and which take into account their personal circumstances are the ones that will survive the 1990s and beyond. Wilkinson (1994) refers to authors such as Handy who have argued that:

> the de-layering within organizations will inevitably weaken obstacles such as the glass ceiling. Firms will change from being 'employing' organizations to becoming 'organizing' organizations with a core of key people managing the firm while operational tasks are sub-contracted to businesses and individuals on the periphery selling their services in the organization. Within the firm feminine values will come to the fore, involving less pyramidal structures, more openness, networking and a higher premium for interpersonal skills (p. 15).

Organizations must introduce policies and strategies to help break down the barriers faced by women in the workplace. These need to be directed at fair selection and promotional procedures, fair training and job experience opportunities, flexible working, and a breakdown of attitudinal barriers in terms of empowering women and

Table 10.2 Strategies for change

Barriers	Strategies
Organizational barriers	
Unfair selection or promotion procedures	equal opportunities policy
	equal opportunities training
	dual interviewing
	precise job specifications
	objective assessment criteria
	external advertising
	equal opportunity audits
	monitoring
	targets
Inflexible working	senior level part-time/ job sharing arrangements
	flexi-time
	working at home
	annual hours
	other flexible arrangements
Mobility	requirement dropped or modified
	dual-career job search
Age limits	requirement dropped
Traditional roles	
Work and family life	career break schemes
	workplace nurseries
	childcare vouchers
	parental leave
	enhanced maternity leave
	other childcare help
Attitudinal barriers	
Lack of confidence	equal opportunity advertising
	headhunting
	internal promotion policies
	women-only training courses
Prejudice	boardroom commitment to change
	equal opportunities training for managers
	awareness training for all staff

Source: Hansard Society Commission (1990).

eliminating prejudiced attitudes and behaviour. Some possibilities are set out in Table 10.2 (from the Hansard Society Commission, 1990).

Organizations should also follow the example of those few which have publicly developed working patterns and practices to encourage family-friendly employment, offer flexible reward packages and provide support and training relevant to family-friendly employment (Industrial Society, 1994a).

In the final analysis, if the position of women at work is to improve, there is a need for stronger legislative programmes to force equal opportunities. Australia, for example, has adopted and adapted the US approach of affirmative action legislation. All private-sector Australian organizations employing over 100 people, and all universities and colleges of advanced education, are legally obliged to adopt affirmative action programmes in order to ensure equal employment opportunities for men and women (Kramer, 1994). In a number of European Union countries the issue of either voluntary or mandatory positive action is now on the agenda. In Greece, for example, it has been suggested that an obligatory quota of 35 per cent be introduced as a minimum target for women in senior jobs in both the public and private sectors. These issues are also being discussed actively in Belgium, Italy and Germany (Davidson and Cooper, 1993).

Until legislative changes occur in Britain and other countries, organizations themselves should develop their own equal opportunities guidelines and positive action programmes. Since 1992 a growing number of companies in the UK have committed themselves to 'Opportunity 2000', a Business in the Community initiative to improve and increase women's participation in the workforce. Recent research published by Opportunity 2000 (1994) showed a significant difference in job prospects for women in the organizations that belong to the campaign. Women now hold 25 per cent of all managerial positions in Opportunity 2000 workplaces, compared with 9 per cent in leading companies as a whole. At director level, women make up 8 per cent of posts in member companies, compared to 3 per cent overall. The campaign now has 275 member organizations employing more than a quarter of the UK workforce, and increasing numbers of its members are introducing flexible working policies.

SUMMARY

The material presented in this chapter has illustrated that on the whole women in employment do not enjoy the same job conditions, pay, status and career opportunities as their male counterparts. The majority of women are concentrated in a limited number of occupations, particularly those dominated by part-time workers. Women's advance into what have been traditionally men's jobs (especially the higher-status roles) is still very limited.

One of the great social paradoxes of the past two decades involves the massive influx of women in the paid workforce and the continuation of inequality in both employment and family responsibilities. Women now represent over 40 per cent of the workforce in Western countries and will be an even more significant component in the future, but organizations have been slow to capitalize on the potential of their female employees. The position of women in employment will improve substantially only through attitudinal, educational, legal and organizational changes and initiatives.

FURTHER READING

The position of women in employment is constantly changing, and recent research studies, surveys and statistics are provided by ongoing issues of *Labour Force Survey*, *Bulletin on Women and Employment in the EU*, *The Equal Opportunities Review* and *Gender, Work and Organization*. Up-to-date research issues relating to women in management are examined in the journal *Women in Management Review* and in books by Davidson and Burke (1994) and Davidson and Cooper (1992).

REFERENCES

Alban-Metcalfe, B. M. and Nicholson, N. (1984). *The Career Development of British Managers*. London: British Institute of Management.

Alimo-Metcalfe, B. (1994). Gender bias in the selection and assessment of women in management. In M. J. Davidson and R. Burke (eds.), *Women in*

Management – Current Research Issues, pp. 93–109. London: Paul Chapman.

Australian Bureau of Statistics (1992). *The Labour Force, Australia*; July, Cat. No. 6203–0.

Balding, J. (1993). *Young People in 1993*. Exeter: University of Exeter.

Bell, E. L. (1990). The bi-cultural life experience of career-oriented black women. *Journal of Organizational Behaviour*, 11(16), 459–478.

Bourantas, D. and Papalexandris, N. (1990). Sex differences in leadership. *Journal of Managerial Psychology*, 5(5), 7–10.

Brannen, J. and Moss, P. (1990). *Managing Mothers: Dual Earning Households After Maternity Leave*. London: Working Mothers Association Newsletter.

Brenner, O. C., Tomkiewicz, J. and Schein, V. E. (1989). The relationship between sex role stereotypes and requisite management characteristics revisited. *Academy of Management Journal*, 32, 662–669.

Brosnan, M. J. and Davidson, M. J. (1994). Computerphobia – Is it a particularly female phenomenon? *The Psychologist*, February, 73–78.

Cartwright, S. and Cooper, C. L. (1994). *No Hassle*. London: Century Books.

Commission of the European Communities (1990). *Employment in Europe, 1990*. Luxembourg: Commission of the European Communities.

Davidson, M. J. and Burke, R. J. (eds.) (1994). *Women in Management – Current Research Issues*. London: Paul Chapman.

Davidson, M. J. and Cooper, C. L. (1983). *Stress and the Woman Manager*. London: Martin Robertson.

Davidson, M. J. and Cooper, C. L. (1987). Female managers in Britain – A comparative review. *Human Resource Management*, 26, 217–247.

Davidson, M. J. and Cooper, C. L. (1992). *Shattering the Glass Ceiling – The Woman Manager*. London: Paul Chapman.

Davidson, M. J. and Cooper, C. L. (1993). An Overview. In M. J. Davidson and C. L. Cooper (eds.), *European Women in Business and Management*, pp. 1–15. London: Paul Chapman.

Davidson, M. J., Cooper, C. L. and Baldini, V. (1995). Occupational stress in female and male graduate managers – A comparative study. *Journal of Stress Medicine*, 11, 157–175.

Department of Employment (1992). *Attitudes to Part-Time Work: A Report on Qualitative Research*. London: Department of Employment.

Department of Employment (1994). *United Nations Fourth World Conference on Women, Beijing, 1995*. London: Department of Employment.

Department of Employment and Equal Opportunities Commission (1994). *Fair Play for Women – Factsheet in Enterprise*. London: HMSO.

Devanna, M. A. (1987). Women in management: Progress and promise. *Human Resource Management*, 26, 409–481.

Earnshaw, J. and Davidson, M. J. (1994). Redefining sexual harassment via Industrial Tribunal claims – An investigation of the legal and psychosocial process. *Personnel Review*, 23(8), 3–16.

Ellison, R. (1994). British Labour Force projections: 1994 to 2006. *Employment Gazette*, April, 11–18.

Employment Gazette (1994). *Mothers in the Labour Market*. November, 403–406.

Equal Opportunity Review (1994). *Women in Unions*. January/February, 53.

Feldman, D. C. (1990). Reconceptualising the nature and consequences of part-time work. *Academy of Management Review*, 15, 103–112.

Ferrario, M. (1994). Women as managerial leaders. In M. J. Davidson and R. J. Burke (eds.), *Women in Management – Current Research Issues*, pp. 110–125. London: Paul Chapman.

Ferri, E. (ed.) (1993). *Life at 33*. London: National Children's Bureau/ESRC and City University.

Greenhouse, J. H., Parasuraman, S. and Warmley, W. M. (1990). Effects of race on organisational experiences, job performance evaluations and career outcomes. *Academy of Management Journal*, 33, 64–86.

Gutek, B. A. (1985). *Sex and the Workplace*. San Francisco: Jossey-Bass.

Hammond, V. (1994). Opportunity 2000: Good practice in UK Organizations. In M. J. Davidson and R. J. Burke (eds.), *Women in Management: Current Research Issues*, pp. 304–316. London: Paul Chapman.

Hansard Society Commission (1990). *Women at the Top*. London: Hansard Society.

Hirsch, W. and Jackson, C. (1989). *Women Into Management – Issues Influencing the Entry of Women into Managerial Jobs*, Paper No. 158. University of Sussex: Institute of Manpower Studies.

HMSO (1991). *British Social Attitudes Survey*. London: HMSO.

HMSO (1995). *Britain 1995, an Official Handbook*. London: HMSO.

Horner, K. (1970). *Femininity and Successful Achievement: A Basic Inconsistency*. Monterey, Calif.: Brooks/Cole.

Industrial Society (1994a). *Family-Friendly Policies*. London: Industrial Society.

Industrial Society (1994b). *Type-Cast*. London: Industrial Society.

Institute of Management (1992). *The Key to the Men's Club*. Bristol: I. M. Books.

Kozak, M. (1994). *Not Just Nine to Five: A Survey of Shift Workers' Childcare Needs*. London: Daycare Trust.

Kramer, R. (1994). Affirmative action in Australian organisations. In M. J.

Davidson and R. J. Burke (eds.), *Women in Management – Current Research Issues*, pp. 277–288. London: Paul Chapman.

Labour Force Survey (1993). London: HMSO.

Labour Force Survey (1994). London: HMSO.

Labour Research (1994). *Still a Long Road to Equality*. London: HMSO.

Lahtinen, H. K. and Wilson, F. M. (1994). Women and power in organisations. *Executive Development*, 7(3), 16–23.

Lefkowitz, J. (1994). Sex-related differences in job attitudes and dispositional variables: now you see them. *Academy of Management Journal*, 37, 323–349.

Lewis, S. (1994). Role tensions and dual career couples. In M. J. Davidson and R. J. Burke (eds.), *Women in Management – Current Research Issues*, pp. 230–241. London: Paul Chapman.

Lownes, S. N. (1994). Summer Quarter Update, July. Croydon: Management Compensation Data Base.

Marshall, J. (1994). Why women leave senior management jobs: My research approach and some initial findings. In M. Tanton (ed.), *Women in Management: The Second Wave*, pp. 4–5. London: Routledge Press.

Martin, J. and Roberts, C. (1984). *Women and Employment: A Lifetime Perspective*. London: HMSO, Department of Employment.

Millar, J. (1992). *The Socio-Economic Situation of Solo Women in Europe*. Women of Europe Supplements, No. 41. Brussels: European Commission.

Nelson, D. L. and Quick, J. C. (1985). Professional women: Are distress and disease inevitable? *Academy of Management Review*, 10, 206–218.

Nicholson, N. and West, A. (1988). *Managerial Job Change: Men and Women in Transition*. Cambridge: Cambridge University Press.

Opportunity 2000 (1994). *Opportunity 2000 – Third Year Report*. London: Opportunity 2000.

Pearn, M. A., Kandola, R. S. and Mottram, R. D. (1987). *Selection Tests and Sex Bias: The Impact of Selection Testing on the Employment Opportunities of Women and Men*. London: HMSO.

Pugliesi, K. (1988). Employment characteristics, social support and the well-being of women. *Women and Health*, 14(1), 35–58.

Repetti, R. L., Matthews, K. A. and Waldron, I. (1989). Effects of paid employment on women's mental and physical health. *American Psychologist*, 44, 1394–1401.

Rotchford, N. L. and Roberts, R. H. (1982). Part-time workers as missing persons in organisational research. *Academy of Management Review*, 7, 228–234.

Rubenstein, M. (1988). *The Dignity of Women at Work: A Report on the Problem of Sexual Harassment in the Member States of the European*

Communities, COM V/412 1087. Luxembourg: Office for Official Publications of the European Communities.

Rubenstein, M. (1991). Devising a Sexual Harassment Policy. *Personnel Management*, February, 8–10.

Rubery, J. and Fagan, C. (1993). *Bulletin on Women and Employment in the European Commission*. Brussels: European Commission.

Rubery, J. and Fagan, C. (1994). *Bulletin on Women and Employment in the EU (No.4)*. Brussels: European Commission.

Rubery, J., Fagan, C. and Grimshaw, D. (1994). *Bulletin on Women and Employment in the E.U. (No.5)*. Brussels: European Commission.

Schein, V. E. (1989). *Sex Role Stereotyping and Requisite Management Characteristics, Past Present and Future*. Working Paper Series, No. WC 98–26. London, Ontario: University of Western Ontario: National Centre for Management Research and Development.

Schein, V. E. (1994). Managerial sex typing: A persistent and pervasive barrier to women's opportunities. In M. J. Davidson and R. J. Burke (eds.), *Women in Management – Current Research Issues*, pp. 41–52. London: Paul Chapman.

Schein, V. E. and Davidson, M. J. (1993). Think manager – Think male. *Management Development Review*, 6(3), 24–28.

Silverstone, R. and Towler, R. (1983). *Secretarial Work in Central London 1970–1981*. London: Manpower Services Commission.

Sly, F. (1993). Women in the labour market. *Employment Gazette*, November, 485–502.

Sly, F. (1994). Mothers in the labour market. *Employment Gazette*, November, 17.

Still, L. (1993). *Where To From Here – The Managerial Woman in Transition*. Sydney: Business and Professional Publishing.

Swiss, D. and Squires, J. (1993). *Women and the Work/Family Dilemma*. Chichester: Wiley.

Tarr Whelan, L. (1994). *Working Women: More Than Time for New Approaches*. Washington DC: Center for Policy Research.

Terbourg, J. R. (1985). Working women and stress. In T. A. Beehr and R. S. Bhagat (eds.), *Human Stress and Cognition in Organisations*, pp. 245–286. Chichester: Wiley.

Terpstra, D. E. and Baker, D. D. (1991). Sexual harassment at work: The psychosocial issues. In M. J. Davidson and J. M. Earnshaw (eds.), *Vulnerable Workers – Psychosocial and Legal Issues*, pp. 179–202. Chichester: John Wiley.

US Department of Labor (1992). *Tabulations from the Current Population Surveys*. Washington DC: US Government Printing Office.

Watson, G. (1994). The flexible workforce and patterns of working hours in the UK. *Employment Gazette*, July, 239–243.

White, B., Cox, C. and Cooper, C. L. (1992). *Women's Career Development*. Oxford: Blackwell.

Wilkinson, A. (1994). *Generations and the Genderquake*. London: Demos.

Wilson, R. (1994). *Labour Market Structures and Prospects for Women*. Manchester: Institute of Employment/EOC.

Working for Childcare (1994). *Survey of Employer-Sponsored Nursery Provision – Britain 1994*. London: Working for Childcare.

Wright, P. C. and Bean, S. A. (1993). Sexual harassment: An issue of employee effectiveness. *Journal of Managerial Psychology*, 8(2), 30–36.

11

Younger and Older Workers

Peter Warr

Many developed countries face a growing imbalance in the age distribution of their working populations. Associated with a temporary increase in the birth-rate in the 1950s and a recent decline in family size, the proportion of older workers will increase and that of younger ones decline. For example, in Britain between 1992 and 2006 the working population above the age of 40 is projected to increase by about 18 per cent, whereas the number aged between 20 and 39 will decline by about 15 per cent (Department of Employment, 1993). This pattern will also be found in continental Europe, the USA, Australia and other countries (Warr, 1994a; World Health Organization, 1993).

The nature of paid work has changed considerably in recent years, so that many older employees are likely to experience task demands that are different from those with which they have been familiar. All developed countries have seen a shift away from agriculture and manufacturing industry to the services sector, which in many cases now accounts for more than two-thirds of all jobs. Hard manual labour is less common in developed countries than it once was, and older as well as younger workers are likely to require cognitive and interpersonal skills rather than physical strength. Furthermore, many jobs now depend on information technology, with associated mental demands on operators (see Chapters 4 and 12); and the pace of change has been increased by greater interaction between companies in different countries and enhanced competition across continents.

This set of developments, in conjunction with an ageing work-force, raises questions that are of both scientific and practical importance. In scientific terms, research in organizations is required to advance knowledge about the processes of ageing more generally; and in practical terms there is need for a sound knowledge-base about the strengths and weaknesses of older and younger employees on which organizations can base their human resource policies. This chapter will review recent findings about work performance at different ages, aspects of training, variations in attitudes and well-being, and the ways in which jobs might themselves influence the process of ageing.

Attitudes to older people in general, and older workers in particular, tend to be relatively negative (Kite and Johnson, 1988). The widespread negative stereotype is associated with extensive experiences of age discrimination by older people in recruitment, selection and promotion (McCauley, 1977). Older individuals who lose their job are particularly likely to remain unemployed for long periods, and as many as 80 per cent of British personnel managers report that age discrimination is a problem in their area of work (Warr and Pennington, 1993). Furthermore, many organizations tend to employ older people primarily in jobs which provide only limited psychological or financial rewards (Warr and Pennington, 1994). Wide-ranging attitudes and behaviours thus restrict the opportunities of older members of the work-force. How far are these consistent with research evidence about effectiveness at different ages?

AGE AND WORK PERFORMANCE

The overall finding from more than 100 research investigations is that there is no significant association between age and work performance. The average correlation coefficient is about $+0.06$, but separate correlations in the literature range from -0.44 to $+0.66$ (McEvoy and Cascio, 1989; Warr, 1994a). It is clear from this wide range that the importance of age varies between different jobs and between different aspects of performance. However, the general pattern is clear: in overall terms, there is no difference between the performance observed for older and younger staff in the same job. Incidentally, in almost every case variations *within* an age-group far exceed the average difference *between* age-groups.

The large majority of studies have assessed performance through supervisors' ratings of specific competencies. This has the disadvantage that performance measures may be subject to some perceptual bias; on the other hand, it permits judgements about multiple aspects

Table 11.1 Age and job performance: examples of research findings through measures of output

	under 25	25–34	35–44	45–54	55 and over
1. Skilled manufacturing operators (USA)	77	85	100	106	106
2. Semi-skilled assembly workers (USA)	89	87	100	105	101
3. Mail sorters (USA)	101	102	100	101	99
4. Office workers (USA)	92	99	100	99	98
5. Manufacturing machine operators (USA)	96	100	100	97	94
6. Equipment service engineers (UK)		99	100	94	

Sources: 1. Giniger, Dispenzieri and Eisenberg, 1983; 2. Schwab and Heneman, 1977a; 3. Walker, 1964; 4. Mark, 1957; 5. Kutscher and Walker, 1960; 6. Sparrow and Davies, 1988.

of work performance. However, in most cases results have been presented only as simple correlation coefficients, so that we cannot identify the pattern of scores (whether they are linear or non-linear) across different ages. Some published results about actual job performance (rather than ratings) at different ages have been brought together in Table 11.1.

Standardizing the scores around those for workers aged between 35 and 44, it can be seen that in these studies there is generally an increase in output up to that age-range, and then either a continuing increase, a plateau, or a small decline. In respect of the equipment service engineers (the last entry in the table), there is a more rapid decline after the middle range. However, it is important to stress that the decline at older ages in that study was found *only* for employees who had not recently been trained; the role of training will be considered later. In general, we can conclude from these and many other studies in the literature that there is no single relationship between age and work performance: positive, negative and inverted-U patterns have been reported. On average, the relationship is around zero, and those positive or negative age-patterns which are found are quite small.

The absence of an overall age effect in the level of job performance contrasts sharply with laboratory evidence of very clear age decrements in many forms of information processing (e.g., Craik and Salthouse, 1992). And it is inconsistent with a widespread negative stereotype about older workers. We clearly need to learn about the factors differentiating between age-patterns in different situations and different behaviours. Some possibilities are reviewed in the next section.

In terms of absence, accidents and labour turnover, the rescarch evidence is as follows. First, although sickness absence is often found to be greater at older ages, the opposite is the case for 'voluntary' absence, when people take time off work without medical or organizational approval (Martocchio, 1989; Hackett, 1990). The overall age-pattern of absenteeism thus depends on the mix of those two effects in a particular organization, and in many cases there is either no overall age difference or younger employees are absent to a greater extent than older ones. Second, accidents are more common at younger ages, especially among inexperienced workers; that significant negative association with age is stronger for men than for women (Dillingham, 1981). And, third, older staff are less likely to leave their employer voluntarily (e.g., Doering, Rhodes and Schuster, 1983), partly, of course, since they tend to be relatively unattractive on the labour market. One implication of the lower staff turnover at older ages is that the financial pay-back from training older employees can be greater than in the case of younger ones, since younger staff are more likely to move away to another employer.

Age and Four Types of Activity

In view of the variations between age-patterns recorded in different studies of work performance, it is necessary to develop models which can explain why different relationships with age occur in different kinds of job. One possibility is to look at combinations of two features: a decline with age in basic capacities, and a gain through age-related experience. This possibility is summarized in Table 11.2, in

Table 11.2 Four categories of job activity and expected relationships of performance with age

Task category	Task requirements exceed basic capacities with increasing age	Performance can be enhanced by relevant experience	Expected relationship with age	Illustrative job content
1. Age-enhanced activities	no	yes	positive	knowledge-based judgements with no time pressure
2. Age-impaired activities	yes	no	negative	continuous, paced data-processing; rapid learning; heavy lifting
3. Age-counteracted activities	yes	yes	zero	skilled manual or cognitive work
4. Age-neutral activities	no	no	zero	relatively undemanding activities

terms of four main types of activity, although the variations are in fact continuous rather than in separate categories as shown in the table.

For the first feature (column 2) we should ask whether the requirements of a particular task exceed basic capacities that are known to decline with age. Those basic capacities ultimately derive from physiological processes, which tend to deteriorate over the years; examples are speed of information-processing or effectiveness of sensory mechanisms. Our concern here is with the years of paid employment, when declines in basic capacities are likely to be smaller than after the age of 60 or 70. Second, we must determine whether the acquisition through experience of knowledge and skills is likely to improve performance with increasing age (column 3). Some activities benefit from accumulated experience, and others do not; in the former case more experienced (and thus, on average, older) employees are likely to be more effective.

In many cases job performance will be a function of both accumulated experience and declining basic capacities, and any observed relationship with age will reflect the relative strength of the two types of age-related influences. There are, of course, empirical problems of specifying in advance for any one task the relative importance of each type of influence. And a single job may be made up of tasks in more than one category, so that age may have different associations with different aspects of performance in the same job.

Age-enhanced activities
In reviewing research evidence in this field, let us start with the category of activities for which a *positive* age-gradient is expected. Category-1 activities (at the top of Table 11.2) are those which remain within basic capacities despite advancing age and in which performance benefits from experience. As indicated in the table, these may be referred to as 'age-enhanced' activities. For example, positive associations between age and job performance are likely in settings that are relatively stable, where knowledge and skills can continue to be developed by older workers (e.g., Maher, 1955). The acquisition of social knowledge and interpersonal skills through accumulated experience was particularly emphasized by Perlmutter, Kaplan, and Nyquist (1990). In their study of food-service employees between 20

and 69, age was found to be correlated +0.36 with performance effectiveness.

Research from several non-occupational standpoints has shown that certain types of cognitive functioning tend to improve with age during the working years. For example, scores on some tests of intellectual ability are regularly found to be higher among older people (e.g., Berg and Sternberg, 1985). Those tests measure what has been referred to as 'crystallized' intelligence (e.g., Horn, 1970), covering cognitive processes and primary abilities that are embedded in learned cultural meanings. Crystallized intelligence (as opposed to 'fluid' intelligence, involved in processing unfamiliar material; see later) is measured through tests of verbal comprehension, analogies and vocabulary; it benefits through practice and new learning. For example, in Stankov's (1988) study of people aged between 20 and 70 crystallized intelligence was correlated +0.27 with age, whereas for fluid intelligence that value was negative (−0.31).

Models of age-related gains in cognitive performance are sometimes presented in terms of 'selective expertise' (e.g., Salthouse, 1985b). The work performance of older employees may remain within an area of maintained expertise, being embedded in familiar settings and operations, although individuals might have more difficulty with new and complex activity. Positive associations with age (category 1 in Table 11.2) are thus often expected.

Other situations in which older employees are likely to be viewed as more effective than younger ones include those demanding personal characteristics which are more often found in older people. For example, Walker (1964) observed in a study of mail sorters a steady increase in consistency, with less variation in output from week to week, across groups from under 25 years to 60 and over. Bowers (1952) reported more positive appraisals of conscientiousness and attendance for older workers in a sample where ages extended into the late 60s.

Age-impaired activities

Second, let us consider category 2 of Table 11.2, activities described as 'age-impaired'. A negative relationship with age is expected in high-demand tasks where basic capacities are exceeded (and more exceeded for older people) and where experience cannot help. That possibility includes continuous rapid information-processing or strenuous physical activity of a kind which becomes more difficult with advancing years.

There are many studies illustrating this negative association outside specifically occupational settings. Some of those deal with sensory processes of visual and auditory functioning, others with motor activity and muscular strength (e.g., Verrillo and Verrillo, 1985), but most research of interest to this chapter has concerned cognitive processes. Non-occupational research into age-impaired activities may be roughly divided into investigations with psychometric tests and studies of particular aspects of information-processing, such as reaction time and learning.

The psychometric tests of interest in this section are those tapping 'fluid' intelligence. These assess performance in situations where new (usually abstract) material has to be processed, often under time pressure. It has long been established that older people within the working population (and, of course, beyond that) perform less well on these tests than do their younger counterparts (e.g., Salthouse, 1985b).

Reaction time in a wide range of tasks is known to be longer as people become older. Salthouse (1985a) illustrated this by presenting more than fifty correlations between age and speed of performance on laboratory tasks (single and choice reaction time, card-sorting, digit-symbol substitution, etc.); the median correlation was -0.45, with a range from -0.15 to -0.64. This reduced speed of information-processing with increased age is potentially able to account for a wide range of apparently diverse findings. Older people's slower handling of information may give rise to poorer performance on any task that requires rapid cognitive processing. That is obvious in the case of reaction time and similar activities, but can also be expected in situations where active mental rehearsal, comparison between alternatives, and temporary storage in memory are needed. Cognitive capacity is limited, and there is need to pass information through the mental system as rapidly as possible before it is lost or overtaken by other material. Particularly complex tasks, requiring a larger number of processing steps, are especially likely to be susceptible to cognitive slowing (e.g., Myerson, Hale, Wagstaff,

Poon and Smith, 1990); those tasks include conventional tests of fluid intelligence (e.g., Vernon, Nador and Kantor, 1985).

What about age differences in learning and memory? Cross-sectional age-impairment is regularly observed. For example, older people tend to be slower in acquiring new skills and knowledge than are younger ones (Sterns and Doverspike, 1989; Warr, 1994a). Salthouse (1985b) collated findings from several dozen laboratory studies (of digit span, free recall of lists, spatial memory, paired associate learning, etc.); these consistently indicate a negative relationship with age. Particular interest has recently been paid to the notion of 'working memory' (e.g., Baddeley, 1986; Salthouse, 1990). Much information-processing requires that mental operations are carried out on one set of material while retaining in temporary storage (one's 'working memory') some information which has to be brought into active operations later in the activity. For example, in a laboratory investigation of working memory people might be presented with a list of words to hold in mind, then asked to carry out a task of logical reasoning before recalling the original list.

Mental activities of that kind (involving simultaneous storage and processing of information) are very common in daily life, in problem-solving, mental arithmetic and many forms of reasoning; and task demands frequently exceed available cognitive capacity. It is known that older people perform less well than younger ones in situations where working memory is heavily loaded (e.g., Campbell and Charness, 1990). That differential effectiveness may underlie age-related decrements in many types of difficult information-processing activities, including those in tests of fluid intelligence (e.g., Salthouse, 1991).

Within specific jobs age-impairment (category 2 in Table 11.2) is expected where job content is changing rapidly, so that previous knowledge and skills can become obsolete. For example, Dalton and Thompson (1971) reported a marked (cross-sectional) decline in the performance of professional engineers after the age of about 40, as their technical knowledge became increasingly out of date. This process was viewed in part as a negative spiral: an older engineer who lacks current knowledge receives poorer appraisals and less challenging assignments, so that he or she comes to feel discouraged and less willing to make an effort for retraining; that discouragement in turn leads to more negative appraisals and further discouragement.

Age-counteracted activities

Many other job activities fall within category 3 of Table 11.2, referred to there as 'age-counteracted'. Older people may have increasing difficulties in some areas because of a decline in information-processing or physical capacities, but they are able to counteract that decline in various ways. This possibility is addressed by models of 'selective optimization with compensation' (Backman and Dixon, 1992; Baltes and Baltes, 1990b). Those are based on the fact that, as people age, they are able to increase their effectiveness in areas of specialization. Continued interest and practice in a limited number of areas permit the growth of knowledge-based competence; and individuals are sometimes able to learn how to compensate as necessary for specific limitations arising from deteriorating basic capacities.

Relevant experience may benefit people in at least four different ways. First is the all-round development of expertise, in the sense of enriched job knowledge and skills, as discussed above in terms of age-enhanced activities. Such expertise (associated with years of experience, but not necessarily linearly) permits more appropriate responses to new situations, generates more rapid and accurate decisions, and also frees cognitive capacity to cope with particularly demanding stimuli (e.g., Charness and Bosman, 1990; Glaser, 1988; see also Chapter 1). The value of expertise in specific areas of knowledge is illustrated by Maylor's (1994) finding that older contestants in the television contest *Mastermind* performed better than younger ones in their specialized areas.

Second, in respect of category-3 activities, older individuals may be able to counteract specific limitations through learned coping behaviours. For example, an older person may take written notes to compensate for possible memory limitations; Birren (1969) has described how middle-aged managers may have learned how to conserve their energy by operating through day-to-day tactics which reduce cognitive and affective load; more generally, older people may simply expend more effort for brief periods in order to keep up with their younger colleagues.

Older people's successful compensation in cognitive activities has been documented in relation to transcription-typing by Salthouse (1984). He examined the performance of experienced typists aged between 19 and 72. Consistent with findings summarized above in relation to type-2 activities, older typists were found to respond more slowly in a reaction-time task and in digit-symbol substitution. However, there was no age difference in the speed with which they typed textual material. By experimentally manipulating the length of preview available (the number of characters visible ahead of the current position), Salthouse showed that older typists in this experienced group looked further ahead in the text than did their younger counterparts. It was that additional preparation time which permitted them to type as rapidly as their younger colleagues.

A third possible application of relevant experience is behavioural accommodation, in which a person alters his or her activities in order to avoid situations which might reveal defects. For example, older employees may to a greater extent actively select tasks known to be within their capacity, avoiding those which now cause them greater difficulty. Or they may have progressed into positions from which they can delegate tasks which they find problematic. In extreme cases, accommodation can be seen in selective migration of older workers out of jobs which they come to find difficult (Teiger, 1989).

Finally, processes of cognitive 'compilation' may occur with increased experience, as activities are assembled into higher-order or more automatic chunks which are relatively independent of demanding lower-order procedures; age-related declines in the latter may be counteracted by the maintenance of effective higher-order skills. For example, only about one-third of the speed-up with practice that Charness and Campbell (1988) observed in a two-digit mental squaring task was due to faster execution of elementary arithmetic operations; most of the speed-up was due to higher-order learning, in terms of chaining together the sub-goals quickly and efficiently.

The precise outcomes from the opposed influence of declining capacities and increasing experience in category-3 activities will depend on the relative strength of each factor in the particular behaviour under study. Research into this relative strength is rather limited. Nevertheless, in many employment situations potential age declines are likely to be of the category-3 kind, counteracted by relevant experience, rather than falling within category 2, in which case experience cannot compensate for impaired capacities.

Age-neutral activities

Last in Table 11.2 are the many 'age-neutral' activities in category 4, where work is routine and non-problematic, requiring either limited skill or skill that is firmly established so that behaviour is fairly automatic. In those circumstances age differences in task performance are not expected. More generally, age-impairment is found only when individuals' capacity is tested at the limits of their competence (Baltes, 1993). In the large number of daily activities away from those limits the performance of older and younger people remains very similar.

Within laboratory studies equivalent performance at different ages is regularly found in easy tasks. For instance, 'primary' memory is apparently unaffected by age; older people are as able as their younger counterparts to hold in memory small amounts of information (within their span of primary memory) that are being used in uncomplicated cognitive activities (e.g., Poon, 1985). Furthermore, while increased age is associated with slower learning of new material, it is unrelated to the forgetting of material after it has been well established (Rabbitt and Maylor, 1991). Most everyday activities are age-neutral in this way.

Age and performance: an overview

The four-part framework summarized in Table 11.2 draws attention to the fact that category-2 activities (those for which we might expect age-impairment) comprise only a minority of job behaviours. Some job tasks are certainly of that kind, but many jobs are made up primarily of the other three types of activity: age-enhanced, age-counteracted or age-neutral. Furthermore, in considering the relationships between age and *overall* job performance, combinations have to be made across a number of component activities. Only in cases where performance is impaired by age in the majority of job components (or in those which are especially salient) will overall performance be lower for older workers; such a situation is likely to be relatively uncommon.

The discussion above has focused upon characteristics within a

319

job itself. It is important also to consider the impact upon an observed age-pattern of possible changes across time in a company's policies for personnel selection and promotion. In some cases differences in organizational practice are more influential than are job features of the kinds discussed so far.

For example, in some organizations the selection standards for a job may have been raised, so that more recent recruits need to possess substantially higher qualifications than those who joined in earlier years. In this situation a cross-sectional comparison between people selected at different times is likely to yield higher performance ratings for the more-qualified staff (who happen also to be younger).

Furthermore, some posts are initial grades for upwardly mobile staff. Very good workers are promoted out after a few years, leaving in the job older individuals who are competent but not outstanding. Once again, a cross-sectional examination of performance at different ages will favour the younger group, because younger staff are all either competent or outstanding whereas the older group has lost its outstanding members through their promotion.

These contextual factors (external to the job itself) need also to be considered when examining age-patterns in job performance. Unfortunately, research reports in this area almost never include information about features of this kind.

THE ACQUISITION OF NEW SKILLS

Perceptions of older workers are structured around three principal features: their physical abilities (which tend to decline with age) (e.g., World Health Organization, 1993), their adaptability (which also tends to decline) and their general work effectiveness (which remains stable or increases with age) (Warr, 1994b). The third component covers behaviours such as thinking before action, hard work, reliability, interpersonal skills, team-working, confidence and overall effectiveness (Warr and Pennington, 1993).

As jobs increasingly require cognitive (rather than physical) competence, physical ability is less salient today than it was previously. In order to take advantage of the wide-ranging effectiveness that has been demonstrated in older staff (the third feature), it therefore

320

becomes necessary to focus attention on the enhancement of adaptability (the second feature). That will often require explicit attention to the training of older people.

Many older workers see themselves as unsuited to substantial new learning and lack confidence in training situations (e.g., Sterns, 1986). Associated with that, they tend to learn more slowly than their younger colleagues (e.g., Sterns and Doverspike, 1989; Warr, 1994a). Paced instruction, where speed of information-transmission is beyond a trainee's control, is particularly problematic, as would be expected from the research into cognitive performance reviewed above; most learning situations exceed people's capacity initially to process and store all the material provided (activities in categories 2 and 3 in Table 11.2). However, it is clear that, given appropriate opportunities, older as well as younger employees can acquire additional job skills and perform effectively in new kinds of work.

What processes are likely to contribute to greater difficulty in learning as one becomes older? Reduced information-processing capacities and a general cognitive slowing have already been described, as have older trainees' anxiety and lower self-confidence as learners. Problems of unlearning initial errors have been stressed by Belbin and Belbin (1972). They argued that older people were better able to learn if their activities were constrained so that errors were minimized early in the process. That procedure has the advantage of sustaining confidence as well as minimizing potential negative interference between material examined at different times.

Older trainees may gain special benefit from 'guided activity (or discovery) learning'. This approach creates situations in which individuals are encouraged to learn by finding out principles and relationships for themselves; the emphasis is on learning by doing rather than through verbal or physical instruction. Discovery learning can be encouraged by asking trainees to generate and answer questions about the subject-matter, rather than merely presenting them with information to be learned. Finding answers to their own questions can permit them to build on individual experience, and a successful process of discovery may encourage a shift from merely extrinsic rewards to more intrinsic achievements (e.g., Knowles, 1984). This form of learning has been shown to be helpful in the training of older workers (e.g., Sterns and Doverspike, 1989).

Older employees are often out of practice at learning itself, and they may need assistance in learning how to learn. Their potential learning ability can be much greater than the actual ability exhibited when they first enter training. Perry and Downs (1985) have considered a number of procedures to develop the skills of learning (for instance, through self-questioning, managing time and testing specific hypotheses), and it may be that those procedures are particularly appropriate for older people.

In most organizations training is directed mainly at younger employees (e.g., Warr, 1994c), partly because of what is in effect collusion between management and older workers themselves. Since many of the latter are nervous about undertaking learning activities and have doubts (not necessarily justified) about their own capacity to acquire new skills, they tend to avoid new training opportunities. There is thus sometimes a self-fulfilling prophecy. Older employees in a particular company may indeed be less adaptable than younger ones, but they receive little assistance to be otherwise. As a result they remain as they are, and the negative age stereotype is reinforced.

In the next few years most jobs will continue to change in response to new customer demands and new forms of product or service. Workers will typically need to change as well, in ways which are not yet predictable. A major organizational requirement is thus to create a culture in which learning and development are given a high priority among older as well as younger employees. To maintain competitiveness many companies need to move older workers laterally into novel and challenging jobs, and provide training which is specially tailored to their needs and which maintains their adaptability in the face of changing requirements.

JOB-RELATED WELL-BEING

Other studies have investigated age differences in well-being, with particular reference to job satisfaction (see Chapter 8). Overall job satisfaction is typically found to be significantly higher among older workers (e.g., Doering, Rhodes and Schuster, 1983), although the positive correlation is not high, usually falling between $+0.10$ and

+ 0.20. The pattern of association is often said to be linear, although the review of early research by Herzberg, Mausner, Peterson and Capwell (1957) pointed to a U-shaped relationship. Their conclusion was that overall job satisfaction was likely to be relatively high for the youngest group of adults, when novelty encourages positive feelings about a job. However, between the ages of 20 and 30 increasing boredom and perceptions of reducing opportunities may lead to some reduction in satisfaction.

In due course, it was suggested, a person comes to terms with his or her job (perhaps having moved out of relatively unrewarding positions) and satisfaction increases significantly, above the level of the youngest group. (That imbalance suggests labelling the pattern as 'J-shaped', rather than 'U-shaped', which implies that the youngest and the oldest groups have equivalent levels of satisfaction.) This J-shape is demonstrated by Clark, Oswald and Warr (1996) in a national sample of British workers, with a minimum job satisfaction level at age 31.

A cross-sectional increase in job satisfaction after the age of about 30 is widely observed, but many investigators have failed to find evidence of raised satisfaction in very young employees, as described in the previous paragraphs. That discrepancy in results may be due to limited sampling at young ages in certain studies. Furthermore, there may be no decline in satisfaction among those young workers who receive training and advancement early in their career; variations in those aspects of a job may determine the pattern of results from any one study.

More focused satisfaction, with a specific job-facet, is related to age in various ways, depending on the facet under investigation. It is generally found that satisfaction with the nature of the work itself is greater in older groups. This relationship remains significant after controlling for job or organizational tenure (e.g., Schwab and Heneman, 1977b) and a range of job characteristics and work values (Clark *et al.*, 1996). Satisfaction with pay is often found to be positively associated with age (e.g., Kacmar and Ferris, 1989; Clark *et al.*, 1996), but an age gradient is usually absent in relation to extrinsic satisfaction, and in relation to satisfaction with promotion, with co-workers and with supervision. That does not exclude the possibility that significant age-relationships are sometimes present, and findings

323

about facet satisfaction are likely to depend on the nature of the sample, the organization and the measures investigated.

As in other parts of this chapter, we might expect factors associated with age, such as income or job level, to account for some of the positive relationship between age and job satisfaction. Older people are often in jobs which pay them more and which have more desirable characteristics. Wright and Hamilton (1978) showed that older workers are more likely to have moved into jobs whose characteristics they value, and that differences of that kind in personally desirable job content can partly explain the positive association between overall job satisfaction and age (see also Clark *et al.*, 1996; Kalleberg and Loscocco, 1983).

As described in Chapter 8, a second important axis of job-related well-being covers feelings of anxiety or strain associated with the job. Maslach and Jackson (1981) found that older members of their human service sample reported lower levels of burnout in terms of emotional exhaustion and depersonalization. Warr (1992) observed an inverted-J relationship between age and job anxiety, with employees between 25 and 34 reporting most anxiety and the oldest group reporting least. In seeking possible explanations of that relationship, additional variables were included in multiple regression analyses. A significant negative correlation between age and job-related anxiety was retained after controlling for differences in job tenure, job level, decision latitude, work demands, working conditions, income, employment commitment, education and other potentially relevant variables.

It thus appears that after controlling for the fact that older people have moved into better jobs, there is still a positive age gradient in occupational well-being. It may be possible to explain part of that relationship by including additional occupational variables, but part of the age-gradient in job-related affect seems to be attributable to *non-job* differences between older and younger people. For example, there is a small but significant cross-sectional increase with age in general measures of life satisfaction (Diener, 1984); and there is generally less non-job anxiety (Warr, 1990) and non-job distress (Clark *et al.*, 1996) among older members of the workforce. The fact that older employees report higher job satisfaction and other forms of occupational well-being than younger people is likely to be partly attributable to broader differences of those kinds; the causes of the positive age-gradient are not entirely occupational.

THE INFLUENCE OF JOBS ON AGEING

Studies reviewed so far have focused primarily on the ways in which age-related processes can influence processes occurring at work: how does ageing affect work behaviour and attitudes? Causal processes in the reverse direction are also important: how do jobs affect the processes of ageing? The emphasis here is upon variations between people which arise from extended exposure to different conditions of employment.

Ageing, as evidenced by changes in physiological and psychological functioning, is not determined solely by a standard set of intrinsic factors giving rise to an unalterable rate of change: changes during the life-course are influenced by social and physical environments and by psychological processes during a person's interactions with those environments. Some environments are more conducive to 'successful ageing' than are others (Baltes and Baltes, 1990a).

Environmental differences are likely to contribute to the increased variability in cognitive performance between people that is typically observed with increasing age. In cases where a negative age-gradient exists in terms of average values, the older sub-sample necessarily contains more low scorers; but it is not unusual for some older people to be as effective as the best young person (e.g., Rabbitt, 1991). This increased inter-individual variability is likely to have developed slowly over a number of years.

In examining possible influences upon the pace of ageing we are in part concerned with the consequences of long-term exposure to certain forms of environmental demands and opportunities. The centrality of paid employment in most people's life means that certain features of jobs can have substantial impacts upon mental health and development (e.g., Warr, 1987). However, jobs are located in the broader network of a socio-economic structure, and it is, of course, difficult to disentangle occupational influences from those arising from a person's place in that structure.

Evidence about the long-term influence of jobs on ageing thus tends to be indirect. However, significant positive associations between extended job experience and individual expertise have been demonstrated in several studies. It is also beyond dispute that short-term training interventions can improve intellectual functioning at all ages, and that some job-holders are exposed to more intellectual stimulation throughout their career than are others. It seems very likely that differences in job demands across an extended period will affect the processes of cognitive ageing.

One source of between-person variability has been discussed in terms of the 'environmental complexity' provided by different jobs. Complex environments expose a person to more varied stimuli, require more decisions and contain greater ambiguity than do simple environments. Research has pointed to the causal importance of this aspect of jobs. Kohn and Schooler (1983) showed that several forms of employees' 'intellectual flexibility' were influenced by the complexity of a person's current job and that held ten years previously. Avolio and Waldman (1987) examined the correlations between age and cognitive functioning in workers (aged 19 to 62) defined as being exposed to different degrees of intellectual stimulation in their work. Within a single company skilled and unskilled employees were compared on a range of tests, including verbal, numerical and mechanical reasoning. Negative correlations with age (holding constant level of workers' education) were greater for the unskilled group (exposed to less complex work environments) than for the skilled workers; for example, values were -0.28 versus -0.05 for numerical reasoning.

A related, simple, example was provided by LaRiviere and Simonson (1965). They recorded the maximum speed with which people between 40 and 69 could copy a sheet of one-digit numbers. For manual labourers and managers, speed of writing was significantly negatively associated with age, but clerical workers (who performed that task regularly in their job) showed no differences in copying speed associated with increasing age.

At present, knowledge and theory in this area are limited. It is obvious in the case of specific physical impairments that continued exposure to certain adverse job demands can affect the way people age physically; this process in respect of psychological ageing now deserves particular attention.

SUMMARY

Against the background of an ageing workforce in many developed countries, this chapter has examined factors associated with age patterns at work. Research has indicated that overall there are no differences between the work performance of older and younger employees, and that there is wide between-person variation at all ages. However, there are differences in the age-performance relationship in different jobs. Four types of activity were described in terms of the combined effects of declining basic capacities and potential gains from experience associated with ageing. Age-impairment was seen to occur in only one of those categories, at least during years in the work-force.

Employee well-being is likely to be associated with age in a J-shaped manner, with lowest well-being occurring between the ages of about 30 and 35; this pattern is caused by non-occupational variations as well as differences in job features at different ages. The acquisition of new skills is more difficult for many older workers, partly because of a slight reduction in speed of information-processing. Given that older workers have positive attributes associated with general work effectiveness, greater organizational attention to learning and training can maximize the value of older (as well as younger) staff.

FURTHER READING

A large number of references have been cited throughout the chapter, and these may be followed up for specific issues. More general treatments of cognitive ageing are provided in handbooks edited by Birren and Schaie (1985), Craik and Salthouse (1992) and Howe and Brainerd (1988). Reviews of specifically occupational issues are by Davies, Matthews and Wong (1991) and Warr (1994a), and in the book edited by Snel and Cremer (1994).

REFERENCES

Avolio, B. J. and Waldman, D. A. (1987). Personnel aptitude test scores as a function of age, education and job type. *Experimental Aging Research*, 13, 109–113.

Backman, L. and Dixon, R. A. (1992). Psychological compensation: A theoretical framework. *Psychological Bulletin*, 112, 259–283.

Baddeley, A. D. (1986). *Working Memory*. Oxford: Oxford University Press.

Baltes, P. B. (1993). The aging mind: Potential and limits. *The Gerontologist*, 33, 580–594.

Baltes, P. B. and Baltes, M. M. (eds.) (1990a). *Successful Aging*. Cambridge: Cambridge University Press.

Baltes, P. B. and Baltes, M. M. (1990b). Psychological perspectives on successful aging: The model of selective optimization with compensation. In P. B. Baltes and M. M. Baltes (eds.), *Successful Aging*, pp. 1–34. Cambridge: Cambridge University Press.

Belbin, E. and Belbin, R. M. (1972). *Problems in Adult Retraining*. London: Heinemann.

Berg, C. A. and Sternberg R. J. (1985). A triarchic theory of intellectual development during adulthood. *Developmental Review*, 5, 334–370.

Birren, J. E. (1969). Age and decision strategies. *Interdisciplinary Topics in Gerontology*, 4, 23–36.

Birren, J. E. and Schaie, K. W. (eds.) (1985). *Handbook of the Psychology of Aging*, 2nd edn. New York: Van Nostrand Reinhold.

Bowers, W. H. (1952). An appraisal of worker characteristics as related to age. *Journal of Applied Psychology*, 36, 296–300.

Campbell, J. I. D. and Charness, N. (1990). Age-related declines in working-memory skills: Evidence from a complex calculation task. *Developmental Psychology*, 26, 879–888.

Charness, N. and Bosman, E. A. (1990). Expertise and aging: Life in the lab. In T. M. Hess (ed.), *Aging and Cognition: Knowledge Organization and Utilization*, pp. 343–385. Amsterdam: Elsevier.

Charness, N. and Campbell, J. I. D. (1988). Acquiring skill at mental calculation in adulthood: A task decomposition. *Journal of Experimental Psychology: General*, 117, 115–129.

Clark, A., Oswald, A. and Warr, P. B. (1996). Is job satisfaction U-shaped in age? *Journal of Occupational and Organizational Psychology*, in press.

Craik, F. I. M. and Salthouse, T. A. (eds.) (1992). *The Handbook of Aging and Cognition*. Hillsdale, NJ: Erlbaum.

Dalton, G. W. and Thompson, P. H. (1971). Accelerating obsolescence of older engineers. *Harvard Business Review*, 49, no. 5, 57–67.

Davies, D. R., Matthews, G. and Wong, C. S. K. (1991). Ageing and work. In C. L. Cooper and I. T. Robertson (eds.), *International Review of Industrial and Organizational Psychology*, vol. 6, pp. 149–211. Chichester: Wiley.

Department of Employment (1993). Labour force projections: 1993–2006. *Employment Gazette*, 101, 139–147.

Diener, E. (1984). Subjective well-being. *Psychological Bulletin*, 95, 1105–1117.

Dillingham, A. E. (1981). Age and workplace injuries. *Aging and Work*, 4, 1–10.

Doering, M., Rhodes, S. R. and Schuster, M. (1983). *The Aging Worker: Research and Recommendations*. Beverly Hills, Calif.: Sage.

Giniger, S., Dispenzieri, A. and Eisenberg, J. (1983). Age, experience, and performance on speed and skill jobs in an applied setting. *Journal of Applied Psychology*, 68, 469–475.

Glaser, R. (1988). Thoughts on expertise. In C. Schooler and W. Schaie (eds.), *Cognitive Functioning and Social Structure over the Life Course*, pp. 81–94. Norwood, NJ: Ablex.

Hackett, R. D. (1990). Age, tenure, and employee absenteeism. *Human Relations*, 43, 601–619.

Herzberg, F., Mausner, B., Peterson, R. O. and Capwell, D. F. (1957). *Job Attitudes: Review of Research and Opinion*. Pittsburgh: Psychological Service of Pittsburgh.

Horn, J. L. (1970). Organization of data on life-span development of human abilities. In L. R. Goulet and P. B. Baltes (eds.), *Life-span Developmental Psychology: Research and Theory*, pp. 424–466. New York: Academic Press.

Howe, M. L. and Brainerd, C. J. (eds.) (1988). *Cognitive Development in Adulthood*. New York: Springer.

Kacmar, K. M. and Ferris, G. R. (1989). Theoretical and methodological considerations in the age-job satisfaction relationship. *Journal of Applied Psychology*, 74, 201–207.

Kalleberg, A. L. and Loscocco, K. A. (1983). Aging, values, and rewards: Explaining age differences in job satisfaction. *American Sociological Review*, 48, 78–90.

Kite, M. E. and Johnson, B. T. (1988). Attitudes toward older and younger adults: A meta-analysis. *Psychology and Aging*, 3, 233–244.

Knowles, M. (1984). *The Adult Learner: A Neglected Species*, 3rd edn. Houston: Gulf Publishing.

Kohn, M. L. and Schooler, C. (1983). *Work and Personality: An Inquiry into the Impact of Social Stratification*. Norwood, NJ: Ablex.

Kutscher, R. E. and Walker, J. F. (1960). Comparative job performance of office workers by age. *Monthly Labor Review*, 83(1), 39–43.

LaRiviere, J. E. and Simonson, E. (1965). The effect of age and occupation on speed of writing. *Journal of Gerontology*, 20, 415–416.

Maher, H. (1955). Age and performance of two work groups. *Journal of Gerontology*, 10, 448–451.

Mark, J. A. (1957). Comparative job performance by age. *Monthly Labor Review*, 80, 1467–1471.

Martocchio, J. J. (1989). Age-related differences in employee absenteeism: A meta-analysis. *Psychology and Aging*, 4, 409–414.

Maslach, C. and Jackson, S. E. (1981). The measurement of experienced burnout. *Journal of Occupational Behaviour*, 2, 99–113.

Maylor, E. A. (1994). Ageing and the retrieval of general knowledge: Performance of Masterminds. *British Journal of Psychology*, 85, 105–114.

McCauley, W. J. (1977). Perceived age discrimination in hiring: Demographic and economic correlates. *Industrial Gerontology*, 4, 21–28.

McEvoy, G. M. and Cascio, W. F. (1989). Cumulative evidence of the relationship between employee age and job performance. *Journal of Applied Psychology*, 74, 11–17.

Myerson, J., Hale, S., Wagstaff, D., Poon, L. W. and Smith, G. A. (1990). The information-loss model: A mathematical model of age-related cognitive slowing. *Psychological Review*, 97, 475–487.

Perlmutter, M., Kaplan, M. and Nyquist, L. (1990). Development of adaptive competence in adulthood. *Human Development*, 33, 185–197.

Perry, P. and Downs, S. (1985). Skills, strategies and ways of learning: Can we help people learn how to learn? *Programmed Learning and Educational Technology*, 22, 177–181.

Poon, L. W. (1985). Differences in human memory with aging: Nature, causes, and clinical implications. In J. E. Birren and K. W. Schaie (eds.), *Handbook of the Psychology of Aging*, 2nd edn, pp. 427–462. New York: Van Nostrand Reinhold.

Rabbitt, P. M. A. (1991). Management of the working population. *Ergonomics*, 34, 775–790.

Rabbitt, P. M. A. and Maylor, E. A. (1991). Investigating models of human performance. *British Journal of Psychology*, 82, 259–290.

Salthouse, T. A. (1984). Effects of age and skill in typing. *Journal of Experimental Psychology: General*, 113, 345–371.

Salthouse, T. A. (1985a). Speed of behavior and its implications for cognition. In J. E. Birren and K. W. Schaie (eds.), *Handbook of the Psychology of Aging*, 2nd edn, pp. 400–426. New York: Van Nostrand Reinhold.

Salthouse, T. A. (1985b). *A Theory of Cognitive Aging*. Amsterdam: North Holland.

Salthouse, T. A. (1990). Working memory as a processing resource in cognitive aging. *Development Review*, 10, 101–124.

Salthouse, T. A. (1991). Mediation of adult age differences in cognition by reductions in working memory and speed of processing. *Psychological Science*, 2, 179–183.

Schwab, D. P. and Heneman, H. G. (1977a). Effects of age and experience on productivity. *Industrial Gerontology*, 4, 113–117.

Schwab, D. P. and Heneman, H. G. (1977b). Age and satisfaction with dimensions of work. *Journal of Vocational Behavior*, 10, 212–220.

Snel, J. and Cremer, R. (eds.) (1994). *Work and Aging: A European Perspective*. London: Taylor & Francis.

Sparrow, P. R. and Davies, D. R. (1988). Effects of age, tenure, training, and job complexity on technical performance. *Psychology and Aging*, 3, 307–314.

Stankov, L. (1988). Aging, attention, and intelligence. *Psychology and Aging*, 3, 59–74.

Sterns, H. L. (1986). Training and retraining adult and older adult workers. In J. E. Birren, P. K. Robinson and J. E. Livingston (eds.), *Age, Health and Employment*, pp. 93–113. Englewood Cliffs, NJ: Prentice Hall.

Sterns, H. L. and Doverspike, D. (1989). Aging and the training and learning process. In I. L. Goldstein (ed.), *Training and Development in Organizations*, pp. 299–332. San Francisco: Jossey-Bass.

Teiger, C. (1989). Le vieillissement différential dans et par le travail. *Le Travail Humain*, 52, 21–56.

Vernon, P. A., Nador, S. and Kantor, L. (1985). Reaction times and speed-of-processing: Their relationship to timed and untimed measures of intelligence. *Intelligence*, 9, 357–374.

Verrillo, R. T. and Verrillo, V. (1985). Sensory and perceptual performance. In N. Charness (ed.), *Aging and Human Performance*, pp. 1–46. Chichester: Wiley.

Walker, J. F. (1964). The job performance of federal mail sorters by age. *Monthly Labor Review*, 87(3), 296–301.

Warr, P. B. (1987). *Work, Unemployment, and Mental Health*. Oxford: Oxford University Press.

Warr, P. B. (1990). The measurement of well-being and other aspects of mental health. *Journal of Occupational Psychology*, 63, 193–210.

Warr, P. B. (1992). Age and occupational well-being. *Psychology and Aging*, 7, 37–45.

Warr, P. B. (1994a). Age and employment. In H. C. Triandis, M. D. Dunnette and L. M. Hough (eds.), *Handbook of Industrial and Organizational Psychology*, 2nd edn, vol. 4, pp. 485–550. Palo Alto, Calif.: Consulting Psychologists Press.

Warr, P. B. (1994b). Age and job performance. In J. Snel and R. Cremer (eds.), *Work and Aging: A European Perspective*, pp. 309–322. London: Taylor & Francis.

Warr, P. B. (1994c). Training for older managers. *Human Resource Management Journal*, 4, 22–38.

Warr, P. B. and Pennington, J. (1993). Views about age discrimination and older workers. In *Age and Employment: Policies, Attitudes and Practices*, pp. 75–106. London: Institute of Personnel Management.

Warr, P. B. and Pennington, J. (1994). Occupational age-grading: Jobs for older and younger non-managerial employees. *Journal of Vocational Behavior*, 45, 328–346.

Wright, J. D. and Hamilton, R. F. (1978). Work satisfaction and age: Some evidence for the 'job change' hypothesis. *Social Forces*, 56, 1140–1158.

World Health Organization (1993). *Aging and Working Capacity*. Geneva: World Health Organization.

12

Job Design and Modern Manufacturing

Sharon K. Parker and Toby D. Wall

Organizations have a wide range of tasks to complete and integrate in order to meet their objectives. They achieve this by allocating tasks and responsibilities to individuals or groups. The term 'job design' denotes the nature of those tasks and responsibilities, how they are grouped together, and especially the degree of discretion afforded to employees over their execution. Organizations have considerable choice in deciding how jobs are designed. One option is to limit jobs to a single task; another is to group a limited number of similar tasks together; and a third is to combine together a variety of tasks which are quite different from each other. For example, the job of a machine operator could involve simply loading and unloading products onto the machine, or it could include other tasks such as checking the quality of the products and carrying out routine machine maintenance. In each case the degree to which individual job holders or groups are given autonomy over the work processes can vary. The machine operator could have little or no control over the scheduling of parts through the machine and the methods of operation, or he or she could be given considerable discretion over these aspects of work. Psychological interest in the processes of job design focuses on how these organizational choices, made deliberately or by default, affect the performance and well-being of employees.

A feature of research in this area is that it is closely tied to practice. Thus, in the interests of applied relevance, the dimensions of jobs that are emphasized are those which are most prominent in reality. A consequence is that current approaches have developed largely in reaction to the dominant trends in industry, which have in recent decades been towards job simplification. At present, however, there are clear signs that this trend is being reversed, bringing with it the need to modify and extend psychological approaches to job design.

This historical link between practice and theory underpins our account of job design, which is in four main parts. In the first two parts we outline traditional job design practice, and the now established body of research and theory to which this has given rise. Then we describe the new manufacturing philosophies, technologies and techniques that are emerging. Finally, we consider how psychological approaches to job design are changing, and need to change further, to meet the challenges of the new manufacturing environment.

TRADITIONAL PRACTICE: JOB SIMPLIFICATION

The Industrial Revolution in the eighteenth century fundamentally changed the pattern of work within society. The manufacture of goods became an increasingly important part of economic activity. Moreover, whereas people producing goods previously worked in trade or craft jobs, alone or in small groups, the invention of large-scale industrial machinery, and the associated development of factories, brought them together in much larger numbers. This concentration of labour raised new issues of how to organize and manage work.

The ideas that were to shape job design practice in the present century are fully described and referenced in historical accounts elsewhere (e.g., Littler, 1985; Wall and Martin, 1987). The core concepts are generally be traced back to the writings of Adam Smith and Charles Babbage, who described the 'division of labour' as the route to enhanced productivity. Their recommendation was that the making of a complex product should be broken down into a series of simple tasks performed by separate employees. This job simplification was held to bring such benefits as: enabling less skilled, and hence cheaper, labour to be recruited; reducing training costs; and improving performance by focusing an individual's attention on one simple operation.

It is difficult to determine the immediate impact of Smith and Babbage's views on practice at the time, but there can be little doubt that their ideas were subsequently taken up enthusiastically from the beginning of the twentieth century. This was largely a result of the work of Frederick Taylor, Frank Gilbreth and others. Most notably, in the development of 'scientific management', Taylor argued that one should not only subdivide work among employees into small discrete jobs, but one should also clearly allocate to management the responsibility for decisions about how the job should be done. The latter included managers carrying out vital 'preparatory acts' to help employees work more efficiently, such as identifying the 'one best way' to do a job by establishing the most effective movements. Having identified the best way, the responsibility of management was to enforce and encourage its practice, primarily through the use of financial incentives. In other words, there was separation between the planning and control of work on the one hand and its execution on the other; and to the original notion of a horizontal division of labour had been added the principle of a vertical division of labour.

Taylor applied this approach to the design of a number of individual manual jobs with spectacular results for output. On a larger scale, Tayloristic principles were implemented by Henry Ford in creating the first car assembly-line at Highland Park, Michigan, in the early 1910s. Here, simplification began to be pushed further towards its limits, to the extent that Ford described half of the jobs within his factories as 'not requiring full physical capacity' (for example, he claimed that 670 jobs could potentially be performed by men without legs!). No mention was made of the use of people's intellectual capacities. In such assembly-line work it is not unusual to find people carrying out a single operation, on a small part of the total product, at a predetermined pace and with little or no discretion over how they perform their task. Cycle times can be as short as two or three seconds.

These ideas were widely absorbed into job design practice. In 1955 a survey conducted by Davis, Canter and Hoffman showed that the principles of scientific management dominated the ways jobs were designed in industry. Of a list of fifteen criteria used by organizations to design jobs, the following were rated as among the most important: minimizing the time required to perform an operation, minimizing skill requirements, achieving specialization of skills and minimizing training or learning times. By the middle of the twentieth century job simplification was the dominant practice for shopfloor jobs (Braverman, 1974; Littler, 1985). As Buchanan and McCalman (1989, p. 13) claim: 'Taylor's ideas have become a central feature of the taken-for-granted organizational recipe that many managers apply to the design and redesign of work, without serious question or challenge.'

ESTABLISHED JOB DESIGN RESEARCH AND THEORY

Not surprisingly, given the prevalence of job simplification, researchers began to question its human consequences. This represented a significant move away from a narrow focus on performance and productivity to an approach which also took account of employee well-being. Some of the earliest investigations of this type were undertaken in the 1920s by the Industrial Fatigue Research Board (later known as the Industrial Health Research Board, IHRB). Emphasis was on the psychological effects of narrowly defined and repetitive jobs such as those of pharmaceutical-product packing and bicycle-chain assembly. These simplified jobs were shown to be dissatisfying, tiring and boring, and subsequent research suggested that they affected employees' mental health. For example, in a study of over 3,000 blue-collar workers, Fraser (1947; cited in Wall and Martin, 1987) found that neurosis most frequently occurred among those who found work boring, who performed jobs that required constant monitoring, or who performed assembly, bench inspection and tool room work. Further studies conducted during the next two decades, many involving the archetypal assembly-line jobs in car factories (e.g., Kornhauser, 1965; Walker and Guest, 1952), showed similar negative consequences of job simplification. To alleviate such problems, researchers recommended that there be job redesign, in the form of *job rotation* (moving people regularly between jobs) or *horizontal job enlargement* (including a greater variety of tasks within a job).

From the above description it is evident that early research was dominated by a concern with the *horizontal* division of labour, and less attention was paid to the psychological implications of restricted responsibility or autonomy. The latter issue, particularly the focus on autonomy, gained greater prominence in the work conducted from around the beginning of the 1960s, which has largely defined the field of job design research to the present day. Three initiatives have been especially influential. The first was the work of Herzberg and colleagues (Herzberg, Mausner and Snyderman, 1959), who proposed the 'motivator–hygiene' or 'two-factor' theory of work motivation. This posited that while some job features extrinsic to the work itself ('hygiene factors', such as work conditions or supervisory practices) affect feelings of dissatisfaction, they are relatively unimportant as determinants of satisfaction or motivation. Instead another group of job features, 'motivators', such as recognition, responsibility and interesting work, should be promoted if people's abilities and motives are to be harnessed for effective work and if they are to find work personally rewarding.

Herzberg's theory commanded considerable attention during the 1960s and put the issue of autonomy high on the job design agenda. However, it was superseded by the more sharply defined Job Characteristics Model (JCM) of Hackman and Oldham (1976, 1980). This specified five core features of jobs salient to both attitudes and behaviour: skill variety, task identity, task significance, autonomy and task feedback. Jobs with higher levels of these characteristics, especially autonomy, were predicted to promote work motivation, work performance and job satisfaction, and to reduce labour turnover and absenteeism. Thus the practical recommendation that emanated from both Herzberg's theory and the JCM was for *job enrichment* – the design of jobs with greater autonomy and responsibility.

The motivator–hygiene theory and the JCM are focused on individual job design. The third main influence on research in the 1960s was that concerned with group work design, and derives from sociotechnical systems theory (Trist, Higgin, Murray and Pollack, 1963). This developed in parallel with, but largely independently from, the previous approaches. In relation to job design, socio-technical systems theory proposed that teams be created around sets of tasks that are varied, form a self-completing whole and have an identifiable value; and that there should be considerable discretion with regard to how those tasks are carried out and to how teams manage themselves (Cherns, 1976). These criteria for group work design correspond closely to those of the Job Characteristics Model. Thus it is unsurprising that there have been calls for a synthesis between the two approaches, and that Hackman (1983) has extended the Job Characteristics Model to group work. The outcome in terms of practice is the recommendation to implement autonomous work groups, alternatively known as 'semi-autonomous work groups', 'self-managing work groups', 'self-managing work teams' and 'self-regulating work teams'.

Research stimulated by these theoretical approaches has been of two main kinds. The first, by far the most common, uses a cross-sectional paradigm. Investigations of this type often draw on the JCM; partly because of the specificity of this model, but also because of the availability of a set of measures of the relevant variables (the Job Diagnostic Survey, Hackman and Oldham, 1975). In cross-sectional studies people are asked to describe the characteristics of their jobs, and the correlations between these descriptions and outcome variables are then examined. Numerous reviews and meta-analyses report a consistent relationship between the extent to which people report they have autonomy and other relevant job properties, and their satisfaction with their jobs (e.g., Glick, Jenkins and Gupta, 1986; Loher, Noe, Moeller and Fitzgerald, 1985; Warr, 1987).

However, this type of cross-sectional study is not without difficulties of interpretation. Roberts and Glick (1981) point out that, because job characteristics have often been measured by self-report methods, findings could reflect the fact that perceptions, rather than actual job characteristics, account for the relationships obtained. For example, people who are most satisfied might also rate their jobs more positively, irrespective of the real characteristics of those jobs. This is also part of the argument behind the social information-processing approach to job design, which posits that social influences affect the way jobs are perceived (Salancik and Pfeffer, 1978). The force of this argument is somewhat reduced by studies showing that perceptual measures provide valid information about job content, and by evidence that independent ratings of job characteristics (such as from supervisors and co-workers) are significantly related to job incumbents' attitudes (e.g., Algera, 1983). However, studies do show stronger relationships with employee reactions for perceptual measures of job characteristics than for independent ones.

The second type of study, although less common, is potentially more instructive. It involves redesigning jobs in line with theory-based recommendations and evaluating the outcomes of this change. An example is the investigation of autonomous work groups in a food factory described by Wall, Kemp, Jackson and Clegg (1986).

The new method of working involved teams of about ten employees, all of whom were required to carry out the eight tasks involved in the production process. Each team worked without supervisors, with members collectively responsible for: allocating tasks among themselves, attaining production and quality targets, recording production data, solving local production problems, ordering raw materials, delivering finished goods to stores, training new recruits and in other ways managing their day to day activities. The effects of these autonomous work groups were assessed by comparing attitudes and behaviours of experimental employees with those of employees in three comparison groups. This was followed up over a further two years during which autonomous work groups were introduced into one of the comparison settings. It was found that experimental employees clearly saw themselves as having more autonomy than their counterparts, and they were much more satisfied with their jobs in both the shorter and longer term. Productivity was also greater since the output of employees in autonomous work groups matched that of those working under conventional job designs, yet in the former case there was no need to employ supervisors.

Several other change studies have been reported (e.g., Cordery, Smith and Mueller, 1991; Locke, Sirota and Wolfson, 1976), most of which demonstrate benefits from job redesign. However, a particular difficulty posed by this type of study is that it is often difficult to ascribe improvements in outcomes solely to the job redesign itself, rather than to associated changes. In other words, the specificity of effects is often unclear. Other problems associated with the literature on change studies are that the research designs of studies are not uniformly strong, many studies consider only short-term effects and it seems likely that failures are under-reported (for critical reviews see Pasmore, Francis, Haldeman and Shani, 1982; Wall and Martin, 1987).

Taking the cross-sectional and change studies together, several observations can be made. There is general support for the proposition that jobs which enhance employees' autonomy or control over their work promote their well-being and job satisfaction. However, findings are less consistent with regard to performance. For example, in a review of twenty-five of the most rigorous case studies and field experiments where jobs were redesigned, Kelly (1992) found clear performance benefits in only twelve. This points to theoretical deficiencies, suggesting there are as yet unidentified factors which inhibit or promote the effect of job redesign on performance. In this respect it might be useful to integrate job design research with organizational theory, since the latter can help specify the contingencies which account for differential effects (e.g., Cummings and Blumberg, 1987). The relationship between job design and psychological strain has also been neglected in recent research, reappearing within a distinct field of inquiry on stress (see Chapter 7). This is an artificial separation given the degree of commonality in both domains with regard to job characteristics, and especially the emphasis on autonomy as an important variable in both cases. Thus, although some critical relationships have been clearly established, there is clearly room in job design research for theoretical development and closer integration with related areas of inquiry.

Our discussion so far has considered job design research from within its own terms of reference. A more fundamental, if somewhat ironic, criticism of job design research is that, like the practice it has sought to explain, the research agenda has been too narrowly conceived. This point was raised in the influential early review of the job characteristics approach by Roberts and Glick (1981), who concluded that 'investigations have become narrower over time. A restricted set of task characteristics . . . have been focused on' (p. 210). The force of this criticism has been underlined by recent developments in manufacturing philosophies, technologies and production methods. In the same way that existing approaches to job design reflect the practices of their day, changes currently taking place in manufacturing create the need to develop this field of research. We describe these changing requirements in the next section, before considering their implications for job design research and practice in the final part of the chapter.

THE NEW MANUFACTURING ENVIRONMENT

In recent years there has been a major change of strategy by leading manufacturing companies. In the face of world-wide economic recession it has become accepted that to succeed, perhaps even to survive, companies have to compete not only on the basis of cost, but also in terms of quality and responsiveness to market demand (Hayes, Wheelwright and Clark, 1988; Lawler, 1992; Storey, 1994). Responsiveness involves offering a wider diversity of products, customizing products, rapidly introducing new product designs and meeting tight delivery times.

As with most changes in strategy, this one did not arise in a vacuum. In addition to economic pressures, the emergence of new technologies and production methods has played a part in shaping the new competitive emphasis. The development of advanced manufacturing technology (AMT) has been an important factor, since this increases potential flexibility in changing between different products and introducing new designs, thus supporting responsiveness to customer demand. Also important has been the introduction of new production methods. Partly inspired by the visibly successful Japanese industries, and reinforced by such influential books as Schonberger's (1986) *World Class Manufacturing*, just-in-time inventory control (JIT), total quality management (TQM) and cellular manufacturing have all become central components of modern manufacturing practice. Next, we briefly describe each of these manufacturing initiatives and their strategic importance.

Advanced Manufacturing Technology

Advance manufacturing technology (AMT) refers to a wide range of manufacturing technologies whose common feature is that they are computer-based. The most common forms are stand-alone computer numerically controlled (CNC) machines. Larger-scale applications, where individual CNC machines and other technologies are linked together by various materials-handling devices, and their operations co-ordinated through shared computer-control, are known as flexible manufacturing systems. The advantage of computer control, over and above the usual benefits of automation (i.e., reduced labour costs, consistent product quality, enhanced output levels), is that it allows for greater flexibility in switching between different processes and products. Each change involves loading different software, rather than physically resetting machines, resulting in greater machine utilization. This 'programmability' creates not only the economies of scale (i.e., being able to produce a large volume quickly) associated with automation in general, but also economies of scope (i.e., being able to produce efficiently a wider range of parts or products), thus permitting the production of customized goods at near mass production cost as well as facilitating more flexible responses to customer demands.

In addition to the computer-based machinery described above, there are two other important types of technology. One is computer-aided design. This supports the design of new products, and, through their being based on a common information technology, allows closer links between the stages of design and production. Other systems, referred to as computer-aided production management, are concerned with the planning and control of production resources. For example, manufacturing resource planning is a computerized order and material-tracking system that has the potential to improve strategic planning, allow for better inventory monitoring and control, and provide on-line data about production schedules.

Just-in-Time Inventory Control

Pioneered by Toyota Motor Corporation, just-in-time inventory control (JIT) has been hailed as a low-investment and 'back-to-basics' approach to manufacturing with the potential for huge benefits. JIT is fundamentally a system for reducing costs by minimizing capital tied up in raw materials, components, work-in-progress and stores of finished goods, thus ensuring minimum delay between the investment in those inputs and the receipt of payment from the customer. Traditionally, manufacturing companies have relied on high levels of inventory so as to accommodate fluctuating demand and unanticipated production problems. Stocks of materials are typically held in case they are needed, buffer stocks are kept between different stages of production so that work is always available at each stage, and finished products are stored on site waiting for the customer to request them. This is essentially a 'push' system in which operations are triggered by the availability of materials and labour, rather than being 'pulled' by customer demand.

The objective of JIT is to remove as much of this inventory as possible by manufacturing to order. It is a pull system, in which each stage of production is carried out 'just-in-time' for the next stage of production until, ultimately, the finished goods are produced 'just-in-time' for the customer (Schonberger, 1986). Materials and components are bought only for immediate use against a specific order. The absence of a stock of finished goods requires short lead times in order to be responsive to customer demands. This means there must be little work-in-progress and close co-ordination between the different stages of production to ensure that products pass quickly from one stage to the next. It also means production involves smaller batches, since no extra is made for stock. This in turn puts pressure on minimizing set-up and change-over times and avoiding disruptions due to problems with the supply of materials or labour, or the unreliability of technology.

Total Quality Management

Traditionally, quality control within manufacturing has involved separate groups of employees who inspect products after they have been made, and who return defects for rework or rectify faults themselves. This separation of production from inspection institutionalizes the expectation of quality problems. The new emphasis of total quality management (TQM) is on avoiding this additional cost and improving quality by making products 'right first time' (e.g., Crosby, 1979). Many methods and techniques are deployed towards this goal, including giving operators responsibility for quality when they are making the product, using various monitoring and problem-solving tools (e.g., cause–effect analyses) to continually improve production processes, and improving product design to reduce manufacturing difficulties. Essentially, quality control is no longer seen purely as a separate policing function but as part of a management strategy in which responsibility for quality is an integral part of, rather than an adjunct to, production planning and work. In practice, there is considerable variation in the focus of TQM initiatives, especially with regard to whether a 'hard' engineering view is taken, focused on the standardization of materials and processes to eliminate problems; or whether a 'softer' approach is adopted based on training employees and giving them responsibility for correcting faults as they arise (Wilkinson, Marchington, Goodman and Ackers, 1992).

Cellular Manufacturing

Historically, the layout of machinery within manufacturing has been organized according to the main stages of production. For example, in an engineering factory all lathes might be in one section, milling and grinding machines in another, drilling in a third, and so on. Materials would be passed from one section to the next, routed as required to make the final product. In cellular manufacturing the different types of machine required to make a particular product or set of products are instead grouped together. The result is called a 'cell', which deals with a narrower range of products but with most or all the stages of their production. By specializing according to product, there is typically a simpler work-flow and easier scheduling, less production time is lost due to machine set-up, and there is decreased work-in-progress. Employees can also more clearly identify with a given product. This makes cellular manufacturing particularly compatible with the aims of JIT and TQM, and it is thus not surprising that the introduction of cells has become increasingly common since the 1980s. Indeed, cellular manufacturing has been described as the 'quiet revolution' of manufacturing (Ingersoll Engineers, 1990).

An Integrated Perspective

The four initiatives described above should not be considered as separate developments. An important factor is the way they combine to allow simultaneous pursuit of the strategic goals of low cost, high quality and responsiveness. Superficially, JIT might be seen as directed at cost reduction, TQM at improving quality, and AMT at responsiveness, with cellular manufacturing representing a facilitating physical arrangement. In reality, the relationships between these initiatives are more complex. For example, AMT not only exploits computer-control to allow responsiveness through a greater diversity of products, but it also helps to control costs (by reduced set-up times and quick changeovers) and quality (by allowing consistent production with tighter error tolerances). Essentially, what these initiatives have in common is an emphasis on linking traditionally separate aspects of manufacturing (such as incorporating quality inspection into production), thus resulting in 'integrated manufacturing' (Dean and Snell, 1991).

In addition, the new manufacturing initiatives should not be considered separately from job design issues of the kind described earlier in the chapter. This is especially the case in light of an increasing recognition that the new initiatives often fail to achieve their full potential, not so much because of deficiencies in the technologies and techniques themselves, but as a result of associated work organization problems. Many practitioners have recognized this link, and there has been a resurgence of interest in job redesign in relation to the initiatives described here (e.g. Lawler, 1992).

The current emphasis is on restructuring jobs to improve employee performance rather than to enhance their well-being or increase attendance. As Littler (1985, p. 21) argues, recent market changes have 'forced many Western corporations to re-examine their philosophy of job design and control from a solid, "down-to-earth" perspective – that of profits'. This in turn means that job redesign programmes are potentially more wide-ranging and important to the organization than those programmes taking place in the 1950s and 1960s (Buchanan and McCalman, 1989; Littler, 1985). They also are typically much more explicitly aimed at facilitating the development of employees' knowledge, skills and orientations, suggesting that such outcomes should be of central interest to researchers. Yet, despite these changing issues for job design practice within the last decade, combined with clear practitioner interest in the topic, there has been little corresponding advance in research on job design. In the final part of this chapter we summarize some key suggestions for extensions to established job design theories. With the current resurgence of interest in job design, the time is ripe to capitalize on opportunities that the new context presents and develop a broader theoretical understanding that serves to inform practice.

MODERN MANUFACTURING AND
JOB DESIGN RESEARCH

Investigations of the relationship between the new manufacturing initiatives and shopfloor work have highlighted many of the limitations of established approaches to job design noted earlier, and suggest at least three important lines of development (Wall and Jackson, 1995). The first, arising mainly from concern about the implications of the new initiatives for employee well-being, relates to the need to expand the range of job content factors taken into account in thinking about this area. The second priority concerns the importance of identifying the contingencies under which job design affects performance or has no effect. Finally, the third requirement is to explicate the processes or mechanisms which may underlie the effect of job design on performance. We consider each of these priorities in turn.

Job Content

The issue of autonomy, or job control, remains a core theme with regard to job design for the new manufacturing initiatives, providing an essential point of continuity with previous research. The dominant concern in early studies of the new initiatives was that they would lead to further job simplification by removing areas of discretion that remained in traditional work systems. Braverman (1974), for example, argued that advanced manufacturing technology, by incorporating the expertise of skilled operators into the program that controlled the machinery, eliminated a key area of job control. Similarly, just-in-time production has been characterized as removing individual control over the timing of tasks, thus 'recreating the rhythm of assembly-line pacing' (Turnbull, 1988, p. 13).

However, research has shown that these fears are too simplistic. The amount of autonomy afforded to employees following the implementation of the new manufacturing systems has sometimes been reduced, but in other cases it has been enhanced (Dean and Snell, 1991; Wall and Davids, 1992). The direction and extent of this change depend both upon the nature of the work systems and the choices made in allocating responsibilities to employees. The varying effect of technology on job control is exemplified by Buchanan and Boddy's (1983) case study of the implementation of a computer-controlled system for baking. For 'doughmen', a new system which precisely determined the recipe for mixing ingredients reduced their control of the process. It removed most of the previous need to rely on human judgement in adjusting the mixture, which had been based on feedback from the sound, touch and colour of the dough. For 'ovensmen', in contrast, the new technology augmented feedback in a way which gave them more control over the baking process. Klein (1991) has similarly described varying effects of just-in-time production (JIT) on job control, and argued that, although increasing individual autonomy might sometimes be incompatible with tightly linked work-flows and JIT principles of standardization, the opportunity nevertheless exists to enhance autonomy at the group level. Supporting this view, in one of the few empirical investigations of the effects of just-in-time production on shopfloor jobs, Jackson and Martin (in press) found that employees in that setting reported reduced control over the timing of their work. The authors argued, however, that this was not a necessary effect of the initiative, and that a strategy of enhancing operators' autonomy 'fits well with the JIT philosophy of increased worker involvement and ownership of production processes'. In light of these observations, it is not surprising that in a large-scale survey Dean and Snell (1991) found no systematic overall relationship between the new manufacturing initiatives and the design of jobs.

Though the evidence shows no uniform effect of the new initiatives on job control, this issue remains of central interest for two reasons. First, job control is known to be one of the most important determinants of employee well-being, and is thus of explanatory value in accounting for differential psychological effects of alternative manufacturing systems. Second, increased job control has been linked to enhanced work performance, although this is likely to be a contingent relationship, as we describe in the next section.

Turning to other aspects of job content, research points to three factors largely ignored by traditional job design theory that now require greater attention. The first of these concerns *cognitive demands*. A common observation is that the new manufacturing initiatives alter the balance between the physical and the cognitive demands of jobs, placing increased emphasis on the latter. An important distinction is between attentional demand (the passive monitoring aspects of the work) and problem-solving demand (the requirements for more active problem-solving and fault prevention). It is clear that both these aspects of work can be affected by the new initiatives. Van Cott (1985), for example, suggests that advanced manufacturing technology 'has rearranged man's [sic] role from an active element to one of passive monitoring' (p. 1140); and total quality management, with its emphasis on 'right first time', can increase the demand for close attention to detail by shopfloor employees (Turnbull, 1988). On the other hand, Cummings and Blumberg (1987, p. 47) argue that new technologies absorb the routine aspects of work while increasing the need for 'employees to manage the unforeseen and non-routine variances that cannot readily be controlled by computer'. Similarly, cases have been reported in which just-in-time production enhances problem-solving demands as a result of pressure on employees to keep the work flowing smoothly. Tailby and Turnbull (1987, p. 17), for example, describe how just-in-time production in a company created for shopfloor employees 'a greater need to use initiative, solve problems and keep production going to prevent subsequent processes being starved of parts'. In the words of a production supervisor within that company, the just-in-time system required 'people who think on their feet not with them'.

The second job content factor deserving greater research attention is *production responsibility*. A feature of many of the new manufacturing initiatives is that they increase the significance and visibility of the individual's contribution to output. In the case of just-in-time production, any disruption to work attributable to an individual is often made more serious and obvious by the absence of buffer stocks, since it directly impedes the work of others. For example, Oliver and Davies (1990, p. 562) describe how problems with one part of the process, tapping threads in an endshield, went unnoticed in a traditional work system because the parts went into buffer stocks. With the introduction of JIT, however, the operator passed the endshield directly to the person working on the next stage. If there were any problems, the person then 'immediately goes over and gives him a bollocking'. Equally, advanced manufacturing technology typically represents a large financial investment and has the capacity to provide a much greater volume of output in a shorter time than conventional technology. As a result, any damage to the technology or downtime which an operator causes, or could have prevented, carries much greater costs.

The psychological importance of these job properties was demonstrated in a field experiment described by Martin and Wall (1987). They recorded the strain experienced by operators as they moved between AMT installations with contrasting levels of attentional demand and production responsibility. For some installations the job involved operating only one machine, whereas in others it involved operating two machines simultaneously. Moreover, production was scheduled so that some installations dealt with less costly products, while others processed work where a single error could result in lost production in excess of £2,000. The findings showed that operators tolerated on their own either the high levels of attentional demand or high production responsibility without negative effects, but that when faced with both demands together they experienced considerable strain. Clearly, the role of cognitive demands and production responsibility invites further investigation, especially given the potential of some modern manufacturing systems to increase these aspects simultaneously.

The final job content factor deserving greater attention is *work interdependence*, which refers to the extent to which employees are dependent on each other and need to collaborate in the execution of their work. Work interdependence was included in early job design theory, but faded from view over time. It returns to prominence because an inherent feature of many of the new initiatives is their integration of traditionally distinct aspects of manufacturing (Dean and Snell, 1991). The elimination of work-in-progress between stages of production as a result of just-in-time, for example, can make employees much more immediately reliant on the performance of others in order to complete their own work. Similarly, total quality management principles, such as getting employees to identify with 'internal' customers and suppliers, explicitly aim to increase employees' awareness of the need to collaborate with other people; and operating problems that occur with advanced manufacturing technology can require shopfloor employees to deal more directly with support staff. Such interdependence, with a resultant need for more tightly linked and co-ordinated efforts, is likely to be important both for employee well-being and for performance. As yet, this possibility remains largely unexplored.

Contingencies

As noted earlier, a problem for established job design theory is to explain why some studies of the effect of increased job control show performance benefits but others do not. One implication is that the effect of job design on performance depends on some 'third factor' or contingency. Recent research applying ideas from organization theory to the design of jobs for operators of AMT suggests that the degree of local *uncertainty* might be a key contingency variable.

Interest in uncertainty stems from the pioneering studies of Burns and Stalker (1961), who observed that the type of organizational structure that worked best in relatively simple, stable and predictable manufacturing environments was different from that needed in more complex and uncertain ones. 'Mechanistic' structures, involving routinized tasks and centralized decision-making, were identified as appropriate for stable and predictable conditions; but 'organic' structures, characterized by flexible practices and decentralized decision-making, were held to be necessary to cater for uncertain environments. Within the latter, for example, it is not possible to have rules and procedures for all the uncertainties; neither is it feasible for a supervisor to make all of the decisions or the best decisions. In other words, the underlying principle is that as the degree of uncertainty increases, so does the need for more devolved decision-making.

Though originally based on an entire organization as the unit of analysis, the uncertainty concept can be applied at the job level. Taking this line, Cummings and Blumberg (1987) analysed the job requirements associated with advanced manufacturing technology. They argued that since these were likely to result in higher levels of production uncertainty, the need was for operators to be 'given the necessary skills, information and freedom to respond to unforeseen circumstances affecting the production system and its task environment' (p. 48). In practice, advanced manufacturing technologies vary with regard to production uncertainty; and it follows that the appropriateness of a recommendation for enhanced operator autonomy will vary accordingly. Thus it is expected that where AMT systems are complex and unpredictable, giving operators greater job control will improve system performance. However, performance gains as a result of enhanced autonomy are not expected where the new systems are predictable and certain.

This hypothesis was confirmed in a longitudinal change study described by Wall, Corbett, Martin, Clegg and Jackson (1990), who examined the impact of increased operator control on the performance of computer-controlled assembly machines. They found that the job changes resulted in a substantial and sustained improvement in output for the systems characterized by the greatest production uncertainty, but that they had virtually no effect with the more stable and predictable systems.

Although empirical evidence remains scant, the potential of this line of inquiry is considerable. Considering uncertainty as a contingency variable has the capacity to explain otherwise apparently inconsistent findings, and provides an important opportunity for integrating job design research into wider organizational theory.

Mechanisms

Perhaps the greatest challenge to emerge from work on the new manufacturing initiatives is the need to better understand the mechanisms by which job design might have its effect. Established job design theory has been relatively silent on the reasons why jobs with greater autonomy are predicted to promote enhanced performance. The implicit assumption is often a motivational one, that increased opportunity for job control affects performance by encouraging greater effort (Campion and McClelland, 1993; Wall and Martin, 1987). Recent developments suggest additional mechanisms worthy of greater attention.

A position now regularly taken is that job design is important because it enables employees to 'work smarter', or solve more complex problems themselves. In an insightful analysis of the 'integrated factory', for example, Susman and Chase (1986) argued that job control promotes performance because it means that 'employees are in a better position to see the relationships between specific actions and their consequences' (p. 268). Lawler (1992) contends that quality improvements accrue because 'employees have a broader perspective on the work process and as a result can catch errors and make corrections that might have gone undetected in more traditional work design in which employees lacked the knowledge to detect them. And, because they have the autonomy to make ongoing improvements, employees become increasingly knowledgeable about how their work can best be done' (p. 85).

There are two mechanisms suggested in the above views. The first is that greater job control fosters the broader and more proactive *role orientations* that are required for effective performance in modern manufacturing environments. For example, employees in integrated manufacturing environments are expected to be aware of, and concerned about, a broader range of team and customer goals; and they are expected to use their initiative to actively seek out, solve and even prevent problems that affect production. This contrasts with employees in traditional manufacturing, who often have a passive and narrow orientation towards their role (for example, they may see their job as operating a single machine and as 'doing what they are told'). Role orientations can thus be distinguished from existing outcome variables used in job design research, such as job satisfaction and well-being, as they assess people's construction of what their job is, rather than their reaction to that job.

Recent studies encourage the belief that greater autonomy promotes the development of such role orientations. Using newly developed scales, Parker, Wall and Jackson (1994) compared the role orientations of employees in autonomous work groups in an integrated manufacturing environment with those of their shopfloor counterparts working under more traditional job designs. The employees in the former group were found to have significantly broader, more proactive and more strategic views of their role than those in the latter group. For example, the employees in autonomous groups reported greater ownership of customer goals (such as delivery times, high quality products) than those working in simplified jobs. The role orientations of employees in the latter group are exemplified in comments such as: 'I'm only responsible for the product until it's put on the floor, like' and 'When I've finished a job, I should just go to the foreman and say "Look, I've finished this, what's next?" and that's as far as I should go, isn't it?' (p. 415).

In a longitudinal study examining the same issue the authors presented strong evidence that the development of new and broader role orientations is dependent on enhanced operator autonomy (Parker, Jackson and Wall, 1993). Some preliminary evidence that orientations are linked to rated performance was also presented, although the design of the study did not permit a definitive test. More research of this type is clearly warranted.

The second mechanism suggested concerns the relationship between job control and specific *job knowledge*. That is, it is assumed that job control releases the use of existing job knowledge and promotes the development of new job knowledge. Evidence that the effect of job control on job knowledge can be a critical link to performance is provided by a study of a robotics system described by Wall, Jackson and Davids (1992). As with many new manufacturing initiatives, the effectiveness of the system was in practice largely a function of how well operating faults were managed. The authors reasoned that by analysing change in the pattern of faults following an increase in operator control they would be able to test for different knowledge-based mechanisms. For example, a reduction in time lost per fault occurring immediately after the job change would indicate gains due to more rapid responses to presenting faults through the application of pre-existing knowledge. On the other hand, a reduction in the incidence of faults which emerged only some weeks or months after the job change would signify a more fundamental development and use of predictive knowledge. The results showed both patterns of change, suggesting that job control has an impact on both the application and the development of performance-related job knowledge. German research in work psychology, guided by Action theory, has resulted in similar conclusions about the importance of cognitive mechanisms linking job control and individual performance (Frese and Zapf, 1993).

We clearly need to know a lot more about the impact of job design on employees' role orientations and their specific job knowledge. This applies not only to the understanding of performance, but also to research investigating mechanisms relating job design and strain. Research of the future will take these issues on board.

SUMMARY

If the psychological study of job design is to be of value, it must both reflect and contribute to practice. In the first two parts of this chapter we described how traditional practice in manufacturing has been towards job simplification; and how this has led to research focusing narrowly on the implications of such job factors as repetitiveness and lack of autonomy for employee motivation and well-being. We argued that although this focus might be adequate in the context of conventional manufacturing environments, it is of more limited use in the face of issues raised by modern manufacturing. In the third part of the chapter we described the strategic changes taking place in manufacturing and the key initiatives these encompass; namely, advanced manufacturing technology, just-in-time production, total quality management and cellular manufacturing. Finally, we considered some implications of those initiatives for job design, summarizing recommendations that research should add cognitive demand, production responsibility and work interdependence to the established emphasis on autonomy; examine the role of production uncertainty as a contingency variable affecting the impact of job control on performance; and investigate whether employee role orientations and job knowledge are among the mechanisms through which job control affects performance.

FURTHER READING

A detailed account of the principles of job design is given in Hackman and Oldham's *Work Redesign* (1980). Many papers and chapters exist, referred to throughout the chapter, that integrate and critique established job design research and theory (e.g., Kelly, 1992; Wall and Martin, 1987). The new manufacturing initiatives, and their implications for job design as well as other aspects of organizations, are described in Storey's (1994) *New Wave Manufacturing Strategies: Organizational and Human Resource Management Dimensions*. Dean and Snell (1991) offer an interesting analysis of AMT, JIT, TQM and cellular manufacturing as part of the more general change in manufacturing strategy, and consider also the implications for shopfloor work. A readable case study of the introduction of new initiatives, which highlights many issues relevant to job design research, is Buchanan and McCalman's (1989) *High Performance Work Systems: The Digital Experience*. The rationale for the recommended lines of development for job design research is more fully described by Wall and Jackson (1995).

REFERENCES

Algera, J. A. (1983). 'Objective' and perceived task characteristics as a determinant of reactions by task performers. *Journal of Occupational Psychology*, 56, 95–107.

Braverman, H. (1974). *Labour and Monopoly Capital: The Degradation of Work in the Twentieth Century*. New York: Monthly Review Press.

Buchanan, D. A. and Boddy, D. (1983). Advanced technology and the quality of working life: The effects of computerised controls on biscuit-making operators. *Journal of Occupational Psychology*, 56, 109–119.

Buchanan, D. A. and McCalman, J. (1989). *High Performance Work Systems: The Digital Experience*. London: Routledge.

Burns, T. and Stalker, G. M. (1961). *The Management of Innovation*. London: Tavistock Publications (reprinted Oxford: OUP, 1994).

Campion, M. A. and McClelland, C. L. (1993). Follow-up and extension of the interdisciplinary costs and benefits of enlarged jobs. *Journal of Applied Psychology*, 78, 339–351.

Cherns, A. B. (1976). The principles of socio-technical design. *Human Relations*, 29, 783–792.

Cordery, J. L., Smith, L. M. and Mueller, W. S. (1991). Attitudinal and behavioural effects of autonomous group working: A longitudinal field study. *Academy of Management Journal*, 34, 464–476.

Crosby, P. B. (1979). *Quality is Free*. New York: McGraw Hill.

Cummings, T. and Blumberg, M. (1987). Advanced manufacturing technology and work design. In T. D. Wall, C. W. Clegg and N. J. Kemp (eds.), *The Human Side of Advanced Manufacturing Technology*, pp. 37–60. Chichester: Wiley.

Davis, L. E., Canter, R. R. and Hoffman, J. (1955). Current job design criteria. *Journal of Industrial Engineering*, 6, 5–11.

Dean, J. W. and Snell, S. A. (1991). Integrated manufacturing and job design: Moderating effects of organizational inertia. *Academy of Management Journal*, 34, 774–804.

Frese, M. and Zapf, D. (1993). Action as the core of work psychology: A German approach. In H. C. Triandis, M. D. Dunnette and L. M. Hough (eds.), *Handbook of Industrial and Organisational Psychology*, vol. 4, pp. 271–340. Palo Alto, Calif.: Consulting Psychologists Press.

Glick, W. H., Jenkins, J. G. D. and Gupta, N. (1986). Method versus substance: How strong are underlying relationships between job characteristics and attitudinal outcomes? *Academy of Management Journal*, 29, 441–464.

Hackman, J. R. (1983). The design of work teams. In J. Lorsch (ed.), *Handbook of Organizational Behaviour*, pp. 70–94. Englewood Cliffs, NJ: Prentice Hall.

Hackman, J. R. and Oldham, G. R. (1975). Development of the Job Diagnostic Survey. *Journal of Applied Psychology*, 60, 159–170.

Hackman, J. R. and Oldham, G. R. (1976). Motivation through the design of work: Test of a theory. *Organizational Behavior and Human Performance*, 16, 250–279.

Hackman, J. R. and Oldham, G. R. (1980). *Work Redesign*. Reading, Mass.: Addison-Wesley.

Hayes, R. H., Wheelwright, S. C. and Clark, K. B. (1988). *Dynamic Manufacturing: Creating the Learning Organization*. New York: Free Press.

Herzberg, F., Mausner, B. and Snyderman, B. (1959). *The Motivation to Work*. New York: Wiley.

Ingersoll Engineers (1990). *Competitive Manufacturing: The Quiet Revolution*. Rugby: Ingersoll Engineers Ltd.

Jackson, P. R. and Martin, R. (in press). The impact of just-in-time on job content, employee attitudes and well-being: A longitudinal study. *Ergonomics*.

Kelly, J. (1992). Does job re-design theory explain job re-design outcomes? *Human Relations*, 45, 753–774.

Klein, J. A. (1991). A re-examination of autonomy in light of new manufacturing practices. *Human Relations*, 44, 21–38.

Kornhauser, A. (1965). *Mental Health of the Industrial Worker*. New York: Wiley.

Lawler, E. E. (1992). *The Ultimate Advantage: Creating the High Involvement Organization*. San Francisco: Jossey-Bass.

Littler, C. (1985). Taylorism, Fordism, and job design. In D. Knights, H. Wilmott and D. Collinson (eds.), *Job Redesign: Critical Perspectives on the Labour Process*, pp. 10–29. Aldershot, Hants: Gower.

Locke, E. A., Sirota, D. and Wolfson, A. (1976). An experimental case study of the successes and failures in job enrichment in a government agency. *Organizational Behaviour and Human Performance*, 5, 484–500.

Loher, B. T., Noe, R. A., Moeller, N. L. and Fitzgerald, M. P. (1985). A meta-analysis of the relation of job characteristics to job satisfaction. *Journal of Applied Psychology*, 70, 280–289.

Martin, R. and Wall, T. D. (1987). Attentional demand and cost responsibility as stressors in shopfloor jobs. *Acadamy of Management Journal*, 32, 69–84.

Oliver, N. and Davies, A. (1990). Adopting Japanese-style manufacturing methods: A tale of two (UK) factories. *Journal of Management Studies*, 27, 555–570.

Parker, S. K., Wall, T. D. and Jackson, P. R. (1994). Job design and work orientations in modern manufacturing: A comparative case study. In S. A. Robertson (ed.), *Contemporary Ergonomics*, pp. 411–416. London: Taylor & Francis.

Parker, S. K., Jackson, P. R. and Wall, T. D. (1993). Autonomous group working within integrated manufacturing: A longitudinal investigation of employee role orientations. In G. Salvendy and M. J. Smith (eds.), *Human-Computer Interaction: Application and Case Studies*, pp. 44–49. Amsterdam: Elsevier.

Pasmore, W., Francis, C., Haldeman, J. and Shani, A. (1982). Socio-technical systems: A North American reflection on the empirical studies of the seventies. *Human Relations*, 35, 1179–1204.

Roberts, K. H. and Glick, W. (1981). The job characteristics approach to task design: A critical review. *Journal of Applied Psychology*, 66, 193–217.

Salancik, G. R. and Pfeffer, J. (1978). A social information processing approach to job attitudes and task design. *Administrative Science Quarterly*, 23, 224–253.

Schonberger, R. J. (1986). *World Class Manufacturing: The Lessons of Simplicity Applied*. New York: Free Press.

Storey, J. (1994). *New Wave Manufacturing Strategies: Organizational and Human Resource Management Dimensions*. London: Paul Chapman.

Susman, G. and Chase, R. (1986). A sociotechnical systems analysis of the integrated factory. *Journal of Applied Behavioral Science*, 22, 257–270.

Tailby, S. and Turnbull, P. (1987). Learning to manage Just-in-Time. *Personnel Management*, January, 16–19.

Trist, E., Higgin, G., Murray, H. and Pollack, A. (1963). *Organizational Choice*. London: Tavistock.

Turnbull, P. J. (1988). The limits to 'Japanisation' – Just-in-time, labour relations and the UK automotive industry. *New Technology, Work and Employment*, 3, 7–20.

Van Cott, H. P. (1985). High technology and human needs. *Ergonomics*, 28, 1135–1142.

Walker, C. R. and Guest, R. (1952). *The Man on the Assembly Line.* Cambridge, Mass.: Harvard University Press.

Wall, T. D., Corbett, J. M., Martin, R., Clegg, C. W. and Jackson, P. R. (1990). Advanced manufacturing technology, work design and performance: A change study. *Journal of Applied Psychology*, 75, 691–697.

Wall, T. D. and Davids, K. (1992). Shopfloor work organization and advanced manufacturing technology. In C. L. Cooper and I. Robertson (eds.), *International Review of Industrial and Organizational Psychology*, pp. 363–398. Chichester: Wiley.

Wall, T. D. and Jackson. P. R. (1995). Changes in manufacturing jobs. In A. Howard (ed.), *The Changing Nature of Work*, pp. 139–174. San Francisco: Jossey-Bass.

Wall, T. D., Jackson, P. R. and Davids, K. (1992). Operator work design and robotics system performance: A serendipitous field study. *Journal of Applied Psychology*, 77, 353–362.

Wall, T. D., Kemp, N. J., Jackson, P. R. and Clegg, C. W. (1986). Outcomes of autonomous work groups: A long-term field experiment. *Academy of Management Journal*, 29, 280–304.

Wall, T. D. and Martin, R. (1987). Job and work design. In C. L. Cooper and I. T. Robertson (eds.), *International Review of Industrial and Organizational Psychology*, pp. 61–91. Chichester: Wiley.

Warr, P. B. (1987). *Work, Unemployment, and Mental Health.* Oxford: Oxford University Press.

Wilkinson, A., Marchington, M., Goodman, J. and Ackers, P. (1992). Total quality management and employee involvement. *Human Resource Management Journal*, 2, 1–18.

13

Working in Groups

Michael West

Living and working together in groups is a fundamental element of our experience. Family groups provide the social support, safety and security necessary for human development, adjustment and mental health. Within work groups people pursue shared objectives by integrating diverse skills, ideally to achieve an optimal use of their resources. It is not surprising, therefore, that psychologists have been fascinated by the study of groups for more than half a century. Social psychologists have focused particularly upon inter-group behaviour such as in racial prejudice and football hooliganism, while organizational psychologists have devoted most attention to work group processes such as communication patterns and decision-making, and to outcomes such as group productivity. In this chapter we will address three sets of questions. What is a work group? What work-group processes typically interfere with effective group performance? And what factors within work groups and organizations most influence group effectiveness?

WHAT IS A WORK GROUP?

It is useful to distinguish between formal and informal work groups, the latter being groups which have no formal organizational identity or function, but which are nevertheless present in all organizations. They may be social groups, such as people who play football together, who meet to share their common religious orientation or who meet to discuss shared grievances about the organization. In this chapter we shall focus on formal groups, those which have an identity and set of functions derived from and contributing to the achievement of the objectives of the organization. Such groups come in many forms. They include project teams, such as a research and development group exploring new ways of putting plastic cabling onto reels; multidisciplinary teams, such as a nurse, physiotherapist and counsellor combining to plan treatment for victims of road traffic accidents; cross-functional groups, for example representatives from marketing, production, sales, and research and development; autonomous work groups, who are responsible for their own work planning and processes; quality improvement groups, such as a team in a manufacturing organization brought together to try to reduce the level of rejects and customer complaints; and functional teams, as seen in surgical and airline cockpit teams.

What characterizes formal groups or teams (the terms 'group' and 'team' will be used interchangeably in this chapter)? There are a number of defining characteristics. First, members of the group have shared objectives in relation to their work. Necessarily, they must interact with each other in order to achieve those shared objectives. Team members have more or less well-defined roles, some of which are differentiated from one another (e.g., in a primary health care team: doctors, nurses, receptionists), and they have an organizational identity as a work group with a defined organizational function (e.g., the public relations team for the pharmaceutical division of a major divisionalized company). Finally, they are not so large that they would be defined more appropriately as an organization, which has an internal structure of vertical and horizontal relationships characterized by sub-groups. In practice, this is likely to mean that a work group will be smaller than about twenty members.

Why do people work in groups, particularly in modern organizations, and what evidence is there for their value? As organizations have grown in size and become structurally more complex, the need for groups of people to work together in co-ordinated ways to achieve objectives which contribute to the overall aims of the organization has become increasingly clear. In large organizations, trying to co-ordinate the activities of individuals throughout the whole organization is like trying to build a sand castle by using single grains of sand one by one.

Clearly, work groups are not appropriate for every task or function within an organization, but there is evidence that the introduction of group goals leads to better performance and productivity in a variety of work settings. Examples cited in a review of more than thirty studies of group goals and group performance (Weldon and Wein-gart, 1994) include loading trucks, performing work safely, harvest-ing and hauling timber, opening mail, operating spinning machines, running a restaurant, processing insurance appraisals, and raising money for voluntary organizations. Specific, difficult goals have been found to improve the performance of groups much more than vague 'do your best' or easy-to-attain goals. When group members feel an attachment to the goal and feel strongly that the group should reach that goal (called 'goal commitment'), not surprisingly, goal attainment is more likely. Weldon and Weingart (1994) suggest a number of factors which may determine the commitment of group members to a group goal. These include the attractiveness of goal attainment (e.g., because the group goal is compatible with group members' personal goals); the fact that membership of the group may lead to satisfaction of individual desires (perhaps simply by being part of a successful or attractive group); having a charismatic group leader; group members' expectations that the group can suc-cessfully complete its task; competing demands which will reduce the likelihood of goal attainment (such as the deleterious effects of con-flicts between seeking to provide excellent patient care in hospitals, demands to reduce health care costs and demands to do work nar-rowly defined according to professional identity – 'that's nurses' work, not doctors''); goal commitment of others in the group; and goal difficulty – if the group goal is perceived to be too difficult to attain, commitment may be reduced.

Weldon and Weingart also describe the importance of planning in groups for achieving group goals, and suggest that group members are characteristically slow to respond to changes in their tasks or their environments that make their strategies ineffective or their goals obsolete. They propose five ways of supporting group work. Goals should be set for all dimensions of performance that contribute to the overall effectiveness of the group; feedback should be provided on the group's progress towards its goal; the physical environment of the group should remove barriers to effective interaction (consider the difficulties faced by cross-national European teams); group mem-bers should be encouraged to plan carefully how their contributions can be identified and co-ordinated to achieve the group goal; and group members should be helped to manage failure, which can damage the subsequent effectiveness of the group.

PROBLEMS OF WORKING IN GROUPS

There is a good deal of research evidence which suggests that, regardless of goals, in some circumstances groups may perform less effectively than individuals working alone, and that certain aspects of group processes can interfere with the attempts of groups to perform optimally in work settings. Early this century a French agricultural engineer attempted to discover whether individuals working alone were more effective than those working in groups (Ringelmann, 1913). He instructed agricultural students to pull on a rope attached to a dynamometer and measured the amount of pull. Working alone, the average student could pull a weight of around 85 kilograms. Ringelmann then assigned them to groups of seven, for whom the average pull was 450 kilograms. The groups were pulling only 75 per cent as hard as the aggregated work of seven individuals.

Further research has involved groups solving conceptual problems, such as how to transport sheep and hungry wolves safely across a river in a boat. Although groups took longer than individuals, they achieved more correct solutions. Other tasks involved 'twenty questions' games. Here a particular object is selected but not identified, and players have to guess the name of the object by asking up to twenty questions, to which they are given only a 'yes' or 'no' answer. Groups have been found to be slightly more effective than individuals in arriving at correct solutions within their twenty questions, but they tend to be less efficient in time use. Individuals took, on average, five minutes to reach the correct solution. Groups of two took seven person-minutes (i.e., three and a half minutes in real time) and groups of four required twelve person-minutes (three minutes in real time). There were no differences between groups of two and four people in the probability of a correct answer (see Brown, 1988, for a review of these studies).

Group functioning can therefore sometimes be less effective than the aggregate of individual efforts. The term 'process losses' is used to refer to the various group processes which hinder effective group functioning (Steiner, 1972). But what are these process losses? One phenomenon identified by social psychologists is called 'social loafing'. Individuals work less hard when their efforts are combined with and masked by those of others than when they are individually accountable (Latané, Williams and Harkins, (1979). The social loafing problem challenges the assumption of group 'synergy', that teams are always more effective than the sum of the contributions of their individual members. So, are problems of group working confined simply to this relative lack of effort amongst group members? Studies of group decision-making suggest that there are other forms of process losses which hinder effective group functioning in very different ways.

Group Decision-making

One of the most important reasons why people work in groups is to use their diverse knowledge, skills and experiences to contribute to achieving the best decisions possible. In determining where and how to drill for oil, the knowledge of geologists, engineers and chemists needs to be co-ordinated. Indeed, a principal assumption behind the structuring of organizational activities into work groups is that groups will make better decisions than individual members working alone. However, research clearly indicates that while groups make decisions better than the average quality of decisions made by individual members (rated by experts external to the group), work groups consistently fall short of the quality of decisions made by their most capable individual members (Rogelberg, Barnes-Farrell and Lowe, 1992). Organizational and social psychologists have therefore tried to identify the processes which impede effective group decision-making. The following issues have been identified.

Personality factors such as shyness can cause some group members to hesitate in offering their opinions and knowledge assertively, thereby failing to contribute fully to the group's store of knowledge. Egocentricity may lead others to be unwilling to consider opinions contrary to their own. Group members are also subject to social conformity effects, causing them to withhold opinions and information contrary to the majority view, especially if that is an organizationally dominant view (Brown, 1988). Members of work groups may lack communication skills and so be unable to present their views and knowledge successfully. There may be domination by particular individuals who take up disproportionate 'air time', or who argue so vigorously with the opinions of others that their own views prevail. It is noteworthy that 'air time' and expertise are correlated in high-performing groups and uncorrelated in groups that perform poorly (Rogelberg *et al.*, 1992). Status, gender and hierarchy effects also can cause some members' contributions to be valued and attended to disproportionately. When a senior executive is present in a meeting, his or her views are likely to have a considerable influence on the outcome.

'Risky shift', or group polarization, is the tendency of work groups to make more extreme decisions than the average of members' decisions. Group decisions tend to be either more risky or more conservative than the average of individual members' opinions or decisions. When individuals discover the position of others, they tend to move along the scale of opinion partly because of a 'majority rule' influence – the largest sub-group tends to determine the group decision. Moreover, a process of social comparison may take place, whereby information about a socially preferred way of behaving leads to polarization. When we compare ourselves with those immediately around us in the organization, we tend to locate our position closer to theirs, rather than retaining the integrity of our initial position. In organizations the dangers of polarization are most likely when the group has just been formed or when the group is confronted with an unusual (often a crisis) situation. Thus shifts in the extremity of decisions affecting the competitive strategy of an organization can occur simply as a result of group processes rather than for rational or well-judged reasons (Myers and Lamm, 1976).

The social loafing effect (see above) can extend to information-seeking and decision-making. Individuals may put less effort into achieving high quality decisions in meetings as a result of their perception that their contribution will be hidden in overall group performance. Diffusion of responsibility can also inhibit individuals from taking responsibility for action when working with others. People often assume that responsibility will be shouldered by others who are present in a situation requiring action (Darley and Latané, 1968).

In organizational settings individuals may fail to act in a crisis involving the functioning of expensive technology, assessing that others in their team are taking responsibility for making the necessary decisions. Consequently, the overall quality of group decisions can be threatened.

The study of 'brainstorming' groups has regularly shown that quantity and often quality of ideas produced by individuals working separately consistently exceed those produced by a group working together (Diehl and Stroebe, 1987). Early studies comparing the effectiveness of brainstorming individually or in groups involved creating 'statisticized' and 'real' groups. Statisticized groups consisted of five individuals working alone in separate rooms who were given a five-minute period to generate ideas on uses for an object. Their results were aggregated at the end and any redundancies due to repetition of ideas by different individuals were taken out. Real groups of five individuals worked together for five minutes generating as many ideas as possible and withholding criticism. The statisticized groups were found to produce an average of sixty-eight ideas, while the real groups produced an average of only thirty-seven ideas. In over twenty studies conducted since 1958 this finding has almost always been confirmed. Individuals working alone produce more ideas of at least as high a quality when they are aggregated than do groups working together. Research by social psychologists clearly indicates that this counter-intuitive finding is due to a 'production-blocking' effect (Diehl and Stroebe, 1987). When people are speaking in brainstorming groups, others are not able to speak and so (temporarily) cannot put ideas forward. Moreover, because they may be holding ideas in their memories, waiting for a chance to speak, their ability to produce more ideas is impaired. Individuals are thus inhibited from both thinking of new ideas and offering them aloud to the group by the competing verbalizations of others.

Another process which occurs during group decision-making is 'satisficing' or making decisions immediately acceptable to the group rather than the best possible decisions (Cyert and March, 1963). Video and audio-tape recordings of group decision-making processes show that groups often identify the first minimally acceptable solution or decision, and then spend time searching for reasons to accept that decision and reject other possible options. They tend not to generate a range of alternatives before selecting, on a rational basis, the most suitable option (Maier, 1970). Finally, Janis (1982, 1989), in his studies of government policy decisions and fiascos, suggested a group syndrome which he called 'groupthink', whereby cohesive groups may err in their decision-making as a result of being more concerned with achieving agreement than with the quality of group decision-making (a process we return to discuss later). This can be especially threatening to organizational functioning where different departments see themselves as competing with one another, promoting 'in-group' favouritism and therefore a greater likelihood of groupthink.

Group decision-making is therefore more complex and problematic than is commonly understood within organizational settings. Recently, researchers have begun to identify ways to overcome some of these deficiencies. For example, research on 'groupthink' suggests both that the phenomenon is most likely to occur in groups where a supervisor is particularly dominant, and that cohesiveness *per se* is not a crucial factor (McCaulay, 1989). This suggests that supervisors could be trained to be facilitative, seeking the contributions of individual members before offering their own perceptions.

WHAT FACTORS WITHIN WORK GROUPS AND ORGANIZATIONS MOST INFLUENCE EFFECTIVENESS?

In an authoritative review of group performance and inter-group relations Guzzo and Shea (1992) conclude that the dominant model for thinking about group performance is an input–process–output model (see Figure 13.1). 'Inputs' include the knowledge, skills, abilities and motivations of group members; the composition of the team in terms of demographic and personality factors; and aspects of the organizational context, such as reward systems, information systems, training and resources. The group's task is also an input factor (though this may be modified as a result of group processes). 'Process' includes the interactions among group members, leadership patterns, information exchange, patterns of participation in decision-making,

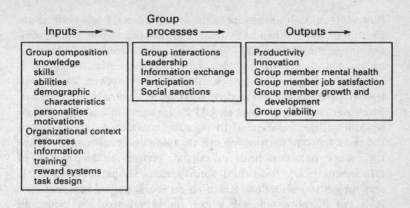

Fig. 13.1 An input–process–output model of group performance.

and social sanctions on individual behaviour. 'Outputs' refers to the products of the group's performance, but may also include group viability: team member growth, satisfaction and well-being; group innovation; and the group's viability for long-term performance (for example, is a cost of their short-term success that the group is no longer willing to work together?) (cf. Goodman and Associates, 1986; Hackman, 1990; Guzzo and Shea, 1992). Recent models suggest that input factors have both direct and indirect (via group processes) effects upon group performance. More sophisticated representations would suggest that group processes will in turn affect input factors (a motivated group may succeed in raising the level of resources available to them in the organization); and outputs will affect both processes (success fosters confidence and perhaps creativity) and inputs (successful groups may win more resources). The factors in this model influencing group effectiveness will be described under these major headings.

Inputs

In relation to task design Guzzo and Shea (1992) make a series of research-based recommendations. First, individuals should feel that they are important to the fate of the group if social loafing effects are to be minimized. When individuals feel that their work is not essential within a team, they are less likely to work effectively with others or make strong efforts towards achieving team effectiveness. It is important, therefore, that roles should be developed in ways which lead group members to see their work as indispensable and unique. Moreover, individual roles should be meaningful and intrinsically rewarding. Individuals tend to be more committed and creative if the tasks they are performing are engaging and challenging. Where their work is monotonous or partial, people are less motivated (Hackman, 1990). Individual contributions should be identifiable and subject to evaluation. Research on social loafing indicates that it is considerably reduced where individual work is evaluated (George, 1992). People have to feel not only that their work is indispensable, but also that their performance is visible to other team members. In laboratory research, where team members know their work performance will be visible to others, they maintain effort to the level they would achieve in individual performance (George, 1992). Teams should also have intrinsically interesting tasks to perform. Just as people work harder if the tasks they are asked to perform are intrinsically engaging and challenging, when teams have interesting tasks to perform they are more committed, motivated and co-operative (Hackman, 1990). Careful design of the objectives and tasks of work groups is therefore desirable. In many companies people work in relatively autonomous self-managing teams, redesigning work themselves to make tasks more meaningful and to improve the quality of performance (e.g., Cordery, in press). There should above all be clear team goals with built-in performance feedback. Research evidence shows very consistently that where people are set clear targets to aim at, their performance is generally improved. For the same reasons that it is important for individuals to have clear goals and performance feedback, so too is it important for the team as a whole to have clear group goals with performance feedback.

In a major research project examining group effectiveness, Pritchard, Jones, Roth, Stuebing and Ekeberg (1988) measured the effects of group feedback, goal setting and incentives on productivity. Five organizational units in the military were studied. One, a maintenance section, repaired a variety of electronic equipment used for aircraft communications. The other four sections together made up a material storage and distribution branch. Productivity baselines were established before each group received new 'treatments' (i.e., performance feedback eight months after the study began, goal setting five months later, and incentives a further five months later) so that the incremental effects of these 'treatments' could be determined.

First, the level of performance of the groups was measured over a period of eight months and then information on their performance was given to each unit for five months. The groups next set clear targets in addition to the performance feedback, and their performance was measured for another five months. Performance feedback was in the form of computer-generated reports, given monthly to the personnel of each unit. Finally, incentives were offered for high performance, in the form of time off from work. Using these approaches, the average increase over baseline productivity was 50 per cent for feedback, 75 per cent for goal setting and 76 per cent for incentives. The results showed a major increase in productivity among the groups, though the unique contribution of each component of the intervention is difficult to estimate accurately. Would incentives have led to a much greater increase in productivity than the additional 1 per cent attributed to them here if this had been the first 'treatment' rather than the third? Whatever the answer to this might be, it is clear that in this careful study goal setting and feedback both had powerful effects on performance.

Another input factor is group composition, which refers not just to the size of the group, but also to its homogeneity or heterogeneity in terms of demographic factors such as age, sex, educational level, training, ability levels, attitudes, personality and values. Research has indicated that different aspects of homogeneity and heterogeneity affect different group outcomes (Jackson, in press; Jackson, Brett, Sessa, Cooper, Julin and Peyronnin, 1991; Guzzo and Shea, 1992). For example, groups composed of people from diverse professional backgrounds seem to produce more creative decisions of higher quality than professionally homogeneous groups. Demographic homogeneity in contrast (similarity of team members in terms of age, sex and educational levels) predicts group cohesiveness and similarity of attitudes and values, but not their effectiveness. Such homogeneity is also a significant predictor of group stability: groups composed of people with similar backgrounds tend to stick together longer. These findings have been demonstrated in groups as diverse as a university faculty, nurses, top-level managers and convenience store field representatives.

What about variations in ability within groups? In problem-solving, group performance appears to be a positive function of the average ability of members, so that the more able are individual members, the better the group's problem-solving ability. However, this is not a simple linear relationship. Though there may be one group member of very high ability, if this person is unsupported, low in status or unpopular, it is unlikely that the group will accede to his or her opinion and will perform relatively badly as a result. Overall, our understanding of the relationship between group composition and group performance is still limited and results are often contradictory. In particular, there is little clear evidence about how the personalities of different group members affect group performance.

In recent years models of group effectiveness have tended to emphasize the organizational context within which teams work (Hackman, 1990). This includes reward systems within the organization in terms of money, promotion and recognition which may be applied either to individuals or teams; and education and training opportunities which may also be available either to individuals or teams. In Hackman's (1990) model, information management systems are highlighted which are thought to impact upon group performance by providing or withholding information necessary for effective task planning and completion. Availability of resources such as people (e.g., too few nurses within the primary care team to administer immunizations), equipment and money, and constraints in the work technology (e.g., repeated malfunctions in the clinic's computing system) will also have a strong impact on the relationship between group processes and group effectiveness. The value of recent models of group performance (described in Guzzo and Shea, 1992) is that they rightly emphasize the role of organizational context in both directly and indirectly determining group performance.

Processes

Group processes include all the social and psychological interactions and exchanges which occur as a consequence of group membership and functioning. According to Tuckman's (1965) model of group development, one of the most important processes in groups is 'norming', which involves 'cohesion exchange', when groups are determining appropriate ways forward in their work and exerting pressures upon group members to conform to these. The powerful effects of these pressures to conform are well established and are beneficial in ensuring that agreed ways of working are followed, thereby building trust and cohesion. However, they are also potentially problematic. When normative influences become too strong, Janis (1982) has argued that they can lead to 'groupthink'. Janis pointed out that where teams have very clear objectives and ideals, and high levels of participation and cohesion, it is possible that their commitment to consensus may override their ability to make good decisions. He analysed the factors leading up to the so-called Bay of Pigs affair in 1961 when the United States presidency was surrounded by an aura of optimism, enthusiasm and vigour.

President Kennedy and his advisers had encouraged the optimism of many Americans, with their commitments to civil rights and democracy. However, at the beginning of this presidency the group was responsible for one of the major foreign policy fiascos of the decade, supporting the invasion of Cuba in what became known as the Bay of Pigs affair. Against much intelligence information, which indicated likely failure, Kennedy and his advisers authorized the CIA to support Cuban exiles in an invasion. The invasion was easily repulsed and the exiles were taken prisoner or killed. Afterwards, many commentators questioned how Kennedy and his advisers could have concluded that the adventure would have been successful.

Janis proposed that Kennedy's cabinet was prone to the detrimental effects of groupthink, which he considers to arise when five conditions are present. First, the team is a tightly bonded group of individuals, who are more concerned with their own cohesiveness and unanimity than with quality of decision-making. Second, the group typically insulates itself from information and opinions from outside and particularly those which go against the group view.

371

Third, members of the group tend not to engage in systematic searches through available options for appropriate solutions, choosing instead to go with the first available consensus option. Fourth, the group is under pressure to achieve a decision; and, finally, the group tends to be dominated by one strong individual. Such groups exert strong pressures on dissenting individuals to conform to the view of the majority, and members may come to share an illusion of unanimity and correctness. Members of the group may also ignore or dismiss cues that there is dissent within the group and actively prevent information from outside the group being admitted to the group's discussion. Clearly, therefore, conformity processes can have a detrimental impact upon work group functioning.

Group processes are also sometimes characterized by conflict, disagreement and controversy. Research evidence suggests that when groups explore opposing opinions carefully and discuss them in a co-operative context, affirming rather than challenging one another's competence, quality of decision-making and group effectiveness are good: 'Controversy, when discussed in a co-operative context, promotes elaboration of views, the search for new information and ideas and the integration of apparently opposing positions' (Tjosvold, 1991). Tjosvold believes that a lack of such controversy can lead to poor decisions such as the Bay of Pigs invasion.

Another important perspective on conflict in group processes is offered by minority influence theory (Moscovici, 1982; Moscovici, Mugny and Avermaet, 1985), which seeks to explain how minorities in groups can have a sustained and powerful impact upon the attitudes and behaviour of others within the group. Minority group influence is the process whereby a numerical or power minority within a group or society brings about enduring change in the attitudes and behaviour of others. Exposure to minority influence can cause private changes in attitudes in the direction of the deviant view as a result of the cognitive or social conflict generated by the minority's disagreement with the dominant view. Social psychological research on minority influence therefore has important implications for understanding work group and organizational behaviour.

Repeated exposure to a consistent minority view can lead to marked and internalized changes in attitudes and behaviours. When people conform to a majority view they generally comply publicly without necessarily changing their private beliefs. Minorities, in contrast, appear to produce a shift in private views rather than mere public compliance (for a review of studies of this phenomenon see Wood, Lundgren, Ouellette, Busceme and Blackstone, 1994). Moreover, some evidence suggests that, even if they do not cause the majority to adopt their viewpoints, minorities encourage greater divergence in thinking about the specific issues they raise (Nemeth and Staw, 1989). For example, Mugny (1982) demonstrated that minority claims, blaming industry for a pollution problem, led those exposed to the minority position to change their judgements on a related issue, the extent to which individuals should take responsibility for pollution. Moscovici argues that minority group influence can be seen in the impact on public attitudes of formerly 'deviant minorities', such as the Green and Feminist Movements in the 1970s and 1980s, which are now accepted as more mainstream movements (Moscovici, Mugny and Avermaet, 1985).

In early studies of minority influence people were shown blue and green slides and asked to categorize them accordingly. In some groups people were exposed to a minority who consistently categorized blue slides as green. This procedure of course had no impact on the majority's correct categorizing of blue slides. However, when members of the majority were subsequently asked to privately rate ambiguous 'blue-green' slides, over half rated the slides in a direction which was consistent with their having been influenced by the minority. In one study (Moscovici and Personnaz, 1980) people were exposed to a minority who identified blue slides as green and were subsequently asked to privately judge the after-image of the slides. They showed a perceptual change consistent with their having been influenced by the minority. This research is important for understanding work group processes, since it indicates that minority influence can lead to very different patterns of group processes than majority influence, and that the conflict and disagreement generated by minorities may lead to new orientations within groups towards group objectives and decisions. However, there is no research evidence to indicate whether, in what circumstances, and how, minorities in groups have an impact upon the effectiveness of performance. These important theoretical ideas, although well-demonstrated in laboratory settings, await empirical testing in work groups.

In describing the problems of working in groups at the outset of this chapter, factors inhibiting effective decision-making were described (such as personality and status effects). Research evidence on structured group decision-making (Rogelberg *et al.*, 1992) suggests that where group members delay suggesting solutions or decisions to allow thinking time and where all members' ideas are presented to and discussed by the group, better decisions are made. Such procedures appear to enable groups to make decisions of a quality at least as good as those of their best individual members. This is also consistent with evidence suggesting that fostering disagreement in a structured way in groups leads to better decisions (Tjosvold, 1985). Such approaches offer one solution to the problem that unless the most accurate group member is assertive and confident, he or she does not influence the ratings of quality of group decisions.

The discussion of group brainstorming earlier also suggested the superiority of *individual* brainstorming (at least in laboratory settings) because of the 'production blocking' effect (the verbalizations of one group member prevent the participation of others temporarily, thus reducing the number of ideas offered). Accepting the fact that production blocking can inhibit performance of brainstorming groups, there are two important advantages of working in group settings when developing new ideas and new ways of doing things. The first is that those who make up teams in organizations have valuable experience of the particular domains of the team's work. For example, a primary health care team contains members with nursing, medical and social work backgrounds; together they bring a broad range of important experience to the team's deliberations. The second argument for brainstorming in groups is the importance of participation. Involving all those affected by organizational change in the change process is vital in order to gain commitment and reduce resistance (e.g., Lawler and Hackman, 1969). In practice, the mechanics of the process can usefully be altered to overcome the production blocking effect. Group members should brainstorm individually to generate their own ideas before bringing them to the group. Then each member should have the opportunity to present all of his or her ideas to the group before evaluation and selection take place.

Another important process element in work groups is their degree of cohesiveness, or interactions which can lead to increased liking, bonding and warmth amongst group members. Many team-building interventions are based on the assumption that increasing cohesiveness will lead to improved group task performance. Analyses reveal that across forty-nine studies of the cohesiveness–performance effect there is indeed overall a statistically significant relationship (Mullen and Copper, 1994). High-performing work groups do appear to be more cohesive than low-performing groups, but the relationship is not strong (an average correlation of 0.25). However, analyses also reveal that the direction of effect seems to be much stronger from performance to cohesiveness than from cohesiveness to performance. In other words, finding ways of getting people to like one another and be warm and supportive in groups is unlikely on its own to have a direct effect upon how well they work in a group. Instead, it is better to help them to work more effectively as a group, for example by clarifying their work goals. Moreover, that process is in turn likely to lead them to like one another and the group to become more cohesive as a result.

So far this discussion of group processes has treated groups as though they were static and enduring entities. In reality, of course, groups begin at one point in time, go through a variety of intra-group processes and at some point in their lives either disperse or dramatically change their composition and function. Group processes vary according to the stage of the group's development. The most widely accepted theory of group development is that proposed by Tuckman (1965). The theory was derived from a careful review of fifty studies of therapy, training, laboratory and natural groups. Tuckman identified changes in the social/emotional and task activities of group members over the life of groups. Social and emotional activities revealed four stages: a dependent stage, when group members sought out someone willing to act as group leader; a stage of intra-group conflict, in which group members argued with one another and with the leader; a cohesion stage, when people were more positive about their group; and finally a role-taking stage, when people adopted particular social roles that made the group a good place for members. Using these data, Tuckman developed a theory which originally contained four stages: 'forming', a stage of dependence and orientation when members are anxious about belonging to the group; 'storming', which involves conflict and emotionality as members become assertive and seek to change the group to satisfy their own needs; 'norming' is marked by the conclusion of negotiations on appropriate ways forward, building cohesion and resolving conflicts; finally comes 'performing', which involves people taking particular roles and solving problems in order to work together to achieve mutual goals. Tuckman and Jensen (1977) later added a fifth stage of group development called 'adjourning', when group members gradually disengage from the group, both socio-emotionally and in terms of task performance, in anticipation of the end of the group.

In concluding this discussion of group processes it is important to point out that many important processes have not been described, such as communication patterns and leadership. These are topics which could merit whole chapters in themselves but they are also areas where, despite considerable research, little theoretical progress has been made. For a fuller treatment of these topics see West (in press). What is clear, however, is the complexity of group processes, which has important implications for those concerned with introducing team-based working in organizations.

Outputs

The final component of the input–process–output model will now be described, along with some consideration of whether team-building interventions have an impact upon group effectiveness. Group effectiveness can be considered in relation to three types of outcome. There is the effectiveness of the group in meeting its organizational goals, including those for innovation; groups may be more or less effective in terms of their long-term viability, i.e., how long they are able to continue functioning; and the effectiveness of groups is also measurable in terms of the mental health and growth and development of team members. If team members are under such pressure at work as a result of team functioning that they are unable to achieve organizational goals satisfactorily, then this can be taken as an indicator of ineffectiveness.

How are productivity and effectiveness to be measured? There are many difficulties involved in identifying appropriate criteria for determining a group's organizational productivity (Brodbeck, in press), partly because a group may have multiple and often conflicting organizational goals (such as meeting production targets to satisfy orders from salespeople, while meeting quality targets set by the quality control department). One way of dealing with these difficulties is to develop a 'constituency approach' to measuring group effectiveness, whereby the criteria used by all of those with a strong interest in the performance of a group within an organization are used (Poulton and West, 1994). For example, within a primary health care team criteria might include confidentiality of patients' records, quality of medical care, effectiveness of liaison with welfare agencies and ease of access for patients to the building.

Do team-building interventions have a significant effect in improving team productivity? Research suggests that such interventions have a reliable and positive impact upon member attitudes and perceptions, but no reliable impact on team performance (Tannenbaum, Beard and Sales, 1992). Team members tend to report changes in how they feel about their team and how they see one another. While this may translate into greater cohesiveness, job satisfaction or team member well-being, studies conducted in organizational settings show no reliable impact of team building upon group performance. In particular, interventions designed to change the interpersonal processes in groups are least likely to effect any change in performance. Some research has been carried out to examine the effect of interventions designed to change task processes rather than socio-emotional features. These aim to help teams define objectives, improve group members' understanding of each other's roles and identify specific performance problems in order to devise action plans to deal with them. Such interventions are more successful in improving team performance than the socio-emotional interventions described above, though not consistently so.

My colleagues and I have been examining the factors which determine innovation in work groups. We have gathered, for example, information on all changes introduced by hospital management teams over a six-month period, had them rated by experts in the National Health Service external to the teams, and determined which factors, of those we measured, predicted innovativeness. The innovativeness of these management teams was inversely related to the size of the teams and the resources available to the team (i.e., the overall budget of the hospitals had a negative relationship to team innovativeness; cf. Andrews, 1979). On the other hand, group climate factors, such as commitment to goals, levels of participation (i.e., interaction amongst team members, information sharing and influence over decision-making), practical support for attempts at innovation, and task orientation (such as constructive controversy and performance monitoring processes in groups) were very effective predictors of the innovativeness of the teams (West and Anderson, 1993). Similar research has been conducted in Sweden with almost identical effects (Agrell and Gustafson, 1994).

Team viability is group members' satisfaction, participation and willingness to continue working together, but this notion can be extended to include cohesion, inter-member co-ordination, good communication and clear norms and roles (Sundstrom, De Meuse and Futrell, 1990). Four social dimensions of team functioning are likely to influence team viability and also to impact upon group members' mental health. These are social support within the team, effectiveness of methods of team conflict resolution, team social climate and support for team member growth and development (West, 1994). However, there has been remarkably little research on the work group factors which predict mental health of members, so most conclusions are based on what is known about organizational and interpersonal influences upon mental health at work. This is another area where a considerable amount of research is still needed.

SUMMARY

Team work in organizations is increasingly the norm, yet the challenges of working effectively in teams are considerable. However, research has also revealed group processes such as how exploration of differing viewpoints within teams can produce better quality of decision-making and more creative solutions to problems. The dangers of team working are also apparent. Conformity to the majority view can lead to 'groupthink', which in turn can result in poor decision-making. Increasingly, researchers are focusing on the organizational context within which groups operate rather than on just intra-team processes. This has revealed how organizations may impede team functioning because of inappropriate structures, reward systems or lack of commitment to training people to work effectively in teams. Yet our understanding of the interaction between inputs, group processes and outputs remains limited, because many major theoretical issues have not been addressed. Despite the long history of group research, there are still many unexplored areas of work group psychology to which researchers have not been attracted. But research on group work in organizations is exciting precisely because it is still at a relatively early stage of development, offering great promise for more understanding of how human beings can most effectively work together.

FURTHER READING

An excellent review of psychological research on teams in organizations is provided in the chapter by Guzzo and Shea (1992). Hackman's (1990) *Groups That Work (and Those That Don't)* offers fascinating accounts of a variety of teams engaged in their daily work, such as cockpit teams, surgical teams and orchestras. *Effective Teamwork* (West, 1994) is a practical guide that covers areas such as setting objectives, ensuring high levels of participation, encouraging team innovation and examining mental health in teams. Finally, *Group Processes: Dynamics Within and Between Groups* (Brown, 1988) is a readable and scholarly account of social psychological research on group functioning. For a comprehensive scientifically oriented review of a wide range of issues related to work group psychology see the *Handbook of Work Group Psychology* (West, in press).

REFERENCES

Agrell, A. and Gustafson, R. (1994). The Team Climate Inventory (TCI) and group innovation: A psychometric test on a Swedish sample of work groups. *Journal of Occupational and Organizational Psychology*, 67, 143–151.

Andrews, F. M. (ed.) (1979). *Scientific Productivity: The Effectiveness of*

Research Groups in Six Countries. Cambridge: Cambridge University Press.

Brodbeck, F. (in press). Work group performance and effectiveness: Conceptual and measurement issues. In M. A. West (ed.), *The Handbook of Work Group Psychology.* Chichester: Wiley.

Brown, R. J. (1988). *Group Processes: Dynamics Within and Between Groups.* London: Blackwell.

Cordery, J. (in press). Autonomous work groups. In M. A. West (ed.), *The Handbook of Work Group Psychology.* Chichester: Wiley.

Cyert, R. M. and March, J. E. (1963). *A Behavioral Theory of the Firm.* Englewood Cliffs, NJ: Prentice Hall.

Darley, J. M. and Latané, B. (1968). Bystander intervention in emergencies: Diffusion of responsibility. *Journal of Personality and Social Psychology*, 8, 377–383.

Diehl, M. and Stroebe, W. (1987). Productivity loss in brainstorming groups: Towards the solution of a riddle. *Journal of Personality and Social Psychology*, 53, 447–509.

Goodman, P. and Associates (1986). *Designing Effective Work Groups.* San Francisco: Jossey-Bass.

George, J. M. (1992). Extrinsic and intrinsic origins of perceived social loafing in organizations. *Academy of Management Journal*, 35, 191–202.

Guzzo, R. A. and Shea, G. P. (1992). Group performance and inter-group relations in organizations. In M. D. Dunnette and L. M. Hough (eds.), *Handbook of Industrial and Organizational Psychology*, vol. 3, pp. 269–313. Palo Alto, Calif.: Consulting Psychologists Press.

Hackman, J. R. (ed.). (1990). *Groups That Work (and Those That Don't): Creating Conditions for Effective Teamwork.* San Francisco: Jossey-Bass.

Jackson, S. E. (in press). Work group heterogeneity and team performance. In M. A. West (ed.), *The Handbook of Work Group Psychology.* Chichester: Wiley.

Jackson, S. E., Brett, J. F., Sessa, V. I., Cooper, D. M., Julin, J. A. and Peyronnin, K. (1991). Some differences make a difference: Individual dissimilarity and group heterogeneity as correlates of recruitment, promotions and turnover. *Journal of Applied Psychology*, 76, 675–689.

Janis, I. L. (1982). *Groupthink: A Study of Foreign Policy Decisions and Fiascos*, 2nd edn. Boston: Houghton Mifflin.

Janis, I. L. (1989). *Crucial Decisions.* New York: Free Press.

Latané, B., Williams, K. and Harkins, S. (1979). Many hands make light the work: The causes and consequences of social loafing. *Journal of Personality and Social Psychology*, 37, 822–832.

Lawler, E. E. and Hackman, J. R. (1969). Impact of employee participation in development of pay incentive plans: A field experiment. *Journal of Applied Psychology*, 53, 467–471.

Maier, N. R. F. (1970). *Problem Solving and Creativity In Individuals and Groups*. Monterey, Calif.: Brooks Cole.

McCauley, C. (1989). The nature of social influence in groupthink: Compliance and internalization. *Journal of Personality and Social Psychology*, 57, 250–260.

Moscovici, G. (1982). *The Power of Minorities*. San Diego, Calif.: Academic Press.

Moscovici, S., Mugny, G. and Avermaet, E. U. (1985). *Perspectives on Minority Influence*. Cambridge: Cambridge University Press.

Moscovici, S. and Personnaz, B. (1980). Studies in social influence V: Minority influence and conversion behavior in a perceptual task. *Journal of Experimental and Social Psychology*, 16, 270–282.

Mugny, G. (1982). *The Power of Minorities*. San Diego, Calif.: Academic Press.

Mullen, B. and Copper, C. (1994). The relation between group cohesiveness and performance: An integration. *Psychological Bulletin*, 115, 210–227.

Myers, D. G. and Lamm, H. (1976). The group polarization phenomenon. *Psychological Bulletin*, 83, 602–627.

Nemeth, C. and Staw, B. (1989). The trade-offs of social control and innovation within work groups and organizations. In L. Berkowitz (ed.), *Advances in Experimental Social Psychology*, vol. 22, pp. 175–210. New York: Academic Press.

Poulton, B. C. and West, M. A. (1994). Primary health care team effectiveness: Developing a constituency approach. *Health and Social Care* 2, 77–84.

Pritchard, R. D., Jones, S. D., Roth, P. L., Stuebing, K. K. and Ekeberg, S. E. (1988). Effects of group feedback, goal setting, and incentives on organizational productivity. *Journal of Applied Psychology*, 73, 337–358.

Ringelmann, M. (1913). Recherches sur les moteurs animés: Travail de l'homme. *Annales de l'Institut National Agronomique,* 2nd series, 12, 1–40.

Rogelberg, S. G., Barnes-Farrell, J. L. and Lowe, C. A. (1992). The stepladder technique: An alternative group structure facilitating effective group decision-making. *Journal of Applied Psychology*, 77, 730–737.

Steiner, I. D. (1972). *Group Process and Productivity*. Orlando, Fla.: Academic Press.

Sundstrom, E., De Meuse, K. P. and Futrell, D. (1990). Work teams: Applications and effectiveness. *American Psychologist*, 45, 120–133.

Tannenbaum, S. I., Beard, R. L. and Sales, E. (1992). Team building and its influence on team effectiveness: An examination of conceptual and empirical developments. In K. Kelley (ed.), *Issues, Theory and Research in Industrial/Organizational Psychology*. London: North Holland.

Tjosvold, D. (1985). Implications of controversy research for management. *Journal of Management*, 11, 21–37.

Tjosvold, D. (1991). *Teamwork: Securing a Competitive Advantage*. Chichester: Wiley.

Tuckman, B. W. (1965). Developmental sequences in small groups. *Psychological Bulletin*, 62, 384–399.

Tuckman, B. W. and Jensen, M. A. C. (1977). Stages of small group development revisited. *Group and Organizational Studies*, 2, 419–427.

Weldon, E. and Weingart, L. R. (1994). Group goals and group performance. *British Journal of Social Psychology*, 32, 307–334.

West, M. A. (1994). *Effective Teamwork*. Leicester: British Psychological Society.

West, M. A. (in press). *The Handbook of Work Group Psychology*. Chichester: Wiley.

West, M. A. and Anderson, N. R. (1993). Innovation, cultural values and the management of change in British hospitals. *Work and Stress*, 6, 293–310.

Wood, W., Lundgren, S., Ouellette, J. A., Busceme, S. and Blackstone, T. (1994). Minority influence: A meta-analytic review of social influence processes. *Psychological Bulletin*, 115, 323–345.

14

The Characteristics of Organizations

Roy Payne

A convenient and simple way of characterizing organizations is to consider the answers to some very basic questions: *What* arc the organizations trying to do? *How* are they trying to do it? *Why* are they trying to do it that way? Answers to the first question lead one to classify organizations according to their goals or purposes. At the broadest level this gives rise to classifications that are so general as to be rather unhelpful, e.g., religious organizations, business organizations, military organizations or voluntary organizations. Clearly, organizations within any of these categories pursue a variety of goals and pursue them in different ways. The study of how goals are chosen and why is a major part of what is now widely termed 'corporate strategy' (Johnson and Scholes, 1994) or 'strategic management'.

Consideration of how organizations attempt to achieve their goals leads to concerns about *organizational structure*. As we shall see, this is not only about the characteristics of organization charts, but also about the structuring of procedures to ensure that people carry out activities reliably and to the desired standard.

Examination of why organizations choose to achieve some goals rather than others, and to achieve them in certain sorts of ways, takes us into the realm of *organizational culture*. Strategy, structure and culture are interrelated in particular organizations, but they tend to have somewhat separate literatures, except where theorists and researchers set out specifically to explore the links between them. However, Mintzberg's work on organizational structure offers a framework that can be used to construct links.

MINTZBERG'S CONCEPTS FOR ANALYSING ORGANIZATIONS

The Five Basic Parts

Mintzberg has written an abbreviated version of his original (1979) book in *Structure in Fives* (1983). The reason for the title will become clear. Mintzberg divides an organization into five basic parts. At the top is the *strategic apex*, where policies are decided, plans made to execute them, resources allocated and orders given to ensure their execution. Below the apex is the *middle line* of employees, who are responsible for carrying out the orders and making sure the policies are pursued. To do the actual work itself (whether it is producing goods or providing a service) there is an *operating core*. In an organization like a university this is the staff of lecturers; in a hospital it is the doctors and the nurses. In other words, the operating core can in some cases consist of highly qualified individuals, though in many manufacturing organizations the role is filled by blue-collar workers, skilled and less skilled. It is perhaps worth noting that the relative size of the middle line and the operating core has changed in many organizations due to the delayering, downsizing or 'rightsizing' that has occurred in recent years, as businesses have striven to reduce costs and improve their competitiveness.

This central part of the structure is assisted by two other groups. Firstly, what Mintzberg calls the *technostructure*. Individuals in the technostructure are analysts or technical advisers. They plan and design work, they select and train people to do the work, they decide strategies for controlling how work is done, but they do not directly produce the main output or service. A major role they have is to create standardization of products and processes and thus improve efficiency. Included here are staff within departments of personnel, work study or systems analysis. The second group to assist the main workflow is the *support structure*. These individuals and groups service the organization's needs by looking after the building, keeping accounts, paying bills and wages, providing meals, distributing mail, etc. These parts and the main tensions/demands amongst them are presented in simplified form in Figure 14.1. While there are considerable advantages in having several groups of specialists providing

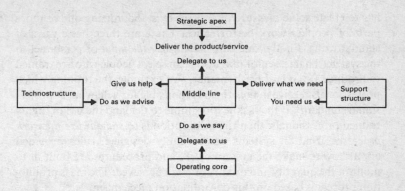

Fig. 14.1 A simplified version of Mintzberg's (1979) five-part model of organization.

expert well-trained services within the organization, it increases the problem of integrating those specialist groups so that they can work together to achieve organizational goals efficiently and effectively. Mintzberg proposed that managers have developed five broad approaches to the problem of co-ordinating these different parts of the organization's structure.

The Five Co-ordination Mechanisms

A major task for the senior managers of an organization is to co-ordinate these different parts so that they function as a purposeful whole. This is achieved in a number of ways; Mintzberg suggests five. The first is *mutual adjustment*. This relies on people communicating regularly, so that they can adjust to each other and to changing circumstances. Much depends on their trust, personal competence and commitment to each other as well as their commitment to the organization's mission and success. Managers of a more autocratic bent, however, might prefer to use another method of co-ordination. They might like to keep a close eye on people, issuing instructions and monitoring their actions to see that the instructions have been carried out. Mintzberg identifies this as *direct supervision*.

If neither of these options is preferred or adequate, the manager has to create some measure of control by standardizing one or more parts of people's work performance. There are three basic ways of standardizing. Firstly, one can *standardize the input* of personnel to the system. That is, senior managers can select people who are trained to produce a standard performance. For example, the training which professionals receive makes them responsible for achieving a 'professional standard'. If the task is too simple to demand the use of highly trained professionals, then the next option is to *standardize the work processes*. That is, systems are carefully designed, rules provided about how to make the system work, and procedures are built in to monitor the quantity and quality of work achieved. The mass production process is based on this co-ordination mechanism.

If it is not possible to standardize either the input or the work process, then the organizational designer is left with *standardizing the output*. Those in the strategic apex produce clear and precise specifications for the quantity, quality and delivery of a product or service. Put simply, standardization of input controls *who* does things, standardization of work processes controls *how* things are done, and standardization of output controls *what* gets done. The social mechanisms for controlling *when* things are done and the *quality* of performance vary in each of these different structures. For organizations employing standardization of input, control of timing and performance is largely dependent on trusting people to behave professionally and to provide services/products on time and to the required quality and value. Standardization of work processes depends on good design of business and operating processes, and standardization of output relies on specification of production standards and deadlines, and the establishment of sanctions associated with failure to meet them.

Mintzberg uses these five basic parts and five co-ordinating mechanisms to create a typology of organizations. In this there are five ideal types. The essential concepts are summarized in Figure 14.2, which is adapted from Mintzberg's revisions of the earlier books (Mintzberg, 1989).

Figure 14.2 gives examples of the kinds of organizations that make up each of the five types. Organizations using a *simple structure* tend to be new, small and entrepreneurial, frequently governed by the owner (often also the founder) and not infrequently managed in a relatively autocratic manner. An *ad hoc structure* (bottom right in the

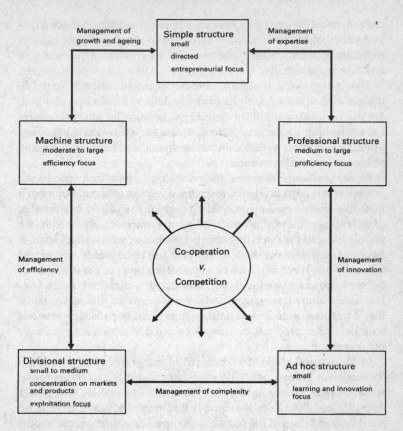

Fig. 14.2 A simplified version of Mintzberg's (1989) five types of organization.

diagram) is often new too, for this is likely to arise in fast-changing ing technologies such as computer companies or other entrepreneurial or creative businesses. Adhocracies are also found in large organizations, where they spring up as separate 'think tanks', examining where the company ought to be in the more distant future. Dealing with rapid change and containing experts who are often from a range of disciplines requires them to put much effort into communication of a free-wheeling, informal kind, so their main co-ordination mechanism is mutual adjustment. Since there is little structure either within the company or the environment, people have to negotiate with each other to agree goals, allocate resources, and give and take responsibility.

The epitome of a traditional industrial organization is found in the *machine structure*, with its formally defined hierarchies and high use of specialists, combined with regulations, rules and procedures for controlling people and activities. Large, white-collar organizations, such as those in government, insurance and banking, also tend to have this sort of structure.

In the *divisional structure* specialization comes from producing just a few standard products under the direction of the directors of a multi-divisional company or holding company which owns a number of different businesses (often called a conglomerate). As a result, the middle line and the operating core predominate, with a small technostructure and support staff to provide for basic needs and expert advice. While there may still be many regulations in the divisions of large companies (deriving from the wider organization), much control comes from the managers and supervisors in the division's middle line. The focus of divisional units is on exploiting particular markets with particular products or services to provide profits for the larger owning group.

In his original book Mintzberg called the *professional structure* a 'professional bureaucracy'. This indicates that it is a structure found in large organizations such as hospitals and universities. The power structure and the values that enable it to work, however, depend on the professionalism of the people in the operating core and the middle line. So the bureaucracy relates more to record keeping and accounting rather than to controlling what the professionals do, for that is left to their professional integrity. This structure is also found in the larger professional practices of lawyers and engineers.

The arrows in Figure 14.2 indicate the main problems and tensions that occur within organizations, as members of the different structural types struggle to adjust to environments which are frequently changing. Consider a small manufacturing organization using a simple structure. As it grows it needs larger manufacturing facilities, and to design and service them it may employ technocrats who begin to exercise their power and influence on how the organization is run.

This threatens the power and influence of the strategic apex. If the organization's simple structure moves towards becoming a machine structure, then the occupants of the strategic apex will have to decentralize some of their power. If they do not, they lose the advantages of standardization of products and economies of scale.

The major conflict within a machine structure is between the technostructure and the middle line. If particular products become very successful, then the route to exploit them may be to set up a separate division to gain the advantages of specialization and business focus. Senior managers in the middle line often benefit from such changes and are therefore often pressing the strategic apex to make them. So the machine structure is threatened by the diversification and growth achieved by its own success, while the divisional structure is always open to the threat of becoming over-specialized, out of date and defunct. The divisional structure comes under pressure from head-office strategists, encouraging it to maintain flexibility in response to changing environments, but its short-term success is often built on keeping internal change at bay to optimize the benefits of specialization and standardization which have been adopted to enable it to exploit its markets effectively.

Although Figure 14.2 summarizes some of the pulls between the five structural types, it is important to recognize that these pulls also exist within single organizations. By their very nature, organizations exist to do something which cannot be done by individuals on their own. This leads to the creation of a range of jobs and duties, and inevitably some jobs are more central to the task than others. Organizational theorists have more and more recognized the wide variety of ways in which politics and power distort the organizational designs that top decision-makers have created (e.g., Pettigrew, 1973; Pfeffer, 1981). Pettigrew's study was one of the first to illustrate how computing departments gained power because of their control of information and their ability to use technological knowledge to pursue computing goals at the expense of the broader goals of the business. This has been shown many times since. In his 1989 book Mintzberg placed politics and co-operation at the centre of his diagram to emphasize that these continually take place in all organizations and create the forces that bring about changes in ideology and culture.

So far I have described a typology of organizations within which may be fitted the wide variety of organizations that exist. It must be recognized that the types in Figure 14.2 are ideal types. Many organizations are hybrids of more than one type, because this reduces some of the conflicts between the different parts of the organization: organizations are continually forced to adjust to the changing technical, commercial and political world that surrounds them. Thus, there are many more kinds of organizations than the five ideal types. British hospitals, for example, are at present striving to reduce costs and improve customer satisfaction, so they have adopted the practices of standardizing and formalizing procedures, but this clashes with the professionalism of the doctors and nurses providing the services, and can result in both machine and professional bureaucracies existing in a rather uneasy alliance. Indeed, many organizations, including the National Health Service, are trying to improve relationships amongst the different professional groups by creating internal markets. Different parts of the organization are set up as separate business units which sell their services to other parts of the organization, and in some cases to competitor organizations. To improve relationships and performance the suppliers have to establish trust and good customer relationships with their clients. Halal (1994) cites a number of examples where profits and innovations have improved considerably using this organizing principle.

The other reason that organizations are not pure types is that they grow and have to change to accommodate growth. They are exposed to changing markets, to changing technologies for producing goods and services, and are also subject to changes produced by legislation from their national governments and from broader political forces, such as the European Union.

Strategic Styles

As we have seen, Mintzberg emphasizes the tensions that exist within organizations, and the environmental forces that act upon them. This combination of forces strongly influences the goals which managers in the strategic apex choose to follow, though their own personal goals will also be a determinant of the organization's direction. A study by Goold and Campbell (1987) illustrates the emergence of what they called 'strategic styles'. They examined divisions of larger companies, but amongst their sample they discovered three distinct strategic styles. The styles were determined by two groups of factors. First was the nature of the business, in terms of the size and schedule of investments and paybacks required by the owning group, and in respect of the hostility of the competition. The second influential factor was the level of resources available to the division. As well as financial resources these included the personality of the chief executive and the skills of the senior management.

The three styles were identified as strategic planning, strategic control and financial control. The strategic planning companies were allowed strong internal leadership, and were given the autonomy to look at multiple products and markets, had a more organic management structure, and were asked to plan the development of the company for the longer term. In contrast, the companies using a financial control strategy were closely monitored financially, had to justify new ventures in financial terms, had leaders who were limited in their autonomy and held strictly responsible for business results. The strategic control style fell between the two. Companies with this style were controlled financially very tightly, but they had more autonomy and were encouraged to plan for longer term strategic positioning.

Hamel and Prahalad (1994) have attempted to predict the strategic choices senior managers will face in the future, and conclude their analysis with a list of the most important questions that will influence the strategy adopted. These emphasize the importance of building structures and cultures that are responsive to the future, not just the present. Answers chosen to those questions will make enormous differences to organizations' cultures and structures. A few examples of their key questions are:

Does the senior management have a clear and collective point of view about how the future will or could be different?

Does the company have a clear and collective agenda for building core competencies and evolving the customer interface?

Do all employees share an aspiration for the enterprise and possess a clear sense of the legacy they are working to build?

Does the firm's opportunity horizon extend sufficiently far beyond the boundaries of existing product markets?

Given these sorts of strategic challenges, what are the characteristics of organizations that succeed in meeting them?

PETTIGREW AND WHIPP'S FIVE CENTRAL FACTORS FOR ACHIEVING COMPETITIVE SUCCESS

Based on intensive, longitudinal studies of organizations in automobile manufacturing, book publishing, merchant banking and life assurance, Pettigrew and Whipp (1993) have shown that higher-performing firms manage themselves differently from others. The study extended over three years and involved 350 interviews. Two companies in each industry were studied, with one company being a much better performer than the other. The better performers were found to have developed a pattern of interrelated activities which concentrate attention on the following five areas: environmental assessment, leading change, linking strategic and operational change, managing human resources as if they were assets and not liabilities, and establishing coherence amongst the different parts of the organization and amongst the other four activities.

Figure 14.3 elaborates these ideas. The dotted line distinguishes the broad characteristics (primary conditioning features) that the high performers had developed from the specific processes and activities (secondary mechanisms) that made those characteristics work. This environmental assessment has to take place at the top of the company and involve all functions; to ensure that it happens, it is necessary to build networks, set up task forces, have a strong planning department, etc. In leading change the senior executives have to do more than give directions and allocate support; they have to detail the agenda, push it through, communicate and reward successful change efforts. Their strategic role needs to be linked to operational change, and that involves training and developing good managers of change throughout the business, designating rewards for achieving change and systems for monitoring progress. It is not adequate to trumpet to the world that 'people are our most valuable asset'; the senior management must empower managers down the line to manage their people as if they really are valuable resources and ensure that all human resource management policies reinforce that process.

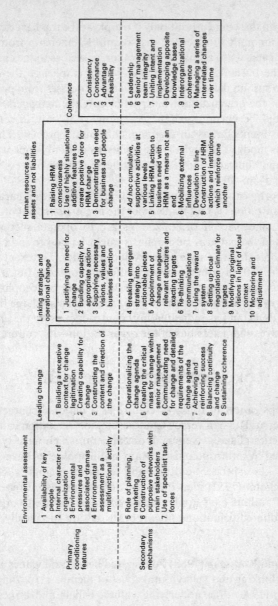

Fig. 14.3 Managing change for competitive success: the five central factors (reprinted with permission).

Finally, all this comes about only if people at the top have achieved coherence amongst themselves; that requires leadership from them all and the capacity to adjust to each other, as well as to the changing needs of the business. Pettigrew and Whipp emphasize the *energy* required to sustain these continuous change processes from people at all levels of the organization, but particularly the managers. 'Managers should be encouraged to see change not only in terms of episodes or events but as an ongoing, continuous process. The key-note of this mode of thought is the ability to not only cope with the dualities and contradictions of the strategic change process but to exploit them' (p. 40).

The importance of this perspective in understanding the characteristics of organizations is that it identifies the five major social processes that must take place if organizations are to operate successfully. Variations in the patterns of emphasis might be said to indicate the organization's strategic style, as introduced earlier. The exact nature of that style will, of course, vary in different contexts. But it is not only the context which will cause variation. The philosophies and values of key participants in the organization will also shape the way things get done, and as indicated in the introduction to the chapter, are themselves characteristics of the organization – its 'culture'.

ORGANIZATIONAL CULTURE

It is perhaps easiest to think of culture as a national characteristic (English versus Russian versus Chinese, etc.) or in relation to smaller tribal societies (Tuaregs versus Trobrianders) which have typically been studied by anthropologists. Many anthropologists have set out to identify key aspects of culture, and the anthropologists Kroeber and Kluckhohn (1952) identified 164 definitions. More recently, a number of authors have applied the concept of culture to organizations and offered definitions of corporate culture specifically. These include:

Cooke and Rousseau (1988): 'the shared beliefs and values guiding the thinking and behavioural styles of members' (p. 245);
Denison (1990): 'the underlying values, beliefs and principles

394

that serve as the foundation for an organization's management system, as well as the set of management practices and behaviours that both exemplify and reinforce those basic principles' (p. 2);

Smircich (1983): 'social or normative glue that holds an organization together . . . the values or social ideals and the beliefs that organization members come to share. These values or patterns of belief are manifested by symbolic devices such as myths, rituals, stories, legends and specialised language' (p. 344);

Schein (1990): '(a) a pattern of basic assumptions (b) invented, discovered, or developed by a given group, (c) as it learns to cope with its problems of external adaptation and internal integration, (d) that has worked well enough to be considered valid, and therefore, (e) is to be taught to new members as the correct way to perceive, think and feel in relation to those problems' (p. 111).

These definitions combine most of the essential components of culture. It is about values, and developing systems and symbols that reinforce and perpetuate those values, so that people behave reliably and predictably to achieve the culture's purposes. Schein would add *artefacts* as an important way in which culture is manifested. By artefacts he means style of buildings, dress codes, speech conventions, nature of the documentation and publicity material, the type of written records kept as well as the 'feel' of the place or its socio-psychological climate.

There is a tendency for authors on culture to assume that all cultures are 'strong' cultures. By a strong culture it is meant that there are clear patterns of values, norms and beliefs and that the vast majority of members of the culture all share them and are guided by them. That is, cultures vary in *strength*, in terms of the degree of consensus/acceptance of the culture by members. They also vary in at least two other dimensions: their content and their pervasiveness. *Content* refers to the topics that the values and beliefs focus on. These include responsibility to others, fairness and justice, contributions to be made, importance of loyalty, the way to treat people, etc. *Pervasiveness* means the range of behaviours and values that organizations attempt to influence. Some organizations focus on a relatively narrow range – how you behave and what you should believe in at work – and others on how you behave and what you should believe in outside of work too. While degree of consensus and pervasiveness are important aspects of understanding culture, it is *content* which most obviously makes one culture distinctive from another.

The Content of Culture

Although in general terms culture is a matter of attitudes, behaviour, values and beliefs, cultures are principally different from each other in respect of the content of these attitudes, values and beliefs. All social groups have to deal with issues about what they are trying to do together, who has power, authority, responsibility, etc., how different roles will be undertaken, what rewards and sanctions will apply and for what values, behaviours, etc.; and ultimately they have to deal with why these purposes and social processes are the ones to value and adopt. An attempt to classify *national* managerial cultures was made by Hofstede (1980).

Hofstede was given access to the survey data collected by IBM from their managers in over forty countries. He showed that managers differed across the countries in the strength of their values about different issues. In examining the answers to the questions, Hofstede found they clustered around four different issues, though he has subsequently added a fifth, identified below as Confucian dynamism (Hofstede, 1991).

> *Power distance*: the degree to which power is concentrated or dispersed throughout different levels in the organization. For example, in IBM power was more concentrated at the top in Indonesia than it was in Austria or Israel.
> *Uncertainty avoidance*: the degree to which deviance from established norms and values would be tolerated. There was low tolerance in IBM Greece and Portugal compared to Sweden.
> *Individualism/collectivism*: the degree to which the culture/climate encourages social cohesion versus individual independence and self-reliance. Australia and the USA were more individualist and Pakistan more collectivist in the IBM sample.

Table 14.1 Hofstede's dimensions of culture in Mintzberg's five types of organizational structure

	Simple structure	Professional structure	Machine structure	Adhocracy structure	Divisional structure
Power distance	high	moderate	high	low	high
Uncertainty avoidance	low	low	high	low	high
Individualism	high	moderate	low	high	low
Masculinity	high	moderate	high	moderate	high
Confucian dynamism	moderate	moderate	high	low	high

Masculinity/femininity: the degree to which assertiveness, dominance of others is approved versus caring and nurturance of others. Within IBM, Japan was more masculine and Sweden and Denmark more feminine.

Confucian dynamism: the degree to which there is concern for the maintenance of traditional social orders (e.g., the family, the dynasty, etc.) versus more individualistic, liberal social orders based on negotiation rather than obligation. Companies in Far Eastern countries tend to be more traditional in this sense than those in Western democracies.

While a handful of dimensions cannot deal with the vast range of cultural types found in the world, they do highlight the central issues found in work organizations. On their own they may miss out crucial aspects of culture and may therefore fail to reveal in detail the way a particular cultural system works, but they are central issues to most cultures and provide an important basis for analysing organization culture.

How do these ideas relate to Mintzberg's five ideal-type structures, described earlier? The latter mainly identify the structural shape of the organization. Those structures have been created in line with the organization's culture, so structures both derive from sets of beliefs and at the same time perpetuate those same sets of beliefs, as do other artefacts mentioned by Schein. Table 14.1 illustrates this by comparing Mintzberg's five structural forms on each of the five Hofstede dimensions. These are not empirical findings, but interpretations of how these different dimensions of cultural values might vary in ideal forms of the Mintzberg structures.

The entrepreneurial goals in a small organization of simple structure would lead to the owner maintaining high levels of control, but simultaneously valuing risk-taking and individualism, backed up by strong masculine values and moderately supportive of traditional social orders. In professional structures education and socialization practices tend to reduce power distance amongst the professionals, especially once they are qualified. On the other hand, moderate to large professional organizations tend to become more bureaucratic, which itself leads to greater power distance; hence power distance is predicted to be moderately strong. Professionalism tends to be founded on reason and rationality, so individualism, masculinity, and traditional social orders are not strongly held, but are likely to exist to some extent. Professionals are trained and paid to absorb uncertainty so uncertainty avoidance is likely to be low.

The classic machine structure is founded on high power distance, high uncertainty avoidance, low individualism, high masculinity and high maintenance of traditional social orders. The learning, innovative adhocracy is based on cultural values rooted in low power distance, high risk-taking, high individualism, low tolerance for traditional social arrangements, and leaning more towards the softness and supportiveness characterized by femininity, though I have been cautious in the Table about just how much that applies. The divisional structure is rooted in power distance much like the simple structure, but the autonomy it is given assumes the division performs well so that uncertainty avoidance is likely to be valued. These values will tend to be supported by high masculinity and support for traditional ways of doing things. Not surprisingly, individualism tends to be lower because of the need for people in the division to pull together to produce quality goods or services.

It is implicit in this framework that the content of the five corporate cultures described above is strongly held, but many organizations fail in convincing large numbers of their members to accept the values they promote. The degree to which cultural values are shared is an important aspect of any culture.

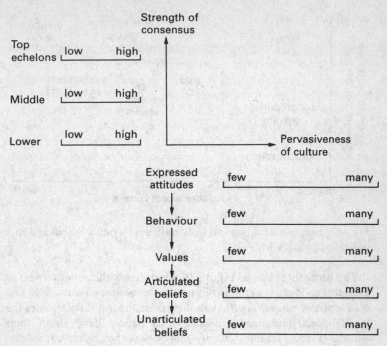

Fig. 14.4 Cultural co-ordinates.

The Strength of Cultures

Figure 14.4 summarizes one way of looking at this issue. The vertical axis represents the *strength of consensus* amongst members of the collectivity (organization, tribe, group, department, etc.). It also indicates that the degree of consensus may vary at different levels of the hierarchy and that these variations influence the overall strength of the culture. It is important to recognize that the consensus must be about the same values/beliefs (content). If the top echelons of a commercial company have high consensus about short-term profits and the lower echelons have high consensus about the importance of job security, overall consensus is likely to be low. A strong culture is one where all levels agree about the same issues.

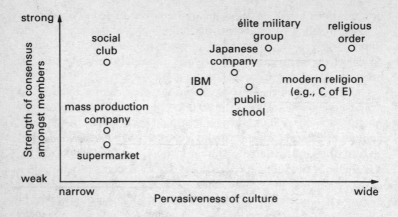

Fig. 14.5 Examples of strong and weak cultures in terms of the cultural co-ordinates of Fig. 14.4.

The horizontal axis in Figure 14.4 represents the *pervasiveness* of the culture. There is variation in pervasiveness in two ways. The first is in terms of *psychic depth*. A culture is stronger if it determines the basic beliefs/fundamental assumptions people have about their worlds. It is less strong if it only shapes how they behave. It is least powerful of all if it affects only what they like or dislike (their attitudes). A powerful religion, for example, will affect all of these. Many work organizations shape their members' behaviour without affecting their values, and may more easily influence the attitudes they are willing to express publicly. The second way in which pervasiveness varies is in terms of the *range* of attitudes, behaviours, values and beliefs that the culture influences. Again, a religion attempts to influence a wide range of all of them; a work organization will seek to influence a narrower range.

Using the cultural co-ordinates in Figure 14.4, it is possible to characterize cultures in terms of these two dimensions. Figure 14.5 gives examples of collectivities with cultures that might be seen to fall in different parts of this space. Collectivities which are low in the pervasiveness of their enculturation practices and which have only low levels of consensus are quite common. Many community clubs, associations, etc. have these characteristics, as do some employing organizations where there are many part-time or seasonal workers (e.g., in building or retailing). As long as people do their job and follow a few basic rules, they are accepted into such a culture. Amongst the permanent staff of such organizations, the culture is often much stronger of course.

Collectivities which do not develop a strong culture but tend to produce high consensus are those that focus on a relatively narrow range of activities. Thus clubs built around particular activities (e.g., hobbies or games) can generate high consensus about the rules, rituals and dramas associated with that activity, but they focus on little else. In work situations this can occur when the company employs a narrow range of specialists, such as scientists who value research highly but are less in agreement about production, marketing or sales as equally valued activities.

Groups that have higher status in society generally, such as doctors, lawyers and the clergy, tend to produce cultures of a higher pervasiveness because they demand that their members behave in particular ways even outside the organization. This is even more true of uniformed organizations such as the police, army and some public schools. Business organizations which are reputed to be higher in both consensus and pervasiveness include organizations such as IBM, Hewlett-Packard and Marks and Spencer. None of these appear at the extreme on the cultural co-ordinates, of course, because they exist in national cultures which value freedom and the private rights of the citizen, so their strength is moderate compared to that achieved by major religions such as Islam, Roman Catholicism and fundamentalist Baptists. In work organizations it seems likely that only those Japanese companies that employ people for life and provide housing and most other benefits would be high on both the dimensions of pervasiveness and consensus; in part, that is possible only because the values in the national culture reinforce the values promoted by such a company.

Measuring Culture

There have been three broad approaches to describing/measuring cultures. The one with the longest history is the anthropological approach. This involves living in a culture and making systematic efforts to describe and explain how it works. In terms of Schein's definition of culture (see above) this would lead to describing the nature and role of artefacts, patterns of expected behaviours and attitudes, the myths and legends of the culture and their functions in it, as well as developing insights into beliefs and values which may be so 'taken for granted' that many members of the culture cannot articulate them clearly themselves. There are not many examples of the anthropological approach in work organizations, but two British ones are Jacques' (1951) *The Changing Culture of a Factory* and Pettigrew's (1985) classic study of twenty years in the history of ICI, *The Awakening Giant*.

The second approach uses questionnaires, examining aspects of organizational 'climate'. In studies of organizational climate people from throughout the organization are asked to say whether a whole range of statements are true or false, whether they describe or do not describe their organization. The questions may cover the physical environment or the structure of the company, but more typically refer to common patterns of attitudes and behaviours. Examples might be about the formality of relationships, attitudes to customers, to risk-taking, how hard people work, the importance of innovation and creativity versus sticking to the rules/playing safe, and how supportive people are to each other. While Hofstede's questionnaire focused on values, it is very similar in style to measures of climate. When people's perceptions are averaged and a score given to each organization, it is possible to show differences in the climates, but this masks a major problem in climate research: it is that people in different parts of the organization often see things very differently. In terms of the analysis of culture presented here, there is low consensus. The empirical and conceptual difficulties this produces are well illustrated in the book edited by Schneider (1990).

The third approach falls between the methods of the anthropologist and those of climate researchers. It attempts to short-cut the anthropologist's prescription to live in and intensively study a culture. These methods attempt to redefine the relatively limited questionnaires designed to study organizational climates and to cast them more directly into cultural concepts (myths, jargon, etc.). For example, Siehl and Martin (1988) first collected qualitative information

402

about a specific company, concentrating on cultural concepts such as values, company jargon, organizational stories, beliefs about practices, etc., and then designed questionnaires to assess what people knew about these. Duncan (1989) studied an organization's culture by a mixture of observational, interview and questionnaire methods. Information derived from these three methods was used in a process of 'triangulation' to provide a more holistic view of the culture.

Some writers would argue that such methods (and climate questionnaires) can never expose the real essence of culture, which ultimately concerns what is described as articulated and unarticulated beliefs (see Figure 14.4): the taken-for-granted. Only a deep knowledge of history, myths and rituals, and their real meaning for the membership of the culture, will fully reveal the true culture. In one sense, anything less than this, such as descriptions of attitudes, norms of behaviour, etc., might be regarded by such writers as not being culture at all. The framework in Figure 14.4 attempts to avoid this argument about conceptual boundaries. Cultures vary from being strong to weak, as defined by degree of pervasiveness, degree of consensus and the range of content they cover. As stated at the beginning of this chapter, any group of people who come together for a common purpose will have to agree on what they are trying to achieve, how they will achieve it, who will do what, how outcomes/rewards will be distributed and why the achievements are of value to them. Some sort of culture will emerge in achieving this, though it might be either a weak or a strong one.

Despite the difficulties in describing and measuring culture/ climate, all three approaches have been able to show that culture influences how well organizations perform and, in extreme cases, whether they survive at all. It is worth noting that some strong cultures affect performance positively while other strong cultures can be the cause of a company's failure. Clashes of corporate cultures are a major cause of failure when companies merge or are taken over. Examples and discussions of these phenomena are to be found in Schneider (1990), Denison (1990) and most comprehensively in Trice and Beyer (1993). As the reader of these books will discover, however, the literature is complex and the links between culture and performance often difficult to tie down in any neat causal model.

If culture is so difficult to define and measure, why has it become so central to managing organizations? From a managerial perspective, the key question has sometimes been defined as: how can you develop a strong culture which is committed to the goals that the members of the collectivity are trying to achieve? Cultures are in part systems of social control. The ultimate system of control is one where people voluntarily act appropriately and monitor their own standards of behaviour. Organizations which can socialize their members to believe, value and behave in accordance with its needs can reliably produce the goods and services it offers. The success of Japanese companies in the last two decades has highlighted the power of a strong culture in achieving quality and reliability. These cultural values are compatible with, and therefore lead to, the high quality, high reliability technology that Japan now produces. But in many cases the culture came first. So where does culture come from?

In the vast majority of cases it seems to derive initially from the influence of a charismatic leader, who defines the basic beliefs, values and patterns of behaviour that epitomize good citizenship (Schein, 1992; see also Chapter 9). The enduring influence of these cultural founders is perpetuated in stories and myths, and reinforced through rituals, regulations and other artefacts. Cultures that endure develop structures, systems and stories that promote the values and beliefs that are central to that culture. When these three harmonize, the culture becomes strong, though, paradoxically, one of the requirements of modern business cultures is that they have strong values about being adaptable, looking for new opportunities and changing their culture to exploit them. Most strong cultures have their origins in the values, ideas and actions of a leader who has shaped these structures, systems and stories. Creating a culture, or changing a culture, depends on a leader or leaders who can persuade people to pursue the vision and provide the structures and systems for enabling them to turn the vision into reality. The processes and actions that bring about organization development and cultural change are dealt with more fully in Chapter 15.

SUMMARY

This chapter has described and defined the main parameters used for characterizing organizations. Using Mintzberg's framework for describing organizations as the linking conceptual scheme, it has shown how different types of organizational strategies relate to different types of organizational structures. Both of these derive from the values and actions of senior managers and owners, and both contribute to the development of cultures which perpetuate, and also reshape, those strategies, structures and cultures. In analysing the concept of culture, emphasis was given to the idea that cultures vary in strength. Drawing upon the work of Pettigrew and Whipp, the chapter describes the five processes which seem most likely to lead to the survival and growth of organizations exposed to an increasing rate of change and increasing degrees of complexity and competition.

FURTHER READING

The academic journals which cover these topics most regularly are: *Academy of Management Journal*, *Academy of Management Review*, *Administrative Science Quarterly*, *Organization Studies*, *Journal of Occupational and Organizational Psychology*, *Journal of Organizational Behaviour* and *Journal of Management Studies*. Less academic, but still well informed journals are the *Harvard Business Review*, the *Academy of Management Executive* and *Personnel Management*.

Mintzberg's (1989) book should be read, and Trice and Beyer's (1993) monograph is set to become a classic text on culture. Handy's (1993) book *Understanding Organizations* covers similar topics but uses some different conceptual frameworks. Most textbooks on organizational behaviour will cover aspects of structure and culture. Johnson and Scholes (1994) provide an excellent introduction to understanding corporate strategy.

REFERENCES

Cooke, R. A. and Rousseau, D. M. (1988). Behavioural norms and expectations: A quantitative approach to the assessment of organisational culture. *Group and Organisation Studies*, 13, 245–273.

Denison, D. R. (1990). *Corporate Culture and Organizational Effectiveness*. New York: Wiley.

Duncan, W. J. (1989). Organizational culture: 'Getting a fix' on an elusive concept. *The Academy of Management Executive*, III, 3, 229–238.

Goold, M. and Campbell, A. (1987). *Strategies and Styles: The Role of the Centre in Managing Diversified Corporations*. Oxford: Blackwell.

Halal, E. (1994). From hierarchy to enterprise: Internal markets are the new foundation for management. *The Academy of Management Executive*, VIII, 4, 69–83.

Hamel, G. and Prahalad, C. K. (1994). *Competing for the Future: Breakthrough Strategies for Seizing Control of your Industry and Creating the Markets of Tomorrow*. Cambridge, Mass.: Harvard Business School Press.

Handy, C. (1993). *Understanding Organizations*, 4th edn. Harmondsworth: Penguin.

Hofstede, G. (1980). *Culture's Consequences: International Differences in Work-related Values*. London: Sage.

Hofstede, G. (1991). *Cultures and Organisations: Software of the Mind*. London: McGraw-Hill.

Jacques, E. (1951). *The Changing Culture of a Factory*. London: Tavistock.

Johnson, G. and Scholes, K. (1994). *Exploring Corporate Strategy*. Englewood Cliffs, NJ: Prentice Hall.

Kroeber, A. L. and Kluckhohn, C. (1952). *Culture: A Critical Review of Concepts and Definitions*. New York: Vintage Books.

Mintzberg, H. (1979). *The Structure of Organizations*. Englewood Cliffs, NJ: Prentice Hall.

Mintzberg, H. (1983). *Structure in Fives: Designing Effective Organizations*. Englewood Cliffs, NJ: Prentice Hall.

Mintzberg, H. (1989). *Mintzberg on Management: Inside our strange world of organizations*. New York: Free Press.

Pettigrew, A. (1973). *The Politics of Organizational Decision-Making*. London: Tavistock.

Pettigrew, A. (1985). *The Awakening Giant: Continuity and Change in ICI*. Oxford: Blackwell.

Pettigrew, A. and Whipp, R. (1993). Managing the twin processes of competition and change: The role of intangible assets. In P. Lorange, B. Chakravarthy, J. Roos and A. Van de Ven (eds.), *Implementing Strategic Processes: Change, Learning and Co-operation*, pp. 3–42. Oxford: Blackwell.

Pfeffer, J. (1981). *Power in Organizations*. Marshfield, Mass.: Pitman.

Schein, E. H. (1990). Organizational culture. *American Psychologist*, 45, 109–119.

Schein, E. H. (1992). *Organizational Culture and Leadership*, 2nd edn. San Francisco: Jossey-Bass.

Schneider, B. (ed.) (1990). *Organizational Climate and Culture.* San Francisco: Jossey-Bass.

Siehl, C. and Martin J. (1988). Measuring organizational cultures: Mixing qualitative and quantitative methods. In M. O. Jones, M. D. Moore and R. D. Snyder (eds.), *Inside Organizations*, pp. 45–59. Beverly Hills, Calif.: Sage.

Smircich, L. (1983). Concepts of culture and organisational analysis. *Administrative Science Quarterly*, 28, 339–358.

Trice, H. M. and Beyer, J. M. (1993). *The Cultures of Work Organizations.* Englewood Cliffs, NJ: Prentice Hall.

15

Organizational Change

Jean Hartley

Since 1980 the scale, scope and pace of change in organizations have increased dramatically. Many organizations have restructured in seeking to become 'more competitive', which has usually involved reorganizing functions and levels, and reducing the number of front-line employees and middle management. In both the private and public sectors, leaders and managers of organizations are trying to find ways to develop stronger emphases on quality, on innovation and on flexibility to respond to and also to initiate change. In addition to these large-scale changes, there are many smaller, incremental changes, which are ongoing because organizations do not stand still. In this chapter we will examine some of the key theories and frameworks which underlie how organizations, groups and individuals change.

To suggest that organizations are always in a state of change is to ignore some important elements of stability and continuity. The very essence of organization is that it implies some patterns of order, structure and power in collective human activity. If organizations are always changing (and they also have some continuities), then what do we mean by organizational change? How much difference does there have to be to constitute an alteration? Change can refer to minor changes in procedures, activities or personnel, but also it can refer to large-scale transformation where the whole purpose, structures and values of an organization are modified (as in, for example, a merger or a major reorientation of the purposes of the organization). This distinction will be elaborated below. In addition, the interpretation of how much (or whether) change has occurred may depend on the person's role in the organization and his or her own personal perspective: organizational change has many subjective as well as objective aspects.

STAKEHOLDERS AND CHANGE

Stakeholder analysis (e.g., Mitroff, 1983) attempts to identify key groups and individuals who have differing perspectives on a matter, in this case organizational change. Internal stakeholders are those who work in the organization itself, though there will be external stakeholders too (the recipients of the organization's products or services, the general public, suppliers to the organization, etc.), who may also try to shape the processes and outcomes of change.

One stakeholder framework is that of Kanter, Stein and Jick (1992), who argue that the experience and preoccupations of change vary according to whether the person is primarily:

- a change strategist (concerned with the connection between the organization and its environment and with the organization's overall direction – often though not always the responsibility of leaders and senior management);
- a change implementer (concerned with the detailed development of the change initiative, e.g., project management and operational execution, rather than primarily the design of change);
- a change recipient (concerned with the effects of the change, often because he or she is on the receiving end of change, sometimes without much opportunity to influence the change plan).

While this classification is rather simple (it seems to imply that organizational members are only in one category, whereas in practice some may move between different roles as the change develops), nevertheless it is useful in emphasizing that organizational change is likely to be experienced differently according to an employee's place within the organization. This is often ignored in writings in this area, which can take a unitarist (generally top management) perspective of the process. However, psychological research has drawn attention to other roles in change, especially the position of the change recipient. Psychologists have even advocated particular techniques to engage recipients in change (for example, participation in aspects of the process of change). The stakeholder groups may, of course, be more numerous than simply those three identified above, for example, trade unions, professional groups or managerial groups.

TYPES OF ORGANIZATIONAL CHANGE

How can we understand and classify the varied changes which occur in organizations? Let us limit our consideration to planned change: organizational change where there is a deliberate intention to create change (though, of course, the process may not go according to plan or it may alter from its original conception). Within this field, writers are increasingly making two types of distinction: changes in the nature and in the scope of change (e.g., Cummings and Worley, 1993).

First, there is the distinction between developmental change, which is concerned with improving the efficiency or effectiveness of the organization from within the general framework of the strategy, mode of organizing and values that are already in place; and transformational change, which is designed to have an impact on the strategy, structure, people, processes and values (or some combination thereof) in a fundamental way. The second dimension of change concerns its scope: whether the change is aimed at a sub-system of the organization or the total organization. The first might be the individual or group level (e.g., team or department) or some organizational sub-system (e.g., information technology system). The second concerns the whole organization. The dimensions of the scope and scale of change, with some examples, are shown in Table 15.1.

This allows a rudimentary classification of organizational change, though the categories are far from robust, given that change may not go according to plan. For example, what senior management intend to be transformational change may end up being merely developmental, or what starts as a minor change in a department may develop to have major change consequences for the organization. Nevertheless, the framework allows us to assess whether change theories are concerned with development or transformation, and whether they are primarily targeted at the whole organization or some part of it.

Until recently, most theory and practice by psychologists has been concerned with developmental change, generally at the level of the

Table 15.1 Types of organizational change

Scale of change	Scope of change	
	development	transformation
Whole organization	e.g.: growth management development improvements in technology pay systems etc.	e.g.: culture change total quality management learning organization
Sub-system	e.g.: job redesign much organization development teambuilding	e.g.: reorganization of department or service

individual or group (see commentaries by Ledford, Mohrman, Mohrman and Lawler, 1989; Porras and Silvers, 1991; Cummings and Worley, 1993). This is an important area of psychological and management theory and research, which will be illustrated below. However, more recently there has been an increasing interest in transformational change. This often requires a more strategic approach than developmental changes (which is not to suggest that some developmental change cannot be strategic). Psychologists are only slowly becoming involved in the strategic management of change (e.g., Sparrow, 1994), though case-study research by sociologists is fairly well established in this area (e.g., Pettigrew, 1986; Dunphy and Stace, 1993).

There are many features of organizations which may be the focus or target of planned change. In broad terms, these may be products and services, strategy and structure, people and culture, and technology. An alternative classification is that by Leavitt (1965), who sees change as being concerned with one or more of tasks, technology, structures and people. Psychologists have tended to focus more on the people and culture aspects of organizational change, though many would recognize the interactions between these aspects of organizations.

THE EXTERNAL ENVIRONMENT

Many researchers argue that the analysis of organizational change needs to start with the external environment. The external environment may provide both pressures and opportunities for the organization to change. These may include:

- political (for example, changes in legislation affecting the organization, such as UK employment legislation or European Union trade legislation);
- economic (for example, changes in the competitive position of the organization, or changes in interest rates, changes in products and services);
- social (for example, demographic changes in the population or higher expectations of customers or users);
- technological (for example, information technologies are modifying many working practices in organizations, and changing standards of product and delivery).

Part of the role of strategic managers is to interpret the meaning and then assess the significance for the organization of the many changes in the external environment which may have an impact at some stage on the organization. The environment may also sometimes be used as a rationale for introducing change, when justification or persuasion is needed.

Dunphy and Stace (1993) argue that the type of strategic organizational change (for example, whether the implementation is primarily top-down and coercive or more distributed and collaborative) will depend in part on environmental demands, including the time which is believed to be available in which to complete the change. The strategic change model of Pettigrew and colleagues (e.g., Pettigrew and Whipp, 1991) also places a strong emphasis on a close analysis of the external context as a constraint on, though not necessarily a determinant of, internal organizational change.

The external environment is mediated through the perceptions, cognitions and value systems of those in the organization who are in boundary-spanning roles and who therefore have contact with the outside. These people include leaders and senior managers as well as many front-line workers (especially in service organizations). The senior managers may choose to act on or ignore the various cues from the environment. Research here has been limited, and there is still much we need to understand about these processes.

Dutton and Dukerich (1991) describe a case study of how a US transport authority dealt with the growing issue of homelessness, showing how the response of the organization to the external environment (growing numbers of homeless people living in the transport facilities) was affected by the identity of the organization (a high-quality institution concerned with transport to which the homeless constituted a threat) and its image (the organization's understanding of how others, especially the media and the customers, saw it). In particular, Dutton and Dukerich argue that the deterioration of the organization's image was an important trigger to action.

Not all change is explicitly related to the external environment. For example, change may be initiated after an internal decision to review the organization's mission and key goals, or it may be promoted by an incoming chief executive, perhaps as a symbolic act of purpose and power.

In sum, a model of organizational change which only examined the influence of external pressures on the organization would play down the scope for human agency, and the role of leaders and managers, as well as others, in influencing the direction and style of change. It would thus be excessively narrow.

TRANSFORMATIONAL CHANGE

Transformational change (at the right-hand side of Table 15.1) involves substantial alteration to the purposes, structure or culture of the organization. For example, many local government organizations are currently grappling with transformational change in moving from being professionally driven to being more citizen- and user-responsive. Transformational change has become more widespread and more urgent in both the private and public sectors in the 1980s

413

and 1990s. It remains a key type of change for organizations. In the private sector competitive pressures have led organizations into re-structuring, using so-called downsizing and delayering as well as heralding changes in values and procedures through initiatives such as total quality management (TQM). There have also been attempts at fundamental change through the modification of culture (see Chapter 14). In the public sector major legislative imperatives and financial pressures have led to massive changes in function, purpose and ways of organizing.

The Role of Leadership

The role of leadership in initiating and managing change is being increasingly explored and is a rich area for psychologists, both as researchers and as practitioners. Early psychological writing tended to be rather vague about the leadership of change, arguing that change initiatives needed 'the support of top management'. However, in the last decade there has been a stronger interest in the strategic management of change, which is often required in the context of transformational change.

Organizational change is here typically initiated and conceived by the leadership of the organization. In private-sector organizations this is likely to be the top management (with an increasing realization that the 'top team' rather than individual managers is likely to be significant here). In public-sector organizations leadership may also be exercised by the politicians and appointees who are accountable to a local community or to ministers for the running of the organi-zation. For example, in a local authority, local councillors are a key part of the leadership of change, working closely with senior managers who are paid employees of the authority.

Effective leadership includes the strategic management of change, which involves the analysis of the environment and the resources, values and capacities of the organization, and the choice between different courses of action which might be taken, which are then implemented either fully or partially. Here we consider strategy only in the context of organizational change. There is increasing evidence that the perceptions, cognitions and values of leaders, and the group dynamics of 'top teams', influence their analysis, choice and attempted implementation of strategies (Sparrow, 1994). The strategic management of change is not just about rational decision-making, however persuasive the *post hoc* rhetoric of strategic managers! There is scope here for more investigations by psychologists, with a remit to explore both the 'cognitive maps' of strategic change-makers and also the social construction of strategy by the senior management team. The research by Dutton and Dukerich (1991) already described is clearly relevant here.

In initiating transformational (and especially organization-wide) change, several commentators have pointed to the importance of developing a vision which can be communicated to the rest of the organization (e.g., Porras and Silvers, 1991). Nadler and Tushman (1989) suggest that, where an organization is undergoing radical change, the leader (they conceptualize the role in the singular, though this is arguable in some organizations) needs several qualities, including the ability to communicate a vision for the future of the organization. They argue that the leader needs to be able to undertake three activities:

- envisioning: the creation of a picture of the future that people can accept and which generates excitement. 'By creating vision, the leader provides a way for people to develop commitment, a common goal around which people can rally, and a way for people to feel successful' (p.105).
- energizing: the leader generates motivation to act among members of the organization. This may be done in different ways, but commonly includes the demonstration of their own personal excitement and energy, combined with enhancement of that excitement through direct personal contact with large numbers of employees. The leader expresses confidence in the ability to succeed and also finds examples of success to celebrate.
- enabling: the leader helps employees to act or perform even under challenging circumstances. Again, this may be done in a variety of ways, but empathy – the ability to listen to, understand and share the feelings of others – has been highlighted.

Nadler and Tushman point out that there are risks with such

leadership. For example, it may create unrealistic expectations of change or excessive dependency on the leader. They emphasize that there is also a need for instrumental leadership, which is focused on clarifying and controlling behaviours, standards, procedures and rewards so that employees are encouraged to behave in ways consistent with the proposed changes.

In this analysis of leadership of major change we see some similarities with the research literature by psychologists on leadership more generally (see also Chapter 9). However, research evidence on leadership in transformational change has not kept pace with commentators' ideas and propositions. While there are case studies of transformational leadership in the literature (e.g., Kanter, Stein and Jick, 1992), these do not demonstrate which decisions, attitudes and behaviours promote successful change. In addition, psychologists have not yet developed operational definitions or measures of such leadership in organizational change, though the concepts are potentially open to measurement in research studies. However, there is an increasing amount of research on the qualities and behaviours of the 'top team' in their leadership capacity (e.g., Sparrow, 1994). In addition, many employees in large-scale organizational change refer to and believe in the importance of the envisioning and energizing roles of leaders (e.g., Hartley, Cordingley and Benington, 1995).

Transformational organizational change is not only about developing a vision of the future state of the organization. The implementation of such change is a major challenge for both managers and change advisers. The idea that change involves developing plans based on the search for optimal solutions and then carrying them out has been effectively refuted by Quinn (1980). Quinn argues that many senior managers engaged in strategic change adopt logical incrementalism. They 'artfully blend formal analysis, behavioural techniques and power politics to bring about cohesive, step-by-step movement towards ends which initially are broadly conceived, but which are then constantly refined and reshaped as new information appears' (p. 65).

Some writers have also criticized the proposal that transformational change is best managed from the top of the organization. Beer, Eisenstadt and Spector (1990), in a study of six large US companies, suggested that some organizations which were successful in creating fundamental changes in values or activities often started with pilot change programmes in peripheral or isolated operational areas. The role of top management may be to support and nurture new innovations and changes which have arisen in operational areas. Lawler (1990) argues that whether change is mainly 'top-down' or 'bottom-up' will depend on a variety of factors, including power relations and the degree of participation which already exists in the organization.

Culture Change

Since the mid-1980s there has been an increasing awareness that fundamental shifts in values and behaviours of organizational members do not occur overnight after redrawing the organization chart. Such structural changes may be important in some circumstances, but many writers have suggested that there is a need for change which is more deep-rooted. Culture change programmes may be of this type. Culture is here taken to be the pattern of basic assumptions, values, norms and artefacts which are shared by organization members and which help them to make sense of the external environment and internal functioning of the organization (see also Chapter 14).

Explicit programmes of culture change are generally linked to a clear strategic vision of the organization. For example, in a programme by British Airways called 'Putting People First' workshops and training on culture change were based on a new vision for the newly privatized airline, part of which focused on seeing the company as concerned with service to customers rather than providing transportation (Goodstein and Burke, 1993). In a British county council a programme of culture change was developed out of the aspirations of the local councillors to develop a more coherent and cohesive organization with a strong emphasis on local democracy, rather than being sectional and professionally dominated (Hartley, Cordingley and Benington, 1995).

Interventions aimed to change an organization's culture are often based on widespread programmes first of management development and then of wider training for staff. For example, in the British Airways programme all staff with customer contact attended off-site training sessions. In addition, task groups worked on suggestions for modifying structures and systems to support the culture change. (There is little point in changing attitudes and assumptions if the management information systems or budgetary procedures reinforce previous habits.) Attention was also paid to symbols of change, including a new company logo, new uniforms and refurbished aircraft. In addition, in culture change, personnel systems may also be modified (e.g., for appraisal and induction) to reflect the selection and socialization of newcomers. Key managers who are not sympathetic to the new culture may be encouraged to leave the organization.

The proposition that fundamental change in values and assumptions can occur on a corporate-wide basis is problematic. It is based on the belief that culture is modifiable by top management actions and policy changes. There are some questions about whether – or to what extent – deeply held assumptions can in fact be altered. How far can culture change be linked to top management's vision and strategy when culture itself concerns fundamental assumptions shared by social groups throughout the organization (which may develop in part through interactions within the group)? Is there a danger that employees learn the 'appropriate' rules of behaviour and expressed attitude but that their fundamental assumptions do not change? In addition, while some management writers have stressed the uniform nature of organizational culture, researchers have suggested that separate sub-cultures may also be important, as, for example, various professional cultures in health and local government, or the sales function compared with production in manufacturing.

Nevertheless, a number of organizations have recently attempted to change their culture. Observers estimate that extensive culture change takes at least five years to complete for a large organization and requires supportive mechanisms in the organizational structure and through organizational processes, including modifications to human resource systems (Tichy, 1983). The impact of culture change on organizational performance is notoriously hard to evaluate (see Siehl and Martin, 1990). However, despite these conceptual and practical difficulties, many organizations have felt it necessary to undertake culture change initiatives in cases where the organization faces a radically different environment, if the organization is performing in a mediocre or worse manner, or if there is rapid expansion or other developments.

Psychologists have been involved in culture change programmes in a number of ways. For example, they may contribute to the diagnosis of the current and desired culture through workshops and discussions or through quantitative climate surveys (sometimes combined with survey feedback). Diagnostic procedures can be used to assess the depth or extent of potential culture change, to help top teams articulate strategic and structural plans to complement and support change and to identify future management competencies which may be needed to support the changed organization. In some cases psychologists design the overall programme of culture change workshops and other human resource aspects, as happened in British Airways (Goodstein and Burke, 1993). Furthermore, process consultation and organization development skills have been valuable in helping senior management, middle management and front-line employees to clarify and understand their values, beliefs and fundamental assumptions about each other and about the organization. This may be especially important for top management, who have often been rewarded in the past for 'old' cultural behaviours.

DEVELOPMENTAL CHANGE

We turn now to examine some of the interventions and theories (often treated in that order) which arise largely in connection with developmental change (see Table 15.1). Much of the work by psychologists has focused on changing the behaviours, attitudes and interactions of individuals and groups, though some interventions have focused on the whole organization.

Theories of, and Approaches to, Individual and Group Change

Psychological writing on organizational change emphasizes the importance of individual and group changes in attitudes, behaviour and learning. Psychological theory argues that this is essential if changes are to be long-term and deep-rooted rather than based merely on behavioural compliance. Individual behaviour change is central to organizational change. The most recent manifestation of this view concerns the notion of a 'learning organization', where the ability of an organization to adapt to future challenges is thought to depend on an organization-wide culture of the acceptance and transmission of learning by individuals, supported by appropriate corporate policies.

However, to say that individual change is necessary for organizational change is not to say that it is sufficient. While individual change is a key part of much long-term and deep-rooted change, there is a danger of some psychological theories being based either on the notion that organizational change is simply the sum of many individual and group changes, or on the idea that theories and frameworks applied to individuals and groups are applicable at the organization level. This is often questionable, for example, in relation to transformational change, where processes concerned with adapting to or shaping the external environment must also take account of the other levers of change described by Leavitt (1965; see earlier): tasks, technology and structures. There is thus a need for theories and approaches which are interdisciplinary. A number of psychological theories have been applied to developmental change (though some are not exclusive to it), and here we will focus on four: Lewin's field theory, organization development theory, systems theory and power-based theory.

Lewin's field theory

Lewin's (1951) field theory is an early and influential psychological theory of change in individuals and groups. It is based on the assumption that the most appropriate way to understand attitudes and behaviour is to view the individual human being in his or her life-space. A key part of the latter is the groups to which a person belongs, both at work and outside work, which influence his or her values, attitudes and behaviours. Therefore, if change is desired (for example, by management) in a person's behaviour, then influence through the group can be a means to achieve change. Lewin and his colleagues applied these ideas to changes in work organization and procedures in manufacturing, which led to the widely held idea (and moral position) that participation in the decision to change promotes effective change (e.g., lower conflict, higher morale and improved performance). However, research results in this area have been equivocal and are open to considerable criticism. Much of the enthusiasm within the organization development movement for active participation by change recipients can be traced to Lewin's work.

Lewin also developed a model of the processes of planned change, which has three stages. The first phase is unfreezing, which consists of reducing resistance to the proposed change and also developing the perception of a need for change. Zaltman and Duncan (1977) view this in terms of the development of the awareness of a performance gap (a gap between the current and desired level of achievement). The second stage involves the change itself (which account does make change seem simple and / or a single step), while the third consists of refreezing: ensuring that the new state of the organization is stabilized, with activities and policies contributing to the new status quo.

This three-phase approach to understanding organizational change has proved very popular, though it is extremely schematic and general. Its value lies in its indication of the early period of preparing for change (perhaps using diagnostic techniques such as force-field analysis or survey feedback) and in the importance of the consolidation, or institutionalization, of change (in refreezing). It has been drawn on by change agents and consultants to develop models for change management (e.g., French and Bell, 1990), though we should recognize that this may make it a theory of change-management rather than a theory of how actual processes of change occur. It does not conceive of change as a dynamic and continuous process but tends to emphasize planned steps towards a final state. Weisbord (1988) has argued that the model may be losing its applicability in any case as the rate of technological and environmental change increases: it is less valid in characterizing an organization in continuous change. It may also be more valuable for describing individual and group processes in a particular and discrete change (for example, a change in working practices or developing customer awareness through a training programme) than it is for thinking about the change of an entire organization.

The continuing popularity of this three-phase model of planned change may speak volumes about the theoretical vacuum, challenging psychologists to develop theoretically rigorous models of organizational change.

Organization development

Organization development (OD) has been a major approach to planned organizational change, especially in its heyday of the 1960s and 1970s. For a time OD had an almost missionary quality and was associated with the growth of humanistic forms of psychology, and an emphasis on employees' feelings and values. It had a strong emphasis on the processes of learning and development, sometimes at the expense of much consideration of outcomes for the organization. Nowadays OD is a more sober and task-oriented activity, with an emphasis on human processes in conjunction with structure, task and systems. However, its early interest in values and processes can be seen as prefiguring to some extent the later interest in organizational culture, and some ideas from OD about developing trust and openness have been prominent in theories about the learning organization.

OD is a general term to cover a wide range of techniques and approaches. An influential characterization is given by French and Bell (1990): 'Organization development is a top-management-supported long-range effort to improve an organization's problem-solving and renewal processes' (p. 17). Beckhard (1969) describes it as planned, organization-wide, managed from the top, used to increase organizational effectiveness and health, using interventions concerned with processes and based on behavioural science knowledge. Its base in behavioural science is varied (and not often specified in any detail), but is seen to derive in part from Lewin's field theory and more generally from a human relations perspective. OD is thus less a theory than a framework (and set of values) about the importance of human interactions and participative management. Writers in this area have tended to emphasize:

- social processes, especially informal behaviours, relationships, feelings and group dynamics. It is argued that shifts in attitudes, values and ways of relating between individuals and between groups will lead to fundamental change: commitment to new ways of working rather than mere compliance to pressures for change.

- experiential learning. OD has developed a variety of techniques to help people learn from their own feelings and experiences, for example in team-building and in conflict management.
- the use of a change agent: someone who is external to the organization who seeks to act as a catalyst for the change, by working with people on the social processes and dynamics in the group and organization. Perhaps more than any other approach to change, OD has examined and emphasized the role of the change agent.

To the extent that it exists, theory in this area has developed largely out of practice. OD has always had a strong interest in developing ideas about, for example, the helping relationship between consultant and client, the use of diagnosis and feedback as part of the process of change, intergroup competition and the processes of managing transitions. (See Cummings and Worley, 1993, for fuller descriptions of these techniques.)

However, the early enthusiasm for OD has not been sustained. While several of the techniques have survived piecemeal, the movement has lost its fervour. In part this may be precisely because it was a movement, with a highly normative framework about what organizations 'ought' to be like. (Openness, trust and sharing were key values.) This had three results. First, OD tended to neglect the analysis of power and politics in organizations. The approach appears to ignore the observation that much organizational change occurs through the use of power and even coercion, and that sometimes this may be the only way to effect and sustain organizational change. Second, the emphasis on human relations and social processes has sometimes been at the expense of consideration of other features which may bring about change; for example, changes in the operational, financial and human resource systems may be essential. While some OD practice had been aimed to reduce the formality of structures and roles in organizations, Brown (1980) noted that some organizations would be aided by more rather than less structure. Third, apart from the pioneers, OD practitioners were less interested in theory than in practice and there was a tendency to neither develop theory nor evaluate results in a systematic manner.

Although OD has claimed to be about organization-wide interventions, in many ways it can be seen to be an approach which is more suited to individuals and small groups – which is where the movement started. On the other hand, the OD movement has done much to demonstrate the importance of people's energy and commitment to both initiate and, especially, sustain change, and many OD techniques are currently used in training and development work as part of a larger scheme of change. OD has also contributed some techniques which can be used both for assessing the need for organizational change and as a first step in that change. For example, survey feedback (Nadler, 1977) has often been used to both collect and feed back data into the organization about its current state of functioning.

Systems theory
Systems theory is based on the assumption that an organization can be viewed as a unitary whole but one composed of parts or subsystems. As an *open* system, the organization interacts with its environment, taking in information and resources as inputs, and transforming these through organizational processes, some of which are turned into outputs into the environment. It is partly because of the prominence of systems theory that so many writers have pointed to the impact of the external environment on the initiation of change processes (see earlier).

Systems theory enables psychologists to move theoretically beyond the confines of the individual and the group to consider both the whole organization and especially the organization in relation to its external environment (e.g., Katz and Kahn, 1978; Nadler and Tushman, 1980). In its emphasis on the relationship of the organization with its environment this approach contrasts with that of OD, whose focus is on the internal social processes occurring within a group or organization. Systems theory is potentially useful in this area in at least two ways. First, it emphasizes that the role of boundary-spanners is important in organizational adaptation and change. So the role of senior or strategic managers is explicitly examined: their perceptions of the environment and the ways in which the organization may try to adapt to that environment (or make the environment adapt to the organization). (This can be of particular significance in transformational change.) Second, systems theory emphasizes the need for careful diagnosis of the external environment and the appropriateness to that of interlocking internal systems (for example, technological, social, human resource management, career and political systems). Change in one part of the internal system of the organization is seen to be likely to have impacts (sometimes unexpected) in other parts.

A specific development of systems theory is socio-technical systems theory. This was developed at the Tavistock Institute in the early 1950s as a result of observations of changes taking place in the organization of work in the coal industry (Trist and Bamforth, 1951). It was later applied to a much larger range of work and organizational settings across the world (Miller, 1993). The approach sets out to achieve organizational change through joint optimization of the technological and the social systems. Rather than merely trying to make people fit technological systems, the socio-technical approach seeks to find ways to maximize the performance of groups through the technological and social features together, appropriately optimized.

However, the very complexity of the systems in any organization makes it difficult to predict what are the key aspects of the internal organizational system which may be affected by any particular change. As with Lewin's approach, the generality of systems theory is appealing but such generality presents problems in application to specific settings. We cannot predict from the theory much more than that the complexity of the system and sub-systems is such that change is unlikely to go as planned. This argues for a process of change which includes regular monitoring and analysis of both the external and internal environment.

Power and organizational change

Relationships based on power are integral to organizations. Power relations flourish especially in situations of ambiguity and uncertainty (Pfeffer, 1981) – just the conditions that exist in programmes of organizational change. Power is inherent in organizations because organizations are coalitions of people and interest groups. Individuals and groups typically have different (as well as some common) values and goals in relation to work, and they may each be trying to shape the direction and process of change. In pursuing those different interests they may use power to persuade others about, or to enforce, their own views and objectives. Managers also have considerable power to reward or sanction which may be exercised at times of change. Stakeholder analysis (see earlier) is one means of attempting to identify power relations through examination of the different interests which may be involved in the context of planned change.

Power can be defined as the ability of a party (an individual, group or department) to control his, her or its environment. Space limitations preclude a more elaborated discussion of the bases, both personal and organizational, which may contribute to the development and application of power. In the context of change, the theme of this chapter, power is likely to be used coercively where there is a major imbalance of power between parties, while more equal distributions of power resources may lead to change being negotiated.

Negotiation may be a key form of change process in many organizations. It requires the ability to impose sanctions on others in cases where interests are thought to be insufficiently met in the agreement for change. Negotiation may be formal or informal, between individuals or between groups. Collective bargaining with trade unions can be important, and in many countries of continental Europe much planned organizational change has been achieved this way. Informal negotiation may be one of the reasons why the managers in Quinn's (1980) study acted with logical incrementalism (see earlier). We still do not know enough about how it occurs in planned organizational change.

Coercive change does not appear in many textbooks about organizational change. Yet it is widely applied, with differing degrees of success. In recent years, for example, the National Health Service and British Rail have been radically restructured using a top-down coercive approach. In some commercial organizations employees may be required to act in response to senior managers who seek to force through change in a short space of time. Psychological theory needs to catch up with reality in researching the processes and outcomes of these types of change.

Although the orientation of many academic psychologists may

predispose them to view coercive change in a negative light (some believe that change should never be forced), there is research evidence that it can be highly effective in particular circumstances, especially where the time-scale for change is very short or where strongly held attitudes from powerful interest groups (e.g., professional staff) may otherwise prevent substantial change occurring. In some cases coercive change may also be in part symbolic, attempting to signal to powerful outsiders – who may provide resources – that change is occurring.

From a psychological perspective, coercive change is unlikely to increase employees' commitment to change in the short-term because some people may feel embittered and resentful. Mechanisms for surveillance and for performance management may therefore be necessary as part of the process. If the change requires a high degree of employee commitment and enthusiasm, a coercive approach has limitations. However, it can in some circumstances lead to attitude change in the longer term (Zaltman and Duncan, 1977).

THE EVALUATION OF CHANGE

What do we know about how *successful* planned organizational change is? What do we mean by success? Is it about achieving the objectives of the original change programme, or can new objectives arise in the course of the change itself? How far does the process of change itself (rather than its outcomes) have to be successful? Achieved outcomes may be of little value if people found the experience so unpleasant they never want to go through something similar again. That could be counterproductive at a time of continuous change.

Some psychological approaches to change incorporate procedures to assist evaluation as part of the assessment of the need for change. Survey feedback was a technique originally developed by OD practitioners to use data generated by the organization itself in discussion about performance gaps and possible ways forward in planning and managing change (Nadler, 1977). Action research uses feedback as part of its approach to both research and practice. However, despite these uses of evaluation in practice, too little of this work has reached the journals as part of a systematic and long-term evaluation of planned change (Porras and Silvers, 1991).

Although the application of pre-change and post-change measures might seem a valuable approach to evaluation, this is complicated by the fact that the change process itself may cause alterations to fundamental perceptions such that conventional scale measures are not easily applicable. Golembiewski, Billingsley and Yeager (1976) identified the need to think about three types of change:

- alpha change: change in the perceived level of a domain within a paradigm (e.g., the perception that our skills as team-workers have improved);
- beta change: change in perceptions of the meaning of the variable, still within a paradigm (e.g., we now have higher standards of what it means to work as a team);
- gamma change: change in definition or conceptualization of a domain in a new paradigm (e.g., good team working no longer means working without any conflict but using conflict constructively to achieve the task).

If there are changes in either the standard or the paradigm (beta or gamma change), then an organization after a programme of change can conceivably score lower on a quantitative measure than at the beginning of the change, despite there being considerable or even radical improvements in performance. This has particular implications for evaluating transformational change and may affect more generally the design of evaluation studies. In some circumstances this argues for 'formative' evaluation. In this case changes in perceptions, actions and processes are studied in an ongoing evaluation such that the evaluation is modified to assess emerging processes of change. In formative evaluation information is gathered and fed back during a programme of change, rather than waiting until after the end of the programme.

Quantitative evaluation has tended to concentrate on the outcome variables of organizational performance and employee well-being, though increasingly there is an emphasis on the long-term preparedness of the organization for further change, should this be seen as necessary. So multiple measures of organizational change are necessary. However, the number of published evaluation studies is small. Porras and Robertson (1992) found only seventy-one studies between 1975 and 1988 which provided both sufficient detail of the study and quantitative data on the outcomes achieved.

This lack of widespread evaluation supports the contention that a great deal of the writing about organizational change is about *managing* change (or being an external change agent) and too little is about its impact at an organizational and, especially, an individual level. We actually know very little about employee reactions to change or what influences those reactions in a systematic way.

Porras and Robertson (1992) classified the seventy-one organizational change interventions as those which focused on organizing arrangements (e.g., goals, strategies, structures, policies); social factors (e.g., culture, interaction processes, networks, individual attributes); technology (e.g., equipment, job design, work flow, technical systems); and physical setting (e.g., space configuration, physical ambience). Over three-quarters of the studies measured either organizational or individual outcomes, with nearly a third measuring both. They reported that there was more 'no change' (53 per cent) than 'positive change' (38 per cent) overall (though perhaps fortunately 'negative change' was the lowest category, occurring in 9 per cent of the cases). These are quite salutary findings after much of the hype about the benefits of organizational change. However, it is heartening to note that positive change was nearly 50 per cent in both the social-factor and organizing-arrangement interventions. In terms of specifically organizational outcomes, nearly 50 per cent were reported as positive, with individual positive change less frequent (38 per cent). Technological interventions were reported to be least successful.

There are a number of possible explanations of these findings, including the possibility of beta or gamma change. One may also note the limitation of simply dividing interventions into four categories, regardless of type of organization, context or presenting organizational issues. However, more specific analyses are precluded by the low number of studies. We also have little information (and no models) of the time-scale over which change might be expected to occur. There is clearly much room for further research here.

SUMMARY

This chapter has explored different approaches to understanding planned organizational change. The field is divided into that concerned with *transformational* change, which generally requires a fundamental change in strategy, structures or values and culture (a paradigm shift change), and *developmental* change, concerned with improving the effectiveness of the organization within the existing set of assumptions and beliefs. A second dimension concerns the scope of change, with some interventions being targeted at the whole organization while others are focused on sub-systems of the organization, such as individuals and groups. This categorization is not entirely robust because much organizational change is complex, involves multiple interventions and occurs over a period of time, but it does provide a means of understanding the different issues for different types of change.

Research into and practice in transformational change are rapidly expanding, but psychologists have only recently become involved. Strategic choice, planning and the management of change depend on the perceptions and leadership abilities of senior management (among others), and psychology is starting to map some of the influences, both individual and social, on these choices. Developmental change is the type of change where psychologists have undertaken more research and practice, and where some valuable theories about individual and group change have emerged. There is a clear need for better theories to understand the complexities of organizational change. However, psychologists have made many contributions to the understanding of human processes in change.

FURTHER READING

A useful introduction to the whole field of organizational change is the book by Cummings and Worley (1993). It includes a valuable chapter on transformational change (though with slightly different labels for the two dimensions of scale and scope of change). It also covers the OD literature in considerable detail. The edited collection by Mohrman *et al.* (1989) on large-scale change covers many of the issues I have described as transformational change. This includes a chapter by Nadler and Tushman on the role of leaders in managing transformational change. Goodman and Associates (1982) produced a thoughtful collection of essays about change, with an emphasis more on theory than on practical implementation. Zaltman and Duncan (1977) still provide one of the best psychological analyses of power-based change.

REFERENCES

Beckhard, R. (1969). *Organization Development: Source Strategies and Models*. Reading, Mass.: Addison-Wesley.

Beer, M., Eisenstadt, R. and Spector, B. (1990). *The Critical Path to Corporate Renewal*. Boston: Harvard Business School Press.

Brown, L. D. (1980). Planned change in underorganized systems. In T. Cummings (ed.), *Systems Theory for Organization Development*, pp. 181 ff. Chichester: Wiley.

Cummings, T. G. and Worley, C. G. (1993). *Organization Development and Change*, 5th edn. St Paul, Minn.: West Publishing.

Dunphy, D. and Stace, D. (1993). The strategic management of corporate change. *Human Relations*, 46, 905–920.

Dutton, J. E. and Dukerich, J. M. (1991). Keeping an eye on the mirror: Image identity in organizational adaptation. *Academy of Management Journal*, 34, 517–554.

French, W. and Bell, C. (1990). *Organization Development: Behavioral Science Interventions for Organizational Improvement* 4th edn. Englewood Cliffs, NJ: Prentice Hall.

Golembiewski, R., Billingsley, K. and Yeager, S. (1976). Measuring change and persistence in human affairs. *Journal of Applied Behavioral Science*, 12, 133–157.

Goodman, P. and Associates (eds.) (1982). *Change in Organizations*. San Francisco: Jossey-Bass.

Goodstein, L. and Burke, O. W. (1993). Creating successful organizational change. In C. Mabey and B. Mayon-White (eds.), *Managing Change*, 2nd edn., pp. 164–172. London: Paul Chapman.

Hartley, J., Cordingley, P. and Benington, J. (1995). *Managing Organizational and Cultural Change in Local Authorities*. Luton: Local Government Management Board.

Kanter, R., Stein, B. and Jick, T. (1992). *The Challenge of Organizational Change*. New York: Free Press.

Katz, D. and Kahn, R. (1978). *The Social Psychology of Organizations*, 2nd edn. New York: Wiley.

Lawler, E. (1990). Strategic choices for changing organizations. In A. Mohrman, S. Mohrman, G. Ledford, T. Cummings and E. Lawler (eds.), *Large-scale Organizational Change*, pp. 255–271. San Francisco: Jossey-Bass.

Leavitt, H. (1965). Applied organizational change in industry: structural, technological and humanistic approaches. In J. G. March (ed.), *Handbook of Organizations,* pp. 1114–1170. Chicago: Rand McNally.

Ledford, G., Mohrman, S., Mohrman, A. and Lawler, E. (1989). The phenomenon of large-scale organizational change. In A. Mohrman, S. Mohrman, G. Ledford, T. Cummings and E. Lawler (eds.), *Large-scale Organizational Change*, pp. 1–3. San Francisco: Jossey-Bass.

Lewin, K. (1951). *Field Theory in Social Science*. New York: Harper and Row.

Miller, E. (1993). *From Dependency to Autonomy: Studies in Organization and Change.* London: Free Association Books.

Mitroff, I. (1983). *Stakeholders of the Organizational Mind.* San Francisco: Jossey-Bass.

Mohrman, A., Mohrman, S., Ledford, G., Cummings, T. and Lawler, E. (eds.), (1989). *Large-scale Organizational Change.* San Francisco: Jossey-Bass.

Nadler, D. (1977). *Feedback and Organization Development: Using Data-based Methods.* Reading, Mass.: Addison-Wesley.

Nadler, D. and Tushman, M. (1980). A model for diagnosing organizational behavior. *Organizational Dynamics*, 9, 35–51.

Nadler, D. and Tushman, M. (1989). Leadership for organizational change. In A. Mohrman, S. Mohrman, G. Ledford, T. Cummings and E. Lawler (eds.), *Large-scale Organizational Change*, pp. 100–119. San Francisco: Jossey-Bass.

Nadler, D. and Tushman, M. (1990). A congruence model for diagnosing organizational behavior. In D. Kolb, I. Rubin and J. McIntyre (eds.), *Organizational Psychology: A Book of Readings*. Englewood Cliffs, NJ: Prentice Hall.

Pettigrew, A. (1986). *The Awakening Giant: Continuity and Change in ICI.* Oxford: Blackwell.

Pettigrew, A. and Whipp, R. (1991). *Managing Change for Competitive Success.* Oxford: Blackwell.

Pfeffer, J. (1981). *Power in Organizations.* Marshfield, Mass.: Pitman Publishing.

Porras, J. and Robertson, P. (1992). Organizational development: theory, practice and research. In M. Dunnette and L. Hough (eds.), *Handbook of*

Industrial and Organizational Psychology, 2nd edn, vol. 3, pp. 719–822. Palo Alto, Calif.: Consulting Psychologists Press.

Porras, J. and Silvers, R. (1991). Organizational development and transformation. *Annual Review of Psychology*, 42, 51–78.

Quinn, J. B. (1980). Managing strategic change. *Sloan Management Review*, 21 (4), 3–20. Reprinted in Mabey, C. and Mayon-White, B. (eds.). *Managing Strategic Change*, 2nd edn. London: Paul Chapman Publishing.

Siehl, C. and Martin, J. (1990). Organizational culture: the key to financial performance? In B. Schneider (ed.), *Organizational Culture and Climate*, pp. 241–282. San Francisco: Jossey-Bass.

Sparrow, P. (1994). The psychology of strategic management: emerging themes of diversity and cognition. *International Review of Industrial and Organizational Psychology*, 9, 147–182.

Tichy, N. (1983). *Managing Strategic Change*. New York: Wiley.

Trist, E. L. and Bamforth, K. W. (1951). Some social and psychological consequences of the longwall method of coal-getting. *Human Relations*, 4, 3–38.

Weisbord, M. (1988). *Productive Workplaces: Organizing and Managing for Dignity, Meaning and Community*. San Francisco: Jossey-Bass.

Zaltman, G. and Duncan, R. (1977). *Strategies for Planned Change*. New York: Wiley.

Subject Index

Author Index

Authors appearing within '*et al.*' in the course of the text are referenced here through page numbers printed in italics.

Abraham, L. M., 235, 249
Ackers, P., 344, 358
Adams, J., 65, 66
Adelson, B., 119
Agho, A. O., 234, *235*, 249
Agrell, A., 378, 379
Ahmed, S., 50, 69
Ainsworth, L. K., 77, 93
Akerstedt, T., 52, 57, 59, 66, 68
Alban-Metcalf, B. M., 291, 302
Aldag, R. J., 165, 185
Alderfer, C. P., 178, 187
Algera, J. A., 338, 355
Alimo-Metcalf, B., 288, 289, 302
Allan, J. S., 50, 67
Allen, N., 170, 185
Alliger, G. M., 90, 93
Allison, G., 117, 118
Allport, D. A., 19, 34
Anderson, C. R., 239, 249
Anderson, J. R., 74, 75, 93, 116,
   117
Anderson, M., 44, 70
Anderson, N. R., 277, 378, 382
Andlaver, P., 54, 70, 71
Andrews, F. M., 378, 379
Angersbach, D., 57, 71
Annett, J., 77, 92, 93, 110, 117
Antonis, B., 19, 34
Appley, M. A., 35
Arendt, J., 64, 68
Armstrong, D., 62, 71
Arnold, J., 168, 171, 172, 182, 185
Arthur, M. B., 162, 181, 182, 185,
   186, 187

Arvey, R. D., 235, 236, 249, 250
Aschoff, J., 40, 46, 47, 67, 70, 72
Ashforth, B., 202, 220
Assouline, M., 164, 182
Atwood, M. E., 112, 118
Australian Bureau of Statistics, 282,
   303
Avermaet, E. U., 372, 373, 381
Avolio, B. J., 269, 275, 326, 328
Ayman, R., 275

Bacharach, A. L., 72
Backman, L., 317, 328
Baddeley, A. D., 7, 11, 19, 29, 34,
   35, 37, 316, 328
Baecker, R. M., 117
Baglioni, A., 195, 206, 218, 219
Baker, D. D., 294, 295, 306
Baker, M. A., 43, 67
Balding, J., 286, 287, 303
Baldini, V., 294, 303
Baldwin, T. T., *227*, 252
Baltes, M. M., 317, 325, 328
Baltes, P. B., 317, 319, 328, 329
Baltes, P. M., 325, 328
Bamforth, K. W., 425, 433
Bamundo, P. J., 227, 250
Bandura, A., 156
Barley, S., 188, 217
Barling, J., 231, 251
Barnes-Farrell, J. L., 363, *364*, *374*,
   381
Barrick, M. R., 150, 156
Bartlett, F. C., 5, 11, 20, 34
Barton, J., 63, 64, 65, 67

442

447